4102

America's Art Museums

Suzanne Loebl

A Traveler's Guide
to Great Collections
Large and
Small

W. W. Norton & Company

New York London

America's Art Museums

For information about permission to reproduce selections from this book, write to Permissions,
W. W. Norton & Company, Inc., 500 Fifth Avenue, New York, NY 10110

The text of this book is composed in Trump Medieval,
with the display set in Trump Medieval and Meta Medium
Composition by Carole Desnoes
Manufacturing by the Haddon Craftsmen, Inc.
Book design by Chris Welch
Production manager: Amanda Morrison

Library of Congress Cataloging-in-Publication Data

Loebl, Suzanne.
America's art museums: a traveler's guide to great collections large and small /
Suzanne Loebl.
p. cm.
Includes bibliographical references and index.
ISBN 0-393-32006-5 (pbk.)
1. Art museums—United States—Guidebooks. 2. Art—United States—Guidebooks.
I. Title.
N510 .L58 2002
708.13—dc21

2001044208

W. W. Norton & Company, Inc., 500 Fifth Avenue, New York, N.Y. 10110
www.wwnorton.com

W. W. Norton & Company Ltd., Castle House, 75/76 Wells Street,
London WIT 3QT

1 2 3 4 5 6 7 8 9 0

For Ernest M. Loebl,

my life and travel companion

And for David, always

Contents

Acknowledgments

Assembling and writing about American art museums was a wonderful and humbling task. Even small museums are so chockful of treasures that I always felt that my summary inevitably short-changed the institution.

Many people answered questions and helped me assemble what is on these pages. First and foremost I want to thank the staffs of the museums described in this book. Without exception, they were enthusiastic, helpful, and forthcoming. It was gratifying to discover that they all enjoyed their jobs, and were devoted to "their" museums. Though their help cannot be overestimated, I alone am responsible for errors, omissions, and misinterpretations.

Thanks are also due to the J. Watson Library of the Metropolitan Museum of Art, the Avery Library of Columbia University, and the New York Public Library. Of these, the Watson Library has the most encyclopedic resources. Given the nature of this book, the sheer number of sources consulted made it impossible to cite them all. The bibliography lists some works that proved especially useful and inspirational.

I also want to thank my friend Doris Lowen for visiting some museums on my behalf. Thanks are due to Joseph Ahearn for his material on the Telfair Museum in Savannah, Georgia, and to Melissa Solomon for the information concerning The Cranbrook Academy, her alma mater.

In the course of my travels, the Convention and Visitors Bureaus of Fort Worth and Houston, Texas, Miami Beach and Orlando, Florida, Pasadena, San Diego, and Santa Barbara, California, and Portland, Oregon, were particularly helpful. The following hotels were kind enough to offer a free bed to a weary traveler: The Abbey Hotel in Miami Beach, the Sheraton Safari in Orlando, the Sheraton Hotel in Pasadena,

California, The Hilton Hotel and the Courtyard Marriott in San Diego, California, The Upham in Santa Barbara, The Warwick Hotel in Houston and The Blackstone Marriott in Fort Worth, Texas, and the Paramount Hotel in Portland, Oregon.

My family as usual was essential to the creative process. I owe a debt of gratitude to my mother, Marguerite Bamberger (1902-1991), whose love of art and of museums was infectious. She taught me to look at pictures long before I could read. During her long, tumultuous life she demonstrated that art transcends time as well as national boundaries and that a museum could make you feel at home no matter where you lived. My husband not only shared many of my museum visits but also carefully went over the entire manuscript.

My editors at W. W. Norton were most encouraging. I want to thank Tabitha Griffin for acquiring the book, and Nomi Victor for her enthusiasm and for shepherding the manuscript through an arduous production process. Thanks are also due to Veronica Johnson for copyediting the manuscript.

As cited, various museums provided the illustrations that enliven the text. I want to thank them all, and hope that the visuals will entice visitors to check out the originals.

Illustration Credits

[p. 41] *Birmingham Persian Wall* by Dale Chihuly, at the Birmingham Museum of Art. Photo courtesy Birmingham Museum of Art, Alabama.

[p. 46] The Central Courtyard of The Heard Museum—Native Cultures & Art. Courtesy of the Heard Museum, Phoenix, Arizona.

[p. 61] The windows of the small Pavilion for Japanese Art. Photo courtesy of the Los Angeles County Museum of Art, Los Angeles, California.

[p. 69] *Still Life with Lemons, Oranges, and a Rose* by Francisco de Zurbarán. Photograph courtesy of the Norton Simon Museum, Pasadena, California.

[p. 72] A *Han Horse* from China. Photograph courtesy of the Pacific Asia Museum, Pasadena, California.

[p. 75] The foyer of the Crocker Art Museum. Photo courtesy Crocker Art Museum, Sacramento, California. © 1989 Van Noy Photography.

[p. 78] Henri de Toulouse-Lautrec, *Jane Avril, 1899*. San Diego Museum of Art (Gift of the Baldwin M. Baldwin Foundation), San Diego, California.

[p. 80] The lobby of the Museum of Contemporary Art, San Diego. Photography by Timothy Hursley. Courtesy of the Museum of Contemporary Art, San Diego, California.

[p. 88] Court of Honor, California Palace of the Legion of Honor, San Francisco, California. Courtesy of the Fine Arts Museums of San Francisco.

[p. 94] The San Francisco Museum of Modern Art, architect Mario Botta. Photo by Richard Barnes. Photograph courtesy of the San Francisco Museum of Modern Art, San Francisco, California.

[p. 97] Rogier Van der Weyden's *Madonna and Child*. Photo courtesy of The Huntington Library, Art Collections, and Botanical Gardens, San Marino, California.

[p. 100] Enrique Chagoya's *1492*. Photo courtesy Santa Barbara Museum of Art, Santa Barbara, California. Museum purchase with funds provided by the SBMA Friends of Contemporary Art.

[p. 104] Richard Diebenkorn's *Ocean Park No. 94*. Photo courtesy Iris & B. Gerald Cantor Center for Visual Arts at Stanford University, Stanford, California. Gift of Phyllis Diebenkorn, 1998.142.

[p. 109] Ralph Earl, *Oliver Ellsworth and Abigail Wolcott Ellsworth*. The Wadsworth Atheneum Museum of Art, Hartford, Connecticut. Gift of the Ellsworth Heirs.

[p. 112] Frederick Childe Hassam, *Le Jour du Grand Prix*, oil on canvas, 37 x 49$\frac{1}{2}$". New Britain Museum of American Art, New Britain, Connecticut. Grace Judd Landers Fund. Photography credit: Michael Agee.

[p. 114] *Pumpkin with a Stable Lad* by George Stubbs. Yale Center for British Art, New Haven, Connecticut. Paul Mellon Collection.

[p. 119] *Veronica Veronese* by Dante Gabriel Rossetti, from the Samuel and Mary R. Bancroft collection. Photograph courtesy of the Delaware Museum of Art, Wilmington, Delaware.

[p. 129] *Self-Portrait Dedicated to Leon Trotsky*, 1937, by Frida Kahlo. Oil on masonite, 30 x 24". Collection of the National Museum of Women in the Arts, Washington, D.C.

[p. 131] Jacob Lawrence, *The Migration of the Negro*, Panel no. 1, 1940–1941. Casein tempera on hardboard. 12 x 18 in. Acquired 1942. The Phillips Collection, Washington, D.C.

[p. 147] Exterior, Museum of Fine Arts, St. Petersburg, Florida. Courtesy Museum of Fine Arts.

[p. 151] The Rubens Gallery. Photo courtesy of the John and Mable Ringling Museum of Art, Sarasota, Florida.

[p. 155] *The Red Foulard* by Pablo Picasso. Photograph courtesy of the Norton Museum of Art, West Palm Beach, Florida.

[p. 157] *The Magnolia Window*. Photograph courtesy of The Charles Hosmer Morse Museum of American Art, Winter Park, Florida. © The Charles Hosmer Morse Foundation, Inc.

[p. 170] Charles Laval, French, *Going to Market, Brittany*, 1888. Oil on canvas. 37.5 x 46 cm. Indianapolis Museum of Art, Indianapolis, Indiana. Samuel Josefowitz Collection of the School of Pont-Aven, through the generosity of Lilly Endowment Inc., the Josefowitz Family, and other Friends of the Museum.

[p. 173] The Cedar Rapids Museum of Art, Cedar Rapids, Iowa, Winter Garden atrium, designed by Charles W. Moore and Centerbrook Architects and Planners, photograph courtesy of French Studios, Inc.

[p. 176] (a) The Eliel Saarinen Building, (b) the I. M. Pei Building, (c) the Richard Meier Building. Courtesy of the Des Moines Art Center, Des Moines, Iowa.

[p. 179] *Kansas Cornfield*, 1913, by John Steuart Curry. The Roland P. Murdoch Collection, Wichita Art Museum, Wichita, Kansas.

[p. 184] Edgar Degas, *The Portrait of Estelle Musson Degas*. Photograph courtesy of the New Orleans Museum of Art, New Orleans, Louisiana. Museum purchase through public subscription.

[p. 189] *Wreck of the D.T. Sheridan* by Rockwell Kent. Photograph courtesy of Portland Museum of Art, Portland, Maine. Picture bequest of Elizabeth B. Noyce.

[p. 191] Fitz Hugh Lane, *Camden Mountains from the South Entrance to the Harbor*. Oil on canvas, 1859. Collection of the Farnsworth Art Museum, Rockland, Maine. Bequest of Mrs. Elizabeth B. Noyce, 1997.

[p. 200] Corsage Ornament, Tiffany and Co., 1900. The Walters Art Museum, Baltimore, Maryland.

[p. 203] Anders Zorn, *Mrs. Gardner in Venice*. Photograph courtesy of the Isabella Stewart Gardner Museum, Boston, Massachusetts.

[p. 207] *The Daughters of Edward D. Boit*, 1882, by John Singer Sargent (US, 1856–1925). Oil on canvas. $87\frac{5}{8}$ x $87\frac{5}{8}$" MFA: 19.124. Courtesy of the Museum of Fine Arts, Boston, Massachusetts.

[p. 210] Claude Monet, *Red Boats, Argenteuil*. Bequest from the Collection of Maurice Wertheim, Class of 1906. President and Fellows of Harvard College (Harvard University Art Museums), Cambridge, Massachusetts.

[p. 222] Norman Rockwell, *Triple Self-Portrait*. The Norman Rockwell Museum, Stockbridge, Massachusetts. © Curtis Publishing Company.

[p. 234] Mural: *Detroit Industry*, South Wall (detail), 1932–1933.

Diego M. Rivera. Gift of Edsel B. Ford. Photograph © The Detroit Institute of Arts, Detroit, Michigan.

[p. 241] West facade, The Frederick R. Weisman Art Museum. Photograph by Don F. Wong © 1993, courtesy of The Frederick R. Weisman Museum, Minneapolis, Minnesota.

[p. 254] George Inness, *Delaware Water Gap*, 1859. Oil on canvas, 32 x 52$\frac{1}{4}$". Gift of Mrs. F. G. Herman Fayen in memory of Mr. Fayen. 1930.2. The Montclair Art Museum, Montclair, New Jersey.

[p. 266] Clyfford Still, *1957-D No. 1*, 1957. Collection Albright-Knox Gallery, Buffalo, New York. Gift of Seymour H. Knox.

[p. 274] *The Moorish Smoking Room.* Photo courtesy of the Brooklyn Museum of Art, Brooklyn, New York.

[p. 279] The Garden Court at the Frick Collection. Photograph courtesy and copyright of The Frick Collection, New York, New York. Photograph by Richard di Liberto.

[p. 282] The Solomon R. Guggenheim Museum, New York. Photograph by David Heald. © The Solomon R. Guggenheim Foundation, New York, New York.

[p. 290] The Jewish Museum, New York, under the auspices of The Jewish Theological Seminary of America, 1109 Fifth Avenue, New York, New York 10128. *Culture and Continuity: The Jewish Journey.* Moritz Daniel Oppenheim, *The Return of the Jewish Volunteer from the Wars of Liberation to His Family Still Living in Accordance with Old Customs*, 1833–94. Oil on canvas. Gift of Mr. and Mrs. Richard D. Levy, the donors maintaining the rights, 1984–61. © The Jewish Museum, New York, New York. Photo by John Parnell.

[p. 302] Audubon, John J. (P)Am. 1 339 p. 0007. *Snowy Owl* (Havell pl. 121), n.d. wc/p, 38$\frac{1}{4}$ x 25$\frac{1}{2}$". © New-York Historical Society, New York, New York.

[p. 304] The *Biblia Latina*, published by Johann Gutenberg and Johann Fust about 1455, at The Pierpont Morgan Library in New York. Photograph by David A. Loggia, courtesy of The Morgan Library, New York, New York.

[p. 328] Frans Hals, *Tieleman Roosterman*. Photograph courtesy Cleveland Museum of Art, Cleveland, Ohio.

[p. 330] George Wesley Bellows. American, 1882–1925. *Blue Snow*,

The Battery, 1910. Oil on canvas. 1958.035. Columbus Museum of Art, Columbus, Ohio: Museum Purchase, Howald Fund.

[p. 337] Claude Monet (France, 1840–1926) *La Berge à Lavacourt*, 1879. Oil on canvas, $23\frac{1}{2}$ x $35\frac{1}{4}$ x $3''$ (unframed). Fred Jones Jr. Museum of Art, The University of Oklahoma, Norman, Oklahoma, Aaron M. and Clara Weitzenhoffer Bequest, 2p. 000.

[p. 340] The Philbrook Museum of Art, Tulsa, Oklahoma, 1993. Photo by R. Greg Hursley.

[p. 344] George Segal's *Helen with Apples*. Photograph courtesy of the Portland Art Museum, Portland, Oregon, the Evan H. Roberts Sculpture Collection.

[p. 349] James Wyeth (b. 1946) *Portrait of Pig*, 1970. Oil on canvas, 48 x 84″. Photograph courtesy of Brandywine River Museum, Chadds Ford, Pennsylvania.

[p. 361] The entrance to The Andy Warhol Museum. Photograph courtesy of the Andy Warhol Museum, Pittsburgh, Pennsylvania.

[p. 364] Edouard Manet, French, 1832–1883. *Le Repos* (Portrait of Berthe Morisot). Oil on canvas. $58\frac{1}{4}$ x $43\frac{3}{4}''$. Museum of Art, Rhode Island School of Design, Providence, Rhode Island. Gift of the Estate of Edith Stuyvesant Vanderbilt Gerry.

[p. 367] The Gibbes Museum of Art. Photograph by Bill Struhs, courtesy Gibbes Museum of Art, Charleston, South Carolina.

[p. 379] 1970.43. Grant Wood, *Parson Weems' Fable*. Oil on canvas, 1939. Amon Carter Museum, Fort Worth, Texas.

[p. 381] (a) Caravaggio, Italian, 1571–1610, *The Cardsharps (I Bari)*, about 1594. Oil on canvas, $37\frac{1}{8}$ x $51\frac{5}{8}''$ (b) Georges de La Tour, French, 1593–1652, *The Cheat with the Ace of Clubs*, about 1630. Oil on canvas, $38\frac{1}{2}$ x $61\frac{1}{2}''$. Kimbell Art Museum, Fort Worth, Texas.

[p. 384] Pablo Picasso, *Femme Couchée Lisant*. Collection of the Modern Art Museum of Fort Worth, Fort Worth, Texas. Museum Purchase, The Benjamin J. Tillar Memorial Trust.

[p. 386] Max Ernst, *Portrait of Dominique*, 1934. Oil, graphite on canvas, $25\frac{3}{4}$ x $21\frac{1}{4}''$. Courtesy of the Menil Collection, 1511 Branard, Houston, Texas 77006.

[p. 398] Georges de La Tour, *Saint Philip*. Photograph courtesy of The Chrysler Museum of Art, Norfolk, Virginia.

[p. 403] *Baby in Red Chair.* Abby Aldrich Rockefeller Folk Art Museum, Williamsburg, Virginia.

[p. 409] The Seattle Art Museum at 100 University Street, with the 48-ft.-tall sculpture, *Hammering Man,* by Jonathan Borofsky. Photo by Susan Dirk. © Seattle Art Museum, Seattle, Washington.

Bibliography

An enormous number of books, magazine and journal articles, catalogs, guides to collections, and museum publications were consulted in the preparation of this book. My thanks go to all the authors and researchers on whose shoulders my work rests. A few of the often used and cited resources are listed below.

Burt, Nathaniel. *Palaces for the People, A Social History of the American Art Museum.* Boston: Little Brown, 1977.

Emerson, Guy. "The Kress Collection, A Gift to the Nation." *National Georgraphic,* December 1961.

Tansey, Richard G., and Fred S. Kleiner. *Gardner's Art Through the Ages.* 10th ed. Fort Worth, Texas: Harcourt Brace, 1996.

Janson, Anthony F., and H.W. Janson. *History of Art.* 5th ed. New York: Harry N. Abrams, Inc., 1995.

Price, Vincent. *The Vincent Price Treasury of American Art.* Waukesha, Wisconsin: Country Beautiful Corporation, 1972.

Saarinen, Aline B. *The Proud Possessors, The Lives, Times and Tastes of Some Adventurous American Art Collectors.* New York: Random House, 1958.

Introduction

The Passionate Sightseer

In 1991, flying from Bar Harbor, Maine, to New York's La Guardia, my puddle jumper landed in Rockland. A stewardess explained that the airline had overbooked the flight, and that anyone willing to get off the plane would get a free ticket to anywhere in the U.S. I grabbed the opportunity. Once I disembarked I took a taxi to the Farnsworth Art Museum. During the next two hours I immersed myself in their collection, so beautifully representing the art of Maine. Thus crystallized the idea for *America's Art Museums*.

At first the guide was to include only small, out-of-the-way jewels like the Farnsworth, neglected treasure-houses like the museums in Newark and Detroit, or great museums in unlikely places like the Toledo Museum of Art in Toledo, Ohio, or the Joslyn in Omaha, Nebraska. But how could I write a guide to American art museums and leave out New York's Metropolitan Museum of Art, my home away from home, or the new Getty Center in Los Angeles that I itched to see? In the end this guide includes 158 museums located in 39 states throughout our Union. This impressive number falls short of the more than 1,330 art museums that dot our land. Time and space limitations are to blame for many lovely museums that were omitted.

The entry for each museum is divided in two. The first, shorter part, provides basic practical information such as:

Address, telephone number, web site, hours, strengths of the collection, special events, activities for children, and parking, as well as information about museum shops, cafés, and restaurants.

The merchandise in most museum shops is especially attractive as are many of the restaurants and cafés. The guide does not list admission prices since these change. Some museums are free; most have free hours or days.

Two of the difficulties encountered in preparing this guide were that America continues to build and improve its museums, and that important works are often in storage. The latter is especially noticeable in small museums, which in order to keep the interest of their local membership and fulfill their mandate, must mount temporary shows even though this means that their best-known treasures are not on view. To find out what is on exhibit and to verify hours, which can change, you may wish to call the museum you're interested in before undertaking a lengthy trip.

The longer portion of each entry gives an overview of the museum's history, the how and why a particular institution came into being. Who provided the money and why? Who assembled the art? Why does one museum own over 100 Renoirs and another none at all? Why do many small New England college museums showcase Assyrian reliefs? Why does the Saint Louis Museum of Art, a bastion of the American Midwest, own the world's largest collection of Max Beckmann, a leading German Expressionist?

The entries also present impressionistic snapshots of the collections, highlighting a few artworks that are representative of the institution or that struck me as especially wonderful.

It turned out that visiting the museums, personally or otherwise, was only half the fun—and labor—of writing this book. To answer my questions, fill in information, and discover the why and how of each museum, I plowed through reams of books, documents, magazine articles, and guides to museum collections. Through my research I became familiar with dozens of the museum directors, curators, collectors, donors, art dealers, and architects to whom this country owes its immense artistic patrimony.

The word *museum* refers to the Greek muses, the nine daughters of Zeus and Mnemosyne who presided over the arts. The Louvre in Paris is generally considered to be the modern world's first great art museum. Until it opened its doors in 1793, as a direct consequence of the French Revolution, most of Europe's art was in the hands of its ruling class—the kings and princes of the land. Gradually Europe's privately owned royal collections gave rise to that continent's major museums: the Prado in Spain, the Uffizi in Florence, the National Gallery in London, and the Hermitage in St. Petersburg, to cite only a few.

America has always been a democratic, pluralistic society, and the story of our museums is different. Even though gigantic fortunes were, and are, accumulated here, many of our wealthy citizens wanted to share their treasures with the general public and so a number of our museums and their contents are the gifts of the captains of industry. That, however, is only part of the story. American museums have also been created and shaped by astute directors, public-minded citizens, devoted curators, passionate collectors, and artists.

As I immersed myself in the study of America's art museums, I discovered many unifying threads. First of all, there was the timeline of their founding. Initially museums were private enterprises. The Pennsylvania Academy of Fine Arts in Philadelphia is usually considered to be America's oldest surviving art museum. In 1781, painter Charles Willson Peale opened a portrait gallery in Philadelphia. It was a general museum displaying art and oddities akin to the Wunderkammern (cabinets of curiosities) beloved by German princes. At the time, most American museums combined natural history and art. (The Berkshire Museum in Pittsfield, Massachusetts, is a modernized survivor of this genre.) Peale's sons also founded small museums in Baltimore, New York City, and Utica, in which spectacles, musical performances, and even freak shows displaced art and natural history. Eventually the Peale museums were taken over by P. T. Barnum, showman and entrepreneur par excellence.

In 1805, Peale and a dozen other respectable Philadelphians founded an art school and museum, the Pennsylvania Academy of the Fine Arts (PaFA), which is still alive and well. In it hangs a huge self-portrait of Peale, showing off the museum he created for the town's Independence Hall. The painter draws back a heavy velvet curtain, revealing portraits as well as cabinets filled with stuffed animals. The New-York Historical Society, founded in 1804, is as old as the PaFA, but at first it had no exhibition space. During the 1850–1860s the New-York Historical absorbed two small private art collections whose public display had failed because of lack of interest.

Connecticut was the next state to create lasting museums. In 1832,

Yale University founded the Trumbull Gallery of Art, to be followed in 1844 by Hartford's Wadsworth Atheneum. The latter is the oldest museum still partially housed in its original building.

America got serious about museums after the Civil War. Boston's Museum of Fine Arts and New York's Metropolitan Museum were both founded in 1870, followed by the Philadelphia Museum of Art in 1876.

One would expect the Old South to have been interested in art. Indeed, Charleston had an art association by 1857 and Savannah's Telfair dates to about 1875. The Civil War, however, depressed the region for a long time and it is only during the second half of the twentieth century that it has joined America's art trail.

Our nation's capital, now the repository of much great art, also got a slow start. William Wilson Corcoran, a serious collector, commissioned a museum building in Washington, D.C., from James Renwick in 1859, but the Civil War delayed its opening until 1874. In 1836, Englishman James Smithson left his fortune to the United States for the purpose of building a museum. For many years the institution concentrated on science, but today the Smithsonian is the guardian of the art owned by the American people. Washington, D.C., also sports several other great museums.

By 1900, America started to sprout museums in earnest. Many of these blossomed in the Midwest. Of this boom Nathaniel Burt, author of *Palaces for the People,* writes: "As a spectacle of esthetic glamour, taste, civic energy, personal generosity, and above all swift accomplishment, there is nothing in the art history of this country or indeed in the whole world to compare with the massive flowering of art museums in the Midwest." Museums in Chicago and St. Louis were founded in 1879, in Cincinnati in 1881, in Detroit in 1885, in Toledo in 1901, in Indianapolis in 1906, and in Minneapolis in 1914. Not only are these institutions well and flourishing today, but other great museums, among them those located in Des Moines, Kansas City, Louisville, Milwaukee, and Wichita, have joined the list.

Eventually, museums spread west, southwest, and south. The oldest museum in California is the Crocker Art Museum in Sacramento, which opened as a private gallery in 1871–1872. Thirty years later the Leland Stanford Jr. Museum (now the Iris & B. Gerald Cantor Center for Visual Arts), which at one time its planners intended to be the largest museum in the world, followed. The great earthquake of 1906 nearly destroyed it and today it is a medium-sized university museum. Today, California is a big museum state and is considered to be New York's only true rival. California's major museums are clustered around Los Angeles and San Francisco, but excellent smaller ones can be found in San Diego and Santa Barbara. Portland, Oregon, too had an early start, forming an art association during the 1890s.

Texas rarely does things half-heartedly. Its oldest museum is in Fort Worth, which calls itself Museum City. Indeed, Fort Worth now has three lovely, noncompeting institutions: the Kimbell, the Amon Carter, and the Modern Art Museum of Fort Worth. Dallas and Houston have good general-survey museums augmented by special collections, as do El Paso, Austin, and San Antonio. Growth in Texas was fueled by oil money, which also built the museums in nearby Tulsa and Norman, Oklahoma.

Today there are excellent art museums scattered throughout America. The Denver Art Museum claims that it is a major art outpost between Kansas City and the West Coast. Several museums in New Mexico and Arizona are showcases for Native American and Spanish Colonial art.

Museums got their starts in several ways. Most often, as in New York and Boston, a group of citizens or an art association decided that their town needed a museum. Some museums, like the Farnsworth, in Rockland, Maine, the Nelson-Atkins in Kansas City, and to a large extent the Getty Center in Los Angeles, resulted from large monetary bequests; it was up to directors and curators to build a museum and assemble a collection. In several cases a World's Fair transmuted a small organization (Chicago, St. Louis, San Diego, and San Francisco) into a large, permanent museum. A great number of delightful museums, such as the Frick, the Hyde, the Isabella Stewart Gardner, and the Marion Koogler McNay, were first created by individuals in their homes for their own pleasure and later became museums. Widows and parents created museums as memorials for husbands or children.

Despite the variety of their histories, America's art museums share many common bonds. Forming one such link are the directors and curators who migrated from one museum to another and the art professors who trained those directors. Take William R. Valentiner. Trained in Germany, he came to New York in 1908 as curator of the Metropolitan's Decorative Arts Department. In 1924 he became the Detroit Institute of Arts's long-time director. Thirty years later he went on to reorganize the collections of the Los Angeles County Museum and from 1954–1955 was involved with the J. Paul Getty Museum in Malibu. He ended up by shaping the North Carolina Museum of Art in Raleigh, and was instrumental in selecting for it a superior Kress collection (see p. 31). James B. Byrnes, his assistant in Raleigh, revitalized the New Orleans Museum of Art and Walter Heil, another of his protégés, became the director of The Fine Arts Museums of San Francisco.

Paul Sachs is another man whose influence is felt throughout America. The scion of a rich New York banking firm, he joined Harvard University in 1915 and for the next thirty-three years taught America's first course in museum administration (museumology). His students (MoMA's Alfred Barr, Rochester's Isabel Herdle, Minneapolis's Samuel Sachs, the Wadsworth Atheneum's J. Everett [Chick] Austin, and scores of others) went on to head some of America's finest museums. In Cambridge, Paul Sachs lived at Shady Hills, the former home of Charles Eliot Norton, Harvard's first professor of fine arts and a lover of works of the Italian Renaissance. A generation earlier Norton had inspired the collector Isabella Stewart Gardner, the art expert Bernard Berenson, and the Hydes, who were to found the museum that bears their name in Glens Falls, New York.

Another unifying factor is the gifts of the wealthy. Of these, the names Mellon, Morgan, Rockefeller, Frick, and Carnegie are most familiar, but there are scores of others. Some names keep recurring. Archer Huntington quipped that "wherever he stepped a museum grew." Indeed, he played a major role in the creation of The Hispanic Society of America, the National Academy of Design in New York, the Huntington Library, Art Collections, and Botanical Gardens in San Marino, the J. S. Blanton Museum in Austin, and the Legion of Honor in San Francisco. The Rockefellers were associated with New York's Museum of Modern Art, the Cloisters, the Metropolitan's Michael C. Rockefeller Wing, The Abby Aldrich Rockefeller Folk Art Museum in Williamsburg, Dartmouth's Hood Museum, the Rhode Island School of Design Museum in Providence, and the Arkansas Arts Center. Andrew and Paul Mellon and Ailsa Bruce-Mellon founded and/or endowed the

National Gallery of Art, the Yale Museum of British Art, the Virginia Museum of Fine Arts in Richmond, and the Carnegie Museum of Art in Pittsburgh. And the industrial titans were not the only benefactors; many museums were founded, and collections assembled, by people with more modest means.

Unlike schools, hospitals, or even libraries, a museum building is a luxury intended to be aesthetically pleasing and beautiful. Taken as a whole, America's art museums represent one of the nation's greatest architectural heritages. Museum buildings include neoclassic palaces of the past, delicate Renaissance buildings, copies of Roman villas, and avant-garde creations. Since a museum is always considered a plum assignment, the buildings are crafted by top architects. McKim, Mead & White, Carrère and Hastings, Cass Gilbert , Paul Cret, John Russell Pope, Frank Lloyd Wright, Eero Saarinen, Philip Johnson, Louis Kahn, I. M. Pei, Richard Meier, and Frank Gehry all designed one or more of America's museums.

However, a building, no matter how beautiful, is only a shell. By the 1920s, many of the larger museums were in place, but their contents were not. As a matter of fact, in the beginning those in charge often had been overenthusiastic in accepting gifts. Cleaning out fakes and "stuff" became a major first task. Today the quality of the art exhibited in America's museums is astounding. America owes many of these possessions to the economic turmoil that reigned in Europe as a consequence of wars and other upheavals (the Franco-Prussian War of 1870, the Russian Revolution, the two World Wars, and the worldwide depression). That, however, is only part of the tale. During the nineteenth century it became fashionable to take a Grand European Tour that often included art-buying sprees. As travel became easier, Americans started to become familiar with and actively supported emerging European artists and bought their works before their prices became sky-high.

Some enthusiastic collectors shipped large objects, including Greek antiquities and entire cloisters, back home to America. Often, such transatlantic transplantations were said to be rescue operations. Mosaic floors and Egyptian artifacts were given to museums as payment for financing and participating in excavations. As late as 1965, Egypt gave the people of the United States the Temple of Dendur in gratitude for their help in salvaging monuments that would have been flooded as a consequence of the Aswan High Dam across the Nile. (The temple was awarded to New York's Metropolitan in 1967 and installed there in 1978.)

Not all of the art on display in museums comes from "away." Increasingly, the art is homegrown. Initially, American art consisted of the portraits, landscapes, and other "folk art" created by limners—itinerant painters with little formal training. America began to produce world-class painters around the time of the American Revolution. American-born Benjamin West went to England in 1780 when he was twenty-one. He never returned home and became a reigning artist in England. He did, however, help train many budding American artists who journeyed to Europe for additional schooling. Slowly America developed art schools of its own. By the middle of the nineteenth century, artists of the Hudson River School had developed America's first major artistic style. Crossfertilization with Europe continued and today art is truly international.

American artists have enriched our museums. Some have bequeathed their estates to specific museums, others—including Isamu Noguchi, Georgia O'Keeffe, Norman Rockwell, and Andy Warhol—now have museums of their own.

Acquiring art, especially great art, is beyond most people's means, but selecting favorites in museums and elsewhere and pursuing the work of particular artists is within everybody's reach. It is a wonderful pastime and I hope that this guide will help you become such a "collector."

Samuel H. Kress

and His Gift to the American Public

Walk into the National Gallery of Art in Washington, D.C., or into any one of thirty-nine other museums in thirty-three states and you will come across works of art donated by the Samuel H. Kress Foundation. During the twentieth century the foundation donated more than 3,000 works of European art, mostly from the thirteenth to the sixteenth century, to American art museums.

Samuel Kress's typically American story can be summarized as "making good and doing good," both carried out with flair and imagination. Samuel Henry Kress was born in 1863, in Cherryville, Pennsylvania, and was named for an uncle who had fallen at Gettysburg three weeks earlier. He finished high school when he was seventeen. During the following seven years he taught school at a salary of $25 a month. He managed to save a bit of money and opened a small notions store in Nanticoke, Pennsylvania, then a wholesale firm. In 1896, Kress opened a five-and-dime store in Memphis, Tennessee, modeled on Woolworth's successful business. The enterprise was a success and rapidly Kress stores opened in thirty states, at a rate of five per year. Samuel Kress crisscrossed America aboard a Pullman sleeper. Eventually the stores were incorporated in New York City and Kress himself moved to a luxurious duplex penthouse on Fifth Avenue. By then, his brothers had joined the family business.

During the early decades of the twentieth century, Samuel Kress went to Italy and there fell in love with art. With the help of Count Contini-Bonacossi he became a collector. According to Nathaniel Burt in *Palaces for the People,* the count convinced Kress "that it was no use to buy just masterpieces by masters . . . but [that he should] evolve a . . . collection representing all the schools and phases of the Italian Renaissance by buying whatever was available." Kress was a quick study. He became highly knowledgeable about Renaissance and Northern European art and availed himself of the services of leading experts and art dealers. These included Bernard Berenson, who also advised Isabella Stewart Gardner, Joseph Duveen, an art dealer, and William Suida, an art historian.

One may wonder how a single individual, no matter how well endowed, could amass thousands of high-quality works of art in a matter of a few decades. According to Kress Foundation archives, the major reason was that many works became available as a consequence of the political and economic upheavals that beset Europe before, during, and after World War Two. (The foundation purchased most of its art between 1927 and 1960.)

The works acquired by the foundation consist of over 1,000 Italian works by 342 identifiable artists. In addition the foundation acquired works by Spanish, French, and Northern European masters including Dürer, Cranach, Rubens, and Van Dyck, to name only a very few. The purchases also include many works by minor painters or unknown artists.

From the beginning Kress intended to share his collection with the American public. He considered founding a museum, most likely located along New York's "Museum Mile." However, when approached, he enthusiastically donated the choice pieces of his collection to the National Gallery of Art in Washington, D.C. In time the National Gallery received over 500 paintings, sculptures, and drawings and a collection of more than 1,300 small bronzes. Speaking at the opening ceremony of the National Gallery in Washington in 1941, Kress said: "I have endeavored to acquire the best examples of the most representative masters of this important [Italian] school beginning with the thirteenth-century painters Giotto and Duccio, and extending through the great periods of Florence, Siena, Umbria, and ending with the Venetians of the eighteenth century."

Shortly after the historic opening of the National Gallery, Samuel Kress developed what everybody described as "a very grave illness" and withdrew totally from public life and involvement with the Kress Foundation. His brothers, especially Rush Kress, continued to buy and distribute the art. Twenty-one museums received "Regional Collections." Cities that had Kress Department Stores were given preference.

The only condition for these gifts was adequate quarters to house them. This requirement enabled many fledgling institutions to obtain funding for improved buildings. Once approved as a Kress collection recipient, the museum's directors were allowed to select their own collection. Typical regional collections included fifty works. Sometimes "Santa Claus" fulfilled special wishes. When Dr. Walter Heil, a former director of San Francisco's de Young Memorial Museum, visited the Kress Foundation in New York he let it be known that what he wanted most of all was El Greco's *St. Francis Venerating the Crucifix*, then available for sale. Heil got the painting of San Francisco's patron saint even though it bore a hefty price tag.

Some works of art remained after the foundation had completed its gifts to regional museums. These were distributed as "Study Collections" of up to twenty works to twenty-three colleges. Numerous other institutions received individual paintings. The money of the foundation is still not exhausted. Today the foundation funds fellowships for young scholars and art conservators, conducts art conservation research, and funds conservation and restoration projects here and in Europe.

American museums would not be the same without Samuel H. Kress and his brothers. As David K. E. Bruce, a former director of the National Gallery of Art, stated at the opening of that museum: "There is not a private collection in the world, and few museums, which can illustrate in as complete a manner as the Kress Collection the development of the Italian school of painting during the Renaissance Period."

How to Visit a Museum with Children

Adults often underestimate the ability of some children to appreciate art. In a September 24, 2000, article in *The New York Times*, Douglas Davis, an artist and art critic, recalls how a museum encounter with the "wild, fiery hues" of a John Marin watercolor when he was eleven determined his life's work.

When we took our eight-year-old son to London's National Gallery he declared, when looking at a Seurat painting, that he had seen it before. "No," we said with authority, "you have never been here." "Yes," David insisted, "out West. . . ." Finally we saw the light. Two years earlier, on a camping trip "out West," we had briefly stopped at The Art Institute of Chicago and had admired Seurat's *A Sunday on La Grande Jatte—1884*. The work at the National Gallery represented a partial scene of that monumental canvas.

Art is part of a child's life. Children love to draw and paint, and the appreciation of pictures and drawing precedes verbal comprehension. Today, museums are prepared for child visitors with treasure hunts, game-filled backpacks, hands-on art exploration rooms, computer terminals, and other goodies. However, though nice, these tools are not essential for a successful museum visit. Here are a few suggestions:

1. Limit the time of the visit.
2. Your own enthusiasm is crucial. If you truly enjoy visiting a museum, your children will too.
3. Do not overwhelm your children with your knowledge and taste. Let them explore on their own.
4. Start out by going to the museum shop and looking at the post-

cards. Then use these images as a treasure hunt. Another variant of this game is to have the children look for particular images: animals, angels, flowers, etc.

5. Pick up a map to the museum. Older children can participate in planning the itinerary with the help of the map. A recent picturebook entitled *Taking Granny to the Museum* is a variant on this theme.

6. Have the children pick out their favorite work of art and let them explain why they like it.

7. Choose museums that feature art your child is interested in. Mummies and Egyptian art fascinate most children. Western pictures and cowboys, model rooms, and portraits of children dressed as if they were adults are also a success. Many children relate to the distorted visions of Surrealist painters. However, do not make any assumptions. The lasting impression that the John Marin watercolor made on Douglas Davis illustrates that the taste of children, like that of adults, is eclectic. Children's response to certain forms of art can be surprising. In 1999, the Brooklyn Museum's *Sensation* show, rejected by many connoisseurs as too avant-garde and sensationalist, was a great success with my grandchildren whose love of fine art can be limited.

8. As you walk through the galleries, talk about specific pictures. For instance, compare a painstakingly realistic landscape or portrait by a Dutch painter with the way these images are rendered by the Impressionists or distorted by Picasso.

9. Remind children of the various purposes of art: a picture of Grandma or of faraway places before there were photographs, a means of telling a Bible story to people who could not read, etc.

10. Encourage the children to buy postcards of the art they liked best.

11. It may also be helpful to provide a guiding structure to the visit by assigning a specific task such as identifying a particular painter or theme.

12. Do not be discouraged when a museum visit is a flop. Like adults, children may be enthusiastic one visit and "hate" museums during the next.

13. Keep art and art books around the house. I still remember the

reproductions that graced the walls of my childhood home—Dürer's *Bunch of Violets,* Van Gogh's *Sunflowers,* photographs of the statues of the kings and queens of Chartres's *Royal Portal.* They have been constant friends, and my heart still beats a little faster whenever I encounter them.

Alabama

BIRMINGHAM

Birmingham Museum of Art

Address: 2000 Eighth Avenue North, Birmingham, AL 35203

Telephone: (205) 254-2566

Web: www.artsBMA.org

Hours: Tues–Sat 10–5; Sun 12–5. Open until 9 every first Thurs. Closed Mon and New Year's, Thanksgiving, and Christmas days.

Strengths: Encyclopedic. Kress collection of Italian Renaissance, Baroque, and Northern European paintings. European, American, and Asian art, with growing collections of African, Pre-Columbian, and Native American art. Decorative arts, including period rooms and the finest Wedgwood collection outside Great Britain. Remarkable sculpture garden.

Birmingham Persian Wall by Dale Chihuly, at the Birmingham Museum of Art.

Other: Free gallery talks, lectures, special exhibitions, films, and concerts. Informative booklets about special collections. Special tours for the visually handicapped in which paste, cloth, feathers, shadow-box relief carvings, aluminum foil, and sand are used to recreate the moods of the art work. Terrace café. Museum shop.

Activities for Children: Hands-on room, featuring a print studio and material to create multimedia drawings and computer art.

Parking: On site.

The Birmingham Art Association was founded in 1908. Forty years later it finally managed to convince the city council that the town needed a museum. It took until 1959 for a permanent, state-of-the-art museum finally to open, on a 3.9-acre site. The museum's collections grew rapidly. The Samuel H. Kress Foundation bestowed thirty-nine works, and other works were donated or purchased. By 1990 the Birmingham Museum of Art (BMA) owned in excess of 18,000 works of art and was bursting at the seams, so Edward Larrabee Barnes, who had designed the Dallas Museum of Art (p. 374), the Walker Art Center in Minneapolis (p. 238), and The Asia Society galleries in New York (p. 271), was asked to build a new wing. He ended up refurbishing and unifying the entire museum.

When illuminated, this new wing looks as if it were a gigantic ocean liner. Through the curved glass facade one glimpses a free-standing staircase which, according to writer Philip Morris (*Southern Accents,* September–October 1994), "nearly steals the show. Elliptical in plan, repeating the window's bow, it becomes highly sculptural in three dimensions and dynamic with movement." The stairs, which are reminiscent of, but different from, the great ramp of the Guggenheim Museum in New York, permit visitors to circulate easily among the museum's three floors.

Barnes preserved and enhanced much of the old museum's glamour. He opened up the former terrazzo and black marble front lobby and installed *Birmingham Persian Wall,* a glass sculpture made specifically for the museum by Dale Chihuly. Large red, yellow, orange, blue, and purple abstract flowers are scattered over an expanse of glass, bathing the entire lobby in vivid colors.

The possessions of the BMA match its building. It has representative paintings from all major European and American schools. There is the Kress collection, of mostly Italian Renaissance, Baroque, and Northern European works. There is also a small but good collection of Impressionist art, abstract art, and representative examples of European and American paintings and sculpture. The museum's twelve bronzes by Frederic Remington celebrate the American West. In addition, the museum owns many Asian works of art (2,500 pieces), and there is also a comprehensive collection of Pre-Columbian art. Selections from the collections—ranging from neolithic times to contemporary—are beautifully displayed in seven redesigned galleries on the ground floor.

Museums grow in unexpected ways, and Birmingham is the proud repository of two major decorative arts collections. The first is the Eugenia Woodward Hitt Collection. The works include more than 800 examples of French furniture, paintings, porcelain, gilt bronzes, and wall clocks dating from 1720 to 1790. These objects are displayed in four period rooms that reflect the donor's interest in the history of French royalty. Ms. Hitt, a native of Birmingham, was very impressed by European nobility (and particularly influenced by her friend the Duchess of Windsor). At one point it was rumored that her collection would leave the U.S. Today we can admire a long-gone lifestyle here in Birmingham.

The second decorative arts highlight, assembled over a forty-year period by Dwight and Lucille Beeson, is the largest collection of Wedgwood china outside England. It includes many early examples (1770–1780) as well as all types of Wedgwood: cream-colored, earthenware, black basalt, jasperware, rosso antico, and caneware.

Most unusual is the BMA's football-field-size Charles W. Ireland Sculpture Garden, designed in 1993 by Elyn Zimmerman, a sculptor, during the museum's renovation. The garden is divided into three uniquely different spaces. The first rests on the foundation of the former museum garden and preserves its beloved old water oaks. It also holds Valerie Judson's newly created *Blue Pools Courtyard*. The second garden is sunken and can be used for temporary exhibits, and the third is a raised plaza designed to hold massive works. Zimmerman's *Lithos, II*, a waterwall constructed of different shades of granite reminiscent of Alabama's geological formations, anchors the end of the plaza. An eight-foot pool catches the water cascading from the sculpture.

Arizona

Fleischer Museum

Address: 17207 N. Perimeter Drive, Scottsdale, AZ 85255
Telephone: (480) 585-3108
Web: www.fleischer.org
Hours: Daily 10–4. Closed major holidays.
Strength: American Impressionism, California School.
Parking: On site.

The small Fleischer Museum opened its doors in 1990, the first museum to be dedicated to American Impressionism, California School. Currently the museum's collection represents works by eighty different artists. Chance, as usual, played a role in the genesis of the collection. Financier Mort Fleischer was drawn to Impressionist paintings but could not afford them. In 1983 he spotted a painting by Franz G. Bischoff, a California Impressionist, in a gallery and was smitten and his collection started to grow.

It may come as a surprise that landscape painting, especially when practiced outdoors, is a relatively late development in art history. During the Renaissance, landscapes often served as background. Realistic landscape painting came into its own during the seventeenth century, and ended up dominating some European schools. The exploration of the breathtaking New World gave rise to a whole generation of American landscape painters. Albert Bierstadt, Thomas Moran, Frederick Church, and others enthralled their patrons with grand visions of Niagara Falls, the Catskills, the Rockies, the Hudson River, the Grand Canyon.

Some painters abandoned heroic visions for small intimate "portraits" of gardens and fields, rocks and streams, domestic life and seascapes. This evolution culminated in Impressionism, first exhibited in France in 1874.

It took about fifteen years for Impressionism to reach America. Visitors to the 1893 Chicago Fair were enchanted by this new way of painting landscapes, portraits, flowers, and still lifes. Since most young American painters were still trained in Europe, some started painting "impressionistic" paintings. They flocked to artists' colonies in Connecticut and elsewhere along the Eastern seaboard. Childe Hassam, J. Alden Weir, John Henry Twachtman, and Ernest Lawson are among the well-known members of these colonies.

It took another fifteen years and another Fair—the Panama Pacific Exhibition in San Francisco in 1915—for Impressionism to reach the West Coast. The California sunlight was an ideal place for the style to blossom. Both Los Angeles and San Francisco had small art colonies, though few of the members were native Californians and most were trained "back East" or in Europe where they learned to paint in an "impressionistic" style.

One's eyes are not accustomed to seeing so many pictures belonging to the same style, and at the Fleischer it takes a while to distinguish the individual characteristics of each painter. The similarities between Impressionist paintings are greater than their differences. Nevertheless, California paintings deal with grander scenery, a more dramatic coastline, and a more intense light than their Eastern counterparts.

The paintings at the Fleischer Museum, such as *Poppies and Lupines (Santa Barbara)* by John Gamble, *Carmel Cypress* by Joseph Kleitsch, *Grand Canyon* by John Bond Francisco, and *Laguna Rocks, Low Tide* by Guy Rose, mirror the magnificent landscape of the Far West.

The Heard Museum

Address: 2301 N. Central Avenue, Phoenix, AZ 85004

Telephone: (602) 252-8848

Web: www.heard.org

Hours: Daily 9:30–5. Closed New Year's, Easter, Memorial, Independence, Labor, Thanksgiving, and Christmas days. Tours daily at 12, 1:30, and 3.

Strength: Native American art and artifacts from prehistoric times to the present.

Special Events: First weekend in March: Annual Guild Indian Fair & Market featuring 500 of the nation's foremost Native American artists. March: Annual World

The Central Courtyard of The Heard Museum.

Championship Hoop Dance Contest. October: Dia de Los Muertos: A Festival for Children. Also Spanish Market featuring music and dance performances, children's craft activities, food, and a "mercado."

Other: Temporary exhibits exploring particular aspects of Native American life. Frequent artisan demonstrations and Native American dance and music events on weekends. Restaurant. Exceedingly large museum shop. All purchases are tax-free. The Heard Museum North, at Pedregal Festive Market Place on Scottsdale Road and Carefree Highway in north Scottsdale: One gallery and a shop.

Activities for Children: Most displays will fascinate children. Treasure hunt maps and other games available. Also see Special Events.

Parking: On street.

At the end of the nineteenth century, as today, Phoenix was a destination for the health-conscious. So it was that Dwight and Maie Heard moved there from Chicago in 1895. At the time, Phoenix was a frontier town numbering 4,000 souls. The Heards successfully engaged in ranching, real estate, banking, farming, and newspaper publishing. They also fell in love with Native American culture, as well as Mexican and Hispanic architecture. Relying on their own excellent taste and increasing knowledge as well as expert advice, the couple started to acquire artifacts. In 1903, they built a large Spanish Colonial house called the Casa Blanca where they shared their ever-multiplying treasures with neighbors and visiting dignitaries, including Herbert Hoover, Theodore Roosevelt, and Harvey S. Firestone.

Fortunately the Heards' interests also encompassed contemporary Native American art. The couple organized yearly invitational fine arts competitions and the art purchased at these events yielded an excellent collection of nineteenth- and twentieth-century Native American art.

By the 1920s the Heards' possessions had overflowed the Casa Blanca and, at the suggestion of daughter-in-law Winifred, the Heards decided to create a museum. Twelve small galleries, surrounding a courtyard, were built adjacent to the family home. In 1929, three months before the museum opened, Dwight Heard died. Maie directed "their" museum for twenty years, watching it become a major institution which in time absorbed the following related collections: the more than 5,000 objects (ceramics, textiles, basketry, beadwork, jewelry, ethnographic material) amassed by Fred Harvey, whose company had opened the American Southwest to tourism at the turn of the last century; Senator Barry Goldwater's collection of 437 katsina dolls dating from 1800 to the 1960s; 600 pieces of Zuni and Navajo jewelry from the early to mid-1900s assembled by C.G. Wallace, a trader at Zuni Pueblo; and Red Mullan's collection of textiles.

The influx of all these treasures (the museum owned 32,000 objects in 1999) necessitated several expansions, the last of which took place in 1999. New museum exhibition techniques have transformed the assorted art and artifacts into an emotionally satisfying showplace. At an exhibit entitled Native People of the Southwest, filled with thousands of baskets, jewelry, pottery, and textiles, visitors journey through various regions and time periods.

The Heard collection bridges the past and the present. This is perhaps best illustrated by a contemporary piece of pottery made by Jean (John) Bad Mocassin, a Hunkpapa Sioux. His grandfather, Bad Mocassin, toured Europe as part of Buffalo Bill's Wild West Show. During the show's stay in France, Bad Mocassin married a French woman. Their grandson's pot clearly is a Native American work, yet its coloring and painting is reminiscent of Miró or Kandinsky. *The Emergence of the*

Clowns (1988) by Santa Clara artist Roxanne Swentzell is another work that reflects traditional tribal figures yet belongs to our own times.

As its founders intended, the Heard Museum is a splendid celebration of the Native American heritage from prehistoric times to the present. It is a peaceful, spiritually nourishing place. Expressed in the words of a man from Taos Pueblo: "We have lived upon this land from days beyond history's record, far past any living memory, deep into the time of legend. The story of my people and the story of this place are one single story."

Phoenix Art Museum

Address: 1625 N. Central Avenue, Phoenix, AZ 85004

Telephone: (602) 257-1222

Web: www.phxart.org

Hours: Tues–Sun 10–5; Thurs 10–9. Closed Mon and major holidays. Tours: (60 min) permanent collection at 1; special exhibits at 2. Both repeated Thurs at 6. Also ArtBreaks (30 min) daily at 12 and Thurs at 7, discussing selected topics.

Strengths: Asian art. American Western art, including painters of Taos and Santa Fe schools.

Other: Audio Guide: A do-it-yourself interactive audio guide that enables viewers to select brief presentations about a specific artist and/or object. Videos on topics relating to exhibits can be viewed in orientation theater. Museum shop. Restaurant.

Activities for Children: The ArtWorks: artworks, books, and hands-on activities for children and their families. Children learn about the behind-the-scene activities of a museum (restoration, shipping art works, budgeting, advertising), and "hang" their own show using magnets. Also family programs every third Sun.

Parking: On site.

As museums go, the Phoenix Art Museum (PAM) is young. The Phoenix Women's Club had sponsored local artists for several decades, but the museum itself dates only from 1959. Like the city of Phoenix, the collection grew rapidly; by 1999 the museum owned 13,000 works of art. A new wing was added in 1965 and in 1997 the museum expanded to about twice its size.

For much of the year Phoenix is hot and so it is pleasant to enter the museum's low-slung building from a sculpture court. Large sculptures by Francisco Zuniega and Leonard Baskin are gathered around a reflecting pool and fountain whose cool waters freshen the air.

Three major themes dominate the collections of the PAM: the Art of Europe and the Americas, the Art of Our Time, and the Art of Asia. Highlights of the European collection include: a portrait of *Adelaïde Labile-Guiard*, a rare masterpiece by Jean Léon Gerôme; a view of Monet's garden in Giverny; and a striking portrait by Kees van Dongen. Henri Rousseau's *La Muse du Poète Guillaume Apollinaire* depicts Marie Laurencin, the poet's companion. Clad in a voluminous black dress, equipped with a large umbrella and a bouquet of flowers, and accompanied by a large angel and a minuscule dog, the cheer-spreading "muse" seems overdressed and lost so far away from her native France.

As expected, the PAM emphasizes paintings of the unique landscape and history of the American West. There are landscapes by Albert Bierstadt and Thomas Moran. A special gallery is devoted to the Taos and Santa Fe schools of painting. This collection includes a striking portrait of *Indian Girl, Santa Clara* by Robert Henri, the charismatic teacher of a whole generation of American painters. When New Mexico became an important art center, Henri was Santa Fe's first "artist in residence." (Also see the Museum of Fine Arts, Santa Fe, p. 264.)

Unrelated to the West are works by Gilbert Stuart, Eastman Johnson, and Winslow Homer. The PAM owns William Merritt Chase's masterpiece, *The White Rose*, a pastel portrait of Miss Josephine Jessup holding a white rose. Works created during the twentieth century are grouped together. Instead of a chronological order, the works are organized according to themes and variations: abstractions, materials, and techniques. Here we find *Flowers, Italy*, a highly stylized fantasy by Joseph Stella, best known for his many views of the Brooklyn Bridge.

A surprise are the museum's major Asian holdings, a portion of which were donated by Dr. Matthew Wong, a U.S.-educated physician who returned to China and collected art and artifacts related to China's imperial court.

Smaller, specialized possessions of the PAM include a fashion design collection with examples from major American and European workshops (Norell, Galanos, Chanel, Dior, and others) and twenty miniature rooms replicating historic American, English, French, and Italian interiors created by Narcissa Niblach Thorne (sixty-eight more are at the Art Institute of Chicago—see p. 163). Imposing portraits of Spanish Colonials by unknown artists of the eighteenth century are displayed in the Spanish Colonial Gallery. The skill of the painter(s) and the opulent clothes of the sitters are striking. An entire gallery is devoted to the work of Philip C. Curtis, a native (born 1907) and lifelong resident of Phoenix.

TUCSON

Tucson Museum Of Art

Address: 140 N. Main Avenue, Tucson, AZ 85701

Telephone: (520) 624-2333

Web: www.tucsonarts.com

Hours: Mon–Sat 10–4; Sun 12–4. Closed Mon from Memorial Day to Labor Day and on major holidays. Tours of entire Historic Block Wed and Thurs at 11 from Oct 1 to May 1. Art Talks most Mon and Thurs at 1:30 from Nov to Mar.

Strengths: Pre-Columbian, Spanish Colonial, and Western 20th-century art.

Special Events: El Nacimiento, a special display of 300 earthenware figurines celebrating Christmas.

Other: Historic Block: the 1860 Romero House; the 1907 J. Knox Corbett Mission Revival style house, furnished with objects from the Arts and Crafts era; the 1867 Edward Nye Fish adobe house; the 1866 Stevens/Duffield adobe house; and the Casa Córdova, a restored Mexican-style adobe house typical of homes built between 1850 and 1880. Museum shop.

Parking: On site.

The Tucson Museum of Art (TMA) stands on land that once was part of a *rancheria* thought to have been established by Father Eusebio Kino during the eighteenth century. He called it Mountain San Cosme del Tucson, a name derived from the Pima Indian descriptive phrase "at the base of the Black Mountains." Indeed, the spectacular mountain range still dominates Tucson, remaining its most spectacular "work of art." In 1775 the Spaniards established a fort, a pueblo, and a presidio on the site. They enclosed an area encompassing twelve or so football fields with a three-foot-thick, twelve-foot-high wall. Eventually, as the railroad and the gold rush brought in a flood of new settlers, the wall crumbled.

It took the Tucson Museum of Art (TMA) a long time to come of age. An outgrowth of the Fine Arts Association formed by the Tucson Women's Club in 1924, the museum occupied various quarters. In 1975, after decade-long deliberations, it was decided that a new building would be erected on the former presidio. Today the museum, whose understated, wood-framed entrance is reached by a dozen platform-like steps, blends in perfectly with the adobe houses of the Historic Block. Of necessity rather small, the museum, with two stories of balconies surrounding the ground floor, has an airy feeling. Now owning 5,000 works of art, the TMA hopes to expand.

As an outgrowth of several major gifts the TMA primarily collects Pre-Columbian, Spanish-Colonial, Western American, twentieth century, and contemporary art. Anthropologist Frederick R. Pleasant donated objects originating in areas of Mexico and Central and South America. Treasured possessions include a stela from Central Mexico (100–300 B.C.E.) and an equally old Olmec *Spoon in the Shape of a Profile Bird Monster*. The Spanish Colonial collection is remarkable for its oil-on-tin retables, its bultos (Mexican wooden figures—also see Museum of International Folk Art in Santa Fe, p. 262), and several portraits.

Closer to our own times is the collection left by Lawrence J. Heller, a lawyer from Washington, D.C. who retired to Tucson. According to museum literature, Heller bought a box of paint to encourage his children's artistic endeavors, then used the unopened box himself. Painting stimulated his own artistic inclinations and he started to collect, buying what he liked regardless of his acquisitions' investment potential. The ninety-two pieces he left to the museum attest to his good taste. We note Marsden Hartley's *Orchid Flowers—Orange Background (Gloxinia)*; Fernando Botero's rotund *Sailor Boy*, whose features disappear in a mountain of pink flesh; Marino Marini's *Horse and Rider*; and Lee Gatch's *Bather*. The Heller gift includes many less well-known artists including a series of color lithographs by José Luis Cuevas, a Mexican artist, and another series by Hans Martin Erhardt, a German artist.

In 1982, Ileen M. and Samuel J. Campbell donated their collection of Western art—both works by Western artists and works on Western subjects—to the TMA. It is of interest to compare Lisa Phillips's jeans-clad, rope-twisting *Cowgirl* (1977) from the Campbell gift with Josephus Gil's *Portrait of Señora Doña Carlota Caspe y Rodriguez* (1816) donated by Henry Pleasant. This young woman wears a rose-embroidered dress; one hand holds a fan, the other points at sheet music. Both women confidently belong to their own times.

The weather in Tucson is usually fine, and in a tour of the sculpture garden and the five houses that are part of the Historic Block it is easy to recapture the atmosphere of the old frontier town.

Arkansas

LITTLE ROCK

Arkansas Arts Center

Address: 501 E. 9th Street, MacArthur Park, Little Rock, AR 72203

Telephone: (501) 372-4000

Web: www.arkarts.com

Hours: Mon–Thurs, Sat 10–5; Fri 10–9; Sun 11–5.

Strengths: American and European works on paper, drawings. French art of the early 20th century. Paul Signac, Will Barnet, George Fischer, Peter Takal. Photographs by Mike Disfarmer.

Special Events: Temporary exhibits.

Other: Decorative Arts Museum located in a historic 1839 Greek-Revival house featuring selections from the museum's large permanent collection of old and new decorative arts.

Activities for Children: Child-friendly. A children's theater is part of the complex.

Parking: On site.

At the dawn of the new century, in February 2000, Arkansas celebrated the opening of its spectacular new art center with a "Big Art Weekend." The center bustled with activity. The galleries—some new, some revamped—were filled with selections from the permanent collections, including special ones such as Toys Designed by Artists, Contemporary Teapots, baskets, and the world's largest collection of works on paper by Paul Signac. Ten free lectures were given in the new lecture hall; *Aladdin and the Wonderful Lamp* was on the boards of the Children's Theater. There were door prizes, artist's demonstrations, guided tours, and gourmet meals.

Little Rock's formal relations with fine art began in 1914 when the Fine Art Club decided to develop the cultural resources of the state. In 1928 the club morphed into the Museum of Fine Arts with quarters in MacArthur Park. Growth was slow. The museum owned 100 works of art in 1934 and 200 in 1937. Matters speeded up in 1957 when the museum joined forces with Little Rock's Junior League. By then, Winthrop Rockefeller, a scion of the art-minded clan, had moved to Arkansas and taken an interest in the museum. The small original building was wrapped in new galleries and the Arkansas Arts Center (AAC) took shape. Forty years later it was again enlarged and today its pillared entrance surrounds a fountain set in a large ornamental pool.

The AAC was fortunate to come under the long-term direction of Townsend Wolfe. As recalled in a February 2000 article in the *Arkansas Democrat Gazette,* "the museum had always lacked an endowment and [when Wolfe arrived in 1968] it was about to close." Putting the institution on a firm financial footing was Wolfe's first task. The mammoth expansion is proof of his success. Since initially his funds were limited, Wolfe decided to concentrate on the acquisition of works on paper and drawings. As a consequence the museum now owns one of the best collections of drawings anywhere in America. Of note are Peter Paul Rubens's *Hygiea, Goddess of Health,* breastfeeding a giant serpent; Edgar Degas's *Three (Nude) Dancers;* Vincent van Gogh's extraordinarily detailed *Man with a Spade, Resting;* Paul Cézanne's *Bath of the Courtesan,* Pablo Picasso's luscious *Les Moissoniers;* and Georgia O'Keeffe's meticulous rendering of a *Banana Flower,* which clearly relates to the artist's sensuous flower paintings.

To celebrate the latest expansion the museum was given 135 works (watercolors and drawings) by Paul Signac, making it the largest single repository of this French Neo-Impressionist. James T. Dyke, trustee and friend of the director, collected the works over a period of fifteen years. When asked why he collected Signac, Dyke said that his initial response to the painter who used dabs of color like Seurat "was visceral, like falling in love. . . . I am struck by Signac's sense of detachment. . . . Signac chooses to record nature at its best." Indeed, looking at the painter's still lives, landscapes, and cityscapes in the AAC's specially designed gallery fills most viewers with a deep sense of satisfaction and peace. It is a rare treat to be able to study one artist in such depth.

The AAC is not all drawings. Among its treasures is Diego Rivera's large *Two Women*, painted in Paris in 1914 during the twenty-eight-year-old artist's Cubist period. It is one of Rivera's rare apolitical works. Another atypical work is Odilon Redon's *Andromeda*. A gift of David Rockefeller, the work depicts a graceful woman chained to a rock. Flowers, Redon's trademark, surround the archway of the painting. Works of American artists working during the first half of the twentieth century are well represented as are contemporary artists. The museum is proud of Alison Saar's *Invisible Man*, the outline of a featureless man holding on to a red chair against a carefully crafted collage background.

California

BERKELEY

University of California Berkeley Art Museum and Pacific Film Archive

Address: 2625 Durant Avenue, Berkeley, CA 94720; also 2626 Bancroft Way
Telephone: (510) 642-0808
Web: www.bampfa.berkeley.edu
Hours: Wed, Fri–Sun 11–5; Thurs 11–9. Closed Mon, Tues, and major holidays.
Strengths: Hans Hofmann. Asian art. Survey of American art.
Other: Pacific Film Archive of 9,000 titles, including the largest collection of

Japanese movies outside Japan. Also, important holdings of Soviet silent film and Eastern European and West Coast experimental film and video. The archive presents 600 public screenings a year. Small café. Museum shop.

Parking: Limited on street, metered; pay garages.

Berkeley is hilly and the University of California Berkeley Art Museum (UCBAM) hugs the ground so closely that it is unobtrusive. Entering it from Durant Avenue, its spacious, wide-open interior comes as a complete surprise. The museum essentially is a concrete shell-like structure rising to a height of six floors. The building is filled with natural light admitted through the above-ground rear facade and translucent ceiling. Galleries, ramps, walkways, and four large balconies unfold like a giant fan into the central space. Sculptures, including Jonathan Borofsky's glossy red *Hammering Man*, a version of the very same work that welcomes visitors at the Seattle Art Museum (p. 407) and also the Museum of Contemporary Art, San Diego (p. 79), occupy the ground floor. It is best to start at the top and descend via the interconnecting galleries.

Chance, as always, plays a major role in the creation of a museum, and to a large extent German painter Hans Hofmann defined UCBAM. Hofmann was born near Munich in 1880, at the time the city was a major cultural center (also see Frye Art Museum, p. 404). As a young artist, Hofmann moved to Paris and was influenced by Cézanne, the Cubists, Fauves, and Robert Delaunay. When Hofmann returned to Munich in 1915, Blue Rider artists and Bauhaus artists, including Franz Marc and Wassily Kandinsky, also impacted his work. Hofmann opened a successful art school of his own that attained some international repute. In 1930, Worth Ryder, the future chairman of UC Berkeley's art department, and other American students invited him to teach at Berkeley. A year later, Hofmann had a solo exhibition at San Francisco's Legion of Honor (p. 87). Hitler was on the rise in Germany, and Hofmann decided to settle in the U.S., founding two influential schools—one in New York, the other in Provincetown. He, however, remained faithful to Berkeley and in 1965 donated forty-seven of his paintings and $250,000 to the university on condition that a proper art museum would be constructed. Twice a year UCBAM presents a selection from its own Hofmann collection, the largest reservoir of his work in the world. Hofmann was the first painter to be called an "abstract expressionist." His paintings are highly varied, joyous, and exuberantly colorful.

The UCBAM is not all Hofmann. Being a teaching museum it tries to present an overview of world art. Several galleries exhibit selections from the museums' large 7,000-work permanent collection, which emphasizes twentieth-century paintings, sculpture, and photography. Highlights include works by Peter Paul Rubens, Auguste Renoir, Jackson Pollock, Andy Warhol, Mark Rothko, Sol LeWitt, Adrian Piper, Cindy Sherman, and Robert Gober. American folk art, portraits, and Hudson River School paintings are exhibited in one gallery whose traditional white plaster walls are embellished with moldings, contrasting with the contemporary ambiance of the museum.

The institution mounts interesting temporary shows such as the long-forgotten submissions to the international competition Phoebe Hearst organized to select an architect for the Berkeley campus.

LOS ANGELES

The J. Paul Getty Museum

J. Paul Getty, the oil tycoon, was born in Minneapolis in 1892 before the family relocated to southern California. His father, George Getty, had accumulated a small oil fortune and J. Paul was educated in England, graduating from Oxford University in 1913. At first he could not quite decide whether to be a playboy or a businessman. He finally chose the latter and in time he made an extraordinary fortune on his own, mostly based on the oil that gushed from wells in Kuwait and Saudi Arabia.

Getty bought his first painting, a Dutch landscape by Jan van Goyen, at auction in Berlin in 1931 for a mere $1,100. Thereafter he collected art sporadically, concentrating on Greek and Roman antiquities and eighteenth-century French decorative art. Though always more interested in decorative arts—pedigreed French furniture and superior Oriental carpets—than in paintings, he acquired a few masterpieces including Rembrandt's portrait of *Marten Looten,* which he later gave to the Los Angeles County Museum of Art (see

p. 60). Getty also bought Greek and Roman sculptures including *Landsdowne Herakles,* a Roman copy of a Greek original.

In 1945 Getty acquired a sixty-four-acre ranch in Malibu, which included a hacienda. Inspired by his friend and neighbor William Randolph Hearst, he even kept a few wild animals. Getty used the hacienda occasionally until 1951, when he left the United States to live at Sutton Place, his castle in the south of England. He lived in England for the rest of his life, writing books, and supervising his fortune and his growing art collection.

In 1953, he founded a small museum in his hacienda, and a trust to operate it. He appointed William R. Valentiner (see Introduction), who had served as his art consultant, as director. Getty and Valentiner did not hit it off too well, and the formal arrangement lasted less than a year. Their relationship, however, remained cordial, and Valentiner continued to advise Getty.

When Getty died in 1976, he left the bulk of his estate—$700 million in Getty Oil stock—to the Getty Trust for "the Diffusion of Art and General Knowledge." By the time the will was settled this amount had grown to more than a billion dollars. This gift stunned both the art world and the staff of the small museum in Malibu. After decades-long deliberations, the Getty Center, a museum complex with wide-ranging activities, was opened in Brentwood in 1999.

The Getty Villa

Address: 17985 Pacific Coast Highway, Santa Monica, CA 90265
Telephone: (310) 230-7075
Web: www.getty.edu/museum/villa.htm
Strengths: Ancient Greek and Roman art.
Parking: Very limited and by pre-arrangement only.

The Villa is closed for renovation and scheduled to reopen in 2003.

California has always been a good place for make-believe. It may thus seem ordinary in Los Angeles to lunch on the patio of a 2,000-year-old

Roman villa, surrounded by plantings and clipped boxwood hedges. Before and after lunch visitors can admire antiquities and marvel at the perfection of intricately laid marble floors, marble mosaics, perfect woodwork, Pompeian type paintings, and other delights.

By 1953, J. Paul Getty decided he had acquired enough art to open a small museum in his hacienda in Malibu. In 1968, when he was seventy-five years old, he decided to replace the hacienda house-museum with a bigger structure. After some soul-searching he chose to model it on the Villa dei Papiri which had been buried by the ashes of Mount Vesuvius in 79 C.E. According to John Walsh and Deborah Gribbon, authors of *The J. Paul Getty Museum,* Getty had observed that though many majestic Roman structures had been re-created, there were "no replicas of private structures." He felt that his villa would "provide a unique experience," and that a visitor would "feel as if I invited him to come and look about and feel at home." No expense was spared during the construction. The results were breathtaking and since the villa-museum opened its doors in 1974, it has been exceedingly popular.

With the opening of the Getty Center in 1999, the Getty Villa was designated a museum for antiquities and closed for renovations. It is scheduled to reopen in 2003. The newly renovated Villa will not only house the Antiquities Collection of more than 50,000 objects, arranged in thematic exhibits, but also have galleries for temporary exhibitions including works from outside the scope of the museum's collection.

The Getty Center

Address: 1200 Getty Center Drive, Los Angeles, CA 90049

Telephone: (310) 440-7330

Web: www.getty.edu

Hours: Tues–Wed 10–7; Thurs–Fri 10–9; Sat–Sun 10–6. Closed Mon and major holidays. Frequent tours on various subjects.

Strengths: Antiquities, selected European paintings, French decorative arts, illuminated manuscripts. Arts education.

Special events: Temporary exhibits. Free concerts, performances, and readings. Family festivals.

Other: Exhibition-related lectures. Gardens. Indoor and outdoor cafés and restaurants with spectacular vistas. Picnics allowed. Comprehensive art bookstore. Art Access, an interactive multimedia resource. Virtual-reality presentations including the reconstruction of a Roman forum based on archaeological excavations.

Activities for Children: Large family room with hands-on activities and various games, puzzles, CD-ROMs, and costumes designed to help children interact with the art works on exhibit. Staffers will help organize a meaningful visit. Materials available in English and Spanish.

Parking: Limited and by reservation only.

The Getty Center sits like an acropolis on a hilltop in the Santa Monica Mountains high above the Los Angeles freeways. Ascending by tram from the parking garage, visitors glimpse the mansions of Bel-Air, urban sprawl, the gray grid of the city, an occasional deer, and the wild canyon—and are reminded of that other California extravaganza: the Hearst castle in San Simeon. Both complexes are located a few miles from the Pacific, dominating the surrounding countryside. Both are grandiose, paying homage to their creators, and both make their visitors feel privileged.

After fierce competition, architect Richard Meier (also see the High Museum of Art, p. 158, and Des Moines Art Center, p. 174) was awarded the task of building the museum. He distributed six two-story pavilions around an open campus filled with fountains, waterfalls, jets, pools, walkways, floating bridges, boulders, stairways, and plantings. Visitors are never far from water, trees, or other beautiful details. The starkly modern buildings are clad in rough-cut stone quarried in Tivoli, fifteen miles east of Rome. Occasionally the stone is alternated with Meier's signature specially treated porcelain panels. The galleries throughout are smallish. Meier took advantage of Southern California's light, and artificial illumination is used only sparingly.

Even with a large sum of money to spend, it is difficult to create an encyclopedic museum at the end of the twentieth century, and the collection of the Getty cannot be compared to those of the great museums of the eastern U.S. The museum nevertheless has a growing number of unique possessions that are perhaps especially enjoyable because they are not drowned in a sea of masterpieces. The museum specializes in the art beloved by J. Paul Getty: European paintings, French furniture, and antiquities. Now the museum also collects Renaissance sculpture, illuminated manuscripts, drawings, and photographs.

Some highlights of the Getty Center include Pontormo's Renaissance portrait of *Halberdier,* an *Annunciation* by Dierick Bouts, early and late Rembrandts, Jan Steen's *Drawing Lesson,* and *Christ's Entry into Brussels in 1890,* long recognized as the masterpiece of James Ensor, Belgium's enigmatic painter. The Getty was also able to acquire Vincent van Gogh's *Irises,* which had been sold at auction for $49 million to an Australian collector who went broke before he could ante up the money. The consignor of the painting was Westbrook College in Maine, which had received it from Joan Whitney Payson (see Colby College Museum of Art, p. 193). Fortunately the Getty could write a big check, enabling *Irises* to stay in the United States. Period rooms displaying Getty's preeminent collection of decorative art are a delight.

Don't leave without visiting the Central Garden, created by Robert Irwin, which overlooks the distant Pacific. It is best to approach it along the gently descending stream that "springs" from a recess in a wall and flows into a pool. From there a stream meanders through trees, eventually cascading into an amphitheater-like pool. A maze of seemingly floating azaleas covers the pool, whose steep banks are a tapestry of flowers and foliage.

Los Angeles County Museum of Art

Address: 5905 Wilshire Boulevard, Los Angeles, CA 90036

Telephone: (323) 857-6000

Web: www.lacma.org

Hours: Mon (including holidays), Tues, Thurs 12–8; Fri 12–9; Sat and Sun 11–8. Closed Wed and Thanksgiving and Christmas days. Very active daily tour program.

Strengths: Encyclopedic. European, American, Asian, Islamic, and decorative arts. Japanese art. Central and South American art, including the largest collection of Rufino Tamayo in the world. Costume and photography collections. Sculpture garden.

Special Events: Extensive temporary shows.

Other: LACMA West, northeast corner of Fairfax and Wilshire Boulevard. Pleasant

The windows of the small Pavilion for Japanese Art at the Los Angeles County Museum of Art resemble giant Japanese rice-paper screens.

restaurants and extensive shops. Free concerts on Sun afternoon and jazz concerts on Fri evenings. Active film and lecture program.

Activities for Children: Every Sun: Family days with live performances and hands-on activities for children 5–12. Also special recorded tours geared to children and a children's gallery at LACMA West.

Parking: Self-parking across from LACMA on the corner of Wilshire and Spalding and on Ogden Drive west of the museum. Also metered, on street.

The five buildings of the Los Angeles County Museum of Art (LACMA) occupy a tightly packed campus on Wilshire Boulevard. Visitors ascend via broad stairs along a cascade of gurgling water to a plaza ringed by tall buildings. White and pale green dominate the scene: The buildings have white walls with large insets of greenish glass; the stairs and the entrance court are covered with a glass canopy held up by three-story-high green-ceramic-covered columns; the railings are green and white. On weekends the plaza is alive with music and dancing, but tourists with little time had better hurry inside, because there is so much to see.

LACMA's forerunner—a hodge-podge museum housing stuffed birds and bison, historical artifacts, and art—dates from 1910. Even though art was not its main focus, the museum gathered a great number of paintings and in 1954 the art division appointed museum maverick William R. Valentiner (see Introduction) to help it achieve world-class status. During his eight-year tenure at LACMA, Valentiner mapped out its future. By then the museum had received major gifts from William Randolph Hearst (Medieval and Renaissance art) Paul Mabury and Allan Balch (Old Masters), George Gard De Sylva (Impressionists), and J. Paul Getty (European paintings, tapestries, and European art). There were also major disappointments. The museum had counted on receiving the striking Arensberg collection of 1,500 works of modern Cubist, Surrealist, and Dadaist art, but it eventually ended up at the Philadelphia Museum of Art (see p. 355). LACMA also expected the Galka E. Scheyer collection of Blue Rider School artists that went to the Pasadena Art Museum (see the Norton Simon Museum, p. 68). With time, however, LACMA assembled 130,000 art objects, many of them superior.

The large Ahmanson building houses the permanent collection. It is a handsome structure with a large central atrium. Start on the second level that houses the art of the ancient world and of Europe. Here are Italian Renaissance paintings, impressive Assyrian bas-reliefs, decorative arts, and much more. You will find Rembrandt's portrait of *Martin Looten*, one of the first art works acquired by J. Paul Getty (see The J. Paul Getty Museum p. 56) and the painter's *Portrait of Hendrickje Stoeffels*, his long-time companion, as well as LACMA's much beloved *Magdalen with the Smoking Flame* by Georges de La Tour, and *Soap Bubbles* by Jean-Baptiste-Siméon Chardin. There are works by Frans Hals, Fredrick Bols, and Pieter de Hooch. Other galleries are filled with the paintings of the Impressionist, Post-Impressionist, German Expressionist, Modern, and other schools. One of LACMA's signature works is Henri Matisse's *Tea, 1919*, in which the painter's daughter and his model are having tea in his garden in Issy-les-Moulineaux on a lazy summer afternoon. Matisse's dog stretches on the sun-dappled ground. Patterned and flat surfaces, light and shade, greens, grays, and browns, alternate in perfect harmony. Ernst Ludwig Kirchner's *Two Women*, black-clad against a yellow and orange background, are less peaceful but equally captivating.

LACMA's American collection, which intermingles decorative arts, sculpture, and painting, is especially appealing. There is Arts and Crafts furniture, Tiffany glass, art pottery, and a thorough representation of works by most American painters. Thomas Hart Benton's huge *The Kentuckian,* depicts father, son, and dog off to hunt in a fantastic landscape. With its rifle and powder horn, the work—a gift of Burt Lancaster—celebrates Americans' "right to bear arms." As much a part of the American tradition is John Singer Sargent's *Portrait of Mrs. Edward L. Davis and Her Son, Livingston Davis.* The portrait is formal, and yet the pose, the expression of the faces, the intertwining of the hands, conveys the tenderness that exists between mother and child. An excellent collection of modern and contemporary American and European art is housed in the Anderson building. Here we come across *Mulholland Drive: The Road to the Studio,* a monumental landscape by David Hockney, as well as works by Frank Stella, Richard Diebenkorn, and Anselm Kiefer.

LACMA's significant Japanese collection is displayed in an architecturally distinct pavilion whose enormous windows are like Japanese rice-paper screens. Beautiful scrolls, paintings, prints, sculptures, textiles, and decorative arts are displayed in diffuse light. A large collection of netsuke—tiny sculptures—invites a prolonged study of these delicate objects.

In 1997 the donation of the Bernard and Edith Lewin Collection of 2,000 Latin American—mostly Mexican Modernist—works catapulted LACMA into the forefront of art from south of the border. The Lewin Collection, which includes the largest holdings of works by Rufino Tamayo in the world, is housed in LACMA West, located in what used to be a Mays department store built in Art Deco style.

Museum of Contemporary Art, Los Angeles

Address: *MOCA at California Plaza:* 250 S. Grand Avenue, Los Angeles, CA 90012; *The Geffen Contemporary at MOCA:* 152 N. Central Avenue, Los Angeles, CA 90013

Telephone: (213) 626-6222

Web: www.moca-la.org

Hours: Tues–Sun 11–5, Thurs 11–8. Closed Mon and New Year's, Thanksgiving, and Christmas days.

Strengths: Art created after 1940 and evolving contemporary art.

Special Events: More than 20 temporary exhibitions a year.

Other: Periodic art talks and dialogues by artists or art experts. Restaurants, coffee bar. Museum shops.

Activities for Children: Artist-led workshops related to exhibitions (periodically, on Sun).

Parking: *At MOCA at Plaza:* SE corner of First Street and Central Avenue; SW corner of First Street and Central Avenue. Weekend parking: California Plaza, Music Center, and Allright lots and garages (have parking tickets validated at museum). *At Geffen:* Low-price public lots.

In 1979 a small group of art lovers realized that Los Angeles was the only major city in the U.S. without a museum of contemporary art. They remedied the situation by creating one. The museum is split between two buildings of widely divergent styles: MOCA at California Plaza and The Geffen Contemporary at MOCA.

The former is housed in an elegant red sandstone building designed by Arata Isozaki (see also Bass Museum of Art, p. 142) and completed in 1986. It is located amidst tall skyscrapers in one of Los Angeles's downtown business centers. The museum and its surroundings are urban and sophisticated. As elsewhere in Southern California, outdoor plazas are interwoven with indoor spaces. Isozaki's building is a carefully balanced combination of cubes, pyramids, and barrel-vault shapes.

The purpose of contemporary art museums is to present the art of our times in all its diversity: paintings, sculpture, photography, video, and film as well as new developments in architecture, music, and the performing arts. It is a tall order and many of the contemporary art museums are non-collecting. Los Angeles's museum does collect and is proud of the 4,600 works of art it owns. A selection of its permanent collection is usually on exhibit. Visitors may for instance view art produced during the 1960s. *Tall Figures I* and *II* by Alberto Giacometti represent 1961. Works produced by Andy Warhol, Jasper Johns, Roy Lichtenstein, and Richard Diebenkorn in 1965 occupy another gallery. One feels like touching a large plate-glass construction entitled *Shatter Scatter* by Barry LeVa that occupies the center of the gallery devoted to

1968. As its name implies, the work reflects and scatters the prevailing illumination. *Friend or Foe?* by Neil Jenny, depicts a big fish pursuing a swimming dog.

While its permanent building in California Plaza was being readied, MOCA-LA's founders mounted exhibits in a vacant warehouse in the nearby Little Tokyo area of Los Angeles. In the 1980s the warehouse was transformed by Frank Gehry into The Geffen Contemporary at MOCA. Gehry, who has emerged as one of the world's best-known museum architects (the Guggenheim in Bilbao, Spain; the Weisman in Minneapolis—p. 240; the refiguration of the Norton Simon in Pasadena—p. 68), here in Los Angeles converted a raw space into a suitable environment for unforgiving contemporary art. According to museum literature: "Gehry's subtle and stunning renovation retained many of the elements that reveal the building's roots. On the outside, the original coat of paint is still barely visible and the massive overhead doors remain in place. . . . To define an outdoor courtyard, Gehry designed a chain-link canopy to span the dead-end street in front of the building. . . . Inside, the vast scale of the space has proven extraordinarily suitable for the exhibition of contemporary art." Indeed, by using existing columns, trusses, beams, and hoists, and by adding platforms and walkways Gehry turned an indifferent warehouse into an exciting space where visitors can view cutting-edge art in all its multiplicity: traditional paintings and sculptures, video art, neon-light constructions, and other media.

OAKLAND

The Oakland Museum of California

Address: 1000 Oak Street, Oakland, CA 94607

Telephone: (510) 238-2200

Web: www.museumca.org

Hours: Wed–Sat 10–5; Sun 12–7; first Fri until 9. Closed: Mon, Tues, and New Year's, Independence, Thanksgiving, and Christmas days. Docent-led tours at 2 on weekdays and by request on weekends. Free 20-min Spotlight Tours for each permanent gallery offered every first and third Sat and second and fourth Sun.

Strength: Californian art and art relating to California.

Other: The Cowell Hall of California History, which documents the settling of the state, the California Missions, the state's Native American heritage, the Gold Rush, and other significant events; the 1906 earthquake and fire and the more recent population explosion are of particular interest. Restaurant. Museum shop.

Activities for Children: Family exploration programs allow adults and children to experience the museum together. Hands-on activities. Many exhibits geared to children. Outdoor play area. Also see Other.

Parking: Pay garage on site (entrances on Oak and 12th Streets).

From the time ships sailed up the Golden Gate, long before the Bay Bridge linked the sister cities, Oakland and San Francisco competed with one another. San Francisco always was the more elegant and arty of the two, while Oakland became its industrial twin with a hard-working port. And yet, the museums of the East Bay, which includes Oakland and Berkeley, hold their own.

Like many other museums, the Oakland Museum is an outgrowth of a fair. When the Panama-Pacific Exhibition opened in 1915 in San Francisco, a number of local California artists were brave enough to exhibit their paintings and sculptures along works of their fellow artists from the East and Europe. A year later, the citizens of Oakland founded a small gallery that exhibited works produced by California artists, and art dealing with California subjects. At about the same time, Oaklanders saw the birth of two other museums: the Oakland Public Museum, which exhibited 12,000 objects of historical and anthropological interest, and a natural science collection assembled by Henry Snow.

By 1950, all three museums had outgrown their quarters and the town decided to build a center that would house all of them. The result is a unique complex of buildings, gardens, leafy terraces, stairs, and sheltered streets. It is difficult to leave the sunny gardens, the sculpture, trees, and terraces that form the outdoor part of the museum and enter the building.

Once inside the Oakland Museum of California, however, the treasures of the museum quickly erase the outdoor memories. The pictures are arranged in chronological order and present an overview of the California art movement from its beginning to the present. There are no

Old Masters here, no Renaissance paintings, no American primitives. The oldest artwork on display consists of some sketches of animals and natives made by the early explorers. There is an impressive panorama of San Francisco in 1849. Portraits of the early settlers—Native Californians, Spaniards, Mexicans, Orientals, and Caucasians—attest that the Golden State was always multi-ethnic.

The heart of the collection celebrates the dramatic California light and scenery. The golden hills, giant trees, meadows, wild coast, and of course the domes, cliffs, and waterfalls of Yosemite. Some of these works may now seem excessively dramatic and pompous. The museum owns Albert Bierstadt's huge painting of Yosemite Valley (1868) as well as works by other Hudson River School painters including Thomas Hill and Keith Scott. The latter two were born in Europe, but were among the first important artists to became permanent residents of California.

Gradually "art for art's sake" overshadows pure documentation. One of Oakland's proudest possessions is a gentle landscape simply called *California*, painted by George Inness (also see the Montclair Art Museum, p. 253), a tonalist influenced by James Whistler. Inness too moved to California and became the teacher of the ever-increasing number of artists living in the Bay area. Proceeding along the chronological path the paintings become infused with sun and light. The California School of Impressionism assails the senses (also see the Fleischer Museum, p. 44).

As in Europe, California Impressionism gave way to other art movements, including the Fauves, characterized by violent, sometimes jarring color juxtapositions. In the East Bay, the Fauves are represented by the Society of Six, including William H. Clapp, a former director of the museum.

The museum also pays homage to the Arts and Crafts Movement's California blossoming. In San Francisco the furniture shop of Arthur and Lucia Matthews produced paintings, furniture, frames, and stained glass windows. The immense Frank Pierce Hammon Memorial Window (1925), depicting small houses, cliffs, flowers, and the ocean, demonstrates their skill. There are fine examples of objects made by Greene and Greene, Stickley, and other important members of the Arts and Crafts Movement.

After you leave the 1920s, the easy part of the museum visit is over. The social realism of the 1930s, the abstractions of the 1940s, the art produced by the Beat generation in the 1950s, and the intermingling of craft and sculpture of the recent past are hard to organize in your mind. But, since art is less well defined today, viewers can more easily rely on their own taste. Exhibitions in this part of the museum change frequently, often featuring specific California artists.

PASADENA

Norton Simon Museum

Address: 411 W. Colorado Boulevard, Pasadena, CA 91105

Telephone: (626) 449-6840

Web: www.nortonsimon.org

Hours: Mon, Wed–Sun 12–6; Fri until 9. Closed Tues and major holidays.

Strengths: European art from the Renaissance to the 20th century, including important works by Botticelli, Rubens, Rembrandt, Zurbarán, Goya, and other Old Masters. Important Impressionist and Post-Impressionist collection, with works by Matisse and Picasso. German Expressionists. Art from India and Southeast Asia spanning 2,000 years. Impressive sculpture garden.

Special Events: Leading temporary exhibits.

Other: Museum shop. Outdoor snack bar.

Parking: On site.

Except for the Rodin sculptures out front, the curious-looking windowless building in downtown Pasadena gives no hint of the treasures hidden behind its fortress-like tile-covered brown walls. Big white letters on the side of the building announce that you have arrived at the Norton Simon Museum. Inside the airy lobby a large Buddha welcomes you, and even visitors already aware of the fact that the museum houses one of the great art collections of the world will be buoyed by its perfection.

Norton Simon bought his first major painting—a Renoir—in 1954, when he and his wife moved into a new house in an affluent section of Los Angeles. According to his biographer, Suzanne Muchnic, Simon had not been interested in or knowledgeable about art before that pur-

Still Life with Lemons, Oranges, and a Rose by Francisco de Zurbarán, is one of many master-pieces owned by the Norton Simon Museum in Pasadena.

chase. His legacy proves that this state of affairs soon changed radi-cally.

As comprehensive art museums go, the Norton Simon is small and not overwhelming, but it is filled with unique examples of European art, a world-class collection from India and Southeast Asia, and exquis-ite examples of post-modern art. Remarkably, most of the art was assembled in a thirty-year period, at a time when "great" artworks were no longer easily available.

Norton W. Simon was born in Portland, Oregon, in 1907 and moved with his family to San Francisco in 1922. He was a financial genius. His brain was a computer, storing information and crunching numbers. He shrewdly specialized in acquiring control of undervalued, poorly man-aged companies and making them profitable. At age twenty-four he invested in a bankrupt orange juice bottling plant in Fullerton, Califor-nia, and that was the beginning of what was to be the Hunt Foods empire, best known for its tomato products. Norton Simon became a multimillionaire.

Thirty years later, Simon used these same skills to assemble his art collection. Simon had excellent taste, and an amazing eye. He also was a quick study, single-minded, passionate, persistent, and paranoid. He endlessly pumped others for information and advice. He drove museum directors, curators, auctioneers, and art dealers to distraction with his endless telephone calls and complex machinations. In the end, he earned every art lover's respect. When he died in June 1993, Franklin Murphy, a chancellor of UCLA and former associate, wrote in the *Los Angeles Times* that Simon was "one the truly great art collectors in American history [bringing together a] fabulous collection of works of art in an astonishingly short time."

In the beginning, Simon bought anything that appealed to him aesthetically, but he rapidly became more selective. At first he was partial to French Impressionists and Post-Impressionists: Edouard Manet, Claude Monet, Vincent van Gogh, Paul Cézanne, Henri Matisse, Paul Gauguin. He developed a special love for Edgar Degas. The museum owns many Degas paintings, drawings, and sculptures, including a group of long-lost wax models.

Thereafter, his scope broadened and Simon assembled the West Coast's best collection of Old Masters. It includes Raphael's *Madonna and Child with Book*; Giovanni di Paolo's *The Branchini Madonna*; Francisco de Zurbarán's *Still Life with Lemons, Oranges, and a Rose*; Rembrandt's *Portrait of the Artist's Son, Titus*; and Lucas Cranach the Elder's paintings of *Adam* and *Eve* that once hung in the Hermitage Museum in St. Petersburg. As time went on, Simon filled in the gaps with fine examples of nineteenth-century art: Camille Corot, Gustave Courbet, Eugène Delacroix, Honoré Daumier, and others.

In 1971, shortly after his longtime marriage dissolved, Simon fell in love with the actress Jennifer Jones. The couple married three and a half weeks after they first met, and eventually honeymooned in India. There he developed a passion for sensuous Indian sculpture. Being Simon, he went on a shopping spree and in record time assembled an outstanding collection that is now breathtakingly displayed on the lower floor of the museum.

When Simon started collecting, Los Angeles did not have an art museum and he was involved in the creation of the Los Angeles County Museum of Art (p. 60). For a while it was thought that he would merge his possessions with that museum, with UCLA, or perhaps with the Getty, or that the Norton Simon collection would become a Western branch of the National Gallery of Art. None of that was to be.

In view of Simon's past as a corporate raider, it is almost ironic that

Simon "took over" Pasadena's about-to-be-bankrupt art institute. Founded in 1924, The Pasadena Art Institute initially occupied the Reed mansion and in 1948 moved to what is now the Pacific Asia Museum (see next entry). It sponsored emerging California artists and in 1953 it received an important and large collection (450 objects) of Bauhaus and Blue Rider art (Wassily Kandinsky, Paul Klee, Lyonel Feininger, Alexei Jawlensky) from Galka E. Scheyer, a European émigré opera singer. A dozen years later the museum commissioned a new building from Ladd and Kelsey—a firm without museum-building experience—which opened in 1969 as the Pasadena Art Museum. The seriously underfunded museum never recovered from the expense of that move. In 1974, Norman Simon acquired the museum, and there followed decades of lawsuits between the old regime and the new concerning exhibition space and deaccessioning.

That, however, was not the only trouble. The building, which had been designed for the large canvases characteristic of modern art, was never quite right for Norton Simon's more intimate works. In 1998, Frank Gehry, best known for the extravagant Guggenheim Museum in Bilbao, Spain, agreed to redesign the museum. (Gehry, an old family friend of Simon and longtime trustee of his museum, also built a museum for Simon's brother-in-law Fred Weisman in Minneapolis— see The Frederick R. Weisman Art Museum, p. 240.) Gehry created smaller galleries, improved lighting, and heightened ceilings and even created outdoor vistas for some of the galleries displaying Indian art. Landscape architect Nancy Goslee Power redesigned the sculpture garden. A large central pond, filled with reeds and water lilies, is reminiscent of Monet's garden in Giverny. Life seems good as you listen to a waterfall and amble among sculptures by Henry Moore, Aristide Maillol, Barbara Hepworth, Jacques Lipchitz, and others, artfully displayed amid tall eucalyptus trees and blooming birds of paradise and iris.

Pacific Asia Museum

Address: 46 N. Los Robles Avenue, Pasadena, CA 91101
Telephone: (626) 449-2742
Web: www.pacasiamuseum.org

A *Han Horse* from China (2nd century c.e.), from the collection of the Pacific Asia Museum in Pasadena.

Hours: Wed–Sun 10–5, Thurs 10–8. Closed Mon, Tues, and major holidays.

Strength: Art of Asia and the Pacific Islands: Chinese, Vietnamese, Tibetan, and Thai ceramics; Buddhist sculptures; paintings from India, China, Tibet, Southeast Asia, and the Trans-Himalayan region; Chinese jade and Japanese netsuke.

Special Events: Celebration of Asian festivals. Lectures.

Other: Research library open to the public 12–4 and by appointment. Many outreach programs designed to familiarize the community with Asian art. Concerts and lectures. Excellent museum store.

Activities for Children: Free family day every third Sat featuring activities celebrating specific themes and cultures. Activity booklets.

Parking: On site.

What is now the Pacific Asia Museum (PAM) has been located in downtown Pasadena since 1924. Its founding is strangely reminiscent of that of the Jacques Marchais Museum of Tibetan Art in Staten Island, New York (see p. 291) except that the Pacific Asia has always had wide community support. Grace Nicholson came to Pasadena from Philadelphia in 1901, when she was eighteen years old. At first she was interested in Native American art and artifacts. She opened a shop and took in typing to supplement her income. Gradually she developed an interest in Asian art. As her expertise grew she sold works of art to private collectors and museums.

In 1924 she commissioned what was to be Grace Nicholson's Chinese Treasure House from Marston, Van Pelt and Maybury. Under their client's directions these local architects built a remarkable two-story Chinese Imperial palace-style abode encircling an authentic Chinese garden. The building pays homage to Chinese myth and traditions. The tile-covered slanted roof is adorned with ceramic dogs to ward off evil spirits and enemies. The courtyard is filled with a profusion of plants and rocks. Humongous carp and goldfish swim in a pond. A metal sculpture of Buddha sits on a bench, keeping a watchful eye on the surroundings.

After Nicholson's death in 1948, her collection was sold for one dollar! The Pasadena Art Institute—founded in 1924—moved into her beloved home, where it organized several ground-breaking exhibits. In 1969 the institute moved into its own building, changing its name to the Pasadena Art Museum (see the Norton Simon Museum, previous entry). After the move the Nicholson house fell into disrepair. In 1974, David Kamansky came aboard as director, restored the building, and spearheaded the task of assembling a world-class collection. Today the museum owns 12,000 objects—including some of the original objects collected by Nicholson—the largest collection of Asian art in Southern California.

The PAM is small and intimate. Three of its dozen or so galleries were restructured in 2000. The cases are filled with Chinese ceramics, divided into burial ceramics, ceramics for the court, and export ceramics. Visitors are reminded that all fine pottery is called china, and that the Chinese had mastered that art of firing and glazing clay at high temperatures when the rest of the world still made do with crude pottery. The examples on display at the PAM are exquisite. The shapes are elegant; the glazes range from dark red to white and include deep blues, yellows, and celadon. A whole case is filled with export ware rescued from a vessel sunk during the fourteenth century.

The objects in the remaining galleries are also graceful. Jade has captivated Asian artists since Neolithic times and the PAM is replete with Chinese jades and Japanese netsuke. Gallery 8, with its Tibetan religious paintings and larger sculptures, some of which were formerly in the collection of Frank Lloyd Wright, is especially elegant. The museum also organizes exhibitions by contemporary Asian American artists.

SACRAMENTO

Crocker Art Museum

Address: 216 O Street, Sacramento, CA 95814

Telephone: (916) 264-5423

Web: www.crockerartmuseum.org

Hours: Tues–Sun 10–5; Thurs 10–9. Closed Mon and major holidays.

Strengths: German paintings, 16th–19th century. Old Master drawings. California paintings, including those capturing the excitement of the California Gold Rush. Ceramics.

Special Events: Temporary exhibits, festivals. Juried exhibition for Northern California artists.

Other: Museum store. The Leland Stanford mansion and the Capitol building in which Thomas Hill's painting *Driving the Last Spike* is exhibited.

Activities for Children: Family Saturdays and sometimes Sundays. Many different programs including a Grandparents' Day.

Parking: On site, metered.

The Crocker is the oldest museum in California. Edwin Crocker was born in New York and grew up near Troy. Edwin and his brother Charles, so the story goes, were fascinated by railroads, which in time would provide their fortune. First, however, Edwin studied law. He practiced in Indiana where he may have met Henry Ward Beecher, the abolitionist. In any case, Crocker defended a group of runaway Kentucky slaves. Though he won the case, the rancor against Crocker was such—he had to reimburse the slave owners—that he decided to join his brothers in Sacramento. Before he left the East, Reverend Beecher married Edwin and Margaret, his second wife, in New York.

The newlyweds arrived in rough Sacramento in 1852 and joined the Crocker Brothers' Store. Edwin became involved in agricultural, political, and cultural affairs, qualified as a California lawyer, and developed a successful practice. He also became a big wheel in the Republican

The foyer of the Crocker Art Museum in Sacramento.

party and sponsored the candidacy of his friend Leland Stanford for governor. Together with his brother Charles, Mark Hopkins, Leland Stanford, and Collis Huntington, Edwin invested in the Central Pacific Railroad. The gamble paid off handsomely and Edwin became a rich man. In 1863, Governor Stanford appointed Edwin Associate Justice of the California State Supreme Court. Eventually, Edwin resigned his judgeship and became the legal counsel and then director of the Central Pacific and Union Pacific Railroad. His name is engraved on the golden spike that marked the joining of the rail spurs that link East and West. In 1869, Edwin suffered a stroke, retired, and devoted the rest of his life to leisure.

By then the family had purchased property in downtown Sacramento, located next to that of the Leland Stanfords. Crocker turned a modest Georgian house into a magnificent Victorian mansion, annexed to a gallery building. According to K. D. Kurutz in *Sacramento's Pioneer Patrons of Art*, Crocker bought art in San Francisco and became interested in collecting on a grander scale. He supported local artists, including Thomas Hill and Charles Christian Nahl, a German-born and -trained painter who came to California to find gold but ended up chronicling the mining life.

In 1869 the Crocker family embarked on a year-long grand European tour, which they spent mostly in Germany. There they purchased four carloads of paintings, which duly arrived in Sacramento. The collection included many German salon paintings from the sixteenth to the eighteenth century as well as a remarkable collection of Old Master prints and drawings that includes works by Albrecht Dürer, Rembrandt, Jacques-Louis David, François Boucher, Jacopo Bassano, and Jean Honoré Fragonard. Some of the paintings were from the Munich School so beloved by the Fryes in Seattle (see the Frye Art Museum, p. 404). Contemporary California paintings, including Thomas Hill's monumental *Great Canyon of the Sierras*, were acquired. The most famous work in the collection is Charles Nahl's *Sunday Morning in the Mines*, which depicts the "good" miners who read the Bible or write home "Dear Mother" and the "wastrels" who carouse and scatter gold dust to the wind.

By 1873 the gallery building, which also contained a sixty-foot-long ballroom, a library, a skating rink, a bowling alley, an indoor swimming pool, and a billiard room, was almost ready. More paintings were purchased and in 1874 the public was invited to view 700 or so works of art. A year later, fifty-seven-year-old Judge Crocker died. In 1885, Margaret Crocker donated the gallery jointly to the City of Sacramento and to the newly formed California Museum Association. The mansion itself was given to the Peniel Rescue Mission.

In 1911, daughter Jennie Crocker Fassett bought the mansion back and gave it to the museum along with an endowment fund. On her trips to the Orient she acquired outstanding examples of Korean ceramics that formed the beginning of the Crocker's superior ceramics collection.

By 1941 the last of the original Crocker family had died, but their museum lives on. Over the years it restored the older sections to their original glamour and added more gallery space. It purchased more art and by now owns 9,000 pieces, of which 10 percent are on view. Over time the museum acquired representative examples of American art (Childe Hassam, Georgia O'Keeffe, Romare Bearden), with an emphasis on Northern California painters (Wayne Thiebaud, Robert Ameson, Joan Brown, Gregory Kondos).

SAN DIEGO

San Diego Museum of Art

Address: 1450 El Prado, Balboa Park, San Diego, CA 92101

Telephone: (619) 232-7931

Web: www.sdmart.org

Hours: Tues–Sun 10:30–6:00, Thurs 10–9. Closed Mon and New Year's, Thanksgiving, and Christmas days.

Strengths: Encyclopedic. European, American, Asian, especially South Asian, and and California art. Toulouse-Lautrec.

Special Events: Temporary exhibits.

Other: Restaurant. Museum shop.

Activities for Children: Quarterly Family Festival Sundays with hands-on activities and live performances.

Parking: Very limited in front of the museum. A free tram runs from outer parking lots to the museum.

In 1868 the city fathers of San Diego set aside eleven hundred acres of parkland and today citizens rejoice in downtown's Balboa Park. In 1915–1916 the Panama-Pacific Exhibition, marking the opening of the Panama Canal, was celebrated in Balboa Park. A loan show was held in a temporary fine arts exhibition hall and a few years later, in 1922, Mr. and Mrs. Appleton Bridges pledged $40,000 for a permanent art building. Mrs. Bridges was a member of the Timken family (of roller-bearing fortune), who later endowed the adjoining Timken Museum of Art (see p. 82).

Mr. Bridges engaged William Templeton Johnson, a local architect, who because of his lack of experience traveled to the East Coast, at his own expense, to study museum architecture. Johnson adhered to the Neo-Spanish style used elsewhere in the park. Artists who had worked on the Panama-Pacific fair created the museum's striking facade. The San Diego Museum of Art (SDMA) opened in 1926.

Reginald Harkness Poland was the founding director. In view of the town's Spanish heritage, he consulted Spanish art expert Archer Huntington, who donated several works, including the spectacular *Maria at La Granja* by his protégé, the Spanish Impressionist Joaquín Sorolla y Bastida (see The Hispanic Society of America in New York, p. 285).

This color lithograph poster of *Jane Avril, 1899* is part of the San Diego Museum of Art's comprehensive collection of works by Henri de Toulouse-Lautrec.

JANE
Avril

H. Stern, Paris

1899

Huntington's Hispanic Society also donated a cast of *El Cid,* a large equestrian sculpture by his wife Anna Hyatt Huntington, which dominates El Prado, the central plaza of Balboa Park.

It was the Putnam sisters—Irene, Anne, and Amy—who put the SDMA on the artistic map of the United States. The sisters' fortune, created by their father and uncle, predates the California Gold Rush. It initially rested on a series of patented household appliances, notably a clothes wringer. The sisters were reclusive and never married. They studied languages and collected art. They each had a wonderful eye, and even today two-thirds of the SDMA's European treasures are Putnam gifts. These gifts are housed on the second floor of the museum and include works by Spanish, Italian, and Dutch masters—Bartolomé Murillo, Francisco de Zurbarán, Jusepe de Ribera, Giorgione, Giotto, Paolo Veronese, Peter Paul Rubens, and Frans Hals. El Greco is represented by a particularly mournful *The Penitent Saint Peter.* The museum also owns an Anthony Van Dyck portrait of *Queen Henrietta Maria,* one of thirteen he painted of the teenage queen.

Eventually the SDMA became truly encyclopedic, with comprehensive collections of American, modern European, and Asian, especially South Asian, art. There is a good selection of European Impressionists, Post-Impressionists, and modern works. In addition to a few works dating back to Colonial times, the American paintings include many by well-known artists of the nineteenth and twentieth centuries. Of special interest is the impressive collection by contemporary California artists donated by Frederick R. Weisman (see The Frederick R. Weisman Museum in Minneapolis, p. 240). The museum has a superior Asian collection, beautifully displayed on the first floor. In addition, Edwin Binnary III gave the museum his extraordinary collection of 1,400 pieces of South Asian art in 1990. According to museum literature, these "works were created between the 16th and 19th centuries . . . and are justly regarded as one of the most important [such collections] in the United States." The narrative paintings and works on paper depict court scenes, religious subjects, lovers in the garden, the divine intermingling with the human, animals, and other scenes with sensuality and humor.

Another special treasure is an extensive collection of works by Henri de Toulouse-Lautrec collected by Baldwin M. Baldwin. The SDMA owns two paintings, eight drawings, and eighty-five lithographs, including a complete set of the artist's thirty-one posters.

Museum of Contemporary Art, San Diego

Address: *MCA La Jolla*: 700 Prospect Street, La Jolla, CA 92037; *MCA Downtown*: 1001 Kettner Boulevard, San Diego, CA 92101

Telephone: (858) 454-3541; MCA Downtown: (619) 234-1001

Web: www.mcasandiego.org

Hours: *MCA La Jolla*: *Labor Day–Memorial Day*: Mon–Tues, Fri–Sat 11–5; Sun 12–5, Thurs 11–8. *Summer:* Mon–Tues, Thurs–Fri 11–8, Sat–Sun 11–5. Always closed Wed. Also closed on New Year's, Thanksgiving, and Christmas days. Tours Tues at 2 and 3, Thurs at 6 and 7, weekends at 2 and 3. *MCA Downtown*: Year-round Mon–Tues, Thurs–Sun 11–5. Closed Wed and major holidays. Tours on weekends at 2 and 3.

Strength: Contemporary art.

Special Events: Temporary exhibitions. Programs for seniors: Artful Conversations on selected Tues at 3.

The star-burst dome of the lobby of the Museum of Contemporary Art, San Diego, designed by Robert Venturi, complements the earlier architecture of Irving Gill, a California architect.

Other: *MCA La Jolla*: Outdoor café. Museum store. *MCA Downtown*: Bookstore.

Activities for Children: *MCA La Jolla*: Free family art workshops first Sun 2–5.

Parking: *MCA La Jolla*: On street. *MCA Downtown*: Underground garage at American Plaza (have ticket validated at museum for special rate). Also metered on street.

Tall, spindly palm trees stand in front of a white, almost Mediterranean-looking building in downtown La Jolla: the Museum of Contemporary Art, San Diego (MCASD). The museum dates from 1941, but part of the building has been here longer. In 1895, Ellen Scripps and some other members of the family who had founded the *Detroit Free Press* relocated to La Jolla and in time endowed their new home with clinics, oceanographic institutes, and other worthwhile institutions. (James A. Scripps had donated eight Old Masters to the infant Detroit Institute of Arts in 1889—see p. 233.) Ellen Scripps built herself a wooden Victorian house on a magnificent bluff in La Jolla. When the house burned down in 1914—one of her ten gardeners was suspected of arson—she asked Irving Gill to build her a new one. Gill was an influential California architect who had studied with Louis Sullivan in Chicago. Gill relied on a combination of square shapes and rounded arches, often fronted by elegant colonnades covered by a trellis. There are several other important Gill buildings in downtown La Jolla next to the museum that, according to architectural critic Paul Goldberger, almost look Italian. Among these, Ellen Scripps's house was the most famous, cited in 1950 by critics "as one of the 50 most important houses built in America."

Ellen Scripps died in 1932, leaving her worldly goods to various La Jolla institutions. Her beloved house stood empty and in 1940 a group of artists asked to use it as an exhibition space. The show was such a success that it led to the formation of what is now MCASD. Its abode underwent various alterations that resulted in a virtual loss of the original house.

Fast forward: In 1988 the museum had to be enlarged once more. After a long search the board of the MCASD selected Robert Venturi and his wife and associate Denise Scott Brown (see Seattle Art Museum, p. 407) as architects. Venturi restored the facade of the Gill building and added a lot of magic of his own, always keeping the spirit of the original builder in mind. Venturi's fat white columns echo Gill's thin ones. The palm trees in front of the house were replanted, the trellis—an essential part of Gill's Mediterranean ambiance—was rebuilt. Visitors enter the museum via a cathedral-like court whose undulating vaults soften the plain architecture and Sol LeWitt's stark, yellow, blue, and red *Isometric Pyramid* wall drawing. The court is an intoxicating place. Venturi describes its dome as a lantern "starburst" and indeed the seven panels that bisect the ceiling frame large windows that admit the bright California sun.

Venturi restored Ellen Scripps's sunroom, from which one watches the waves of the blue Pacific and a strip of white beach. Soon one simply must step into the garden, once cultivated by Miss Scripps with a large staff. Today it is smaller. The vegetation is scraggly Southern California and the art is contemporary. Nobody can fail to be amused by Niki de Saint Phalle's large, stomping elephant frightened by a small mouse. (The French sculptor moved to California and her unique humorous creatures are found throughout San Diego and La Jolla.) There are other works with a sense of humor, including Richard Fleischner's *Froebel's Blocks* and chains of polyethylene *Doll's Heads* by Nina Levy.

In 1986, MCASD established a branch in downtown San Diego, now located in a two-story building. In its own way this structure, and especially its location, is also quite remarkable. The museum is across the street from the city's seventy-five-year-old railroad station that looks like a Spanish-style church. In addition the museum abuts the terminal of the San Diego trolley line, whose imposing steel superstructure, dating from another era, almost looks like an abstract sculpture. Jonathan Borofsky's *Hammering Man* (also see the Seattle Art Museum, p. 407, and the University of California Berkeley Art Museum, p. 54) stands in front of the museum.

MCA Downtown sometimes exhibits works from the museum's vast permanent collection, such as Claes Oldenburg's flesh-colored *Alphabet/Good Humor*. A docent is overheard saying that contemporary art often relies on shock value and the label explains that "by transforming two American icons—the alphabet and the Good Humor Bar—into an intestine-like pink mass, Oldenburg created an art rich in irony, humor and psychological overtones." The label of David Hammons's *Champ, 1989*, constructed from red boxing gloves and a draped inner tube, reads: "Champ is a wry commentary on the legacy of African-Americans in boxing . . . the sleek black 'skin' of the cut rubber inner tube hangs limply, echoing the body language of an exhausted fighter, but also suggests flayed skin . . . and complex notions of weakness and power, freedom and oppression, ambition and defeat. . . ."

One museum, two locations, as the MCASD likes to describe itself—a combination of elitism and down-to earth realism. It is good to have them both.

Timken Museum of Art

Address: 1500 El Prado, Balboa Park, San Diego, CA 92101
Telephone: (619) 239-5548
Web: http://gort.ucsd.edu/sj/timken
Hours: Tues–Sat 10–4:30; Sun 12–4:30. Closed Mon, and for the month of Sept.

Strengths: 16th- to 19th-century Italian, Spanish, Dutch, Flemish, French, and American art. Russian icons.

Special Events: Temporary exhibits. Concerts.

Parking: Very limited in front of museum. A free tram runs from the outer parking lots to the museum.

Adjoining the Neo-Spanish Roccco–style San Diego Museum of Art (see page 77) is an unobtrusive one-story structure, the Timken Museum of Art, which opened its doors in 1965. Here is how it all came about.

In 1950, after San Diego Museum director Reginal H. Pollard retired, the surviving Putnam sisters, Anne and Amy, became disenchanted with the museum to which they had given so much art. However, they continued to collect magnificent pictures, which they lent to other museums throughout America. It was feared that after their death the works would leave San Diego permanently, but fortunately for their hometown, their lawyer, the Honorable Walter Ames, arranged matters differently. Ames had other wealthy clients, the Timkens, whose roller-bearing fortune had already built the original SDMA. The Putnams and the Timkens actually lived across the street from one another (the Timkens in a house built by Irving Gill—see previous entry), but they had never met. Ames, however, convinced both parties to create a small boutique museum, with the Timkens providing the physical structure and the Putnam Foundation supplying the art. Frank Hope, Sr., designed an elegant building. Natural light filters in from the ceiling, illuminating about sixty timeless masterpieces, mostly dating from the fifteenth to the nineteenth century. Introspection and intimacy is the common denominator of the art on view. Currently the museum owns about 110 works of art.

The Timken encourages visitors to linger and understand the meaning of each picture with the aid of long labels and special displays. A highlight is Peter Bruegel the Elder's *Parable of the Sower* (1557) from the Gospels of Matthew, Mark, and Luke. "One of only three Bruegels in America," a guard declares with pride. A high school teacher is busy explaining Bruegel's dream-like, mystic landscape, dominated by blue mountains, to his class. He points to the diminutive seed-scattering peasant in the foreground and a small crowd on the other side of the river. "If you take a magnifying glass you can make out Christ preaching to his flock. What is remarkable, however, are the mountains," the teacher continues, "which young Bruegel saw as he journeyed to Italy to study painting. . . ."

In another gallery is the largest known painting by Petrus Christus, the *Death of the Virgin*. Like the Bruegel, which it predates by a century, the painting is filled with details. The Virgin lies on a bed holding a burning candle, a symbol of her faith. She is attended by the apostles, her soul is ascending to heaven, and through the window we glimpse an angel dropping her girdle to St. Thomas, a proof of her Assumption. As in the *Birth of the Virgin* by Francisco de Zurbarán in the nearby Norton Simon Museum in Pasadena (p. 68), the central portion of the picture is a crimson-covered bed.

The Timken is partial to portraits painted by Peter Paul Rubens, Rembrandt, François Clouet, Bartolomeo Veneto, Frans Hals, Nicholas Maes, and Jacques-Louis David. The museum is particularly proud of the portrait of Mrs. Thomas Gage by John Singleton Copley. Painting the new wife of the commander-in-chief of the British forces in North America was a plum assignment for the thirty-three-year-old Boston-born painter. He took great care to detail the beautiful lady's red silk Turkish-style caftan, her lace-like chemise, and her pensive pose. The museum also owns a few choice landscapes, seascapes, and still lives. The selections again emphasize serenity and harmony. John F. Peto's *In the Library* depicts a mess of books and a candle; Fitz Hugh Lane is represented by a view of *Castine Harbor and Town*, and even Albert Bierstadt's view of *Cho-looke, the Yosemite Falls*, is small.

Amy Putnam studied Russian and a selection from her collection of icons fills one gallery. Eastern Orthodox icons are religious images created for prayer and liturgical use. Some are large, most are small. They are little gems, reminiscent all at once of Siennese art and illuminated manuscripts. Lavish use of gold endows them with a feeling of luxury, their lack of perspective lends them touching naïveté, and their spirituality explains their almost supernatural power. The Timken owns *The Royal Gates*, six images that include the annunciation and the four evangelists. Other icons depict *The Savior Enthroned*, from the fifteenth century, a typically Byzantine image of *The Jerusalem Mother of God*, and *The Last Judgment*. Viewing the icons, beautifully displayed against ancient green velour, is a fitting conclusion to an inspiring museum visit.

SAN FRANCISCO

The Asian Art Museum

Address: Civic Center Plaza, San Francisco, CA 94102

Telephone: (415) 557-6966

Web: www.asianart.org

Strengths: Comprehensive collection of Asian art spanning 6,000 years of Oriental history. The collection extends from early Chinese bronzes, pottery, and ceremonial objects to the great ages of Chinese art; also Indian temple figures, jade, Chinese bronzes, jewel-encrusted altarpieces from Tibet and Nepal, screens, Buddhas, Khmer sculpture.

Museum closed until fall 2002.

It is fitting that Asian art plays a major role in California, America's gateway to the East. San Francisco's Asian Art Museum, the gift of Avery Brundage, got there by accident. Brundage (1887–1975) was born in Detroit. He studied civil engineering, founded a construction company which built many of the tall buildings that line Lake Michigan in Chicago, and made a fortune. Early in life he discovered Greek philosophy and with it adopted the Greeks' love of competitive sports. Quite naturally, he participated in reviving the Olympic Games. Brundage excelled in high jumps and discus and weight throwing and represented the United States at the 1912 Olympics, in Stockholm. He might have become a world champion, but the games scheduled for 1916 had to be canceled because of World War One. After the games resumed, Brundage headed the Olympic Committee for twenty-six years.

During the 1920s, Brundage fell in love with the serenity and spirituality of Oriental art, feeling that it demonstrated that body and soul are one. Moreover, he believed that the impatient West could profit from the ancient spirit of the East. At an international exhibit in London he caught "collector's disease" and started amassing Asian art. His timing was propitious. By then there were tools and techniques to excavate and evaluate ancient works. The local Asian governments, however, did not yet appreciate the aesthetic and monetary value of their vast art treasures. Brundage could buy Oriental art and export it freely.

During the next forty years, Brundage assembled a total of more than 6,000 art objects from China, Japan, Korea, Thailand, Cambodia, India, and Vietnam. Quite understandably, he wanted his possessions to stay together and loyally offered his collection to the Art Institute of Chicago. The institution declined because it did not have enough space to accommodate it.

Brundage then offered the collection to the city of San Francisco, on condition it would be properly housed. In 1960, using money from a special bond issue, the west wing of the de Young Museum (see p. 91) was converted to the Asian Art Museum (the Asian). In 1975, Brundage bequeathed his remaining holdings to San Francisco and today the Asian owns 12,000 objects spanning 6,000 years of Asian history and is one of the largest museums outside Asia exclusively devoted to Asian art. Maps help the visitor understand how the various Asian cultures relate to one another. The sculpture, paintings, bronzes, jades, textiles, and decorative objects look splendid in their old setting, though they are about to move to new quarters.

San Francisco is on a museum-building spree. The San Francisco Museum of Modern Art (p. 93) occupied its new quarters in the early 1990s. The Legion of Honor (see next entry) was completely refurbished and expanded in 1998. The de Young is being razed and rebuilt, and the Asian has been given San Francisco's old Main Library. The latter is located in the city's familiar Civic Center, consisting of one of the nation's most complete collection of Beaux Arts buildings. What is more, the 1917 structure is being converted by Gaetana Aulenti, the Milanese architect who turned a Paris train station into the magnificent Musée d'Orsay. The Asian is Ms. Aulenti's first North American project. According to museum literature: "An indoor sky-lit court incorporating the historic entrance and grand staircase provides a dramatic focus . . . while reworked walls afford views into galleries, creating a sense of openness," permitting visitors to circulate and look down into the court. Those who have visited the Musée d'Orsay can hardly wait for the old-new San Francisco Asian to open.

The Fine Arts Museums of San Francisco

The California Palace of the Legion of Honor
The M. H. de Young Memorial Museum

The Fine Arts Museums of San Francisco represents the merger, in 1970, of the city's two rival art museums: The California Palace of the Legion of Honor and the M. H. de Young Memorial Museum. The collections were rearranged so that each museum would have its own areas of concentration.

The California Palace of the Legion of Honor

Address: 100 34th Avenue (at Clement Street), Lincoln Park, San Francisco, CA 94122

Telephone: (415) 863-3330

Web: www.legionofhonor.org

Hours: Tues–Sun 9:30–5. Tours daily.

Strengths: French art. European Old Masters. Kress and Rodin collection. Period rooms. Achenbach collection of 80,000 works on paper.

Special Events: Excellent temporary exhibits.

Other: Theater, concerts (the museum owns a pipe organ). Magnificent surroundings overlooking San Francisco. Very pleasant restaurant. Museum shop.

Activities for Children: Most Sat at 2, two family programs: Doing & Viewing Art (ages 7–12) and Big Kids/Little Kids (ages 3 1/2–6). Each week participants visit a different museum gallery, then participate in related hands-on activities.

Parking: On site, very limited.

The California Palace of the Legion of Honor (known as the Legion of Honor) is in Lincoln Park on a headland high above the city's famed "golden-gated" harbor. The small French palace that houses it almost looks incongruous among the typically western splendor of rocks and windswept cypresses. Walking across the plaza for a look at the Golden Gate Bridge and the wild, untamed ocean, the visitor's steps are arrested by a lonely plaster figure staring out from behind a barbed wire fence. Behind him lies a jumble of corpses. This is *San Francisco's Holocaust Memorial,* created by George Segal. The juxtaposition of the memory of

Court of Honor, California Palace of the Legion of Honor.

one of humanity's most heinous crimes with the glorious site highlights the frailty of life and the ephemeral quality of art and beauty.

Two equestrian statues—*Jeanne d'Arc* and *El Cid*, the Spanish folk hero who lived from 1040 to 1099—flank the museum itself. They are the work of Anna Hyatt Huntington (also see The Hispanic Society of America in New York City, p. 285). A large Mark DiSuvero sculpture entitled *Pax Jerusalem*, welded from orange-painted I-beams, adds a contemporary note. Auguste Rodin's brooding *Thinker* welcomes visitors in the Legion's Court of Honor. The Court is pierced by a small version of the famous glass pyramid I. M. Pei developed for the Louvre.

The Legion of Honor is the gift of Adolph B. and Alma Emma Charlotte Corday Lenormand de Brettville Spreckels. Their fortune, like that of the New York Havemeyers, was built on sugar. The Legion of Honor was the outgrowth of the Panama-Pacific Exposition of 1915 whose French pavilion was modeled on the Hotel de Salm, a small Parisian palace built in 1788 and later used by Napoleon as headquarters for his Legion of Honor. After the fair, Mrs. Spreckels, who loved anything French, offered to build a permanent version of the palace and use it as a museum. She was not the first American to be impressed by the Legion of Honor—Thomas Jefferson copied its dome for his Monticello mansion.

The ground for the new museum was broken in 1921. Marechal Foch, the French hero of World War One, attended and planted a Monterey cypress. The museum was given on Armistice Day 1924 to the City of San Francisco "to honor the dead [California men who fell in the war] while serving the living."

Now the museum had to be filled. Alma Spreckels's dancer friend, Loïe Fuller, had introduced her to Rodin, and she fell in love with his work. She bought many objects directly from the sculptor's studio and today the Legion owns more than seventy of his works. Many of these are now displayed in a large rotunda decorated with French and American flags. Mrs. Spreckels convinced others to help her museum. Archer M. Huntington, a distant Spreckels in-law, presented the Legion with eighteenth-century French paintings, sculpture, tapestries, porcelain, and furniture essembled by his mother, Arabella Huntington, also a devotee of French art (also see The Huntington Library, Art Collections, and Botanical Gardens, p. 96). Another major gift came from her friends Mr. and Mrs. Henry K. S. Williams, who lived in Paris collecting paintings and other treasures. Alma Spreckels persuaded them to leave their estate to the Legion. To begin with, seventy works of art arrived in Lincoln Park on the eve of World War Two. The Williamses also left an endowment for acquisitions which has doubled the number of works donated by the couple.

During the first decades of its existence, the Legion and San Francisco's other art museum, the de Young, were rivals, mirroring the feud of their founders (see next entry). Both museums attempted to build general art collections. Since both founders intended to leave their museums to the city there was a movement toward unification during the 1930s when Walter Heil, a protégé of Detroit's William Valentiner, directed both institutions. According to Nathaniel Burt in *Palaces for the People*, Alma Spreckels grew weary of Heil during the Nazi era when she learned that during World War One he had been in the Luftwaffe and was the roommate and best friend of Hermann Göring. Thereafter, Heil's role was confined to the directorship of the de Young.

In 1970, two years after Alma Spreckels's death, the administration and the collections of the two museums merged. Today the Legion of Honor houses mostly antiquities of European art and works on paper, while the de Young displays "the rest."

The Legion of Honor is an easy museum to visit. The collections are arranged in a logical, relaxed fashion, older European paintings interspersed with period rooms, tapestries, sculpture, decorative arts, and even a fabulous fifteenth-century Moorish ceiling from Spain. The Legion is famous for its Kress collection selected by the aforementioned Walter Heil. When Heil visited the Kress Foundation's offices in New York he said that El Greco's *Saint Francis Venerating the Crucifix* was at the top of his wish list. The Kress Foundation purchased the picture for Heil and visitors can now admire the city's mysteriously lit patron saint silhouetted against a dark mountain. Other great paintings of the Kress gift include Pieter de Hooch's *Interior with Mother and Children* and works by Jacob van Ruysdale, Titian, and Giovanni Tiepolo.

The Flemish and Dutch Baroque paintings—many donated by Roscoe and Margaret Oakes to the de Young and transferred to the Legion after the merger—represent another highlight. Of particular note is Anthony Van Dyck's imposing portrait of *Marie Claire de Croy, Duchess of Havré, and Child,* painted in 1634. Mother and daughter are dressed to the nines, the little girl wearing a cumbersome red dress and mom showing off her pearls and lace. Rembrandt's *Joris de Caulerij* is also resplendent in his military garb and Peter Paul Rubens's *The Tribute Money* refers to material possessions of this opulent period. The Legion also owns two rare paintings by Georges de La Tour.

From 1992 to 1995 the Legion underwent an extensive renovation and underground enlargement resulting in the creation of large galleries for temporary exhibits and elegant, smaller galleries for the permanent collection. Thanks to the hilly character of the site the galleries are lit by daylight. Greek vases, glass, antiquities, and a large porcelain collection are on display as well as selections from the large Achenbach collection of works on paper (80,000 items spanning the period from the end of the fifteenth century to the present and including Old Master prints and drawings, Japanese prints, Persian and Indian miniatures, photographs, and modern and contemporary graphics).

The M. H. de Young Memorial Museum

Address: 75 Tea Garden Drive, Golden Gate Park, San Francisco, CA 94118
Telephone: (415) 750-3614
Web: www.deyoung.org
Hours: Tues–Sun 9:30–5.
Strengths: American art. Art of the Americas, Oceania, and Africa. Decorative arts, Oriental rugs.

The museum is closed for renovation until 2005, but the de Young Art Center, located near Golden Gate Park at 2501 Irving Street (at 26th Avenue), remains open.

For eighty-one years the M. H. de Young Memorial Museum (the de Young) occupied a pink stucco building fronting on a small reflecting pool—the Pool of Enchantment—in which bronze frogs and nymphs frolic among aquatic plants. Inside, thirty-five-plus galleries clustered around the large Hearst Court, and visitors ambled among its superior collections of American, African, Native American, Oceanic, Decorative Art, and Art of the Americas. The building, however, was damaged by the 1989 Loma Prieta earthquake and instead of being patched it has been razed and a new museum is being built in its place.

In 1892, M. H. de Young, the editor of the *San Francisco Chronicle,* visited the Columbian Exposition in Chicago and decided that his hometown, then suffering from financial depression, needed its own world's fair. De Young convinced a reluctant city to let him mount such an exhibition in Golden Gate Park and the fair opened in 1893. It was such a success that the city agreed to let de Young keep the Fine Arts Building. In 1919, de Young replaced the original building with a Spanish-type building that was enlarged in 1925.

De Young created the new museum's collection. Not being very knowledgeable about art, he mixed art, bric-a-brac, and exotica. At one time the museum owned 23,000 stuffed birds, a German World War One plane, and a room full of shoes, silverware, and similar items. San Franciscans enjoyed their museum, and an attendance of 6,000 on a Sunday afternoon was the norm. Later curators cleaned out the original collection but some early acquisitions are still on view. One of these is an eleven-foot-high vat-like vase by Gustavo Doré called *Le Poème de la Vigne*. The Mexican and South Sea collection, neglected during the early years of the museum, turned out to be really valuable.

M. H. de Young was a muckraking journalist and his battles with the Spreckelses—the founders of the rival California Palace of the Legion of Honor (see previous entry)—are fun to revisit. At one time reporters from the *San Francisco Chronicle* photographed a philandering Adolf Spreckels at a San Francisco Hotel. Spreckels was so outraged that he beat up the detective and photographer and tried to shoot de Young in his office. Since, however, both de Young and the Spreckelses deeded their museums to the city, the institutions were merged in 1970. By then the founders had died and their treasures were then arranged in a logical fashion. The Kress collection, which was given to the de Young, is now in the Legion, and non-European art traveled in the reverse direction.

One of the de Young's areas of concentration is American art. In 1978 the museum's holdings were enhanced by the donation from Mr. and Mrs. John D. Rockefeller III of a hundred-plus works. The museum's collection covers American art from Colonial and Federalist times (John Singleton Copley, Gilbert Stuart, and the Peales). The museum is proud of George Caleb Bingham's *Boatmen on the Missouri*. Once more we share the vision of the Hudson River School painters. Thomas Moran's *Yellowstone*, with its waterfalls, rocks, and pines, is lyrical. A large rainbow frames the Andes in Frederick Church's *Rainy Storm in the Tropics*. In William Bradford's *Scene in the Arctic*, we visit icebergs at the other end of the earth. There are paintings by Childe Hassam, Mary Cassatt, and other American Impressionists and by California artists of the late nineteenth century. There is Thomas Hart Benton's humorous *Susanna and the Elders*, in which a modern woman sitting on the banks of a brook, takes off her hat and high-heeled sandals under the watchful eye of two farmers hiding amid fantastic vegetation. The de Young is a big museum with a variety of collections from Africa, South America, and Mesoamerica. There are also a magnificent rug collection, a collection of Native American totem poles, and examples of Tiffany glass.

The old de Young was much beloved, but the plans for the new museum are exciting. Switzerland's Herzog and De Meuron, who built

London's Tate Gallery of Modern Art, are the architects. The plans envision a three-story exhibition space (basement and two floors). To minimize the building's impact on Golden Gate Park, pathways will weave through the museum itself, accessing an interior court which can be visited without entering the museum proper. According to museum literature, there will be a tower reminiscent of the old de Young which will house arts education programs and provide an "expansive view of the city's skyline stretching from downtown to the ocean."

San Francisco Museum of Modern Art

Address: 151 Third Street, San Francisco, CA 94103

Telephone: (415) 357-4000

Web: www.SFMOMA.org

Hours: Mon–Tues 11–6; Thurs 11–9; Fri–Sun 11–6. Opens at 10 Memorial Day–Labor Day. Closed Wed, New Year's Day, Independence, Thanksgiving, and Christmas days.

Strengths: Modern (American Abstract Expressionism, German Expressionism, Fauvism, especially the works of Henri Matisse) and contemporary art, architecture and design, digital and media art, and photography.

Special Events: 20 temporary exhibits annually.

Other: Indoor/outdoor café. Museum shop.

Parking: Numerous pay garages, including those on Mission Street and SFMOMA's garage at 147 Minna Street.

During the 1990s, downtown San Francisco—which was often compared to New York's old "Hell's Kitchen"—underwent a spectacular rebirth of which the San Francisco Museum of Modern Art (SFMOMA) is an important part. The museum is housed in a severe, windowless, stepped-back red-brick building, which sports a black-and-white striped turret. From afar one wonders at the function of its eye-like "observatory." The building is the work of Mario Butto, the Swiss architect well known for the dramatic effects of his creations. Indeed, inside and out SFMOMA is like a piece of sculpture. Stripes—alternating shiny black marble and dull granite—dominate the exterior and the

The San Francisco Museum of Modern Art, architect Mario Botta.

interior, an effect enhanced by the huge Sol LeWitt murals that grace the lobby (also see the High Museum of Art, p. 158). The building is so powerful that it threatens to overshadow the art, and for a while it did.

Though the SFMOMA actually is a "senior citizen" with old roots, it only recently came into its own. During the last part of the nineteenth century San Francisco had a somnolent art association, which according to Nathaniel Burt in *Palaces for the People,* was "more famous for its receptions than for anything else." Nevertheless the association had assembled an exhibit for the magnificent Palace of Fine Arts Bernard Maebeck built for the Panama-Pacific Exhibition of 1915. That dome-shaped palace survived the fair and now is a landmark, but it is not an art museum. In 1935 a museum devoted solely to the art of the twentieth century opened its doors in San Francisco's neoclassic Civic Center.

Spiritually the core of the institution was the Matisse collection of Michael and Sarah Stein, whose family fortune derived from cable cars. Early in the twentieth century Michael and Sarah moved to France, where they joined their expatriate siblings Leo and Gertrude Stein, the avant-garde art patrons. Michael and Sarah were particularly fond of Henri Matisse and assembled many of his works. In 1935, when Hitler rose to power, the Michael Steins and their collection returned to a large house in Palo Alto. Michael died and Sarah showed her great paintings to those who asked (see the Iris & B. Gerald Cantor Center for Visual Arts, p. 102). Unfortunately, Sarah's descendants played the horses and she had to sell most of her Matisses before her death in 1953. By then, however, several other San Franciscans had become very fond of Matisse. Sarah's good friend, Mrs. Walter A. Haas, whose husband catapulted Levi jeans to fame, bought several of her best Matisses and eventually they, as well as other collections, were given to the SFMOMA. Central to the Matisse collection are a Madonna-like portrait of Sarah and a more conventional one of Michael donated to the SFMOMA by friends "in honor of [the Stein's] role in bringing the work of Matisse to the Bay Area." Also included is the exuberant *Woman with a Hat*. In *The Proud Possessors* Aline B. Saarinen reports that when Sarah showed the picture to visitors in her Palo Alto home she habitually added: "and to think that when she posed for those frenzies of colors, Madame Matisse was wearing a black dress . . . and a silly black hat loaded with feathers."

SFMOMA's permanent collection also includes the *Flower Carrier*, one of Diego Rivera's best-known works. It hangs next to Frida Kahlo's double portrait of herself and Rivera. We also note an abstract Franz Marc *Gebirge* (mountains), and a version of Joseph Stella's *Brooklyn Bridge*. The postwar European and American collection includes a very youthful portrait of George Washington by Roy Lichtenstein, Andy Warhol's *National Velvet*, and works by, among many others, Clyfford Still, Jackson Pollock, Richard Diebenkorn, and Robert Motherwell.

The collection continues to grow. When David A. Ross took over its directorship in 1998, he announced a major acquisitions plan, and since then the museum has enlarged its collection by acquiring twenty-two seminal works by Ellsworth Kelly, fourteen important works by Robert Rauschenberg, and major works by René Magritte, Piet Mondrian, and Marcel Duchamp.

Notable among other permanent possessions is the growing Carl Djerassi collection of works by Paul Klee (130 in 2000)—some of them already donated, some promised—a selection of which is on view.

There are also many works by emerging and established Bay Area artists.

Appropriately—since Silicon Valley is in its back yard—the museum is an important media arts center. The museum acquires and sponsors film, video, and other electronic and time-based art. The top floors of the museum are always occupied by good and frequently changing temporary shows.

But museum art is only one of the pleasures of the visit. Crossing the museum on flying bridges or descending the stairs, visitors can admire the changing views inside the museum and outside. The small fourth floor balcony dedicated to Steve Silver, founder of Beach Blanket Babylon and a victim of AIDS, overlooks Buena Yerba Park. The park is a new address for art in San Francisco: A Mexican museum, to be built by Gaetana Aulenti (see San Francisco's Asian Art Museum, p. 85) and a Jewish museum, designed by David Liebkind, who created the world-famous Jewish Museum in Berlin, are scheduled to open there within the decade.

SAN MARINO

The Huntington Library, Art Collections, and Botanical Gardens

Address: 1151 Oxford Road, San Marino, CA 91108

Telephone: (626) 405-2100

Web: www.huntington.org

Hours: Tues–Fri 12–4:30; Sat, Sun 10:30–4:30. *Memorial Day–Labor Day*: Tues–Sun 10:30–4:30. Closed Mon and most holidays including Christmas Eve. Extended hours may be in effect during vacation times.

Strengths: British and French art of the 18th and 19th centuries; Van der Weyden's *Madonna and Child*; a small survey of American art. Decorative arts. Rare books and illuminated manuscripts, including a Gutenberg Bible and the Ellesmer manuscript of the Canterbury Tales.

Other: 150 acres of botanical gardens featuring fifteen specialized settings. Restaurant. English tea served overlooking the rose garden.

Activities for Children: Ask for the "Kid's Stuff" activities sheet at front desk. Look for the Plant Discovery Cart at the lily pond equipped with nature crafts,

Rogier Van der Weyden's *Madonna and Child*, at The Huntington Library, Art Collections, and Botanical Gardens in San Marino, is a rare example of this Northern Renaissance master's works.

watercolor, and collage projects for children 4–14 (schedule varies). Also see Web site for Virtual Reality Tour of garden and Plant Trivia Timeline.

Parking: On site.

Collis P. Huntington was one of four principals present when the last spike of the Central Pacific was driven into place in Utah. It is to his nephew and fellow railroad tycoon, Henry, that we owe The Huntington. The institution bills itself as a library, art collection, and a botanical garden, and it is indeed all of these on a very grand scale.

To begin with there was the land, a vast ranch named San Marino, which had a spectacular view of the San Gabriel Mountains. Henry bought it in 1902. Ten years later, when he was sixty, he built a spectacular Beaux Arts mansion. By then he had married his uncle's widow, Arabella Huntington, the mother of Archer Huntington (see Introduction). The two devoted their energies and fortunes to collecting rare books and art and to transforming a working ranch into a botanical wonderland. Even for a dedicated art lover it is difficult to leave the gardens and go indoors.

Henry admired all things English, and his art gallery is best known for a group of twenty full-length paintings created between 1770 and 1800 by Joshua Reynolds, Thomas Gainsborough, George Romney, and Thomas Lawrence. Many of the works, including Gainsborough's portrait of Jonathan Buttall known as *The Blue Boy*, Lawrence's *Sarah Barrett Moulton, "Pinkie,"* and Reynolds's *Jane, Countess of Harrington*, are very familiar. Today they hang in a separate gallery, but when the Huntingtons were in residence they were scattered throughout the spectacular mansion. It is hard to see where they would have fit, because the walls of the residence are filled with smaller, charming works: some European genre scenes called conversations, landscapes by William Turner and John Constable, and Sporting Art. There is also fine furniture, silver, and porcelain. Even though the house is palatial, the best parts are the deeply shaded loggias from which one can admire the gardens and mountains.

American art, housed in the beautifully detailed, classic Virginia Steele Scott Gallery, complements and contrasts with the English portraits of the mansion. The collection, spanning 300 years, is a real gem. Portraits of the Colonial and Federal periods are scarce on the West Coast, but those on display here are a joy. Among the earliest is Pieter Vanderlyn's charming picture of a finely attired *Cornelius Wynkoop*, shown on his father's extensive lands in Albany. John Smibert's portrait of *Benjamin Lynde, Sr.* is paired with that of his daughter-in-law *Mrs. Benjamin Lynde, Jr.* by Robert Feke. There are grand American portraits by John Singleton Copley, Thomas Sully, and John Singer Sargent that invite comparison with their English counterparts; and sweet ones, such as George Bellows's *Portrait of* [his wife] *Laura*. Here we also find George Caleb Bingham's beloved genre painting *In a Quandary* and works by Thomas Moran and Frederick Church as well as more recent works by Mary Cassatt, Edward Hopper, and the Ashcanners. A great joy of the Scott gallery is a reconstructed dining room by Greene and Greene, California Arts and Crafts architects. The room, with its inlaid furniture and stained glass, dates from 1906.

Some French and Flemish paintings are exhibited in the Arabella Huntington Memorial Gallery. Among these, Rogier Van der Weyden's

Madonna and Child is both exquisite and important because so few works by this fifteenth-century painter have come down through the years. Henry's vast library is filled with rare books and illuminated manuscripts: Chaucer's *Canterbury Tales,* a Gutenberg Bible, atlases, Books of Hours. Selections from these are on view in special exhibits.

Like the Blisses buried at their Dumbarton Oaks in Washington, D.C. (see p. 123), which resembles the Huntington in many ways, Arabella and Henry are buried in an orange grove on the grounds of their estate. Their mausoleum was designed by John Russell Pope, architect of the National Gallery of Art and the Jefferson Memorial in Washington, D.C., which the California structure resembles. On a clear day there is a view of the gardens and the mountains from the steps of the Greek-inspired temple: a perfect spot to remember with thanks those who in their good fortune have left this country a legacy of beauty.

SANTA BARBARA

Santa Barbara Museum of Art

Address: 1130 State Street, Santa Barbara, CA 93101

Telephone: (805) 963-4364

Web: www.sbmuseart.org

Hours: Tues–Thurs, Sat–Sun 11–5; Fri 11–9. Closed Mon and major holidays.

Strengths: Extensive collection of Latin American art. European and American 19th- and 20th-century art. Antiquities. Asian art, photography.

Special Events: Temporary exhibits.

Other: Library open to public Tues–Fri 12–4. Café. Museum store.

Activities for Children: A special gallery with hands-on activities and dress-up clothes.

Parking: Low-priced public lots.

During the 1940s, when the museum-building boom intensified in California, prominent citizens of Santa Barbara lobbied for a museum. In 1941 the Santa Barbara Museum of Art (SBMA) opened its doors in the town's former post office, a dignified structure dating from 1914. At the time the museum owned sixty-five pictures. A new wing was added in 1998.

Enrique Chagoya's *1492*, at the Santa Barbara Museum of Art.

As museums go, the collection of the SBMA is small but choice. At first the institution concentrated on collecting American art of the past and present. Soon devoted and affluent citizens of this California seaside town left the museum some of their precious possessions, including antiquities, eighteenth- to twentieth-century European and Asian art, and a superior Latin American collection.

Fine classic sculptures (Egyptian, Greek, Roman), grouped around a large central amphora, are displayed in a small entrance court. They are the gift of Wright S. Luddington. As a young man Luddington traveled widely. He had a good eye, shopped for paintings in France and America, and eventually left much of what he owned to the museum.

The French Pre-Impressionist, Impressionist, and Post-Impressionist paintings are especially enjoyable. Many are small and intimate. Berthe Morisot's beach scene is particularly appropriate to Santa Barbara, except that the frolicking woman and her two little girls are fully clad. An early Henri Matisse painting of the *Pont Saint Michel* has an almost Cubist simplicity except that it is painted in Fauve colors. There are two Georges Rouault *Acrobats*, created before the painter became ultra-religious. Piet Mondrian's orange, white, and violet *Blooming Rhododendrons* were executed before that painter concentrated on the geometric shapes of Neoplasticism. One of Marc Chagall's charming creatures strides across the canvas with a cane, oblivious of the woman hiding in her hair. The museum is proud of its three paintings by

Claude Monet, which were purchased by International Harvester's McCormicks on their honeymoon. Mrs. McCormick donated the Monets in memory of her husband, Stanley. These happy pictures are well suited to Santa Barbara's sunshine.

The museum has a comprehensive American collection, including portraits by John Singleton Copley, James Peale, and Thomas Sully. The Ashcan artists contributed East Coast scenes, and George Inness's large *Morning in the Catskill Valley*, with its orange-colored trees, reminds viewers that outside Southern California the year is governed by changing seasons. A fine, well-displayed Asian collection occupies the balcony of the museum, some of it assembled by Charles Henry Luddington, father of Wright.

The most remarkable possessions of the SBMA, however, are its steadily growing holdings of Latin American art. The beginning of the collection dates from the 1950s, when Dr. MacKinley Helm, a pioneering scholar of Mexican modernism, donated core objects. More acquisitions were made during the 1990s and the focus was broadened to include works from other Central and South American countries as well as from the Caribbean.

The Latin American artists were influenced by the prevailing European and American art styles, but nevertheless their work retains a characteristic power of its own. The SBMA owns major and minor works, in all media, by familiar and unfamiliar artists. Of the great Mexican masters, Rufino Tamayo is the least political. The SBMA's deceptively simplistic *Moon Dog* and *Jackal* contrast with his *Night and Day*. Whereas the former are in primary colors and hark back to Pre-Columbian art, the latter is lyrically sophisticated. Its muted blues, yellows, and browns symbolize the mystery of the heavens and the constellations, perhaps recalling the astronomy that was so important to Pre-Columbian civilization. The title of Enrique Chagoya's large-scale cartoon-like drawing, *1492*, refers to the discovery of the Americas by Columbus and the colonialism that followed. Two angry fists, resembling those of Disney's Mickey Mouse, occupy almost the entire canvas, one clutching a bloody sword, the other a crucifix, while a small Pre-Columbian figurine strides along the bottom. The face and clenched hands in David Alfaro Siqueiros's *The Aesthete in Drama* are heart-rendingly tragic. José Clemente Orozco is represented by his portraits of women. The donkey and the man in Diego Rivera's *Loading Wood* are funny and Francisco Zuniega's onyx sculpture *Bent Nude* is classically beautiful.

STANFORD

Iris & B. Gerald Cantor Center for Visual Arts

Address: Lomita Drive at Museum Way, Stanford University, Stanford, CA 94305
Telephone: (650) 723-4177
Web: www.stanford.edu/dept/SUMA
Hours: Wed, Fri–Sun 11–5; Thurs 11–8. Closed Mon, Tues, and major holidays.
Strengths: Encyclopedic. Asian, African, Native American art. American landscapes, contemporary American art. Rodin collection. Richard Diebenkorn. Stanford family memorabilia.
Special Events: Excellent temporary exhibits. Lectures, theatrical performances.
Other: Restaurant. Museum shop. Sculpture garden.
Activities for Children: Family tours on selected Sat.
Parking: Metered, on site.

When it was first built in 1898 the Leland Stanford Jr. Art Museum was to be the biggest and the best museum in the world. Leland Stanford, Jr., the only child of Jane and Leland Stanford, had been interested in antiquities. In New York he had visited with the director of the Metropolitan Museum in New York and in Athens with the legendary Heinrich Schliemann. His ambitions apparently included creating a museum. After he died of typhus in Florence in 1884 at the age of sixteen, his grief-stricken parents decided to create a university as well as a museum in his memory. His mother supervised the museum portion of the project. She modeled the building on the rather stark neoclassic design of the National Archeological Museum in Athens. The entire structure was built from reinforced concrete using a method patented by E. L. Ransome, who served as engineering consultant. According to Paul Venable Turner in *Museum Builders in the West,* the structure not only ushered in "a new phase of American museum architecture, but represented the first monumental use of reinforced concrete as the principal building material of the 20th century."

The entrance of the museum was flanked by four monumental ionic columns. The interior and exterior were decorated with thirteen intricate mosaics made by the Salvatti Company of Venice. The floors were covered with marble and there was a central and two peripheral rotundas. The central structure was enlarged by long wings, and for a brief time the museum was the largest in the United States.

Filling such a large space with art was a problem, but Jane Stanford was diligent. By opening day she had assembled 15,000 objects, including duplicates from the Cesnola collection in New York, American landscapes, European Old Masters, and Egyptian artifacts.

It is said that "Man proposes, God disposes." Governor Leland Stanford died in 1893, five years before the opening of the museum, and Jane Stanford died in 1905. A year later, in 1906, her beloved museum was partially destroyed, and her house on Nob Hill in San Francisco totally destroyed, by the San Francisco earthquake. Much of the art lost in each place remained unaccounted for and the quality of the original collection had never been evaluated. Only the central portion of the museum remained usable, and the museum limped along until it was closed in 1945. It was reopened in 1963, but nature was not done with it. The 1989 Loma Prieta earthquake closed it once more. This time, Iris and B. Gerald Cantor came to the rescue. Slowly and thoughtfully they restored the main building and the rotundas and added a new wing. The museum was refounded in 1999 and renamed the Iris & B. Gerald Cantor Center for Visual Arts (the Cantor).

Today, visitors enter the original, majestic entrance hall, at times occupied by one of Deborah Butterfield's horses, whose rough texture contrasts with the formal mosaic floor and marble walls. A grand staircase ascends to the second floor.

The Stanford family is still much in evidence. There are imperial-looking portraits and two large galleries of memorabilia, including the last spike driven into the ground by Governor Stanford when the eastern and western sections of the transcontinental railroad were joined in Utah in May 10, 1869 (also see the Crocker Art Museum, p. 74).

The museum owns excellent collections of ancient Mediterranean (Egypt, Greece, Cyprus, and Rome), Asian, African, Oceanic, and Native American art, each beautifully displayed in its own gallery. The two small, double-height rotundas that survived the earthquakes are

Richard Diebenkorn's *Ocean Park No. 94*, at the Iris & B. Gerald Cantor Center for Visual Arts at Stanford University.

especially pleasing. One is filled with Asian jades and ceramics echoed in the Salvatti mosaics that adorn the walls.

Paintings, including striking landscapes of the American West, are housed on the second floor. Leland Stanford, Sr., was particularly fond of Thomas Hill, the British artist who lived and died in California, and owned more than twenty of his works. A breathtaking view of *Yosemite Valley*, including Bridal Veil Falls and El Capitan, is on view. Two tiny figures on horseback add a human note to the painting.

The Cantor's collection of modern and contemporary American art is strong. Richard Diebenkorn, who attended Stanford University, donated a large oil called *Window* to the museum of his alma mater. The label and museum literature note that the painter discovered Matisse when he visited Sarah Stein in her house in Palo Alto (see the San Francisco Museum of Modern Art, p. 93). Indeed, the influence of the French master can be seen in the railing and colors of Diebenkorn's painting. The museum also owns several of the painter's *Ocean Park* series. There are works by other Bay-based artists including Wayne Thiebaud, Robert Hudson, and Manuel Neri as well as examples by major post-1960s American painters.

The work of Auguste Rodin is the Cantors' special passion. The French artist, a contemporary of the Impressionists, liberated sculpture from its strict academic conventions. His sculptures are fluid and impressionistic and some experts consider him the greatest sculptor since Michelangelo. In 1945, B. Gerald Cantor, founder and chairman of a large international security firm, came upon Rodin's *The Hand of God* in New York's Metropolitan Museum of Art. Cantor bought the first of approximately 750 Rodin works in 1947, eventually giving most of these to over seventy museums. It is not surprising that 187 of these ended up in his own museum. There is an early maquette of *The Burghers of Calais* in which the six men assume heroic stances. Rodin fortunately changed his concept. As described in museum literature: "The figures are [now] barefoot, wearing sackcloth, and their anguish is evident from their despondent poses and gestures." The large Rodin sculptures are outdoors in a beautifully landscaped sculpture garden. Most striking among the twenty or so works is *The Gates of Hell*, inspired, no doubt, by Lorenzo Ghiberti's *Gates of Paradise* in Florence. Rodin's gates are a powerful work in which tormented souls float and weave freely over the entire surface of the doors. In the lintel is an image of the familiar *Thinker,* the figure which at the sculptor's request stands guard over his tomb in France.

Colorado

DENVER

Denver Art Museum

Address: 100 W. 14th Avenue Parkway, Denver, CO 80204

Telephone: (720) 865-5000

Web: www.denverartmuseum.org

Hours: Tues–Sat 10–5; Wed 10–9; Sun 12–5. Closed Mon and most major holidays. Tours Tues–Sun at 1:30; Sat at 11 and 1:30. In-depth tours of different areas of the museum Wed and Fri at 12. Overview tours (45 min) twice daily during the summer.

Strengths: Encyclopedic. Native American, Spanish Colonial, Pre-Columbian art. Art of the American West. North West Coast Indian art. Contemporary art, architecture, design, and graphics with an emphasis on American contemporary and Italian design.

Special Events: Jazz concert first Wed.

Activities for Children: The Just for Family Center, on the first floor, has five play stations focusing on particular collections. Backpacks (Sat 10:30 and 4; Sun 12 and 4) filled with hands-on games and activities designed for the exploration of different areas of the museum. Two "discovery libraries" (Western and European art) in which children can explore art by rummaging through artifacts, dressing up like specific subjects shown in paintings, or by using CD-ROMs. Specific child-oriented activities throughout the museum are highlighted by a mascot based on a monkey from Pre-Columbian Peru.

Other: Museum shop. Restaurant.

Parking: Low cost, on site.

At the end of the nineteenth century, Denver was a remote frontier town. Nevertheless, in 1893 a group of citizens founded an art association that organized lectures and temporary shows. By 1917 the association became the Denver Art Museum (the DAM). The venerable museums of the Eastern U.S. advised the fledgling institution to specialize in Western and Native American art, but the founders persevered in assembling a comprehensive collection. They received fifty artworks from the Samuel H. Kress Foundation, and obtained other fine art, and today the DAM boasts that "it is the largest encyclopedic museum between Kansas City and the West Coast."

It took many years for the institution to display its treasures properly. In 1971, however, when the new museum opened its doors, it astounded the public. The building, designed by Gio Ponti, a Milanese architect, has been compared to a "fortress," a "concrete brute," and an "Italian castle wrapped in aluminum foil." The last refers to its skin of highly reflective tiles that shimmer in tones of silver and gold when hit by the Colorado sun.

The two seven-story towers actually are very serviceable buildings, totally different from more traditional arrangements. The design was partially necessitated by the smallness of the site in downtown Denver, but it was also hoped that the limited size of each floor would prevent museum fatigue.

Tours of the museum start on the sixth floor, which houses several of the museum's perennial favorites: Frederic Remington's *The Cheyenne*, Thomas Cole's *Dream of Arcadia*, Adolphe William Bouguereau's carefully executed *Childhood Memories*, and Claude Monet's sketchy and colorful *Water Lily Pond*. According to museum literature: "Bouguereau and Monet would have been surprised to *both* be selected as visitor favorite's. . . . Bouguereau warned his students against the heretical ideas of the Impressionists, whom he deemed 'color blind.' Monet, on the other hand, explaining his technique to a colleague said, 'when you go out to paint, try to forget what objects you have before you . . . and think in terms of a little square of blue, here an oblong of pink, here a streak of yellow. . . .'"

On the fifth floor, docents point out a Chinese *Incense Lacquer Box* of the fourteenth–fifteenth century, a *Chinese Scholar's Table* from the sixteenth–seventeenth century, and a Japanese *Suit of Armor* of the eighteenth century. The fourth floor combines Pre-Columbian and Colonial art of the Americas. The contrast between the ornate figure of *St. Ferdinand, King of Spain, 1730* and the simple *Moche Portrait Vessels* (100 B.C.E. to 700 C.E.) is striking. The second and third floors present art and artifacts produced by Native Americans. Of great significance is the *Pawnee Bear Claw Necklace* that played an important role in wars between the Sioux and Pawnees. The contemporary art is exhibited on the first floor. The museum is proud of Deborah Butterfield's sculptured horse *Orion*, and of Jim Dine's *Wheatfield*, a giant construction of disparate objects—a skull, tools, a Venus, a parrot—supported on an axle and two tractor wheels, all of which relate to the artist's life.

In 1990 the DAM embarked on the ambitious creation of a new design and architectural department that concentrates on the design of the last quarter of the twentieth century. The rapidly growing contemporary design collection is placing Denver in the forefront of this type of art.

The DAM continues to grow. In 2001, the museum unveiled to great fanfare plans for a strikingly modern new wing in glass and titanium designed by Berlin-based architect Daniel Libeskind. The building is scheduled to open in 2005.

Connecticut

HARTFORD

Wadsworth Atheneum Museum of Art

Address: 600 Main Street, Hartford, CT 06103

Telephone: (860) 278-2670

Web: www.wadsworthatheneum.org

Hours: Tues–Sun 11–5; first Thurs (most months) 11–8. Closed Mon and New Year's, Independence, Thanksgiving, and Christmas days. Frequent tours.

Strengths: Encyclopedic. Renaissance and Baroque paintings. Hudson River School. American portraits. European and American Impressionists. 20th-century European and American art. African American art. Leading decorative art collections including Meissen porcelain, 17th-century American furniture and silver, and regional folk art objects.

Special Events: Ground-breaking temporary exhibits. Theater and dance performances. Lectures.

Other: Excellent free print guides to various permanent exhibits (Hudson River Galleries, American silver, etc.). Indoor-outdoor restaurant. Museum shop.

Activities for Children: Maps for treasure hunts. 8 Sun per year, special, low-cost family programs teaching children how to enjoy museums and art.

Parking: Metered, on street; pay garages. Free parking on weekends in Travelers Lot # 7 on Prospect Street.

Hartford's inner city is alive and well. Its art museum, the Wadsworth Atheneum, has the distinction of being America's oldest continuously operating museum, still using its original building. The turreted Gothic Revival–style edifice contrasts with the gilded dome of the Connecticut capitol and the even more recent mirror-covered skyscrapers. The banners outside the museum, announcing temporary exhibits sponsored by Aetna, Travelers, Massachusetts Mutual, and others, never let you forget that Hartford is the hub of America's insurance industry.

Daniel Wadsworth founded the museum in 1842. He was the son of Colonel Jeremiah Wadsworth, the Commissioner-General of the Amer-

Ralph Earl's portrait of *Oliver Ellsworth and Abigail Wolcott Ellsworth* at the Wadsworth Atheneum in Hartford. The couple's estate is seen through the window.

ican Forces during the War of Independence. A plaque outside the Atheneum states that on "June 6, 1775 George Washington visited with Jeremiah Wadsworth in his house, which then occupied the site." When the museum opened its doors, it owned seventy-eight paintings, one miniature, and three sculptures.

The Atheneum continually outgrew its original quarters. Four new buildings were added, each in a different style: the Tudor-Revival Colt Memorial (the gift of the widow of the inventor of the revolver), the Renaissance-Revival Morgan Memorial, the neoclassical Avery Memorial, and the modern Goodwin Building. During a 1960s renovation the floors above the original grand hall were removed and the entrance now soars upward. Throughout the museum most galleries remain small and human-sized.

Initially the museum collected mostly American art. Its first purchase was John Trumbull's (also see Yale University Art Gallery, p. 116) five large canvases depicting the Revolutionary War. Other early treasures include John Singleton Copley's likeness of the *Jeremiah Lees* and Ralph Earl's large double portrait of *Oliver Ellsworth and Abigail Wolcott Ellsworth*, with their beloved and imposing home Elmwood showing through the window.

Daniel Wadsworth was a personal friend of Thomas Cole. He bought six of the Atheneum's dozen works by this seminal American painter, including a scene from *The Last of the Mohicans*. The talent of the seventeen-year-old Hartford-born Frederick Church impressed Wadsworth, and today the Atheneum owns an early impressive Maine seascape, its thundering waves foreshadowing Impressionism. Albert Bierstadt's powerful *In the Mountains* is reminiscent of the exciting, pre-camera times when dramatic landscapes were being discovered by the painters of the Hudson River School.

Another mood reigns in the galleries devoted to American Impressionism, one of whose centers was Connecticut. The light-infused works of George Inness, Childe Hassam, William Merritt Chase, John Singer Sargent, Ernest Lawson, and others contrast with the more grandiose views of their elders. A *View of West Hartford* by William J. Glackens makes us realize how much our landscape has been altered during the past seventy-five years. There are also wonderful examples of more recent American artists: Maurice Prendergast, Norman Rockwell, Ben Shahn, and Milton Avery, to name only a few.

The European collections are also strong. Notable Old Masters include: Lucas Cranach the Elder's *The Feast of Herod*, Peter Paul Rubens's *The Return from the Flight into Egypt*, Michelangelo da Caravaggio's *The Ecstasy of St. Francis*, and Francisco de Zurbarán's *St. Serapion*. America was not built by Caucasians alone; the Atheneum is home to the Armistad Collection of works by African Americans. Selections from the extensive holdings are always on view.

Hartford's possessions were shaped by a succession of distinguished directors and curators. One of the most colorful was A. Everett "Chick" Austin, Jr. (also see John and Mable Ringling Museum in Sarasota, Florida, p. 150), who served from 1927 to 1944. The year he was appointed, the Atheneum received the Sumner Fund of two million dollars. Austin used the fund, in part, to build one of America's most impressive Baroque, Modern, and Surrealist art collections.

In 1934, Austin added a theater, a first for an American museum. Austin had sponsored George Balanchine's immigration to the U.S. and in 1934 the choreographer's infant dance company, the future New York City Ballet, gave its first public performance in Hartford. That same year witnessed the Atheneum-hosted world première of Gertrude Stein's *Four Saints in Three Acts*. Himself a professional magician, Austin gave benefit performances to fund art classes for children.

At every turn the Atheneum provides pleasant surprises. There are period rooms, displays of magnificent silver, and galleries full of chairs, chests, and highboys. Elsewhere visitors come across a lion with a startlingly human face, painted for a tavern by William Rice (1773–1847), Hartford's preeminent sign painter; a provocative display of hats in the small Costume Institute; Morgan's collection of Meissen porcelain; Colt's collection of firearms—too much to see in a few hours!

NEW BRITAIN

New Britain Museum of American Art

Address: 56 Lexington Street, New Britain, CT 06052

Telephone: (860) 229-0257

Web: www.nbmaa.org

Hours: Tues–Fri 12–5; Sat 10–5; Sun 12–5. Closed Mon and major holidays.

Strength: American art, especially of the Hudson River and Ashcan schools.

Special Events: Exhibitions by contemporary artists.

Other: Small museum shop.

Activities for Children: The Hands-on Alcove, stocked with books, crayons, and other arts-and-craft materials and dress-up clothes.

Parking: On street.

Like many of America's small museums, the birth of the New Britain Museum of American Art (NBMAA) seemed amateurish. The museum was founded in 1903 by a group of local art-minded citizens. During the first twenty-four years of its existence it was housed in the library of the New Britain Institute. In 1937, Mrs. Grace Judd Landers bequeathed the museum her pleasant house, abutting a large park designed by Frederick Law Olmsted. As time went on the museum

Frederick Childe Hassam, *Le Jour du Grand Prix*, at the New Britain Museum of American Art.

increased its holdings from two dozens paintings to 4,500 works ranging from early eighteenth century to the present. From early on the
museum decided to concentrate on the acquisition of American art.

The museum is a delight to visit. Over the years, wings were added
to the original quarters, yet the intimate feeling of visiting somebody's
private home has not vanished. Oriental carpets are on the floor, the
fireplaces have been left in place, and the walls are painted in different
colors or covered with wood paneling or grass cloth. Individual rooms
are given over to Portraiture, Hudson River School Landscapes, Genre,
Impressionists, Seascapes, Ashcan School, Early Modernism, Realism
Between the Wars, and so on.

There are representative works of the "grand old men" of American
portraiture—John Singleton Copley, William Merritt Chase, Charles
Willson Peale, John Singer Sargent—and of the Hudson River School—
Frederick Church, Albert Bierstadt—as well as lovely works by less
familiar artists.

Since Connecticut was one of the centers of American Impressionism, it is not surprising that the museum owns a superior collection of
these works. It owns twelve paintings by Childe Hassam alone. Note

the presence of one of America's icons: *Niagara In Winter* as painted by John Henry Twachtman. Another familiar landscape is a view of *Monhegan* by George Bellows. Ashcan School painters are particularly well represented.

Thomas Hart Benton's mural *The Arts of Life in America* was commissioned for the library of the Whitney Museum of American Art in 1932. In 1953, when the Whitney moved, half the mural was sold to the NBMAA, the other half to The Chrysler Museum of Art in Norfolk, Virginia (see p. 397). The Connecticut portion of the mural occupies a small gallery and though it would be nice to see it from a greater distance, Benton's imagery retains its bite.

Unhurried contemplation is one of the goals of the NBMAA. Each of its two floors has a small sitting area overlooking the giant maples and verdant lawns of Olmsted's park. These unobstructed outdoor views suit much of the art on display. Art books and catalogs available in these lounges encourage visitors to linger.

NEW HAVEN

The Yale Center for British Art

Address: 1080 Chapel Street, New Haven, CT 06510

Telephone: (203) 432-2800

Web: www.yale.edu/ycba

Hours: Tues–Sat 10–5; Sun 12–5. Closed Mon and major holidays.

Strengths: British art, particularly William Turner, George Stubbs, and Sporting Art.

Special Events: Temporary exhibits featuring British artists.

Other: Films, concerts, lectures, and gallery talks. Museum shop with English flavor.

Activities for Children: Special programs.

Parking: At the Chapel-York garage on York Street; also metered, on street.

According to the title of his autobiography, Paul Mellon never forgot that he was "born with a silver spoon in his mouth"; he spent a large fraction of his very long life ensuring that his fellow Americans could share his love of fine art. When he was in his late twenties he helped his father, Andrew Mellon, create the National Gallery of Art in Wash-

Pumpkin with a Stable Lad by George Stubbs, at the Yale Center for British Arts, was the first painting that Paul Mellon purchased. The museum owns more paintings by this particular British painter than any other institution in the world.

ington, D.C. (p. 125). Paul Mellon was also an important force in revitalizing the Virginia Museum of Fine Arts in Richmond (p. 400). No one knows which one of the institutions he endowed he loved best, but it may very well have been the Yale Center for British Art (YCBA).

Paul Mellon attributed his love for all things British to his English mother and the part of his childhood that he spent in England's peaceful countryside. He attended Yale, graduating in 1929, and then went on to study at Cambridge, England. He became a skilled hunter and horseman, and it is not surprising that, in 1936, when he bought his first oil painting it was George Stubbs's *Pumpkin* [a horse] *with a Stable Lad*. The work is now one of the YCBA's fifteen Stubbses and the first of many of Mellon's Sporting Art works. Today the museum has the largest collection of George Stubbs in the world. The next British artist to captivate Mellon was William Blake, whose nightmarish inner visions—also at Yale—contrast with Stubbs's orderly ones.

In 1950, Paul Mellon started to assemble British art systematically with a view to leaving it to a museum. The collection, the largest aggregation of British art outside Great Britain, is very personal and low key. It eschews the grandiose, full-length portraits beloved by Collins Huntington (see Huntington Library, Art Collections, and Botanical Gardens, p. 96) and the romanticism of Pre-Raphaelite art. The YCBA features genre paintings (William Hogarth, Arthur Devis, George Hayman, Thomas Gainsborough), landscapes (John Constable, William Turner, Canaletto), portraits (Anthony Van Dyck), Sporting Art, lots of wonderful paintings of horses and much, much more, including works by contemporary artists.

In 1966, Paul Mellon decided to donate his collection to his alma mater. He endowed it generously. The university appointed Louis Kahn as architect. Kahn, who just then was completing the Kimbell Art Museum in Fort Worth, Texas (p. 380), was no stranger to New Haven. He had been a professor at Yale and had enlarged the university's Art Gallery across the street. Before embarking on a design for the YCBA, Kahn studied British art and Paul Mellon's collection. He also investigated the manner in which the paintings had been displayed in the English country homes for which they had been created. Kahn and his client decided on intimate settings, small galleries, long corridors, and natural light.

The museum is wedged between existing buildings and is located on busy city streets. It has a concrete, steel, and glass exterior. The shiny surfaces reflect the mood of the sky. The visitor enters via a large glass-covered court dominated by a Barbara Hepworth sculpture. Inside the soft woods and woolen carpets contrast with the hard exterior shell reiterated in the elevator shaft and the stairs. Comfortable sofas are distributed throughout the galleries and dark places are lighted ingeniously.

It is best to start your visit on the fourth floor, usually filled with the Turners, the Stubbses, and works from the sixteenth to the early nineteenth century. The third floor is given over to temporary exhibits, the second to more recent artworks.

The Yale Center for British Art was Louis Kahn's last work. He died in 1974, three years before the museum opened. Others carried on for him. The plans he drew worked exceedingly well. According to the museum staff, "they are suitable for the third graders from New Haven's public schools, Yale students, scholars, and the general public."

Yale University Art Gallery

Address: 1111 Chapel Street, New Haven, CT 06520

Telephone: (203) 432-0600

Web: www.yale.edu/artgallery

Hours: Tues–Sat 10–5, Sun 1–6. Closed Mon and major holidays.

Strengths: Encyclopedic. Italian Renaissance. Old Masters. American 18th- and 19th-century art, including part of the "modern" art assembled by Katherine S. Dreier's Société Anonyme.

Other: Sculpture garden. Museum shop.

Activities for Children: Sporadic family days with entertainment, music, and hands-on art activities.

Parking: At Chapel-York Garage on York Street; also metered, on street.

The Yale University Art Gallery (YUAG) was founded in 1832, long before anyone knew that Yale would become a world-class university and that its museum would receive masterpieces from its devoted, distinguished, knowledgeable, and wealthy alumni.

In 1832, Jeremiah Day, Yale's president, arranged to buy twenty-eight paintings and sixty miniatures from John Trumbull, who chronicled the American Revolution in these pre-camera days (also see the Wadsworth Atheneum, p. 108). In 1901, Trumbull agreed to design a fire-proof art gallery and was awarded a pension—America's first university art grant. The Trumbull Gallery, an elegant neoclassical structure, was demolished in 1901.

In 1872, Yale acquired, at auction, the collection assembled by James Jackson Jarves, the American pioneer enthusiast of quattrocento paintings, who had acquired a stunning collection of what were then called "Italian Primitives." Jarves had exhibited the paintings in New York, then had hoped to sell them at a profit. Instead his "fire sale" netted only $23,000 (also see the Cleveland Museum of Art, p. 327), allegedly a third of what it had cost him. According to Francis Steegmiller, in *The Two Lives of James Jackson Jarves,* "The acquisition conferred considerable distinction on Yale, for at the time no other institution, and no individual in the country, possessed pictures at all comparable in interest."

Today the YUAG occupies two connecting, widely disparate buildings. The first, designed in 1928 by Edgerton Swartwout, resembles an Italian Gothic palace; the other was built in 1953 by Louis Kahn, who also built the neighboring YCBA. New Haven thus is the site of the distinguished architect's first and last museums.

To begin with, Yale owned fewer than a hundred paintings; as of the latest count, it owned more than 80,000 objects, many unique. It has an encyclopedic collection comprising ancient, pre-Columbian, African, Asian, and European art.

Yale is well known for its American paintings and decorative arts. In 1930, it was given Mabel Brady Garvan's collection of 10,000 examples of early American silver, furniture, pewter, and ceramics, as well as paintings, prints, and sculpture. Two years later, it received the Whitney Collection of Sporting Art, depicting almost every known sport. The works complement those of the adjacent Yale Center for British Art (see previous entry). Yale owns remarkable works by John Singleton Copley, John Smibert, Thomas Eakins, Frederick Church, Winslow Homer, Childe Hassam, and many others.

The European collections grew as well, mostly because of a generous bequest from alumnus Stephen C. Clark. There are prime examples of European Pre- and Post-Impressionism (Camille Pissaro, Edouard Manet, Edgar Degas, Auguste Renoir). Yale owns Vincent Van Gogh's *The Night Café*, a painting so well known that it is surprising to discover where it actually "lives."

In 1941, to its surprise, Yale received part of the collection assembled by Katherine S. Dreier and her Société Anonyme (more than 1,000 works by 180 different artists). From about 1913 until 1929, when MoMA opened in New York and she deemed her efforts superfluous, Dreier championed modern art in America. A close friend of the Surrealist Marcel Duchamp, Dreier bought, exhibited, and lectured about Wassily Kandinsky, Kasimir Malevich, Joseph Stella, Piet Mondrian, Constantin Brancusi, and many other by now familiar artists, all of whom can now be seen at Yale. Other parts of the Dreier Collection went to The Museum of Modern Art (p. 297) and The Solomon R. Guggenheim Museum (p. 281), both in New York.

CONNECTICUT

Delaware

Delaware Art Museum

Address: 2301 Kentmere Parkway, Wilmington, DE 19806

Telephone: (302) 571-9590

Web: www.delart.org

Hours: Tues, Thur–Sat 9–4; Wed 9–9; Sun 10–4. Closed Mon except Martin Luther King, Jr., Presidents', and Columbus days. Closed New Year's, Thanksgiving, and Christmas days.

Strengths: American art (1840 to 20th century), with emphasis on magazine illustrations, cartoons, and Brandywine School. Important works by Howard Pyle; N.C., Andrew, and Jamie Wyeth; and artists of the Ashcan School. The largest Pre-Raphaelite collection in the United States.

Special Events: Wed 4–9: Guided tours, films, lectures, and films. Thurs 12:15–1:15: Tours and lectures free with purchased box lunch. Special happenings on selected weekends.

Other: The 40,000 volume Helen Farr Sloan Library is open to the public. Museum shop. Art rental gallery. The art exhibited at the Brandywine River Museum, in nearby Chadds Ford, Pennsylvania (p. 348), is complementary and can easily be visited at the same time. Café.

Activities for Children: Pegafoamasaurus, an interactive exhibition gallery for children with hands-on activities.

Parking: On site.

The Delaware Art Museum (DAM) goes back to 1912, the year Howard Pyle died. He had been born in Wilmington in 1853, and lived there most of his life. He was one of America's top illustrators and his work appeared regularly in *Colliers, Harper's Monthly,* and other leading magazines. Children and adults were captivated by the books he illustrated and often wrote. His painting and illustrations are at once realistic, romantic, fantastic, and a bit frightening. They are so powerful that his reputation reached Europe. In a letter to his brother Theo, Vincent

Veronica Veronese by Dante Gabriel Rossetti is part of the Delaware Art Museum's magnificent collection of Pre-Raphaelite works.

Van Gogh commented on the "wonderful illustration in *Harper's* by Howard Pyle."

In 1894, Pyle, often called the father of American illustration, founded what would become known as the Brandywine School of painting. Newell Convers (N.C.) Wyeth, Maxfield Parrish, Frank Schoonover, and others who would become important artists and illustrators in their own right attended his classes. When Pyle died, his students wanted to keep forty-eight of his most treasured works in Wilmington. Their efforts eventually resulted in the Delaware Art Museum.

The museum, in suburban Wilmington, is small and accessible. Light streams in through big windows. Emphasis is on works by Pyle and his followers, including three generations of Wyeths: N.C., Andrew, and Jamie (also see the Brandywine River Museum, p. 348, and The William A. Farnsworth Art Museum, p. 190). Together with the Peale family, who hail from neighboring Philadelphia, the Wyeths are the closest America comes to having a painting dynasty. N.C.'s painterly illustrations for classic tales have great power and imagination. His precocious son Andrew, mainly taught by his father, exhibited in New York City when he was only twenty years old. Andrew's starkly realist portraits, still lifes, and landscapes reflect a deep psychological insight. Like his father's work, his paintings have a narrative quality that makes the ordinary seem extraordinary. Andrew's son Jamie, also taught by his father, continues in the family tradition. Favorite subjects are lighthouses, seascapes, flowers, portraits, and animals.

Museums grow in many unexpected ways. So it is that the DAM owns America's largest Pre-Raphaelite collection. The Pre-Raphaelites flourished in Victorian England during the 1850s. Members of the group were discontent with the shallow, meaningless academic and realistic art of the day, and harked back to the spirituality and idealism of the "pre-Raphael" Middle Ages and early Renaissance. The story goes that Samuel Bancroft, a Wilmington industrialist, became captivated by Pre-Raphaelite art while having tea in a private home in England. Thereafter, he and his wife, Mary, assembled a major collection of Pre-Raphaelite paintings and decorative objects. Bancroft befriended the artists and collected related archival material. Eventually the entire collection was willed to the DAM.

All major painters of the Pre-Raphaelite Brotherhood are represented: Dante Gabriel Rossetti, William Holman Hunt, John Everett Millais, Edward Burne-Jones, and Marie Spartali Stillman. The carefully crafted, symbolic works are displayed in a Victorian setting that enhances their sumptuous feeling. Most of paintings depict women in dramatic situations. The women with their mournful faces are beautiful, light glancing off their golden hair and their dramatic clothing. In their own way, the pictures relate to the mythical vision so evident in the Brandywine School of art. The Pre-Raphaelite movement was short-lived, but its ideas were absorbed by William Morris, a designer whose fabrics and wallpaper patterns are still used today, and by the Art Nouveau and even the American Crafts movements.

The DAM's extensive collection of nineteenth- and twentieth-century American art includes some familiar masterpieces: Winslow Homer's *Milking Time* and Edward Hopper's *Summer Time*. The museum is well known for works of The Eight, also known as the Ashcan artists, a turn-of-the-twentieth-century anti-academic group. Members include Arthur B. Davies, William Glackens, Robert Henri, Ernest Lawson, George Luks, John Sloan, and Maurice Prendergast, all of whose works are on display at the museum. Of these, the DAM established a close relationship with John Sloan and his wife, Helen Farr

Sloan. After the painter's death the museum received the residual estate from his widow, who also endowed a comprehensive library. Galleries exhibiting recent and contemporary American art complete the visit to this charming museum.

District of Columbia
(Washington, D.C.)

The Corcoran Gallery of Art

Address: 500 17th Street NW, Washington, D.C. 20006
Telephone: (202) 639-1700
Web: www.corcoran.org
Hours: Mon, Wed, Fri 10–5; Thurs 10–9. Closed Tues and New Year's, Thanksgiving, and Christmas days. Tours daily—except Thurs—at 12:30; Thurs at 7:30.
Strengths: American art, especially contemporary. Also European art, sculpture, Greek antiquities from 8th to 1st century B.C.E. Italian majolica, bronzes. Honoré Daumier.
Special Events: Family day, concerts.
Activities for Children: Family program about every other Sun, with diverse art-oriented activities and docent-led tours geared to children.
Other: Café, featuring jazz, and gospel music on Sun. Museum shop.
Parking: Metered, on street; pay garages.

Compared to the other Washington museums the Corcoran is strangely old-fashioned. Its collection was assembled by William Wilson Corcoran, a native of Georgetown, D.C. A successful banker at the time of America's Industrial Revolution, Corcoran intended to donate his collection to the American public. Since there was no museum, he commissioned one from James Renwick, the builder of St. Patrick's

Cathedral in New York City, in 1859. The Civil War erupted before the building was finished, and Corcoran, a Southern sympathizer, fled for the duration. The museum was officially founded in 1869, an institution, in the words of its donor, "dedicated to art, and used solely for the purpose of encouraging the American genius." The galleries finally opened in 1874, depriving the Corcoran of the honor of being America's oldest big-city museum. It lost out to Boston and New York by a year.

Unlike most of his contemporary collectors, Corcoran befriended American artists. As a consequence, his museum now is the lucky owner of paintings by Albert Bierstadt (*Mount Corcoran, The Last of the Buffalo*), Frederick Church (*Niagara Falls*), George Inness, and others. Corcoran also established an art school and organized a biennial art competition. Paintings bought at the event enriched the collection. Today the museum owns representative works by most major American artists from colonial times to the present. The galleries in which these paintings are displayed are very satisfying and impressive.

In 1897, Corcoran commissioned a larger Beaux Arts building designed by Ernest Flagg, a Paris-trained New York architect. It is still one of the best examples of this style in America. The museum was expanded in 1925 and a final wing, designed by Frank Gehry, was commissioned in 1999.

Fifty years after it became public, the Corcoran attracted the collection of Senator William A. Clark, Montana's "Copper King," shown in a beautiful portrait by William Merritt Chase. Clark had been on the board of the Corcoran since about 1900. A Francophile, Clark bought his art—good, bad, and indifferent—on his own from a variety of art dealers. Most amusing is a group of small sculptures by Honoré Daumier, the painter-cartoonist. It is fitting that these caricatures of the French politicians are displayed in such close proximity to our own legislators.

The Corcoran also owns the *Salon Doré,* a French period room. The sumptuous room, paneled from ceiling to floor with Corinthian pilasters, trophy panels, garlands, and large framed mirrors, is a reminder of what life of the privileged few was like during the eighteenth century in Paris. An elaborate clock, from the private sitting room of Marie-Antoinette at the Tuileries Palace in Paris, stands on the mantelpiece.

The Cocoran's European collection is famous for its Dutch seventeenth-century and French mid-nineteenth-century works and also for its tapestries, rugs, and textiles. European holdings include works by Auguste Renoir, Claude Monet, Gustave Courbet, and Camille Pissaro.

In addition, the museum owns many examples of work by twentieth-century American painters. The collection of American Impressionists—Mary Cassatt, Childe Hassam, and James Whistler, among others—is particularly strong. The John Singer Sargents—especially *The Oyster Gatherers of Cancale,* painted in 1878—are curator Dorothy Moss's special favorites. The painting was the first our famous expatriate exhibited back home. There is a good selection of Ashcan painters as well as works by Thomas Hart Benton, Arthur Dove, John Marin, Philip Pearlstein, Josef Albers, and Mark Rothko. The Corcoran also has a superior and growing collection of photographs.

Dumbarton Oaks

Address: 1703 32nd Street NW, Washington, D.C. 20007

Telephone: (202) 339-6400

Web: www.doaks.org

Hours: *Collection:* Tues–Sun 2–5. Closed Mon and holidays. *Gardens:* Open daily as follows: March 15–Oct 2–6; Nov–Mar 2–5. Call to find what flowers bloom when.

Strengths: Byzantine and Pre-Columbian art. The music room of this sumptuous Georgian mansion reflects the intellectual and social atmosphere of the capital from 1920 to 1940. Gardens by Beatrix Ferrand. Libraries.

Other: Museum shop.

Activities for Children: This small museum and its gardens are child-friendly.

Parking: On street.

Robert Woods Bliss and his wife, Mildred Bliss, had exquisite taste. Together they assembled a small, unique collection of art, and created a parklike garden which is a joy for anyone fortunate enough to visit. Dumbarton Oaks, in Washington's Georgetown, is named for the Scottish farmer from Dumbarton-on-the-Clyde who received the land grant in 1702. Like the Frick in New York (p. 278), the Gardner in Boston (p.

202), and the Pierpont Morgan Library in New York (p. 303), Dumbarton Oaks is so personal that even today, sixty years after it opened to the public, visitors feel like privileged guests.

Robert Bliss limited his collecting to Byzantine and Pre-Columbian art. He selected his 500-piece Pre-Columbian collection with extreme care, weighing the aesthetic values of each piece. There is lacy gold jewelry from Colombia (1000–1500 C.E.), sculptures of the gods, and ceremonial objects. The works are displayed in eight circular glass bays in a small pavilion built by architect Philip Johnson. The larger Byzantine collection is equally appealing to the senses. It includes a large collection of seals (13,000) and coins (more than 11,000), and early mosaics, textiles, jewelry, ceremonial silver, religious objects, ivories, and bronzes, including the *Statue of a Horse* from the late Roman period. In addition, Dumbarton Oaks houses the world's greatest library related to Byzantine studies.

As remarkable as the house and its art are, landscape architect Beatrix Ferrand's masterpiece, the sixteen-acre garden, is even more so. It was developed by Ferrand and Mildred Bliss over a period of twenty-five years. The garden is divided into a series of intimate rooms filled with flowers, ornamental pools, immense trees, statuary, stairs, and fountains. One such room is the Pebble Garden, in which smooth beach stones are used to depict the family arms, a sheaf of wheat. The design is defined by a groundcover of thyme, and the walls are hung with wisteria. Elsewhere are the large Rose Garden, the Beech Terrace, an Ellipse, and a walk bordered by flowering fruit trees. There are putti playing in small pools, surrounded by grass and flowers. There are majestic old trees and a stream meandering from a small outdoor theater down to a lower, more open section of the garden.

Mildred Bliss's interest in gardening led to the Garden Library, a collection of 11,500 works on landscape history, including many rare examples.

In 1940 the couple donated their life's work to Harvard University and it became the institution's world-renowned center for Byzantine studies. They continued to live nearby and visited almost daily. Eventually, like the Smiths of the Springfield Museums in Massachusetts (p. 219) they were laid to rest in one of the walls of their beloved gardens. The wall bears the Dumbarton Oaks motto: *Quod Servis Metes* (As ye sow, so ye shall reap). Elsewhere a tablet honors Beatrix Farrand, creator of this Eden.

National Gallery of Art

Address: On the National Mall at Constitution Ave and 4th Street NW, Washington, D.C. 20565

Telephone: (202) 737-4215

Web: www.nga.gov

Hours: Mon–Sat 10–5; Sun 11–6. Closed New Year's and Christmas days. Hourly introductory tours of the collections and frequent tours of temporary shows.

Strengths: Encyclopedic. Prime examples of European and American art.

Special Events: Important temporary exhibits.

Other: Lectures, films, Sun evening concerts (admission on a first-come basis). Prints, drawings, and rare books not on exhibition can be viewed by prior arrangement from 10–12 and 2–4 (call 202-842-6380). Micro Gallery: A comprehensive multimedia computer system that provides in-depth information on works owned by the National Gallery. Restaurants, including the particularly nice Terrace Café, located on the upper level of the East Building, and the Espresso bar. Museum shops. Wheelchairs, strollers, and assistive listening devices for use in the large auditorium are available. Sculpture garden. Ice skating rink.

Activities for Children: Special web address: www.ngskids.gov. Also many activities, some drop-in, others requiring preregistration (call 202-842-6880). Low-cost booklets for self-guided tours are available.

Parking: Limited metered; pay garages.

Of the several ways of entering the museum, it is most impressive to arrive at this "Palace for the People" from the National Mall. The entrance is a majestic rotunda, whose huge black columns soar to a cupola. Potted flowering plants ring a fountain topped by a statue of Hermes, the Greek messenger of the gods. Two long corridors extend from the center rotunda, each terminating in a smaller, plant-and-fauteuil-filled rotunda. Small galleries open along these airy, light-filled passageways. No visitor can fail to be swept away by the magnificence of our National Gallery of Art (NGA) or by its collections.

The NGA is the gift of Andrew W. Mellon, a banker and former Secretary of the U.S. Treasury. In 1927, when he was seventy-six years old, he decided that his country needed a national art gallery. Aided by the top art dealers of the day, he started buying high-quality art. His biggest coup was acquiring priceless treasures from St. Petersburg's Hermitage museum, sold by the financially strapped Soviet Union. The secret transaction yielded Raphael's *Alba Madonna,* and two Annunciations, one by Sandro Botticelli, the other by Jan van Eyck. Mellon's other acquisitions—130 in all—are equally magnificent. Then he commissioned John Russell Pope, the foremost museum architect of his time, to build a museum. Pope designed a sumptuous six-block-long building which, according to Aline Saarinen in *The Proud Possessors,* "required eight hundred carloads of Tennessee marble of twenty-three shades ranging from deep rose to pearly pink." Other colors of stone were used for the interior.

Mellon was both modest and smart. In order to encourage other donors, he refused to have the gallery bear his name. Even before the National Gallery opened in 1941—on the eve of World War Two—Samuel H. Kress (see p. 31) had donated a magnificent collection of European Old Master paintings and decorative arts to the NGA. Early on, the NGA was also the recipient of the Widener and Chester Dale collections. Philadelphia's P. A. B. Widener—whose immense fortune rested on supplying the Union Army with mutton and then on trolley cars—and his son, Joseph, had assembled a fantastic collection of Old Masters. The Philadelphia Museum of Art coveted the riches, but after much soul-searching the Wideners gave them to the NGA instead. The NGA also was the recipient of the collection—consisting of mostly the art—French Pre-Impressionism, Impressionism, and Post-Impressionism, stopping short of Cubism—assembled by Chester Dale, a New York financier, and his wife, Maude.

The National Gallery is not as exhaustive as other big museums, but its works are of extremely high caliber and the displays are well organized. Every room is equipped with well-written guides explaining the art on display. The west galleries are filled with older art. Almost immediately visitors realize that the National Gallery is the home of many of the world's best-known pictures. Samuel Kress's red-and-gold Byzantine and Renaissance paintings and artifacts (1,815 in all) fill entire galleries. The Kress Foundation would eventually distribute an equal number of objects to eighteen regional museums. Raphael's *Alba Madonna* gazes happily from her round frame. There is Botticelli's portrait of Giuliano de Medici, whose family were the art patrons of Florence. There is the lovely face of *Ginevra de'Benci*, the New World's only painting by Leonardo Da Vinci. There are luscious Titians and regal Anthony van Dycks. A few steps further on we are immersed in Northern Europe's more somber art: Rembrandt's self-portrait, Jan Vermeer's interiors, Jacob van Ruysdael's landscapes, and imposing portraits by George Romney and Thomas Gainsborough.

Retracing our steps through the great rotunda to the East Wing, we are engulfed by the French Impressionists, works by Vincent van Gogh and two of Claude Monet's Rouen cathedrals among them. Unlike most other encyclopedic museums, the National Gallery only displays art. There are no period rooms, and very few decorative objects or antiquities. Every object is choice. Indeed, Andrew Mellon stipulated that the gallery could only accept gifts that were of the same high caliber as the art he had donated.

Andrew Mellon died before Franklin Delano Roosevelt could open the museum. Mellon's children, especially his son Paul, took an immense interest in his father's legacy. For many years Paul Mellon was chairman of the board.

Big as it was, the National Gallery eventually outgrew its space. Fortunately, an odd-shaped piece of land across Fourth Street had been reserved for expansion. Ailsa Bruce Mellon and Paul Mellon volunteered to expand their father's gift. After an extended search, they engaged I. M. Pei to design an additional building (the "East Building"). Whereas the West Building harks back to elegance, warm woods, and sumptuous marble, the East Building is a soaring open glass-and-concrete structure. Galleries surround the open center, dissected by floating bridges. Long vistas and sharp edges add excitement. Escalators carry visitors from floor to floor. A huge Alexander Calder mobile hangs from the ceiling some 150 feet above the ground floor. A restaurant clings to the top-most floor. From this height the ground floor, with its milling crowd, trees, and Max Ernst's Capricorn sculpture, looks distant and small. An immense wall hanging, based on a Joan Miró painting, hangs down from an upper gallery.

The East Building is well suited to display the twentieth-century art for which it was built. The building also has galleries for temporary exhibits. A magical series of small French paintings, again given by Paul Mellon and Ailsa Bruce Mellon, is often displayed in the smaller galleries on the ground floor of the East Building.

National Museum of Women in the Arts

Address: 1250 New York Avenue NW, Washington, D.C. 20005

Telephone: (202) 783-5000

Web: www.nmwa.org

Hours: Mon–Sat 10–5; Sun 12–5. Closed New Year's, Thanksgiving, and Christmas days.

Strength: Brings the work of women artists to the attention of the general public.

Special Events: Active temporary exhibit schedule (about 12 a year) related to women in the arts.

Other: Extensive library and research center whose resources are geared to educate the public about the contributions of women to visual- and book-related arts; open to the public by appointment. Restaurant. Museum shop.

Parking: Limited on street; pay garages.

Throughout most of history, there have been few women artists, and these few were mostly anonymous and unseen. All this unrealized talent is one of humanity's great losses. The National Museum of Women in the Arts (NMWA) does its share in redressing the balance. During the 1960s, Wilhemina C. and Wallace F. Holladay started to assemble artworks executed by women. Twenty years later the collection was big enough for a museum. The NMWA was incorporated in 1981 and six years later it moved to Washington's former Masonic Grand Lodge, an elegant 1906 Renaissance Revival structure.

The permanent collection provides a few examples of older works. There is a *Holy Family with St. John* from the sixteenth century by Lavinia Fontana. A label, based on an old commentary, oddly states that: "This Flemish painting will appeal to the devout better than any painting of Italy, [including] women, especially the very old and the very young, and also to monks and nuns." There is a still life by Judith

Self-Portrait Dedicated to Leon Trotsky, by Frida Kahlo, from the collection of the National Museum of Women in the Arts.

Leyster (1609–1660). There are botanical and zoological prints. An alligator devouring a snake by Maria Sibylla Merian (German 1647–1717) is so amusing that it fails to frighten.

The excellent labels stress what is extraordinary about the women artists, who succeeded in spite of restrictions and prejudice. We marvel at the display of silver made by women silversmiths; at Camille Claudel's fine bronze of a young girl; and at a painting by Mary Jane Peale, the daughter of Charles Willson Peale, the founder of the American Peale painter-dynasty. We learn that Rosa Bonheur, France's famed animal painter, avoided harassment by disguising herself as a man while practicing her craft.

Another explanatory tablet, next to paintings by the Impressionists Berthe Morisot and Mary Cassatt, explains that these two paved the way for women artists. Indeed, their numbers increased. We admire a painting of a sturdy black tree with yellow leaves by Georgia O'Keeffe and a self-portrait of an all-dressed-up Frida Kahlo. As always, Kaethe Kollwitz's mournful children tug at one's heart. There are paintings by Lee Krasner, the wife of Jackson Pollock, and Elaine de Kooning, the wife of Willem de Kooning, and tablets that wonder how the art of these women was affected by their husbands' fame. There are examples of works by Marie Laurencin, Suzanne Valadon, Gabrielle Münter, Tamara de Lempicka, and Louise Nevelson.

The NMWA also maintains an impressive research center, a library with a resource file on over 17,000 artists from all nations. Like other museums in our nation's capital, the NMWA pays a belated tribute to a neglected "minority."

The Phillips Collection

Address: 1600 21st Street NW, Washington, D.C. 20009

Telephone: (202) 387-2151

Web: www.phillipscollection.org

Hours: Tues–Sat 10–5, Sun 12–5, Thurs 10–8:30. Closed Mon and New Year's Day, Independence, and Christmas Day. Tours Wed and Sat at 2.

Strength: An intimate collection of 12th- and 20th-century American and European art.

Special Events: Sun afternoon concerts at 5 (Sept–May). Temporary exhibits related to strength of museum. Special talks first Thurs at 12:30.

Other: Café. Museum shop.

Activities for Children: Free Family Fun Pack; before-hours special guided tours; occasional 3-hour hands-on art workshops.

Parking: Limited on street. Also Washington Hilton Embassy Row Parking at 2105 Massachusetts Avenue NW.

As you enter the red-brick Georgian-revival house on a tree-lined street in the nation's capital, you immediately sense the quiet reserve, the restrained elegance that characterized the closing years of the turbulent nineteenth century. The four-story Phillips Gallery was built in 1897 as a home for the Phillips family, inheritors of the Laughlin steel fortune.

Already at Yale, Duncan Phillips, an English major, was fascinated by art. After graduation his interest intensified. In 1916, he and his brother convinced their parents to spent $10,000 annually on buying art. When Duncan's father and brother died within a year of each other, he and his mother (born Laughlin) decided to establish an art gallery in their memory.

The Migration of the Negro was the first epic cycle by Jacob Lawrence, then a young unknown African American painter. In 1942 The Phillips Collection in Washington, D.C., acquired half of the 72 paintings and The Museum of Modern Art in New York City acquired the other half.

From the very first, art rewarded Duncan Phillips handsomely. At an early exhibition of his fledgling collection he met Marjorie Acker, a painter and art enthusiast. After their marriage, building the Phillips collection was central to their lives. While scholarly, it is also a statement of their personal taste.

Initially Phillips favored paintings by a few French artists: Jean-Baptiste Siméon Chardin, Alfred Sisley, Claude Monet, and Henri Fantin-Latour. Then he added works by contemporary American painters: John Henry Twachtman, Robert Weir, Albert Pinkham Ryder, James Whistler, Ernest Lawson, George Luks, and Childe Hassam. By 1921, Phillips owned 240 paintings, enough to open what he described as "America's first Museum of Modern Art" in two rooms located off the family mansion. He hoped that the works, hung in an intimate, homelike setting, would "provide a joy and help people see [the art] . . . as true artists see it."

Duncan very rapidly became a passionate collector and a trusted friend of contemporary artists. A photograph shows a happy Duncan aboard ship setting out for one of his European art-buying sprees. By 1930, he owned 600 works, many of them epoch-making: Auguste Renoir's *The Luncheon of the Boating Party*, Honoré Daumier's *Upris-*

ing and *Three Lawyers*, Pierre Bonnard's *The Palm*, and Edgar Degas's *Dancer at the Bar*. Other European favorites include Georges Braque, Paul Cézanne, and Paul Klee. He bought El Grecos because he felt that the painter was "the first impassioned expressionist," and Edouard Manets because he was fascinated by the artist's novel technique for applying paint.

Some of Duncan's acquisitions were daring. In the 1940s he and The Museum of Modern Art in New York City shared Jacob Lawrence's epic cycle depicting the migration of African Americans from the rural South to the industrial North. Lawrence was a young black painter trained in Harlem at a PWA workshop. The thirty-six small, intense paintings fit the Phillipses' love for art on a human scale. Duncan and Marjorie Phillips were staunch supporters of American modernists including John Marin, Georgia O'Keeffe, Marsden Hartley, Arthur Dove, Milton Avery, and Mark Rothko.

By 1930, 2,400 works of art crowded the Phillipses out of their house. Extensive remodeling turned the mansion into a full-fledged museum. The directorship of this jewel was taken over by their son Laughlin, who had majored in art history. An annex connected to the original museum doubled the exhibition space.

Like the Freer in Washington (p. 134), the Frick in New York (p. 278), and the Gardner in Boston (p. 202), Sterling and Francine Clark in Williamstown (p. 223), the Phillips Collection reflects the taste and passions of the individual collectors. Duncan and Marjorie Phillips concentrated on artists of the nineteenth and twentieth centuries. Their collection stresses artistic continuity, evolution, and innovation. To help museum visitors grasp certain interrelationships, paintings at the museum are arranged in "Units." Other experts might see different or additional associations, but the Units chosen by Duncan and Marjorie Phillips work well. The art at the Phillips is gentle. The paintings are on a human scale. As Duncan wrote: "We are skeptics about extremist fads, such as so called pop art and optical art . . . and of abstract expressionism."

As the founder hoped, the museum still teaches, provides enjoyment, and bestows peace. He fulfilled his vision. In the seventy-five years since its opening, the collection has given immeasurable joy to the many who come to see it.

The Smithsonian Institution

Freer Gallery of Art
Hirshhorn Museum and Sculpture Garden
National Museum of African Art
Smithsonian American Art Museum

As of the latest count the Smithsonian Institution operates fourteen different museums, a zoo, and three gardens. Twelve of the museums are in Washington, D.C., and two in New York City.

Let us go back to 1847, when the cornerstone of what became known as "the Castle" was laid, and recall the strange story of how this came about. James Smithson was born in England in 1765, the natural son of Hugh Smithson, the Duke of Northumberland. James studied at Oxford, and became an expert in "Chymistry and Mineralogy." He identified and presumably mined a particular type of zinc ore, which was named in his honor. Along the way he amassed a fortune. When he died, in 1829, he left his earthly goods to his nephew. His will, however, stipulated that if the nephew died without heirs the balance of the legacy would pass "to the United States, to found at Washington, under the name of the Smithsonian Institution, an establishment for the increase and diffusion of knowledge. . . ." In 1835 the nephew died childless. During the next ten years, Congress debated on how to utilize the generous bequest of a man who had never visited these shores.

To comply with his wishes Congress decided to create a multi-faceted organization involved in research and dispersal of academic findings. The fledgling institution asked James Renwick, Jr., the architect of St. Patrick's Cathedral in New York City and also of the first home of Washington's Corcoran Gallery of Art (p. 121), to build it a building on the National Mall. For years the Norman-style "Castle," at variance stylistically with most other Mall buildings, served as headquarters for the institution and exhibition hall for its collections. Today the Castle houses the administrative offices, an information center (telephone: 202-357-2700; web: www.si.edu), and, strangely, a crypt that holds the reinterred remains of benefactor James Smithson. Visitors to the Castle, an opulent structure clearly dating from another era, can pay tribute to this stranger who felt a kinship with our young nation. The Smithsonian's collections are now housed in satellite museums, several of which are also on the National Mall. The satellite museums include, in addition to those listed above: the National Museum of Natural History, the National Air and Space Museum, and the Cooper-Hewitt Museum of Decorative Arts and Designs in New York City, to name just a few.

The Smithsonian's three gardens—the Enid A. Haupt Garden, the Mary Livingston Ripley Garden, and the Butterfly Habitat Garden—are all within easy reach of the Castle.

Freer Gallery of Art and Arthur M. Sackler Gallery (Smithsonian)

Address: 1050 Independence Avenue SW, Washington, D.C. 20560

Telephone: (202) 357-4880

Web: www.si.edu/asia

Hours: Daily 10–5:30. Closed Christmas Day. Tours daily (except Wed) at 11:30.

Strengths: Exquisite Asian collection comprising mostly historic bronzes, jades, sculptures, painting, scrolls, metalwork, manuscripts, glass, lacquerware, and ceramics from China, Japan, Korea, Iran, India, Egypt, Arabia, Greece, and Syria. Early Christian art and manuscripts. American paintings of the 19th and early 20th century, including the largest collection of James Whistler in the world. Also Whistler's *Peacock Room.*

Special Events: Temporary exhibits drawn from the museum's vast holdings as well as loan shows.

Other: Museum shop. Informal talks Thurs 5:30–7:30 in conjunction with "Art Night on the Mall.

Activities for Children: Two free guides, *In the Footsteps of Buddha* and *Fly with Me,* available at information desk.

Parking: Limited on street; pay garages.

The Freer and Sackler galleries together form the Smithsonian's national museum of Asian art. The Freer was the Smithsonian's first satellite museum. It is the gift of Charles Langston Freer, one of America's railroad tycoons. Charles Freer was of French Huguenot extraction. He was born in 1856 and started to work when he was fourteen years old. Good with figures, he accompanied his boss, Frank J. Hecker, to Detroit where they made a fortune building railroad cars. In 1900, when he was only forty-four years old, Freer retired and dedicated himself to living well.

Charles Freer was a fastidious man. In *The Proud Possessors*, Aline B. Saarinen reports that he was painstakingly particular about his food, the mixture of the tea he drank, the vintage of his wine, the quality of his caviar, and the color of the flowers that decorated his house. It is not surprising that he fell passionately in love with the refined, genteel art of China, Japan, and the Near East.

Freer opted against leaving his treasures to the new Detroit Institute of Arts. In 1904, fifteen years before his death, he offered his collection, and money to erect a building to house it, to the Smithsonian Institution. This was a novel move and the Regents of the Smithsonian debated the matter ad infinitum. President Theodore Roosevelt finally settled the question in 1906 in Freer's (and our) favor. The museum, designed by Charles Platt in the Italian Renaissance Style, opened in 1923, four years after the donor's death. Freer had specified that only a small part of the magnificent collection, consisting of more than 2,000 objects, would be on display at any one time, and visiting the uncluttered museum is relaxing and spiritually nourishing.

Freer started traveling to the Orient in 1895 to learn more about his chosen field and also befriended experts in Oriental art, especially those associated with Harvard. The collection is of unusually high quality. It includes bronzes, jades, sculptures, paintings, metalwork, lacquerware, ceramics, prints, and glass from China, Japan, Korea, India, Iran, Egypt, and Syria, as well as a rare collection of early Christian manuscripts.

His museum, however, is not entirely devoid of Western art. Before Freer became totally captivated by Asian art, he collected a few American artists, including James (Abbott McNeil) Whistler, the expatriate painter. Freer bought his first Whistler in 1887. The two men became close friends and when Whistler died in 1903, Freer was a pallbearer. By then, Freer owned more Whistlers than anyone else. An amusing story concerns one he did not own until later. Fredrick Leyland, a British shipping magnate, owned Whistler's painting *The Princess of the Land of Porcelain,* that harmonized with his collection of blue and white Chinese porcelains. In 1876, Leyland asked Whistler to decorate his London dining room. Whistler obliged. While Leyland was on vacation, Whistler overpainted the embossed leather that lined the room with a turquoise background and gold-leafed peacocks. Birds spread their feathers from side panels, the ceiling, and window shutters. Upon his return, Leyland was horrified and reduced Whistler's fee by more than half. Outraged, Whistler added two more peacocks, one representing the filthy rich, money-grabbing Leyland, the other a poor, proud Whistler. After Leyland's death Freer bought the paneling of the *Peacock Room* as well as the painting of the Princess. They are now in the Freer, and the room adds its luster to the aesthetically pleasing museum.

By the 1980s the Freer had outgrown its quarters, and the nation gratefully accepted the four-million-dollar gift of Dr. Arthur M. Sackler (also see Harvard University Art Museums, p. 208) to build an adjoining museum, the Arthur M. Sackler Gallery, which opened in 1987. Sackler also donated 1,000 works from his collection of early Chinese bronzes and jades, Chinese paintings and lacquerware, ancient Near-Eastern ceramics and metalware, and sculptures from South and Southeast Asia, all of which complement Freer's original gift.

Hirshhorn Museum and Sculpture Garden (Smithsonian)

Address: On the National Mall at Independence Avenue and 7th Street SW, Washington, D.C. 20560

Telephone: (202) 357-2700

Web: www.hirshhorn.si.edu

Hours: Daily 10–5:30. Closed Christmas Day. *Sculpture Garden*: 7:30 to dusk. Tours: *Museum*, Mon–Fri 10:30 and 12, Sat–Sun 12 and 2; *Sculpture Garden*, May–Oct, Mon–Sat 12:15.

Strengths: Modern and contemporary European and American sculpture and painting.

Other: Outdoor café, summer only. Museum shop.

Activities for Children: Especially good Family Guide.

Parking: Limited; metered, on street.

Sitting catercorner across the National Mall from the National Gallery of Art is a forbidding-looking concrete doughnut-shaped building resembling a giant flying saucer on stilts. The museum and its contents are the gift of Joseph Herman Hirshhorn. In 1905, when Herman was six, his mother, Amelia, immigrated to the U.S. with her thirteen children. The family was among the poorest of the poor. Amelia worked in a sweatshop; food was scarce and at times scavenged. Nevertheless, learning, intellectual pursuits, and art were highly prized. At fourteen, Hirshhorn was a twelve-dollar-a-week office boy, and at seventeen he was a stockbroker. He quit before the crash of 1929 and made a fortune as North America's "Uranium King." An inscription in the lobby of "his" museum records his gratitude:

It is an honor to have given my art collection to the people of the United States as a small repayment for what this nation has done for me and others who arrived here as immigrants. What I accomplished in the United States I could not have accomplished anywhere else in the world.

According to Aline B. Saarinen in *The Proud Possessors*, Hirshhorn was "a little man in a big hurry." He was decisive and bought lots of art, fast. Art dealers recall Hirshhorn buying half a dozen works by a single artist. Hirshhorn collected modern art and sculpture. The bulk of his collection dates from the twentieth century.

Today, works by Henry Moore, Emile Bourdelle, Auguste Rodin, Pablo Picasso, Alberto Giacometti, Marino Marini, David Smith, and others fill the large circular galleries of the Hirshhorn. The small scale of these sculptures is satisfying. There are playful sculptures by Elie Nadelman, gyrating mobiles by Alexander Calder, a terrifying *General Nuke* by Robert Arenson, stark sculptures by Barbara Hepworth, and the lifelike *Bus Riders* by George Segal.

Paintings by the top American artists of the twentieth century fill the smaller galleries radiating off the center. We note works by Indiana Jones, Edward Hopper, Walter Kuhn, Childe Hassam, Reginald Marsh, George Bellows, John Sloan, and others.

In the Hirshhorn's multilevel sculpture garden, with its reflecting pool, fifty or so large sculptures dating from 1880 to 1960 are displayed amid trees and plantings. Many of the works are familiar: Moore's

Draped Reclining Figure, a stabile by Calder, Marini's life-affirming horse and rider, Giacomo Manzú's sleek *Cardinal,* Francisco Zuniega's *Seated Yucatan Woman,* Joan Miró's zany *Lunar Bird,* and Auguste Rodin's *Balzac* and *Burghers of Calais.*

Unlike paintings, which are unique, sculptures can be cast and recast. So it is that our hearts can break repeatedly over Rodin's *Burghers of Calais,* the five men who, during Europe's Hundred Year War, would go to their death rather than hand over the keys of their city. The work, more than any other, symbolizes ordinary people's resistance to oppression.

National Museum of African Art (Smithsonian)

Address: On the National Mall at 950 Independence Avenue SW, Washington, D.C. 20560

Telephone: (202) 357-4600

Web: www.si.edu/nmafa

Hours: Daily 10–5:30. Tours Mon–Thurs at 1:30; Sat–Sun at 11 and 1. Closed Christmas Day.

Strength: Traditional arts of Africa south of the Sahara. Contemporary African art.

Other: Variety of programs facilitating the discovery of the many traditional arts and cultures of Africa. Library and photographic archives are open by appointment. A bazaar-like museum shop with merchandise from Africa.

Activities for Children: An excellent Family Guide; various programs (storytelling, hands-on activities) at irregular intervals.

Parking: Limited on street; pay garages.

During the first fifteen years of its existence the forerunner of the National Museum of African Art (NMAFA) was a private museum. It was founded in 1964 by Warren M. Robbins, a former cultural attaché of the U.S. Foreign Service. Like others, he had noted how much African tribal art had influenced modern art, especially the work of Pablo Picasso, Paul Klee, Amedeo Modigliani, and the German Expressionists. When Robbins returned to Washington, he opened the museum, using his small collection of African and modern art as a starter. Appropriately the museum was located in the former Capitol

Hill residence of Frederick Douglass, the nineteenth-century abolition-ist, editor, and government official. Robbins served as director until 1982.

In 1979 the museum became part of the Smithsonian Institution and in 1987 it moved to the National Mall. Like its neighbor, the Arthur M. Sackler Gallery, most of the exhibition space is underground. Six small Moorish-type domes top an entrance pavilion. The visitor only becomes aware of the nature of the museum when faced by two large, contemporary sculptures in the airy entrance, one of a warrior with a boat headdress.

Africa is a vast continent, comprising fifty-plus nations. Its art, cre-ated by hundreds of ethnically distinct groups or tribes is interwoven with daily life in ways quite different from most Western art. It expresses religious and cultural beliefs in masks, ceremonial figures, and practical objects for daily usage. Moreover, African art, most often made of wood, fibers, and ceramics, is highly perishable. In spite of these difficulties the NMAFA has been able to assemble a splendid array of sculpture, textiles, household objects, architectural elements, and decorative arts. The dark ebony wooden figures, masks, and animals, dating mostly from the nineteenth and twentieth centuries, are both glorious and terrifying. It is easy to pick out the relationship of these abstract figures and Cubism. Objects used in everyday life—wooden head rests, snuff spoons, textiles—fill entire galleries.

During the fifteenth and sixteenth centuries, art flourished in the western African kingdom of Benin. The museum has an excellent col-lection of these works crafted from ivory, wood, bronze, and brass, including the familiar naturalistic cast-copper heads of its rulers (obas). Here as elsewhere the continuity of African art is striking.

The earliest works in the museum date from 1750 to 1570 B.C.E. They were found in excavations of the royal tombs of Kerma—a neigh-bor of ancient Egypt. Indeed, before reading the labels, one would assume that the objects had originated in ancient Egypt. The collection is on permanent loan from the Museum of Fine Arts, Boston (p. 205), which displays the balance of this spectacular find.

On the ground level of the NMAFA is small fountain, surrounded by a bamboo-filled pool. Here, surrounded by panoramic photographs of contemporary Africa, visitors can relax and dream of faraway places.

Smithsonian American Art Museum (formerly the National Museum of American Art) and Renwick Gallery

Address: 8th and G Streets NW, Washington, D.C. 20560; *Renwick Gallery*: Pennsylvania Avenue at 17th Street NW, Washington, D.C. 20560

Telephone: (202) 357-2700; *Renwick Gallery*: (202) 357-2531

Web: www.AmericanArt.si.edu

Hours: Daily 10–5:30. Closed Christmas Day.

Strengths: 37,500 works in all media spanning more than 300 years of America's artistic achievement, in particular works from the Colonial and Federal periods, Hispanic colonial art, portraits of Native Americans, landscapes, American Impressionism, works from the PWA sponsored by the New Deal, a large collection of works by African American artists, and 20th-century realism and abstract art.

Other: Restaurant, appropriately called Patent Pending.

Activities for Children: Before the renovation the museum had an activity room and tours for different age groups.

Parking: Limited; metered on street or private garages.

Museum closed for renovation until 2003; Renwick Gallery remains open with increased activity.

The sixteen-foot-tall galloping fiberglass and epoxy cowboy (*Vaquero* by Luis Jiménez, 1980) looks out of place on the steps of the grand Old Patent Office Building, home of the Smithsonian American Art Museum (SAAM), formerly the National Museum of American Art. Beginning in 1820, a date that predates Smithson's bequest (see p. 133), artworks were given to what a group of public-minded citizens hoped would eventually be a national art gallery. According to the *History of the National Museum of American Art*, published by the Smithsonian, in 1829 John Varden, a Washingtonian, started to exhibit this small collection in his own house. In 1841 the art moved to the newly constructed Patent Office Building, coincidentally the present home of the museum, and Varden became curator of the "National Institute" for government-owned artistic and historic items. That institute was disbanded in 1846, when the works became the property of the newly founded Smithsonian Institution. The latter neglected the collection for decades, but it nevertheless grew. In 1906 the probated will of Harriet Lane Johnston, an art collector and niece of President James Buchanan, forced the Smithsonian to form what it called a "National Gallery of Art." Thereafter, by gift or purchase, the Smithsonian acquired rare collections, including 400 paintings of American Indians by George Catlin and 1,300 works by William H. Johnson, an African American primitive painter who spent much of his professional life in Europe. Today the collection includes choice examples of almost every American artist from the Colonial period until today, among them the portraits of *Sea Captain Murphy* and of his wife *Barbara Baker Murphy* by Joshua Johnson, *Matthias and Thomas Bordley* by Charles Willson Peale, the portrait of *Elizabeth Winthrop Chambers* by John Singer Sargent, *Cape Cod Morning* by Edward Hopper, *The Library* by Jacob Lawrence, and *Malibu* by David Hockney.

The historic Old Patent Office Building, whose cornerstone was laid in 1836, was designed to be "a temple to the industrial age." Completed in 1867, it is arguably the finest example of Greek Revival architecture in America today. It was slated to be demolished in 1958, to make way for a parking lot. Fortunately, the building was saved and given to the Smithsonian Institution, which used it to house its homeless collections as the National Museum of American Art and the separate National Portrait Gallery. The building served the two institutions well for forty years. In January 2000, however, the Smithsonian embarked on a major $60 million renovation. The renamed SAAM as well as the Portrait Gallery will be closed for two to three years. While the museum is closed, eight shows, entitled *Treasures to Go*, will visit seventy museums throughout America. The themes of these exhibits—Young America, Lure of the West, American Impressionism, The Gilded Age, Scenes of American Life, Modernism and Abstraction, Contemporary Folk Art, and Arte Latino—hint at the treasures of its collection. The SAAM's extensive web site provides an itinerary of the show and also displays more than 4,000 of the museum's works.

During the renovation the associated Renwick Gallery remains open with increased programming. The Renwick is housed in an impressive Second Empire style building that was the first home of the Corcoran Gallery of Art (p. 121), designed by James Renwick, Jr., the architect of

St. Patrick's Cathedral in New York City. One hundred and seventy paintings and sculptures belonging to SAAM's permanent collection now hang in the Renwick's Grand Salon—one of two period rooms. Pictures, including Thomas Moran's three monumental views of Yellowstone Park, are hung salon-style, one atop another and side by side. The Renwick Gallery also houses a permanent collection of craft, design, and decorative art.

Florida

MIAMI REGION

Bass Museum of Art

Address: 2221 Park Avenue, Miami Beach, FL 33139

Telephone: (305) 673-7530

Web: www.bassmuseum.org

Hours: Tues–Sat 10–5; Sun 1–5; second and fourth Wed 1–9. Closed Mon and major holidays.

Strengths: Overview of European paintings, sculptures, and textiles, including tapestries and ecclesiastic vestments. Modern design collection. Architectural photographs of Miami Beach.

Special Events: Special exhibits.

Activities for Children: Family days.

Other: Restaurant. Museum shop.

Parking: Metered, on street.

In 1963, John and Johanna Bass donated their 500 works of European art and an endowment to the city of Miami Beach provided the collection would be properly housed. The city offered—and remodeled—its by then outgrown Art Deco library.

John Bass, a highly musically and artistically talented man, was born in Vienna in 1891. After some detours, he followed his father's advice and made money in the sugar industry. Together with his wife he assembled an impressive art collection, most of which was given to Miami Beach. Two thirty-foot-long Flemish tapestries had to be hung in a special addition to the museum. Other favorite works in the collection include Sandro Botticelli and Domenico Ghirlandaio's *The Coronation of the Virgin*, Peter Paul Rubens's *Holy Family with St. Anne*, Hans Makart's *The Valkyrie*, Michiel von Musscher's *Self-Portrait*, and more modern works. The founding collection also included works on paper by Rembrandt, Albrecht Dürer, Honoré Daumier, and Henri de Toulouse-Lautrec, and decorative arts from the seventeenth to the nineteenth century.

Some experts considered the attributions of some of these works controversial; nevertheless, the core collection stimulated growth in other areas (Japanese, Chinese, Korean, Afro-Brazilian, and photography). Most remarkable perhaps is the modern design collection of 1,000 objects by Charles and Ray Eames, Richard Meier, Robert Stern, and other leading architects and designers of the twentieth century.

The original library building was located in Miami Beach's elegant Art Deco neighborhood. Urban decline set in during the last decades of the twentieth century and there where fewer visitors. Now, however, the neighborhood is experiencing a rebirth. A renovated and expanded Bass Museum—designed by the same Arata Isozaki responsible for the Museum of Contemporary Art, Los Angeles (p. 63)—opened its doors in May 2001. The museum is to be a centerpiece of Miami Beach's new cultural center. An expanded sculpture garden, with works that emphasize Florida's proximity to Cuba and Latin America, and a broad allée of trees leading down to the Atlantic Ocean, will increase the pleasure of a city long one of America's leading playgrounds.

Lowe Art Museum, University of Miami

Address: 1301 Stanford Drive, Coral Gables, FL 33124

Telephone: (305) 284-3535

Web: www.lowemuseum.org

Hours: Tues–Wed, Fri, Sat 10–5; Thurs 12–7; Sun 12–5. Closed Mon and New Year's, Thanksgiving, and Christmas days, and major holidays.

Strengths: Small encyclopedic museum. Kress collection of Italian Renaissance, Baroque, and Northern European paintings. Native American art.

Special Events: 6 temporary shows annually. Outdoor arts festival each Jan.

Activities for Children: Brochures and games that help children appreciate art.

Other: Museum shop.

Parking: Metered, on campus.

Even though it dates only from 1950, the Lowe Art Museum (the Lowe) is the Miami region's oldest. Thanks to devoted patrons, and a gift of forty-seven works from the Samuel H. Kress Foundation, its collection is now substantial (9,000-plus objects). To house it, the original museum, designed by Robert Little, has repeatedly been enlarged. Today, seven of its twelve galleries are devoted to the permanent collection.

The collections are arranged chronologically. The walls of the two galleries occupied by the Kress collection are burgundy red. The Byzantine Madonnas and saints painted so long ago on their golden backgrounds look familiar and at home. Other familiar European painters are represented—Jusepe de Ribera, Jacob Jordaens, Thomas Gainsborough, Claude Monet—as are some well-known American painters—James and Rembrandt Peale, Albert Bierstadt, George Inness.

The Native North American collection is particularly fine. Ceramic vessels of the late Mississippian period (1200–1700) from the southeastern United States are on view, as well as beadwork, rugs, finely woven baskets, and an animal skin covered with small drawings that serves as a war record.

The largest gallery is given over to more recent American painters such as Walter Kuhn, Louise Nevelson, Adolph Gottlieb, Deborah Butterfield, and others. The museum is justly proud of *Las Frutas* by Fernando Botero, the Colombian painter whose monumental style defies classification. Duane Hanson's sculptures *Security Officer* and *Football Player* look so real that one wonders why they don't move.

The Lowe is located on the Coral Gables campus of the University of Miami, for which it serves as a teaching resource. Its galleries surround a small Mexican-style courtyard. The plant-filled oasis is constructed from recycled bricks and tiles. As you listen to the softly flowing fountain and watch a lizard scurrying to safety along a bench, you forget about present-day urban Miami.

Museum of Contemporary Art

Address: 770 N.E. 125th Street, North Miami, FL 33161

Telephone: (305) 893-6211

Web: www.mocanomi.com

Hours: Tues–Sat 11–5; Sun 12–5. Closed Mon and major holidays. Tours Sat at 2.

Strength: Contemporary art.

Special Events: Last Fri: Free jazz concerts. Annual exhibition of highlights of the permanent collection. Lectures.

Others: Museum shop specializing in hard-to-find art books, and original work by local artists.

Activities for Children: First Sat two hands-on workshops: Start Together (ages 4–6) and Creative Arts (ages 7–12). Periodic workshops for adults and teens.

Parking: Free, adjacent to museum.

The Museum of Contemporary Art (MoCA) is a feisty, fun museum. In 1996, the fledgling museum acquired a new building designed by Charles Gwathmey, the architect who had the difficult task of enlarging New York's Guggenheim Museum. He described his Miami building as a "Cubist collage in [both] color and structure." Actually, the ocher building, dwarfed by enormous palms, one of which stands in a large reflecting pool, looks pleasantly surrealistic. Its interior navelike space, which can be subdivided by movable walls, is unusual because it can accommodate the enormous pieces characteristic of some contemporary art.

The museum's permanent collection, which includes works by John Baldessari, Dan Flavin, Dennis Oppenheim, Louise Nevelson, Edward Ruscha, Julian Schnabel, and others, is on view once a year. Recently, MoCA was awarded twenty-nine works from the collection of Peter and Eileen Norton. These well-known Los Angeles collectors distributed part of their contemporary arts collections because they wanted to strengthen awareness of experimental art throughout the U.S. The MoCA received a package entitled *Contemporary Sculpture,* which includes works by Jason Rhoades, Peter Shelton, and Ursula von Rydingsvard.

The MoCA prides itself on being "the museum where new art is discovered." Indeed, it offers eight to ten "provocative" and "innovative" shows a year, and promises to become an important institution in Florida.

ST. PETERSBURG

Museum of Fine Arts, St. Petersburg

Address: 255 Beach Drive, St. Petersburg, FL 33701

Telephone: (727) 896-2667

Web: www.fine-arts.org

Hours: Tues–Sat 10–5, Sun 1–5, 3rd Thurs each month (except summer) until 9. Closed Mon and New Year's, Independence, Thanksgiving, and Christmas days. Tours Tues–Sat 11, 2, and 3; Sun 1 and 2.

Strengths: Encyclopedic. European art of the 19th and 20th centuries. Ashcan School. Photography.

Special Events: Temporary exhibits. Tea in the garden on Tues (Feb–April). Luncheon concerts, lectures, and much more.

Other: Museum shop.

Activities for Children: Family days.

Parking: On site.

Centuries of discrimination and gender bias may have "done in" women painters, but women art collectors and museum builders have not been affected. St. Petersburg owes its charming museum to Margaret Acheson Stuart (1896–1980). Her dad, Edward Goodrich Acheson, invented and/or developed synthetic graphite, carborundum, and tungsten products that helped his associate and friend, Thomas Edison, develop incandescent lightbulbs. In 1928 the Acheson Corporation merged with Union Carbide and Acheson's children became wealthy. Margaret, the youngest of eight, studied interior decorating, bookbinding, and even, to overcome her shyness, acting. Her real love, however, was fine art and museums. To those who knew her it seemed inevitable that she would become a collector of art and perhaps establish a museum in St. Petersburg.

Originally called Point Pinellas, the town was named after St. Petersburg in Russia by a Russian political exile who arrived in 1881. It started to flourish four years later when a well-known physician proclaimed at a meeting of the American Medical Association that its climate was especially healthy.

The Art Club of St. Petersburg was established in 1919, and occupied a building on the site of the present museum. In 1961, Mrs. Stuart

Exterior, Museum of Fine Arts, St. Petersburg, Florida.

decided to establish a museum in the town where her family spent winters, and eventually summers too. She asked John L. Volk to design a Palladian-style one-story building with two curved, columned porticos flanking the entrance. Great pains were taken to arrange the museum like a residence.

The museum is an absolute gem. Mrs. Stuart was particularly interested in nineteenth- and twentieth-century art, and works from that period fill the largest gallery of the museum. We note Francis Picabia's *The Church at Montigny, Effect of Sunlight, 1908,* an early work of the future Dada painter; Paul Gauguin's *Goose Girl, Brittany,* rendered in the vivid tones more closely associated with his Tahitian works; Berthe Morisot's *Reading;* Eugene Fromentin's *Arabs Charging Through a Forest Path;* and Claude Monet's *Houses of Parliament.* Excellent works of lesser-known artists are also on display, including some by Henri Lebasque, Emile Othon Friesz, Jean Hélion, and Elisabeth Vigée-Lebrun.

American paintings are displayed in a "dining room" around a long table. There are works by Georgia O'Keeffe, John Sloan, Georg Luks, and Robert Henri. One is surprised to see *The Café Madrid,* the 1926 portrait of Mr. and Mrs. Chester Dale by Guy Pène du Bois. The Chrysler-Garbisches donated two stunning American folk art paintings and there are small collections of antiquities and Renaissance, Indian, and Native American art.

The manner in which some of the museum's possessions are displayed is striking. One small gallery is devoted to Pre-Columbian art. One or two statues are displayed by themselves in a highlighted niche. The display of a Steuben glass collection is equally dramatic. An exhibit entitled *The Elegant Table* highlights a selection of silver, glass, and China.

Tampa Bay can be glimpsed from two interior courts. Linger in the Moorish Court, with its Persian tiles, Portuguese vases, and huge tree, and listen to the fountain. *War* and *Peace,* two romantic sculptures by Antoine-Louis Barye, are in the other court.

Mrs. Stuart's museum is in good, loving hands. They slowly expand on the founder's vision by adding photographs and more contemporary art, while shying away from the rude and shocking.

Salvador Dali Museum

Address: 1000 Third Street South, St. Petersburg, FL 33701

Telephone: (727) 823-3767

Web: www.daliweb.com

Hours: Mon–Sat 9:30–5:30; Thurs 9:30–8; Sun 12–5:30. Closed Thanksgiving and Christmas days.

Strength: Extensive holding of Salvador Dali's oeuvre.

Special Events: Shows of related Surrealist painters.

Other: Extensive museum shop with reproductions of Dali's cane, watches, perfumes, and even food.

Activities for Children: The art itself.

Parking: On site.

Salvador Dali (1904–1989) was an artistic child prodigy, and the Salvador Dali Museum (SDM) lets us experience the full range of his talent, from a landscape he did when he was thirteen to the large canvases he painted fifty and sixty years later.

Success for Dali came early. He had his first one-man show in Madrid when he was twenty-one. In 1928, he achieved international fame when three of his paintings were exhibited at the third annual Carnegie International Exhibition in Pittsburgh. One of the three, *The Basket of Bread*, now at the SDM, is typical of the artist's super-realistic style. Dali moved to Paris in 1929, joined the Surrealist group, and met Gala, then the wife of the poet Paul Eluard.

The Surrealists based much of their work on dreams and the unconscious. Dali immersed himself in Freud, and his work certainly reflects the fantastic and irrational. His paintings, however, are deeply intellectual and studied. They also are autobiographical, most containing images or references to himself, his alter-ego Gala, his childhood memories, and the coast of his native Spain.

Viewing his work is both emotionally and intellectually rewarding, and the experience is amplified by listening to the extremely well informed docents of the museum. So we learn that many of Dali's works are based on those of other artists. We come across *Archeological Reminiscence of Millet's Angelus*, in which, according to Dali, the couple does not pray over a basket of vegetables but the coffin of a child. The museum is subdivided into chronological sections—the last of which contains five of the twenty paintings the cofounder of the museum, Reynolds Morse, called "masterworks." Each of these enormous canvases is an intellectual, allegorical, and technical tour de force which took a year to complete. In *The Discovery of America by Christopher Columbus*, Dali pays homage to Spain, America, and the Catholic Church. His beloved Gala, as St. Helen, is on a banner carried by Columbus and Dali himself is shown as a monk carrying a crucifix.

The seeds of the Salvador Dali Museum were sown in 1941 when Eleanor Reese, an art student, and Reynolds Morse, a plastics engineer, came upon a Dali exhibit. It was love at first sight. Two years later the young married couple bought *Daddy Longlegs of the Evening—Hope!*. The Morses also met the painter and his wife-muse, Gala, and established a life-long, though sometimes difficult, friendship.

It is rare to come upon a museum so closely based on the intimate relationship between artist and patron. The Morses closely followed Dali's career. As you visit the museum you will learn of Reynolds escorting Dali in America or discussing the genesis of particular paintings with the painter in his studio. In 1980 the Morses realized that their collection of 95 oils, over 100 watercolors, and nearly 1,300 graphics, sculptures, and objets d'art—then worth $350 million—would have to be dispersed upon their death. Their tax dilemma and search for a museum was reported in the *Wall Street Journal*, where it caught the eye of a St. Petersburg attorney who contacted the Morses. During a visit to the city Morse noticed an abandoned marine warehouse on the shores of Tampa bay. The bobbing white boats, the vegetation, and the Florida sun were reminiscent of Dali's beloved Mediterranean. The simple, beautifully "recycled" building suits Dali's work to perfection.

SARASOTA

John and Mable Ringling Museum of Art

Address: 5401 Bay Shore Road, Sarasota, FL 34243

Telephone: (941) 351-1660

Web: www.ringling.org

Hours: Daily 10–5:30. Closed New Year's, Thanksgiving, and Christmas days. Tours. Free admission to museum on Sat.

Strengths: Baroque art. Largest collection of works by Rubens in the U.S. Other European art of the 17th to 19th century. Period rooms.

Others: Rose, Dwarf, and Secret gardens. Circus museum. Cà d'Zahn, the Venetian-style winter residence of the Ringlings. Restaurant. Museum shop.

Special Events: Temporary exhibits. Annual medieval fair.

Activities for Children: Hands-on interactive gallery. Childrens Art Festival (a day-long event). Friends and Family days with activities related to special exhibitions.

Parking: On site.

It is not surprising that when John Ringling, creator of "The Greatest Show on Earth," became a collector during the 1920s, he fell in love with works of the flamboyant Baroque School of Art. He housed his possessions in a pink Venetian palace, and used the same style to build a mansion for himself and his wife, Mabel. Fronting on Sarasota Bay it recalls the palace of the Doges in Venice.

Within a short time the Ringlings amassed a huge collection of art, most famous for having the largest number of works by Peter Paul

The John and Mable Ringling Museum of Art in Sarasota is justly renowned for its impressive collection of works by Peter Paul Rubens. Here is a glimpse of the Rubens Gallery.

Rubens in any collection in America. Many of the other paintings are by less-well-known, mostly Italian, painters. The works are displayed in twenty-one galleries arranged along two axes framing an enormous interior courtyard. The galleries are top-lit and, in addition to paintings, contain some decorative art. The museum developed what it calls "long labels," and a diligent visitor can became extremely well informed about the purpose, trend, style, and interrelationship of the works exhibited. So we learn that during Rubens's life Western Europe was torn by wars between the Catholic Church and the Protestants and paintings were used to promote faith.

Given their style, the Baroque painters, and Rubens in particular, clad their subjects in sumptuous silks and satins, embellished by jewels and precious objects. Except for their naked feet, it is hard to imagine that the men and women in Rubens's *The Departure of Lot and His Family From Sodom* are fleeing for their lives. That, however, does not detract from the mastery of the painting, the movement of the cloth, and the expression of the faces. Living in Catholic Flanders, Rubens received many commissions from the church. The Ringling owns four of eleven full-scale cartoons for the tapestry series *The Triumph of the Eucharist*, which was woven in Brussels during the seventeenth century. The only painting cycle by this artist outside Europe, the cycle includes scenes from the Old and New Testaments. Notable is *The Triumph of Divine Love,* in which a Madonna-like figure of Charity stands in an ornate chariot drawn by two spirited lions; delicately molded putti surround the smiling main figure and the landscaped background is breathtaking. This being Ringling's legacy, it is amusing that the jewel-encrusted chariot of the painting could easily have been part of his circus.

Leaving the Rubens galleries one enters a room displaying intimate German art of the fifteenth century. The gallery is filled with small gilded statues of angels, various icons, and Lucas Cranach the Elder's portrait of *Cardinal Albrecht as Saint Jerome.* This painting, like the Rubens tapestry, is filled with domesticated animals, including a cheerful lion. The Ringling owns other masterpieces, among them Paolo Veronese's *Rest on the Flight to Egypt,* Frans Hals's *Pieter Olycan,* Jan Steen's *The Rape of the Sabine Women,* two grand English portraits by Thomas Gainsborough and Reynolds, and a selection of Cypriot antiquities from the Cesnola Collection sold by New York's Metropolitan Museum. The courtyard is filled with bronze replicas of ancient Greek, Roman, and Baroque sculptures. An immense copy of Michelangelo's David surrounded by palm trees guards an elaborate fountain.

The museum opened in 1930, six years before Ringling's death. Ringling had left all his possessions to the State of Florida, but his will was contested and the museum closed, to reopen ten years later. The first director hired by the state was none other than A. Everett Austin, the flamboyant long-time director of the Wadsworth Atheneum in Hartford, Connecticut (see p. 108). Austin was not only an expert in Baroque art, but also an amateur showman. Austin added wisely to the collection. He also turned the Ringling mansion into a "historic house," created the neighboring Circus Museum, and bought the internal structure of an eighteenth-century Italian theater which the city transformed into an active playhouse. Since a visit to these are included in the ticket price, visitors will have a good idea of what life in Sarasota was like during the 1930s, when it was the winter quarters of the circus and hosted some of America's rich and famous. A new wing for the exhibition of modern art was added in 1966.

TAMPA

Tampa Museum of Art

Address: 600 N. Ashley Drive, Tampa, FL 33602

Telephone: (813) 274-8130

Web: www.tampamuseum.com

Hours: Tues–Sat 10–5; Thurs 10–8; Sun 1–5. Closed Mon and major holidays.

Strengths: Greek and Roman antiquities. Sculptures by C. Paul Jennewein. Contemporary art. Art glass.

Special Events: Temporary exhibits. Third Thurs: "After-dark" (5–8) events.

Other: Museum shop.

Activities for Children: Child-oriented museum with Family Fun days. Workshop from 10–12 on Sat for children 3–8; older children (9–13) sketch in galleries.

Parking: Underground pay garage.

Contemporary and sleek, the Tampa Museum of Art (TMA) contrasts starkly with the Dali's marine storage facilities (p. 148) and the Fine Arts Palladian-style building (p. 146) in nearby St. Petersburg. Tampa's low-slung building fronts on a large reflecting pool embellished by two very disparate sculptures: *Strands of Mirror,* a contemporary work by Beverly Pepper, and *Triton,* by C. Paul Jennewein. Surrounded by Tampa's towering office buildings, the white limestone museum looks small and elegant. It was founded in 1979 and extensively renovated in 1986.

In view of its modern shell, it is surprising that one of the museum's cornerstones is the superb collection of antiquities assembled by Joseph Veach Noble. Greek vases—black on red and red on black—marble sculptures, personal ornaments in bronze and gold, coins, and ancient glass vessels are beautifully displayed in accessible Plexiglass cases.

Another cornerstone of the museum is its sculpture collection. Jennewein (1890–1978), a major American academic sculptor, left the TMA his estate of 2,150 works. Some examples of his elegant academic works, including a one-third scale painted plaster maquette of the pediment for the Philadelphia Museum of Art from 1926–1933, are on display. The museum also owns works by other major sculptors, including Hiram Powers, Charlotte Dunwiddie, and Jacques Lipchitz.

Some of these works are displayed in the large glassed-in Terrace Gallery, which fronts the Hillsborough River. From there, visitors have an unobstructed view of the 1891 Tampa Bay Hotel, built in the Moorish Revival style. The view of the building's three domes and thirteen minarets crowned by gilded crescents—representing the thirteen months of the Islamic calendar—is breathtaking. The building, surrounded by tropical vegetation and unfortunately partly obscured by newer indifferent structures, is now part of the University of Tampa. Examples of the museum's extraordinary art glass collection, such as Toots Zynsky's *Dark Street,* are on view in the Terrace Gallery.

The museum's main focus is to further enlarge its holdings of contemporary artists such as Chuck Connelly, Jim Dine, Judith Glantzman, Robert Mapplethorpe, Robert Motherwell, James Rosenquist, Frank Stella, and many others. The museum has a large collection of works on paper and photographs.

WEST PALM BEACH

Norton Museum of Art

Address: 1451 S. Olive Street, West Palm Beach, FL 33401

Telephone: (561) 832-5196

Web: www.norton.org

Hours: Tues–Sat 10–5, Sun 1–5. Closed Mon (May–Oct) and New Year's, Independence, Thanksgiving, and Christmas days. Tours daily at 2. Also lunchtime lecture at 1:30.

Strengths: European, American, contemporary, and Chinese art.

Special Events: Interesting temporary exhibits.

Other: Indoor/outdoor restaurant. Museum shop.

Activities for Children: Special tours on selected Sun. Special web site: www.kids.norton.org

Parking: On site.

Like most Florida museums the Norton is small. It was the creation of two people: Ralph H. Norton, the head of the Acme Steel Company, and his wife, Elizabeth C. Norton. The Nortons had assembled a sizable collection of art "back home" in Chicago. They were not passionately devoted to any one painter or school, but according to Mr. Norton himself their tastes "were reasonably Catholic. . . . Our aim was to

The Red Foulard by Pablo Picasso, a gift of R. H. Norton, at the Norton Museum of Art in West Palm Beach, Florida.

select pictures which gave us aesthetic satisfaction." The modesty of this statement belies the Nortons' excellent taste and their ability to select defining works of the artists they liked.

When the Nortons retired to West Palm Beach in 1939 they decided to share their possessions with the public and built a charming museum whose style is described as "stark, late Art Deco/Neo Classic." It served well and underwent a massive refurbishing and expansion in 1997. Its buff exterior, terrazzoed floors, and interior court fit the semitropical vegetation of Florida. Elizabeth Norton died in 1947 and her husband in 1953. A devoted, knowledgeable staff and patrons continue their efforts.

The permanent collection is divided into four areas of interest—European, American, Contemporary, and Chinese—each filled with notable examples. It is refreshing that the time span covered by the artworks is circumscribed. There are no Hudson River landscapes or early American portraits. The European collection concentrates on art created between 1870 and 1945, and there are examples of all major art movements of that time: Impressionism, Post-Impressionism, Neo-Impressionism, Symbolism, Fauvism, Cubism, Dadaism, and Surrealism. Here are stunning works by Claude Monet, Paul Cézanne, Fernand Léger, Robert Delauney, Edgar Degas, Henri Matisse, Pablo Picasso, and Chaim Soutine, to name only a few. The American collection includes works by Winslow Homer, John Marin, George Bellows, Marsden Hartley, and Georgia O'Keeffe. The Contemporary collection includes work by Robert Motherwell, Sam Francis, Jacob Lawrence, and Deborah Butterfield.

The Chinese collection ranges from 1500 to 500 B.C.E. The museum owns a distinguished group of ancient jades, which are displayed a few at a time to highlight specific pieces. There are also outstanding examples of Buddhist sculpture.

The works are beautifully displayed. The entrance hall, with its soaring roof and intricately inlaid floor, and the palm-filled interior courts are appropriate for a state that treasures a relaxed lifestyle.

WINTER PARK

Charles Hosmer Morse Museum of Art

Address: 445 Park Avenue North, Winter Park, FL 32789

Telephone: (407) 645-5311

Web: www.morsemuseum.org

Hours: Tues–Sat 9:30–4, Sun 1–4. Sept–May: Fri 9:30–8. Closed Mon and major holidays. Tours available during public hours.

Strengths: Comprehensive Tiffany collection. Arts and Crafts. Rookwood Pottery. American paintings from the 1850s to 1914.

Other: Museum shop.

Parking: On site.

Passion for their chosen subject is a must for collectors. We are fortunate that the McKeans fell in love with Tiffany. It was also lucky that both McKeans were artists, that Jeannette had inherited a fortune from her industrialist grandfather, Charles Hosmer Morse, and that as a student Hugh had spent two months at Laurelton Hall, Tiffany's summer home. Hugh never forgot the glory of that place. He recalled his arrival there in 1930 in his book *"Lost" Treasures of Louis Comfort Tiffany:* "The evening was spiced with the fragrance of petunias. The pools,

The Magnolia Window, now in the Charles Hosmer Morse Museum in Winter Park, Florida, once adorned Louis Comfort Tiffany's own residence at Seventy-second Street and Madison Avenue in New York City.

fountains, terraces, and gardens were unlike anything I had ever seen." You can imagine the McKeans' shock when they arrived to view Laurelton in 1957, after it had been ruined by fire. ". . . charred timbers and twisted pipes made bizarre patterns against the sky," McKean wrote, "the lawn was strewn with the lovely gray furniture from the dining room," and one of the sections of the *Four Seasons* window leaned against a tree. The McKeans also found the remains of the chapel designed for the World Columbian Exposition in Chicago in 1893, windows, and the immense columns of the loggia, their capitals still "blooming" with wine red poppies and glass daffodils. Before the couple left they had bought "everything the fires had spared."

After a meteoric career Tiffany had become a forgotten man. His flamboyant Art Nouveau style was at odds with a harsh world and the sleek, no-nonsense modernist furniture. So in 1942, when Jeanette McKean organized a small museum at Rollins College in Winter Park and exhibited works by Tiffany, it made news. In 1955, she curated a more extensive Tiffany exhibit, the first since the turn of the century. It sparked a Tiffany revival.

At first the McKeans did not know what to do with their Laurelton Hall goods. They donated some important pieces to the American wing of the Metropolitan Museum in New York. Eventually, however, the couple created a larger museum in Winter Park, which now owns the most comprehensive Tiffany collection in the world. It evokes the artist in all his glory. Tiffany had kept or reacquired many of his finest works. There are the *Butterfly* and *Magnolia* windows from the Tiffany Mansion on Seventy-second Street in Manhattan, the first in hues of yellow and brown, the second using the artist's white "drapery glass." There are the four panels of the *Four Seasons*. There are columns from Laurelton Hall, lamps, vases, paintings, and even the gray furniture from the dining room. And then there is the chapel, reconstructed in all its overornate glory. Multilayered Roman arches and mosaic-encrusted columns frame the peacocks depicted in the reredos. The baptismal font, which has been compared to a giant Fabergé egg, stands in a side chapel against a lily window.

In addition to Tiffany the museum also displays important American paintings mostly from the 1850s to World War One, and works of the Arts and Crafts Movement. Most impressive is the large selection of Rookwood Pottery, an enterprise founded in 1880, almost accidentally, by Maria Longworth Nichols Storer of Cincinatti, Ohio (also see Cincinatti Art Museum, p. 322). There is also furniture by Stickley, naive paintings, and—touchingly, perhaps—gowns worn by three generations of Morses: the wedding gown worn by Martha Owens (Morse) in 1868, a reception gown worn by her daughter Martha around 1896, and the wedding dress worn by granddaughter Jeannette Genius (McKean) in 1945.

Georgia

ATLANTA

High Museum of Art

Address: 1280 Peachtree Street NE, Atlanta, GA 30309

Telephone: (404) 733-4400

Web: www.high.org

Hours: Tues–Sat 10–5; Sun 12–5; Closed Mon and holidays. Tours Sun at 1 and 2.

Strengths: Encyclopedic. European paintings and sculptures from the 14th through the 19th century including a Kress collection, German Expressionists, American landscape painting, and a growing body of contemporary works. Decorative arts, including outstanding 19th- and 20th-century American furniture. Dramatic African masks and ceremonial figures and extensive sub-Saharan art. Folk art. Photography.

Special Events: Temporary shows. Lectures, Wed noon luncheon program.

Other: Satellite gallery in the business and convention district exhibits folk art and photography. Restaurant. Museum shop.

Activities for Children: Visual arts learning space with interactive, hands-on activities. Also special audio tours for younger audiences. Toddler's Day (ages 1–4) every Thurs: At this popular event small children can participate in a variety of arts-related experiences. Sat workshops at 10 (reservations required). Sun studio workshop 1–3 (ages 6–12).

Parking: Limited paid parking in Arts Center garage.

In 1926, Hattie High donated her house to a twenty-year-old organization whose mission was to promote "interest in the applied and fine arts [in Atlanta], to give lectures and practical instruction, and to found a museum." Since these early days, the High Museum of Art (the High) has become one of the leading small encyclopedic museums of the South.

The museum remained in Mrs. High's Tudor home until 1955, when it was replaced by a larger air-conditioned structure. This building, too, was outgrown and in 1979 the time seemed right to replace the old museum. Coca-Cola magnate Robert W. Woodruff jump-started the project with a $7.5 million challenge grant. From the many architects competing for the commission, the museum selected Richard Meier, partially because he was the only candidate who did not overwhelm the committee with a team, but explained his plans unassisted. Shortly thereafter, Meier enlarged the Des Moines Art Center (p. 174) and twenty years later Meier would obtain an even larger museum commission, that of building The Getty Center in Los Angeles (p. 58). There are many architectural similarities between the three institutions.

The new museum, like the old, shares its site with Atlanta's Memorial Arts Building, built in 1968 to commemorate the 114 Georgians who had perished during a museum-sponsored European art tour. Atlanta's large First Presbyterian Church is another neighbor. Meier oriented the new museum so that the three buildings form a harmonious urban space.

The museum's skylit entrance is a clear reference to Frank Lloyd Wright's Guggenheim. As in New York, a ramp climbs up inside the atrium, but it is not an exhibition space. Visual excitement, however, is provided both by views of Atlanta through the outer glass wall, and glimpses into the central atrium. Throughout the building Meier refers to the architecture of Le Corbusier, his mentor. Specific allusions are the pipe rails and nautical forms that are also prominent at the Getty Center. In celebration of its tenth anniversary the museum installed Sol LeWitt's *Irregular Bands of Color*, a sixty-four-foot-high mural from 1993. The angular star-shaped work magnifies the drama of the large atrium.

A well-designed museum should not overwhelm the art. The High's excellent collection lives happily in spatially varied galleries that radiate out from the atrium. The High's Kress collection includes a number of particularly fine examples. *Saint Catherine of Alexandria,* painted in Sienna during the fourteenth century, is somberly silhouetted against a gold background. Giovanni Bellini's serene *Madonna and Child* is shown against a hilly Italian landscape. The forceful, serious face of *Duke Henry the Devout of Saxony* by Lucas Cranach the Elder is awe-inspiring, especially when contrasted with the almost frivolous paintings by later French and Italian masters. The High's Hudson River landscapes are peaceful. Though it currently concentrates on the acquisition of post-1970s American art, the High owns two Surrealist masterpieces: Max Ernst's *Tree of Life* (1928), a dreamlike image of an underwater world, and Arshile Gorky's Miró-like image *Garden in Sochi* (1940–1941), which the artist based on his childhood memories from Armenia. The museum also owns a great and comprehensive collection of American decorative art ranging from Colonial days to the present.

The High displays some of its art in a thematic rather than chronological fashion. "Life in Art," for example, pairs a traditional eighteenth-century portrait of a wealthy Georgia family with a decorated stoneware cooler (ca. 1840) depicting a slave wedding. In "Abstractions," Claude Monet's *Houses of Parliament* (1905) is paired with John Henry Twachtman's *Along the River* (1889) and Ellsworth Kelly's *White Panel, II* (1985). This experimental approach, which forces viewers to see art in a novel way, has proved so popular that it is now permanent.

SAVANNAH

Telfair Museum of Art

Address: 121 Barnard Street on Telfair Square, Savannah, GA 31401

Telephone: (912) 232-1177

Web: www.Telfair.org

Hours: Mon 12–5, Tues–Sat 10–5, Sun 1–5. Closed major holidays. Tours daily at 2.

Strengths: Decorative arts. American paintings of the 19th and 20th centuries.

Special Events: Juried art fair in fall. Theme-related concerts.

Other: Owens Thomas House (124 Abercorn Street on Oglethorpe Square, Savan-nah, GA 31401. Hours Mon 2–5, Tues–Sat 10–5, Sun 10–5): A fine, rare example of English Regency architecture in America, built by English architect William Jay in 1816–1819. An outstanding collection of decorative arts, mostly dating from 1790–1830, is on display. The attached carriage house, now an educational center, housed the slave quarters.

Activities for Children: 4 Family Sundays a year with hands-on activities, special tours, artist demonstrations, and music.

Parking: On street.

In 1818, Alexander Telfair commissioned a grand Regency-style mansion from William Jay, an English architect. The elegant white building still looks as it did then, with its entrance door shielded by a large rectangular porch and four Corinthian columns surmounted by a large semicircular window. In 1875, Miss Mary Telfair, one of his sisters and the last of the Telfair line, bequeathed the house, its furnishings, and an endowment to the Georgia Historical Society. She specified that the mansion had to be used as a museum. It took a while for the plan to become a reality because relatives contested Miss Telfair's will. Eventually the U.S. Supreme Court upheld the original bequest.

The first director of the museum was Carl Brandt, a German portrait painter who was partial to casts and German salon art. Brandt remodeled the mansion into a museum, adding the Sculpture Gallery and Rotunda, which now house the permanent collection. The four murals

Brandt painted at the time, honoring sculpture, architecture, painting, and graphic arts, are still in place. He also painted a posthumous portrait of a black-clad Miss Telfair, enthroned on a red velour armchair looking as if she was watching over her possessions. Brandt fortunately preserved much of the mansion's unique architecture. Today the octagonal parlor, with its trompe l'oeil oak paneling, and the dining room are filled with exquisite period furniture.

Many of the casts assembled by Brandt have disappeared. A reminder of these early days is a reproduction of the frieze of the Parthenon which still resides in the upper portion of the entrance hall, and one of *Laocoon and His Sons* struggling with giant serpents.

The Telfair, billed as the oldest art museum in the Southeast, opened in 1886, with Jefferson Davis, former President of the Confederacy, and other luminaries attending the ceremonies. Carl Brandt died in 1905. Eventually the directorship was taken over by Gari Melcher, a native of Detroit who had relocated to Savannah, his wife's hometown. Melcher was a successful painter and friend of many American artists, particularly the Impressionists and Ashcanners. From them, Melcher acquired a delightful collection of American paintings, including Robert Henri's *La Madrileñita*, a fancily dressed Spanish woman; *Snow Capped River*, a winter landscape by George Bellows; *Savannah Nocturne Ships in Harbor*, by Eliot Clark; and works by Edward W. Redfield, Childe Hassam, Frederick Frieseke, and other well-known and lesser-known artists.

There is a modest collection of European paintings. The museum is particularly proud of Julian Story's huge picture entitled *Black Prince of Crécy*, which depicts a fourteenth-century battle scene.

Sylvia Shaw Judson's sleek sculpture of the *Bird Girl* welcomes visitors in the Drawing Room Gallery. It attained world fame when a photograph of it by Jack Leigh was used on the cover of John Berendt's *Midnight in the Garden of Good and Evil*. This best-selling book rekindled interest in Savannah, a lovely southern city whose historic district—the largest in the entire U.S.—has escaped the ravages of modernization.

The Telfair's collections of works on paper, sculpture, and photographs are fine and growing. The latter includes works by Jack Leigh, a native of Savannah, whose images, in his own words, "capture not only the beauty of the place and her people but also the emotional grip the South has on those who call her home." It is, however, the decorative arts collection—in the main museum and in the nearby Owens Thomas House—that is most appropriate to these spectacular antebellum houses.

The Telfair has outgrown its quarters and an additional museum building is in the process of being built within walking distance. The new structure, designed by Moshe Safdie—the architect of the National Gallery of Canada—will include galleries, a library, a sculpture garden, and an auditorium, permitting the museum to display more of its permanent collection and host bigger traveling and temporary exhibitions.

Illinois

CHICAGO

The Art Institute of Chicago

Address: 111 S. Michigan Avenue, Chicago, IL 60603

Telephone: (312) 443-3600

Web: www.artic.edu

Hours: Mon, Wed–Thurs, Fri 10:30–4:30; Tues 10:30–8; Sat, Sun 10–5. Closed Thanksgiving and Christmas days.

Strengths: A well-rounded, encyclopedic museum renowned for its French Impressionists and Old Masters. Also glass paper weights, Chagall windows, Thorne miniature rooms, Sullivan's Chicago Stock Exchange.

Special Events: "Blockbuster" exhibits, as well as well-designed smaller shows.

Other: Once or twice a day, museum curators give general tours and specialized 1-hour lectures as well as shorter "Object Lessons" concerning a single work of art. Upscale dining room with waiter service; nice cafeteria. Museum shop.

Activities for Children: On weekends, a variety of free programs (gallery talks for specific age groups, workshops, performances) that introduce children and families to the museum and its collections. For more details call (312) 857-7161 or check the web site.

Parking: Pay lots.

Chicago proudly hosted the World's Columbian Exposition of 1893, which celebrated the 400th anniversary of Columbus's discovery of America. It was an important event for the United States. The country had recently emerged from the Civil War and was establishing a leadership role among the globe's industrialized nations. The then twenty-five-year-old Art Institute of Chicago (AIC) convinced Chicago's Park District Board to help it build suitable quarters. A neoclassic fine arts palace was erected on Michigan Avenue. It has been the AIC's home ever since, though it has undergone many expansions. The director of the fine arts component of the fair was Halsey Ives, who put his Chicago experience to good use when he did the same thing for his beloved Saint Louis Art Museum in Missouri (see p. 244).

A sense of history and surprise grips visitors as they pass through the arched entryway and ascend the grand stairs. One would expect such an old space to be dark. In 1980, however, during one of the museum's numerous expansions and rebuildings, the old roof was replaced by glass, thereby providing the "dowager" with an up-to-date ambiance. Architectural fragments from Chicago's past surround the skylight. They include an elevator grill by Louis Sullivan, a stained glass window by Frank Lloyd Wright, and many anonymous works.

Another leading figure organizing the Columbian Exposition was Bertha Potter Palmer, an art collector. Mrs. Palmer mostly acquired "safe" French pictures of the Barbizon School. Like New York's Louisine Havemeyer, she was, however, a friend of Mary Cassatt, the expatriate American Impressionist, who convinced her to buy Impressionist paintings by Auguste Renoir, Claude Monet, Edgar Degas, Edouard Manet, and others. These purchases were eventually bequeathed to the AIC, contributing to its unequaled holdings of Impressionist paintings in America. Among numerous other masterpieces the AIC owns are four of Monet's Grain Stacks, Georges Seurat's *A Sunday on La Grande Jatte—1884*, Gustave Caillebotte's *Paris on a Rainy Day*, and Renoir's *Two Little Circus Girls*.

From its beginning, prominent benefactors showered the AIC with gifts. Charles L. Hutchinson, the institute's first director, and Martin Ryerson, the museum's most generous donor, helped it to become one of the world's great museums. Both men had wide-ranging tastes and built superior collections of American and European art. Among their many important European purchases was the Demidoff Collection of Old Masters that included Rembrandt's *Girl at the Dutch Door* and Meindert Hobbema's *Watermill.* The two friends also acquired El Greco's magnificent *Assumption,* refused by Louisine Havemeyer because, according to Nathaniel Burt in *Palaces for the People,* it was too big to hang in her house. After their deaths the staff of the AIC and devoted patrons continued their work. The museum's Post-Impressionist, Modern, and Contemporary collections are strong. Specially beloved pictures include Grant Wood's *American Gothic,* René Magritte's *The Banquet,* early and late Picassos, examples of the Blue Rider School, and much more, all exhibited in spacious galleries interspersed with sculptures by modern masters.

The museum has top-notch Indian, Southeast Asian, Chinese, Ancient Egyptian, Greek, Etruscan, Roman, Japanese, Korean, African, and Ancient American collections. Also included are American and European decorative arts, arms and armor, and even a collection of old firearms. There is also a delightful paperweight collection; beautifully displayed clear globes of glass enclose small worlds filled with abstractions, flowers, fruits, and even snakes.

An amble around the AIC reveals many special treasures. Six immense stained glass windows were commissioned from Marc Chagall to commemorate Chicago's Mayor Richard J. Daley. The windows, executed in shades of blue highlighted with yellow and orange, celebrate music, art, literature, liberty, theater, and dance. Made between 1974 and 1977, they are Chagall's last major work. The windows are alive with the magical imagery the artist used throughout his long life.

Near these windows you will find Louis Sullivan's transplanted trading floor from the old Chicago Stock Exchange, a prime example of the architect's carefully crafted style. The wooden floor and paneling are gleaming as are the brass rails, stained glass ceiling, and small lamps. Its big slate blackboard, with spaces for quotations from the New York Stock Exchange, is a reminder of the pre-computer age. There are no period rooms, but the sixty-eight famous Thorne Miniature Rooms (also see the Phoenix Art Museum, p. 48) illustrate the development of architecture and decorative styles.

Chicago Museum of Contemporary Art

Address: 220 E. Chicago Avenue, Chicago, IL 60611

Telephone: (312) 280-2660

Web: www.mcachicago.org

Hours: Wed–Sun 10–5; Tues 10–8. Closed Mon and New Year's, Thanksgiving, and Christmas days.

Strength: Contemporary art of the second half of 20th century.

Special Events: First Fri evenings: Live music, experimental films, other performances. Also a summer solstice celebration; concerts, lectures. Temporary (sometimes controversial) exhibitions by contemporary artists.

Other: Tours by well-informed volunteers. Art TalkBack invites visitors to express their opinion about exhibitions and video presentations. Unusually good Asian-inspired food is served in a large lake-front café covered by a canopy-like artwork entitled *An Infinite Expanse of Sky*, by Jacob Hashimoto. A large "culturecounter" store sells artist-designed jewelry, clocks, mobiles, ties, unusual home gifts, books, magazines, and videos.

Activities for Children: Children are invited to climb on the artworks in the sculpture garden, or to use a small playhouse.

Parking: Paid, in museum garage and public lots.

Art has always been important to Chicago. So it was that in 1967 a handful of its citizens opened a Kunsthalle—German for "a hall for Art"—in a building that had first served as a bakery and later was the headquarters for Playboy Enterprises. The initial, ground-breaking exhibits of the future Museum of Contemporary Art (MCA) featured Dada artists, art of the Russian avant-garde, and photographs by Robert Mapplethorpe. In 1968 the museum had itself wrapped by Christo, an exponent of "art of the moment." The MCA continues to feature up-and-coming artists. Unlike many other contemporary art museums, MCA opted to build a permanent collection. Today it owns work by Franz Kline, René Magritte, Bruce Nauman, Claes Oldenburg, Robert Rauschenberg, Andy Warhol, and many others.

During the 1990s the MCA outgrew its space in the old bakery and the renowned Berlin-based architect Josef Paul Kleihues erected a new, sleek glass-and-metal building. Wide, grand stairs ascend from a plaza to the first floor. The museum and the skyscrapers of modern Chicago contrast with the city's medieval-looking landmark Water Tower that sits across the street. Exciting views are glimpsed from the MCA's five floors and terraces. Indeed, the juxtaposition of the old brick-clad buildings of Northwestern University, Lake Michigan, traffic flowing on Lake Shore Drive, and the immense John Hancock tower, complements the contemporary art displayed within the museum.

The permanent collection of the MCA is displayed on the fourth and fifth floors. Visitors may ascend via an elliptical staircase that rises from a small pebble- and goldfish-filled pool to a skylight. The beautifully crafted black and white stairs are an obvious reference to Frank Lloyd Wright's Guggenheim Museum in New York (p. 281). The contrast between square and elliptical shapes is stressed throughout the building.

Selections on display from the permanent collection change every six to eight months and may include a group of early Alexander Calder mobiles and stabiles, sculptures by Marisol, collages by Robert Rauscheberg, paintings by Anselm Kiefer, and other now-classic examples of contemporary art. Some of the works have an obvious emotional impact, while others are more difficult. "Contemporary art relies on the participation of the viewer," a guide explains as his flock contemplates the emotion-laden work of Willie Cole, an African American artist who based some of his work on the irons his grandmother, a laundress, used to make a living.

The Terra Museum of American Art

Address: 664 N. Michigan Ave, Chicago, IL 60611

Telephone: (312) 664-3939

Web: www.terramuseum.org

Hours: Wed–Sat 10–6; Tues 10–8; Sun 12–5. Closed Mon. Daily half-hour tours at 12; Sat–Sun also at 2.

Strengths: American art up to the 1950s, American Impressionism, Prendergast.

Special Events: Last Fri 5–7: Live folk music, appetizers, open bar.

Other: Small, choice loan shows featuring special aspects of American art. Museum shop.

Activities for Children: Family Guides explaining current exhibitions. Family Fair one Sun a month for parents and children (5–12). The Terra is ideal to visit with children. "The museum is straight up and down," a staff member explained; "they cannot get lost. And then it is small and its art is representational."

Parking: Public lots.

Daniel J. Terra, who revolutionized the printing ink business, founded the Terra Museum of American Art in 1980. A U.S. Ambassador-at-large for Cultural Affairs, Terra started collecting American art during the 1950s, when it still was affordable. His collection of 700 important American works is all-inclusive, ranging from Ammi Phillips's cheerful *Girl in a Red Dress* to works of the mid-twentieth-century. There are eighteenth-century portraits, nineteenth-century landscapes and sea-scapes, genre paintings, and still lifes including works by Thomas Cole, Frederick Church, George Caleb Bingham, James Whistler, John Singer Sargent, and Thomas Eakins. Twentieth-century artists—Edward Hooper, Georgia O'Keeffe, Marsden Hartley, Stuart Davis, Reginald Marsh, Rockwell Kent, and Milton Avery—are also represented. Major emphasis, however, is on paintings of the Hudson River School and American Impressionism. The Terra owns sixty-nine works by Maurice and Charles Prendergast. Only the Williams College Museum of Art, in Williamstown, Massachusetts (p. 226)—recipient of their estate—owns more.

The Terra occupies two five-story former office buildings on North Michigan Avenue, dubbed "the Magnificent Mile." As you move from floor to floor within the museum, you can observe Chicagoans partaking in our nation's favorite pastime: upscale shopping.

The inside of the Terra is free-flowing and luxurious. The floors are carpeted; gently sloping ramps connect intricately stacked floors. Spaces are always intimate. Like that other Midwesterner, Henry Clay Frick (see The Frick Collection, p. 278), Daniel Terra surrounded himself with pleasant, mostly normal-scale art.

The Terra's best-known work is *The Gallery of the Louvre* by Samuel F.B. Morse. The painting dates from 1831–1833 and depicts miniatures of about fifteen well-known masterpieces from the Louvre. The work, which Morse hoped would teach Americans about "great" art, was sent on tour; viewers were to pay a 25-cent admission fee. The enterprise was a flop and Morse went on to invent the code that bears his name. His great painting languished in storage for one hundred years. Then, when Terra wanted to buy it at auction, he had to compete with the National Gallery and ended up by paying $1.3 million, a tidy sum during the 1950s. Before hanging it, Terra sent it on a successful tour, fulfilling its creator's ambition.

Because of his great interest in American Impressionism, Daniel J. Terra also founded the Musée d'Art Americain in Giverny, France, which commemorates the American art colony established in Monet's hometown when Impressionism was at its height.

Indiana

INDIANAPOLIS

Indianapolis Museum of Art

Address: 1200 W. 38th Street, Indianapolis, IN 46208

Telephone: (317) 920-2660

Web: www.ima-art.org

Hours: Tues–Wed, Fri–Sat 10–5; Thurs 10–8:30; Sun 12–5. Closed Mon and major holidays. Tours daily.

Strengths: Asian, American African, and European art. William Turner (largest collection outside England). Neo-Impressionism (works by Gauguin and Pont-Aven School). Studio glass. Regional artists.

Special Events: Sun afternoon recital. Outdoor festivals. Films.

Other: The 52-acre grounds are filled with magnificent formal and informal gardens, statuary, fountains, and even a "Better Than New" shop. Also on the grounds are the restored 1930s Lilly mansion, greenhouse, and gardens. Restaurants. Museum shops.

Activities for Children: Family day every third Sun.

Parking: Free outdoor; limited pay indoor.

The Indianapolis Museum of Art (IMA) was founded in 1883 as part of America's remarkable wave of museum building. In the beginning, as

Charles Laval, French, *Going to Market, Brittany*, 1888, at the Indianapolis Museum of Art.

in other Midwestern states, there was an exhibition-organizing art association. In 1895, John Herron, an English-born farmer who had "made good" in Indiana, died, and left his considerable fortune to the association, even though no one there remembered meeting him. A Mission-style museum—the John Herron Art Institute—opened in 1906, but it lacked a collection. At first it was filled mostly with mediocre art, but gradually matters improved. Early contributors included the curious Indiana "Gamboliers," who "gambled" by buying the art of what they considered promising artists. Their purchases included works by Henri de Toulouse-Lautrec and Henri Matisse. Indianapolis citizens, including the family of Eli Lilly, the drug manufacturer, and Dr. George H. A. Clowes, a collector of great art, were good to their museum and today the IMA owns a interesting, encyclopedic collection.

In 1968, Josiah Lilly gave the museum Oldfields, a fifty-two-acre estate on the outskirts of town. A new building was erected, which eventually grew into a series of interconnected pavillions.

Most of the museum's Old Masters were Clowes's gift. The IMA is especially proud of Neroccio dei Landi's *A Madonna and Child* from about 1495. Also noteworthy is a Rembrandt self-portrait of a very young man wearing a jauntily perched velvet cap. The work is infused with the painter's characteristic light, but lacks the obvious introspection and pain of later self-portraits. Another highlight is three of El Greco's Apostles: *Saint Matthew, Saint Simon,* and *Saint Luke.* The museum's American collection is strong and comprehensive. It includes portraits by Gilbert Stuart, works by native son William Merritt Chase, landscapes by Hudson River painters, and works by Luminists, Tonalists, Impressionists, Regionalists, and Realists. The IMA's collection of art after 1945 is growing.

Most remarkable are the other complete collections that have been given to or bought by the museum. Passion created Kurt F. Pantzer's William (J. M. W.) Turner collection of 3,000 prints, 43 drawings and watercolors, 3 major oils, and 7 portraits. It is the largest Turner collection outside Great Britain. In 1914, Pantzer took an art history class at Harvard and became captivated by Turner. He returned to Indianapolis to practice law and in 1937 bought the first of many works and related material. In 1972, Pantzer transferred his beloved collection to his hometown museum where a selection is on view in three galleries devoted to the master watercolorist.

The IMA's Asian holdings are strong, and include sixty-nine works by the Japanese painter Hiroshige (1787–1858), the major Chinese art collection assembled by Eli Lilly, and the Alan Strassman Collection of ninety-five Japanese works from the Edo period (1615–1848), including twenty gloriously painted screens acquired by the museum in 2000. The Neo-Impressionists (followers of Georges Seurat) are well represented. In 1999 the museum acquired by grant/purchase Samuel Josefowitz's extraordinary collection of works from the little-known Pont-Aven School, which formed around Paul Gauguin in Brittany during the 1880s. According to Helen Lee, IMA's chief curator, "the works, with their vibrant colors, decorative patterns, and vivid images of Breton life, offer a superb look at a fresh and powerful approach to painting." The school illustrates the transition from the Impressionists to the Fauves and German Expressionists. In addition to Gauguin the collection includes works by lesser-known artists, among them Emile Bernard, a special favorite of Josefowitz.

Museum fatigue vanishes when visiting Oldfields, a gracious home built around 1912, and the formal and informal gardens of the Lilly estate. They were laid out in 1910–20 and include a Ravine Garden, with a stream that cascades into rock-rimmed pools, a Border Garden, and a Formal Wood Garden. Spending a day at the IMA is an escape from the stresses and strains of ordinary life.

Iowa

CEDAR RAPIDS

Cedar Rapids Museum of Art

Address: 410 Third Avenue SE, Cedar Rapids, IA 52401

Telephone: (319) 366-7503

Web: www.crma.org

Hours: Tues–Wed, Fri–Sat 10–4; Thurs 10–7; Sun 12–4. Closed Mon and major holidays. Noontime lectures by staff and guests (bring lunch). Tours by prearrangement.

Strengths: Regional artists, in particular Grant Wood, Marvin D. Cone, and Mauricio Lasansky. Also sculpture by Malvina Hoffman, and Roman portrait busts.

Special Events: Temporary exhibits.

Other: Art Discovery Center for all ages offers CD-ROM tours, interactive computer programs, and hands-on activities. Museum shop.

Activities for Children: Family day one Sun a month. Hands-on gallery.

Parking: Free, near museum.

Cedar Rapids is not generally considered an artistic hotbed. Yet it has had an active art association since 1890, and now sports one of America's most innovative museums. It is also the hometown of several well-known artists—Grant Wood, Marvin D. Cone, and Mauricio Lasansky—and its museum had the good fortune of being headed by Joseph S. Czestochowski, a man with a vision.

Czestochowski, the museum's first professional administrator, came

The Winter Garden atrium at the Cedar Rapids Museum of Art.

to Cedar Rapids in 1978 after having served at the Memphis Brooks Museum of Art in Tennessee (p. 372). When he arrived, according to *The Iowan*—a local newpaper—the Art Center had an annual budget of $121,000 and owned 453 works of art. Within a few years, Czestochowski had acquired the world's largest collection of works by Iowa's native sons and had raised enough money to build a new museum. However, instead of starting from scratch, the museum restored the city's beloved, vacant Carnegie Library, built in 1904, and twinned it with a new two-story, state-of-the-art building connected to the old library by a "winter garden," a soaring plant- and light-filled space defined by forty-five-foot-high columns and roofed by a glass canopy. The red columns, with their red-and-lilac-striped bases, imbue the space with a fiesta-like atmosphere.

Grant Wood and Marvin D. Cone were classmates and lifelong friends. It is fitting that so much of their work is now part of the Cedar Rapids Museum of Art's permanent collection. Like Thomas Hart Benton, Wood defined himself as a Regionalist painter, hoping that his style expressed the unique character of the Midwest. Though

Wood's best-known satirical and/or whimsical works, including *American Gothic, Daughters of Revolution,* and *Parson Weems' Fable,* are now in Chicago, Fort Worth, and Cincinnati respectively, the CRMA owns the artist's estate of 250 works. Especially noteworthy are *Woman with Plant,* a portrait of the artist's mother, and *Young Corn,* a typically "regional" landscape. Wood's oeuvre shares most of the first floor with Cone's haunting, fantasy-laden landscapes and cityscapes.

Both Wood and Cone spent some of their time teaching art in Iowa. So did Mauricio Lasansky, a native of Argentina who came to the University of Iowa in 1945 on a one-year appointment and stayed. Lasansky revitalized intaglio printmaking after World War Two and became, according to *Time,* "the nation's most influential printmaker." He donated much of his epoch-making work, as well as his private art collection, to the CRMA. The work of Bertha E. Jaques and James Swann, two printmakers with Iowa connections, and sculptures by Malvina Hoffman, who worked extensively with Rodin in Paris, are also on display.

Along totally different lines, the CRMA owns twenty-one Roman portrait busts created 2,000 years ago. The collection, donated by Tom and Nan Riley, is a reminder of artists' perennial task of rendering likenesses. The busts include the emperors Augustus, Hadrian, Antoninus Pius, and Marcus Aurelius as well as those of unknown women and children.

DES MOINES

Des Moines Art Center

Address: 4700 Grand Avenue, Des Moines, IA 50312

Telephone: (515) 277-4405

Web: www.desmoinesartcenter.org

Hours: Tues–Fri 11–4; Thurs 11–9; Sun 12–4. First Fri 11–9. Closed Mon and major holidays.

Strengths: Art of the 20th century. Sculpture, including works by Arp, Moore, Smith, Chamberlain, and others.

Special Events: Temporary exhibits. Lectures, films.

Other: First Fri 5–9: Arts After Hours—dance performances, concerts, cash bar, etc.

Activities for Children: Good activity books for children in English and Spanish.

Parking: On site.

If you were to create a building highlighting museum architecture of the twentieth century, you might call upon Eliel Saarinen, I. M. Pei, and Richard Meier. Each of these actually contributed to the Des Moines Art Center (DMAC). Such a seriatim collaboration might have resulted in a disastrous hodge-podge. Fortunately, each architect respected the work of his predecessor, and the DMAC is a joy to behold.

For Des Moines, incubation time from art club to museum was particularly long. In 1916, upon learning that seventy-eight-year-old James D. Edmundson, a wealthy, reclusive Des Moines-based lawyer, might endow a museum, a group of art-minded citizens formed an association that organized temporary shows and bought some art. Edmundson lived to be ninety-five years old, and thereafter it took ten years to execute his will.

After due deliberation, the Edmundson trustees declared that "Des Moines will not want, in the years to come, [a museum built in] imitation Greek, Gothic or English architecture." They selected Eliel Saarinen—the Finnish-born architect and director of the Cranbrook Academy of Art in Michigan (see Cranbrook Art Museum, p. 231)—to design a contemporary-style museum. The finished museum, located in Des Moines's Greenswood Park, was U-shaped, encircling a reflecting pool.

The original museum—the first U.S. museum built after World War Two—opened in 1948. It proved so serviceable that it has needed little modification. More space, however, was required, so I. M. Pei built a dramatic two-story addition in 1966. The spacious, soaring wing was designed to display the DMAC's growing sculpture collection. By the mid-1980s the museum had again outgrown its space. Richard Meier added yet another major component. He relied on the architectural vocabulary he had used for Atlanta's High Museum (p. 158), and would later use at The Getty Center in Los Angeles (p. 58): an exterior of white porcelain-coated metal panels, white railings, balconies, dramatic stairs, and glassed-in corridors.

For years the cumbersome governing body of the museum, as well as a succession of directors, could not agree on the type of art the museum

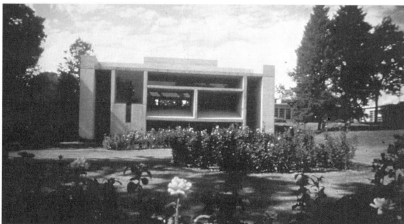

The Des Moines Art Center: (a) The Eliel Saarinen Building, (b) the I. M. Pei Building, (c) the Richard Meier Building.

was to collect. Eventually it was decided to concentrate on art of the last 150 years, since it was unrealistic to try to assemble a superior collection of Old Masters.

Fortunately, money was available. In 1937, Winnie E. Coffin, a Des Moines native, had left the still nonexistent museum a large acquisitions endowment. The fund, named for her husband, Nathan Coffin, another successful Iowa lawyer, has enabled Des Moines to acquire world-class art, including Robert Henri's *Ballet Girl in White* (actually bought by the art club in 1927) and Edward Hopper's enigmatic *Automat,* so typical of the artist's work that it was chosen as a commemorative stamp by the U.S. Postal Service. Appropriately, the DMAC owns Red Grooms's *Agricultural Building,* a construction depicting animals and people at the Iowa State Fair. There are also works by Oscar Kokoschka, Francisco Goya, Francis Bacon, Marsden Hartley, Anselm Kiefer, and James Ensor, to name only a few.

The museum has always favored sculpture. Not only will you find works by Henry Moore, Alberto Giacometti, Jean Arp, David Smith, and John Chamberlain, but also George Segal's plaster casts and motor-driven marionettes by Dennis Oppenheim. Bruce Nauman's twelve-foot-high *Animal Pyramid,* including seventeen separate animals, stands outside the Meier building, an exuberant match for Carl Milles's life-affirming *Man and Pegasus,* standing in the reflecting pool. Mary Miss's six-acre *Greenwood Pond: Double Site* is a pioneering piece of art-cum-landscape which links the environment, the viewer, and the artist in a very special relationship.

Kansas

WICHITA

Wichita Art Museum

Address: 619 Stackman Drive, Wichita, KS 67203
Telephone: (316) 268-4921
Web: www.wichitaartmuseum.org

Hours: Tues–Sat 10–5; Sun 12–5. Closed Mon and major holidays.

Strengths: American art with an emphasis on paintings from 1900–1950. American and European prints. Porcelain birds. Pre-Columbian and Mexican artifacts. British watercolors. Outdoor sculpture display.

Special Events: Family ArtFests. Temporary exhibits.

Other: Every Sun at 1:30: Gallery talks, usually discussing the work of a particular artist. Video Breaks.

Activities for Children: A 3,000-square-foot gallery offers hands-on art exploration for children of all ages. WAM for Kids encourages children to find meaning in the museum's collection.

Parking: On site.

The museum is closed for expansion until 2003.

It is surprising how many of America's museums were created by women. The Wichita Art Museum (WAM) owes its existence, and the beginnings of its extraordinary collection of American art, to Louise Caldwell Murdock (1852–1915) and her associate, Elizabeth Stubblefield Navas (1885–1979).

In *Towards an American Identity*, Novelene Ross, WAM's chief curator, describes Louise Murdock as a "woman from the generation which, at the turn of the century, transformed Wichita from a 'cowtown' to a 'civilized' cultural center." In a larger sense, Murdock was also what she called "A New Woman," and contributed to this nation's emerging feminism. Louise Caldwell moved to Wichita when she was fourteen and married Roland Pierpont Murdock, the owner of Wichita's first major newspaper, in 1877. During their travels, Louise discovered art, educated herself, and started to share her knowledge with her fellow citizens. Widowed at fifty-four, she studied interior decorating and returned to Kansas, where she started a decorating business using her professional skills to help rich and poor to have tasteful homes.

Bringing art to Kansas remained her mission. She organized loan shows and eventually left her residual estate for the purchase of an American art collection, provided Wichita would build a suitable museum. To satisfy this requirement the town bought 7.65 acres of farmland on the Little Arkansas River during the 1920s, and in 1935 erected a simple Art Deco structure on the site. Because of the Depres-

Kansas Cornfield, 1913, by John Steuart Curry, at the Wichita Art Museum.

sion the museum was smaller than intended. It was enlarged in 1963 and 1977, and will again grow in 2002.

Before her death, Louise Caldwell Murdock had asked her young assistant, Elizabeth Navas, to implement her will. Navas, self-educated like Murdock, became a connoisseur of American art. Between 1939 and 1962 she bought 167 paintings, graphics, sculpture, and decorative objects for the Murdock collection in Wichita. During much of that time Navas lived in New York, befriending art dealer Edith Halpert (also see the Abby Aldrich Rockefeller Folk Art Museum, p. 402, and the Marion Koogler McNay Art Museum, Texas, p. 390).

Significantly, Navas's first purchase for Wichita was John Steuart Curry's *Kansas Cornfield* (1913). The image of a monumental stalk of blooming corn, silhouetted against other stalks, is still one of the WAM's signature pieces. Curry, whose art is related to that of other Midwestern Regionalists, said of this work: "I have tried to put into this painting the drama that I feel in the presence of a luxuriant cornfield beneath our wind-blown Kansas skies. . . ." In her careful purchases, Navas acquired works of then avant-garde artists: Edward Hopper, Stuart Davis, Georgia O'Keeffe, Reginald Marsh, and Jack Levine. She also acquired the American "ancestors" for her contemporary collection: folk art, and an oil painting by Horace Pippin, an African American artist. WAM also owns stunning works by lesser-known painters, including Henry Koerner's *Pond*, Russell Cowles's *County Fair*, and Yasuo Kuniyoshi's *Season Ended*.

In time others joined Navas's efforts. In addition to American art of 1900–1950 the museum owns European prints and drawings, British watercolors, porcelain birds by Dorothy Doughty and Edward Marshall Boehm, and Pre-Columbian Mexican artifacts. The museum amply fulfills its founder's dream of bringing art to Kansas.

In 2001, the WAM closed to the public in order to undertake a $10.5 million expansion project. The new facilities will include glass works made especially for the museum by Dale Chihuly, additional public areas, and a new visitor-friendly entrance.

Kentucky

LOUISVILLE

The Speed Art Museum

Address: 2035 S. Third Street, Louisville, KY 40208

Telephone: (502) 634-2700

Web: www.speedmuseum.org

Hours: Tues–Fri 10:30–4; Thurs until 8; Sat 10:30–5; Sun 12–5. Closed Mon and major holidays.

Strengths: Survey of world art. Northern European tapestries of the 15th–17th centuries. Decorative art. Northern European art. American Renaissance art. Kentucky artists.

Special Events: Third Thurs after-hours music, refreshments 6–9.

Other: Temporary exhibits. Art Sparks, a novel interactive computer system. Restaurants. Museum shop.

Activities for Children: A large state-of-the-art learning center makes visits fun. Interactive computers are programmed with 30 different activities, some of which are suitable for the very young. Highlights include the creation of digital artworks. The center also supplies more traditional art-making supplies like oils, pastels, charcoal, and clay. Also tapes, Art Backpacks, and dress-up materials. Families First: selected Sat.

Parking: On site.

The Speed Art Museum (the Speed), the southernmost of the Midwestern museums, was founded by Mrs. J. B. Speed in memory of her industrialist husband. The Greek Revival–style building opened its doors in 1927. Mrs. Speed and her niece directed the museum until 1946, when the first professional director came aboard. Support by the Speed family continues. In 1996, J.B.'s granddaughter, Alice Speed Stoll, donated over $50 million, enabling the Speed to become a major national museum.

It took the Speed a while to fulfill its mission. Today it owns a respectable encyclopedic art collection, spanning 6,000 years of civilization, with some specific highlights. New wings were added in 1973 and 1986, and in 1997 the institution underwent a major renovation.

The centerpiece of the museum is the Tapestry Gallery of the Preston Pope Satterwhite Wing. Satterwhite (1867–1948), like his fellow collectors W. R. Hearst and J. P. Morgan, had tastes that ran to the grand. He decorated his lavish homes in Palm Beach, Florida, New York City, and Long Island with Renaissance furniture and seventeen spectacular tapestries woven in Europe between the fifteenth and the seventeenth centuries. Eventually, he willed his possessions to his native town, where they are displayed along with a magnificent carved fireplace, chasubles and ecclesiastic vestments, stained glass windows, paintings, and sculpture. One of the museum galleries is the heavily carved Manor House Hall from the Grange, Devon, England. It dates from the Elizabethan period and was transplanted to Louisville during the 1940s.

The museum has a superior collection of Old Masters. During the recent renovation, curators have regrouped the works so as to stress their similarities and differences. For example, educational materials explain the relationship of Nicholas Tournier's (1590–1639) *Five Men Playing Dice* to the work of Michelangelo da Caravaggio (1573–1610), whose realistic style, unorthodox perspective, dark colors, and dramatic illumination profoundly influenced artistic development. Another beloved possession is Lucas Cranach the Elder's portrait of *Herodias*, wife of King Herod and mother of Salome. Recent cleaning indicated that originally the picture included the severed head of John the Baptist, which undoubtedly would have detracted from the charm of this elegantly dressed Renaissance beauty. Best known among these works is Rembrandt's *Portrait of a Woman* coiffed and collared with the heavy lace fashionable during the seventeenth century. There are English and French Salon paintings as well as more recent European artists including Jacob van Ruysdael, Camille Corot, Claude Monet, Paul Gauguin, Georges Seurat, Constantin Brancusi, Marc Chagall, Pablo Picasso, Henri Matisse, and Paul Klee.

American painters are well represented. Of special interest is the Kentucky collection that includes paintings of nineteenth and early twentieth century and sculpture, silver, and furniture made by or for Kentuckians. Rarely encountered elsewhere but present here is a solid representation of works from the American Renaissance (1876–1917), whose inspiration was derived from the Italian Renaissance as well as from the classical work of Greece and Rome. The museum has adequate collections of classical antiquities and Native American and African art.

Museums cannot stand still. The Speed is actively acquiring twentieth-century art. It is an avid collector of glass, including works by Dale Chihuly, whose lyrical free-form glass pieces are spreading across America. The museum is also acquiring photographs. The sculpture court sports a Henry Moore and Juan Munoz's humorous *Piggyback*. For those familiar with the original, John DeAndrea's *Manet: Le Déjeuner sur l'Herbe* is extremely amusing.

Louisiana

NEW ORLEANS

New Orleans Museum of Art

Address: 1 Collins C. Diboll Circle, New Orleans, LA 70179

Telephone: (504) 488-2631

Web: www.noma.org

Hours: Tues–Sun 10–5. Closed Mon and major holidays. Tours Tues–Sat at 11 and Sun at 2.

Strengths: French art. Kress collection. French and Spanish Colonial art. Decorative art, including a comprehensive glass collection, Newcombe College Pottery, and a Fabergé collection. Contemporary American art, including Louisiana artists.

Special Events: Annual festivals: Art in Bloom, Home and Art Tour; Masterpiece Motorcade, Odyssey Ball, and Going for Baroque.

Other: Café. Museum store.

Activities for Children: StART point gallery, an interactive process of creativity.

Parking: Free, on site.

Like San Francisco's Legion of Honor (p. 87) and the Metropolitan Museum's famous Havemeyer Collection (p. 293), a sugar fortune built the New Orleans museum. Sugar-broker Isaac Delgado, a Jamaican immigrant, gave the city money for a building to house his aunt's beloved collection of art and artifacts. The city donated a piece of its City Park and the Isaac Delgado Museum of Art opened its doors in 1911. Then, as now, the ocher facade of the neoclassical edifice abuts a lagoon and is surrounded by live oaks and subtropical vegetation. It was, as the donor hoped, "a temple of the arts for rich and poor alike." The newspapers of the day hailed it as the "city's [new] splendid possession." Picturesque courtyards, embellished by metal gates and sculptures, endow the museum, like much of New Orleans itself, with an air of mystery.

For a long time, the museum had a minuscule endowment and its finances were strained. It almost closed in 1931, when the city of New

The Portrait of Estelle Musson Degas, 1892, painted by her brother-in-law and first cousin Edgar Degas, is one of the proudest possessions of the New Orleans Museum of Art.

Orleans cut its funds. Matters improved slowly, but even during bad times the museum received a few notable gifts, made a few good purchases, and hosted remarkable temporary shows.

In 1964, James B. Byrnes, who helped William R. Valentiner revitalize the North Carolina Museum of Art in Raleigh (see p. 320), was appointed director and worked hard at doing the same for the Delgado. A year later the new director had a bit of luck. He learned that a British collector wanted to sell Edgar Degas's *Portrait of Estelle Musson Degas,* a cousin and sister-in-law of the painter. The portrait of the young woman, arranging flowers in a vase, was painted in 1872–1873, during the artist's visit to New Orleans, his mother's birthplace. "Bringing Estelle Home" became a rallying cry for the museum, and spearheaded monetary and other donations. The painting was acquired for $190,000. Degas' wonderful painting of the New Orleans *Cotton Office,* unfortunately, hangs in the museum of Pau, France. In 1968 the citizens approved a bond issue, and the museum underwent a major expansion. Soon thereafter the museum changed its name to the New Orleans Museum of Art (NOMA).

To celebrate its seventy-fifth anniversary in 1985, and to reaffirm once again the roots of America's most Gallic city, the museum purchased the picture of yet another French woman, the monumental *Portrait of Marie Antoinette* by Elisabeth Vigée-Lebrun (see the Kimbell Art Museum, p. 380). Today the likeness of the ill-fated queen greets visitors as they ascend the grand stairs from NOMA's majestic white-columned Great Hall to the upper floor. Though not French, the *Portrait of Mrs. Asher B. Wertheimer,* one of the thirteen epoch-making portraits of this London family by John Singer Sargent, is another celebrated possession.

Today the NOMA is a large, lively museum, boasting 40,000 objects displayed in forty-six galleries. The Kress Foundation gave it twenty-nine Renaissance and Baroque paintings. The museum has always been partial to French art and features many nineteenth-century Salon and Barbizon School paintings as well as Impressionists and Post-Impressionists. Another sentimental favorite is a bronze horse by Degas, donated by his nephew, Michael Musson, in 1948.

The American collection includes a comprehensive collection of works by Louisiana artists, as well as examples of modern and contemporary American artists. Decorative art is another strength of the museum. The comprehensive glass collection (6,000 pieces) includes pieces from Egyptian times to the present. As in Cincinnati, women pioneered the development and manufacture of art pottery in New Orleans and the museum features many examples of the city's own Newcomb College Pottery, often decorated with native flora, such as chinaberries, or fauna. Much beloved by the public is the museum's collection of Fabergé (on permanent loan). These luscious, precious-stone-encrusted Easter eggs and jewels appeal to a universal love of the exotic and extravagant. Collections featuring Spanish and Colonial art; photographs, prints, and drawings; and African, Asian, Native American, Oceanic, Indian, and Pre-Columbian art are satisfying.

Maine

BRUNSWICK

Bowdoin College Museum of Art

Address: Bowdoin College, Walker Art Building, 9400 College Station, Brunswick,
ME 04011

Telephone: (207) 725-3275

Web: www.bowdoin.edu/artmuseum

Hours: Tues–Sat 10–5, Sun, 2–5. Closed Mon and major holidays.

Strengths: Superb portraits from the Colonial and Federalist periods. Maine
painters, especially Rockwell Kent.

Other: 15 or more temporary exhibits annually. Museum shop. The Peary-Macmil-
lan Arctic Museum, in Bowdoin's Hubbard Hall, established in 1967 to celebrate
Bowdoin's involvement in the northern frontier of the world.

Parking: On campus in areas reserved for visitors.

In its classic American Renaissance-style building, the small Bowdoin
College Museum of Art sits like a jewel on a fairy-tale New England college campus. The collection was started during the initial decades of the
nineteenth century, making it the oldest college museum in America.

Bowdoin College was founded in 1794, when Maine was a district of
Massachusetts. It was named for James Bowdoin II, a governor of the
state and a member of a politically prominent family. His son, James
Bowdoin III, the college's first benefactor, in 1811 left it 70 paintings and
a box of 141 drawings, which form the nucleus of the collection. Gifts
from other family members followed. Today, these Colonial and Federalist portraits by Gilbert Stuart, Robert Feke, John Singleton Copley,
and John Smibert are known throughout the art world. The fact that the
works were mostly painted in the New World demonstrates the patri-
otic pride of the donor. Jefferson had appointed him ambassador to Spain
and in 1805 Bowdoin III commissioned a portrait of Jefferson from
Gilbert Stuart for our Spanish embassy. Our third president, wearing a
simple black suit and lace jabot, is seated on a chair placed in front of a

massive column and heavy velvet curtain. "The portrait," says V. Scott Diamond in *The American Art Review* (May–June 2000), "is a quiet icon of America's belief in future greatness." Other great portraits in the collection include *Brigadier General Samuel Waldo* by Robert Feke, commemorating the general's victory over the French at Louisbourg, and *Thomas Flucker* by John Singleton Copley. Most charming is Stuart's portrait of *Mrs. Thomas C. Upham*. Bowdoin also owns a rare portrait by Joshua Johnson, painted after 1795. Most likely Johnson was an ex-slave who had lived in the household of Charles Willson Peale's brother-in-law, Robert Polk. After the latter's death, Johnson may have entered the Peale household where he assisted the painter. Later, Johnson worked independently, becoming one of America's earliest known African American artists (also see The Baltimore Museum of Art, p. 195, and Pennsylvania Academy of the Fine Arts, p. 353).

Nobody at Bowdoin paid much attention to its artistic possessions until the college's centennial in 1894, when Harriet Sarah and Mary Sophia Walker donated a small building in memory of their uncle, Theophilus Wheeler Walker, who is shown in a bas-relief by Daniel Chester French displayed in the entrance. The museum, built by McKim, Mead & White in American Renaissance style, is reminiscent of J. P. Morgan's Library in New York, built by the same architects at about the same time. The rotunda at Bowdoin, which serves as the entrance hall, is decorated with lunettes painted by four leading American artists: Elihu Vedder, Kenyon Cox, Abbott H. Thayer, and John La Farge. Here we find also five large Assyrian reliefs from the ninth century B.C.E., the gift of an alumnus. The Walker sisters were knowledgeable art collectors and enriched the museum most notably with works by Winslow Homer and other contemporary American painters. Eventually, James Bowdoin's box was unpacked and its lovely drawings, one attributed to Pieter Breugel, formed the beginning of the museum's works on paper (numbering, in 2000, 1,300 drawings, 4,000 prints, and 1,300 photographs). The museum also owns landscapes and seascapes: Notable are Martin Johnson Heade's *Newbury Port Marshes: Passing Storm* from 1865–1870 and William Trost Richards's extremely detailed but dreamlike *Into the Woods* from 1860.

The Walker building is small. Its second gallery is filled with excellent antiquities, including Greek vases and other objects from the ancient Mediterranean collection and some other European art, including works from the Italian Renaissance.

The collections of any worthwhile museum enlarge with time. In 2000, Bowdoin owned 14,000 art objects, many related to artists working in Maine. Its holdings include Ashcan artists, especially works by John Sloan. Bowdoin owns the nation's primary holding of Rockwell Kent. The artist's *Sun, Manana, Monhegan* is hard to forget. According to Diamond, in "reducing Monhegan's rocky terrain to stark forms and casting them under the glare of the sun, Kent invokes the primitive rhythms of daily and seasonal change." Bowdoin's enormous collection also encompasses many works by Eva Hesse, who in her very short life produced an amazing oeuvre of abstract expressionist works. Because of Bowdoin's small size, any one of these works is only rarely on view. Six underground galleries were added in 1975 and another expansion is planned.

PORTLAND

Portland Museum of Art

Address: 7 Congress Savare, Portland, ME 04101

Telephone: (207) 775-6148

Web: www.portlandmuseum.org

Hours: Tues–Wed, Sat–Sun 10–5; Thurs–Fri 10–9. Closed Mon and New Year's, Thanksgiving, and Christmas days. *Memorial Day–Columbus Day*: also open Mon 10–5. Tours daily at 2; Thurs, Fri also at 6.

Strengths: Paintings by Maine artists, including Winslow Homer, George Bellows, and Andrew Wyeth. American and European art.

Special Events: Shows often featuring Maine artists. Meet-the-artist talks. Series of Sunday Morning Jazz breakfasts

Other: Café. Museum shop. McLellan-Sweat House: One of Portland's grandest houses of the early 1800s and the former home of the museum. Attached to the museum, it houses state-of the art interactive computers which allow visitors to explore the social, economic, political, and art history of the 1800s.

Activities for Children: Learning Laboratory, an interactive visitor's center in the L.D.M. Sweat Memorial Galleries. Family Guide entitled "Seeing the Museum Together."

Parking: Pay lot next to museum; also metered, on street.

M
A
I
N
E

Wreck of the D.T. Sheridan by Rockwell Kent, at the Portland Museum of Art. Kent is one of many artists captivated by Maine's spectacular coastline.

Portland, Maine's largest city, has fewer than half a million inhabitants. It is thus particularly proud of its award-winning museum building and excellent collection. In a way this is not surprising. Maine, whose automobile license plate's motto is "Vacation Land," has been an inspiration to artists since the 1850s when Frederick Church discovered its mountains and rocky shores and Fitz Hugh Lane painted its harbors. Since then the state has been the inspiration and a summer or year-round residence for John Marin, the Wyeth family, Marsden Hartley, the Zorachs, Robert Henri, Winslow Homer, and Robert Indiana, to name only a few.

The Portland Museum of Art (PMA)—a proud showplace for Maine artists—was founded in 1882. At first it used a variety of exhibition spaces. In 1908, Mrs. M. J. M. Sweat bequeathed the museum her three-story mansion and money to transform it into a museum. It was enlarged in 1911. The museum's collection gradually outgrew this space. In 1976, Charles Shipman Payson, a native of Maine, came to the rescue. He gave the museum his incomparable collection of seventeen paintings by Winslow Homer and eight million dollars toward a new building. Henry Nicholas Cobb of I. M. Pei and Partners designed it.

When entering the red-brick building, which so perfectly matches

189

Portland's rejuvenated downtown, one is surprised to find the interior light, open, and airy. One's eyes immediately travel up five floors to an octagonally shaped skylight, a unifying motif repeated throughout the building. Everything is on a human scale and the interconnection between the different levels suits the open spaces evident in many of the paintings.

Take the elevator to the top floor. Against the walls are portraits of Maine's ancestors. Major General Henry Dearborn, who fought in the Revolutionary War, looks imposing in his resplendent, beribboned uniform. There are two portraits by Gilbert Stuart, and a few choice decorative art objects. As you descend via shallow stairs to the main gallery you glimpse the ocean through a round porthole window.

The largest gallery is filled mostly with Maine art, and those familiar with the state's landmarks may grow wistful. There are two views of Mount Katahdin, Maine's biggest mountain, by Frederick Church. There are seascapes by Winslow Homer, and the *Wreck of the D.T. Sheridan* on Monhegan Island by Rockwell Kent. Edward Hopper painted *Pemaquid Light,* George Bellows *Matinicus,* and Andrew Wyeth *Raven's Cove.* The U.S. Postal Service lent the museum a door decorated with Waldo Pierce's painting *Woodsmen,* one of twelve art projects the Federal Works Program funded in Maine during the Great Depression.

Not all the art in the PMA relates to Maine. Joan Paine Whitney, Shipman Payson's first wife, bequeathed the museum twenty-six Impressionist and Post-Impressionist paintings. Other Maine collectors have also bestowed gifts. The collection of world art was further enhanced by Albert Otten and Maine-native Scott M. Black. In 1996, Elisabeth B. Noyce (also see the next entry) bequeathed it sixty-six works of American art carefully selected to fill existing gaps. A stunning glass collection enhances the café.

ROCKLAND

The Farnsworth Art Museum

Address: 352 Main Street, Rockland, ME 04841
Telephone: (207) 596-6457
Web: www.farnsworthmuseum.org

Hours: *Columbus Day–Memorial Day:* Tues–Sat 10–5, Sun. 1–5; closed Mon. *Memorial Day–Columbus Day:* Mon–Sat 9–5. Closed on major holidays.

Strengths: 19th- and 20th-century American representational art, especially landscape and marine paintings by artists working in Maine, including Winslow Homer, Marsden Hartley, George Bellows, and Rockwell Kent. Louise Nevelson's early work. The Wyeth Center, devoted to the Maine works of the Wyeth family.

Special Events: Exhibits related to the collection and/or artists associated with Maine.

Other: Museum shop. Wyeth Center, on the museum campus. The Farnsworth Homestead, a Victorian house across the street, provides a glimpse of how a well-to-do shipping magnate lived in a small Maine seaport during the 19th century. The Olson House, in the nearby town of Cushing, Maine, is a classic Maine farmstead. The Homestead and the Olson House are open Memorial Day–Columbus Day daily 10–12, 1–4.

Parking: On street.

Lucy Farnsworth would have liked her museum. From the outside the main building looks like a slightly overgrown New England home. It sits in the middle of the small town of Rockland, where Lucy lived frugally for her entire ninety-seven years. Lucy Farnsworth would also have been thrilled that her trustees bought the core of the museum's priceless collection at bargain-basement prices.

Fitz Hugh Lane, *Camden Mountains from the South Entrance to the Harbor*, at The Farnsworth Art Museum.

Lucy Farnsworth may never have visited a museum, nor was she a collector, and her museum does not reflect her taste, nor is it burdened with her possessions. But when she died in 1935, she left $1.3 million to her hometown. Her will instructed her trustee, the Boston Safe Deposit and Trust Company, to build a library and a one-room art museum in memory of her younger brother and her father, William A. Farnsworth, a shipping magnate. Since tiny Rockland already had a library, the entire endowment went into building a museum. The bank appointed Robert P. Bellows, a retired architect, to buy the art.

Bellows and his advisors decided to concentrate on realistic landscape and marine paintings. These were out of favor in the 1940s and hence inexpensive. Bellows bought a painting attributed to William Turner for $29.50, a Maurice Prendergast for $65, a John Constable for $850. Bellows splurged when he spent $1,000 for a Winslow Homer, but all in all, he bought 696 paintings at an average cost of $71.43 per work. Today, most museums could not afford to pay the contemporary value of Bellows's purchases.

It was logical that the Farnsworth concentrate on artists inspired by Maine's spectacular coast. The sunny views of headlands, surf, lakes, and meadows by artists living or summering in Maine make up a large part of the Farnsworth's collection. But life in Maine is not always happy. There is poverty, hard work, foul weather, shipwrecks, and storms. Paintings by the Zorachs, George Bellows, Winslow Homer, and many others depict the mundane, the sad, and the catastrophic as well as the picturesque.

The Farnsworth always had a good relationship with the Wyeth family, whose summer home was nearby. During his shopping spree, Bellows had bought seven watercolors from twenty-six-year-old Andrew. In 1951, the museum gave Andrew his first solo museum retrospective and in 1968 it did the same for his son Jamie. These exhibitions put the Farnsworth on America's art map. Eventually the museum bought additional Wyeths, most notably Andrew's *Her Room* for $65,000, then a very high price for a painting by a living artist. It was still a bargain of sorts because it is now considered one of the painter's most important works. In 1991 the museum acquired the Olson House, the setting of some of Andrew's major paintings in nearby Cushing.

In 1995 the Farnsworth bought the former Pratt Memorial

Methodist Church, a simple New England structure with a clapboard exterior and a stark interior. With the cooperation of the Wyeth family it became the Wyeth Center. Patriarch N. C. Wyeth's paintings occupy the first floor; Andrew's and Jamie's share the second floor. "Maine paintings look better in Maine," Andrew once said. "It involves something as simple as the slant of the light across the landscape." The work (several thousand items) of the three Wyeths indeed looks great, the emotional experience amplified by the view of downtown Rockland and its harbor through the arched windows of the church. (Also see Brandywine River Museum, p. 348.)

In 1979 the Farnsworth featured the work of another local artist, Louise Nevelson. Though born in Russia, the sculptor grew up in Rockland, where her father, and later her brother, owned businesses. The Farnsworth bought several Nevelson sculptures; the artist and her brother, Nathan Berliawsky, donated others, enough to fill the Nevelson-Berliawsky Gallery. The museum also buys the work of contemporary artists associated with Maine, including Robert Indiana, Will Barnet, and Carolyn Brady.

In 1996 the museum received seventy works of Maine-related art assembled by Elizabeth B. Noyce, an artist and philanthropist. The gift included older works by Edward Hopper, Fitz Hugh Lane, Marsden Hartley, Eastman Johnson, and Rockwell Kent that complement the Farnsworth's holdings. In 2000 the Moorehouse family donated another large wing used for Maine-related temporary exhibits.

These riches have transformed the Farnsworth from a lovable regional museum into one that has international stature. Fortunately, the size of the galleries and the intimate art itself, preserve its small-town atmosphere.

WATERVILLE

Colby College Museum of Art

Address: Colby College, 5600 Mayflower Hill Drive, Waterville, ME 04901
Telephone: (207) 872-3228
Web: www.colby.edu/museum
Hours: Mon–Sat 10–4:30; Sun 2–4:30. Tours.

Strengths: 18th-, 19th-, and 20th-century American art. American folk art. Small European collection. John Marin, Alex Katz.

Other: Museum shop.

Parking: On street.

Founded in 1959, the Colby College Museum of Art (the Colby) was a small teaching collection until the arrival in 1966 of Hugh J. Gourley III. Thanks to his enthusiasm, loyal art patrons, artists, and alumni have turned the Colby into the largest museum in the state of Maine. The museum, and its three major additions (1973, 1996, and 1998), blends in well with the Neo-Georgian architecture of the campus. Currently the entrance is marked by William Zorach's sculpture *Mother and Child*.

The 1998 addition was built by Frederick Fisher, the prize-winning California architect who rebuilt New York's P.S.1. Contemporary Art Center (p. 306) and the municipal art museum in Berlin, Germany. Intended for Colby's permanent collection of eighteenth-, nineteenth-, and twentieth-century American art, the thirteen new galleries are intimate and brightly colored, "because," as architect Fisher said, "most of this art was created for domestic environments." The collections are arranged chronologically. Paintings of trustworthy-looking burghers, sea captains, women, and children, many of them by anonymous painters, gaze at us from the deeply colored walls. All major American artists are represented. Among many paintings worthy of note are John Singleton Copley's portrait of *Mrs. Metcalf Bowler,* William Merritt Chase's view of *Prospect Park, Brooklyn,* Childe Hassam's *Harvest Time, Brittany,* and Mary Cassatt's *Meditation.*

The John Marin collection of twenty-six paintings, watercolors, drawings, and etchings is the heart of the collection of Maine artists. Marin's oil *From Seeing Cape Split* (1935) is director Gourley's favorite. Looking at the view of the ocean, land, and sky, Gourley explained: "Marin has really captured the energy one sees on Cape Split on a windy day. . . . The way he applied the paint conveys the feeling of the day it was painted." Marin's other work is equally wonderful, including *Stonington, Maine; Weehawken, NJ;* and *The Brooklyn Bridge,* one of America's icons. There are also works by other Maine painters: George Bellows, Rockwell Kent (his painting *Black Head, Monhegan* is a gift of the Phillips Collection in Washington, D.C., p. 130, illustrating the spirit of cooperation that can exist in the American museum art world), Maurice B. Prendergast (*Barn, Brooksville, Me.*), Marsden Hartley, Andrew Wyeth, Marguerite Zorach, and a sculpture by Gaston Lachaise entitled *The Ogunquit Torso*. Louise Nevelson, who spent her childhood in Maine, donated thirty-five of her works to the museum.

Colby owns over 400 paintings by Alex Katz, who summers in Maine. His works are on rotating display in several galleries large enough to accommodate the artist's billboard-scale paintings. Frequently exhibited works include *Pas de Deux*, a series of five couples on five canvases; the elegantly dressed, blue eyed-women are entwined with their partners at what seems to be a cocktail party. The portrait of poet Allen Ginsberg, seen in multiple views from the front, back, and two sides, is another unusual work. In 1999 the *Boston Globe* declared that the art of Alex Katz alone was worth a trip to Waterville.

Most other major twentieth-century American artists are also represented: George Luks, Georgia O'Keeffe, Claes Oldenburg, Childe Hassam, Jacob Lawrence, and Robert Henri, to name a few. The museum also owns a few twentieth-century European artists: Emil Nolde, Henri Matisse, George Grosz and Raoul Dufy among them.

In addition, together with Portland and Westbrook College, Colby shares—on a rotating basis—the Joan Whitney Payson Collection of French Impressionists (see Portland Museum of Art, p. 188).

Maryland

BALTIMORE

The Baltimore Museum of Art

Address: 10 Art Museum Drive, Baltimore, MD 21218

Telephone: (410) 396-7100

Web: www.artbma.org

Hours: Wed–Fri 11–5; Sat–Sun 11–6. First Thurs until 8. Closed Mon, Tues, and

New Year's, Independence, Thanksgiving, and Christmas days. Lectures every Thurs, Sat, and Sun at 2.

Strengths: Cone collection of Post-Impressionist art, especially Matisse. Cubist, Surrealist, and contemporary art. Superb American furniture, art, and period rooms. Art from Africa, the Americas, and Oceania. European Old Masters. An extensive collection of prints and photographs.

Special Events: First Thurs (5–9): Freestyle art and fun activities (tours, talks, live music, dances) for all ages. Family program 6–8.

Other: Restaurant. Museum shop.

Activities for Children: Thurs, Sat, 1–5 Art + Fun = BMA. Visitors pick up one of three BMA packs (costumes, sounds, or sketching) at a kiosk whose contents are related to the art on view.

Parking: Metered, on site; additional on weekend at Johns Hopkins University lots.

Portions of the museum are closed until 2002.

In 1904 a great fire devastated downtown Baltimore, and the master plan for its rebuilding included an art museum, which was finally established in 1914. Until 1924, when a million-dollar appropriation was voted upon, the museum occupied rented quarters. John Russell Pope, who ten years later would construct the National Gallery in Washington, D.C. (p. 125), designed a neoclassical structure. Initially growth was slow, but in 1949, after the museum received the collection assembled by the Cone sisters, the Baltimore Museum of Art (BMA) became a world-renowned institution.

Upon entering the Cone Wing, color enraptures the senses—the blue and yellow of Paul Gauguin's *Vahine no te Vi;* the Prussian blue, white, and black of Pablo Picasso's *Woman with Bangs;* the sturdy brown of Vincent van Gogh's *A Pair of Boots.* But it is Henri Matisse's work that is totally captivating. Few artists were able to capture the joyous sensuality of life as he did. Whether clad or naked, stretched out or sitting, his women, often surrounded or accompanied by plants, flowers, fish, or dogs, exude sensuality. The patterned walls and floors of his artfully constructed interiors are a delight.

Today, when women can do almost anything, it is difficult to appreciate the extraordinary lives led by Dr. Claribel (born in 1864) and Miss

Etta (born in 1870) Cone. They were the daughters of Herman Cone, a German Jewish immigrant who founded a financial empire. His daughters snubbed tradition. Claribel attended the Women's Medical College affiliated with the Johns Hopkins University, where she befriended Gertrude Stein and her brother Leo. The Steins moved to Paris, where they became important figures among expatriate writers and the French Post-Impressionist painters.

After graduation, Claribel accepted medical research fellowships in France and Germany, but gradually her medical interests were displaced by art. Starting in 1901, Miss Etta too voyaged to Europe. The Steins introduced the sisters to avant-garde art. The Cones became major patrons and friends of Matisse, who came to Baltimore to pay a condolence call on Etta after Claribel's death in 1929.

Claribel left her share of their avant-garde collection to Etta, hoping it would go to the BMA, but its fate was by no means certain. Alfred Barr, of New York's Museum of Modern Art, and other museum directors tried to tell Etta that Baltimore was not ready for modern art. She was not swayed, however, and bequeathed 3,000 works of art and a sizable endowment to the BMA, stipulating that the collection remain intact. Included were forty-two paintings by Matisse, eighteen of his sculptures, and dozens of works on paper. In addition, there were works by Picasso, Paul Cézanne, Gauguin, Auguste Renoir, and van Gogh, all of them feasts for the eyes.

The sisters had not particularly liked Cubism. Fortunately, Saidie A. May, another Baltimorian, collected twentieth-century Cubist and Surrealist art, including works by Juan Gris, Georges Braque, Picasso, Joan Miró, Max Ernst, and others. She also acquired American Abstract Expressionist art during the 1940s, when these painters were still relatively unknown. Thanks to the gift of her collection and judicious purchases, the museum's collection of twentieth-century art is stunning and comprehensive.

The BMA has other strengths. Together with other American art museums (see Worcester Art Museum, p. 228), the BMA participated in the excavations in ancient Antioch (Antakiya, Turkey). This enterprise yielded mosaic floors and floor fragments from private villas.

A possession that made front-page news in the *New York Times* is Anthony van Dyck's *Rinaldo and Armida*, painted for the ill-fated King

Charles I. Exportation of this national treasure from England almost caused a riot. Nevertheless, the painting arrived in Baltimore where it joined similarly grand eighteenth-century portraits from England and France and superior Old Master works. Rembrandt is represented by *Titus, the Artist's Son*. Frans Hals by the *Portrait of Dorothea Beck*, and Botticelli by a *Madonna with Child and Angels*.

The BMA expressed an early interest in African art, mounting an exhibition in 1936. Three years later it held a full-scale exhibition entitled *Contemporary Negro Art*, which at the time was a bold statement for a southern U.S. city. The museum owns Joshua Johnson's *In the Garden*, painted ca. 1805 by one of America's earliest known African American artists (also see Bowdoin College Museum of Art, p. 186, and Pennsylvania Academy of the Fine Arts, p. 353). The BMA's collections of art from Africa, Asia, the Americas, and Oceania are outstanding.

The museum's 40,000-plus works-on-paper collection (prints, engravings, drawings), ranging from the fifteenth century to the present, is an almost complete record of the world's output. It is among America's best.

Museums are in the habit of outgrowing their quarters. The Pope building was enlarged several times. Two contrasting sculpture gardens—with a total of thirty-four sculptures—were added in 1980 and in 1988. The Wurtzburger Garden is formal, consisting of a series of outdoor rooms, while the Levi Garden occupies a steep, bowl-shaped site filled with beech, tulip, and oak trees. Both gardens are a welcome respite from city life and museum fatigue. In spring the ground is covered with thousands of blooming narcissus. (The gardens can be visited free during museum hours.)

The latest addition to the BMA is the West Wing (1994), whose sixteen galleries are filled mainly with post-1945 American art, including many works by Andy Warhol. The BMA's excellent collection of decorative arts and period rooms were reinstalled in the Pope building.

The Walters Art Museum

Address: 600 N. Charles Street, Baltimore, MD 21201

Telephone: (410) 547-9000

Web: www.THEWALTERS.org

Hours: Tues–Fri 10–4; Sat–Sun 11–5; first Thurs until 8. Closed Mon and New Year's, Memorial, Independence, Thanksgiving, and Christmas days. Gallery talks Wed at 12 and Sun at 1:30.

Strengths: Superior collection of art, artifacts, and decorative objects spanning 5,500 years: Ancient and medieval art, illustrated manuscripts, Old Masters, Renaissance and Post-Renaissance art, Impressionism. Collections of Egyptian, Roman, Greek, Chinese, Japanese, Southeast Asian, and Indian art are also remarkable.

Other: Free, extensive, random-access audio guide. Café. Museum shop. Hackerman House, a gracious old mansion adjacent to the museum, contains the museum's extensive Asian collection.

Activities for Children: Family programs most Sat (ArtWard Bound, 1–4, or festivals). Also special programs some first Thurs.

Parking: Lot at the corner of Center and Cathedral Streets; fee reduced when ticket is validated in museum.

For over a century Baltimorians have flocked to The Walters Art Museum (the Walters) to escape their daily routine and look at art. Even though it owns 30,000 works of art and has been repeatedly enlarged, the museum has retained some of the intimacy of the original family home-museum.

The Walters is the gift of William T. Walters and his son Henry. In 1824, when William was five years old, he is said to have spent his first five dollars on a Swiss artist's view of *Napoleon Crossing the Alps.*

During the 1850s, William, a wealthy wholesale liquor merchant and banker, supported local artists, among them Alfred Jacob Miller, a Baltimore native who accompanied a Scottish adventurer out West (see the Joslyn Art Museum, p. 249). The Walters owns Miller's *Interior of Fort Laramie,* where fur trappers traded pelts.

Because of alleged mixed loyalties the Walters family had to move to Paris during the Civil War. Here, William built an extensive collection of nineteenth-century French art, including Ingres's *Betrothal of Raphael and the Niece of Cardinal Bibbiena, 1813* (also see Fogg Art Museum, p. 209), as well as key works by Théodore Géricault, Honoré Daumier, Camille Corot, and Eugène Delacroix. While in Europe, Walters discovered Japanese and Chinese art. He also became enchanted with the

The Tiffany iris brooch, at The Walters Art Museum, Baltimore.

work of Antoine L. Barye, the French animal sculptor, and after his return to America commissioned works for Baltimore's parks.

In 1874, Walters opened his luxurious residence to the public. Ten years later, his possessions overflowed the house and he added a picture gallery. Paintings were hung, three high, above glass cases filled with Chinese ceramics, Japanese lacquerware, and jewelry. After his death his son Henry took over the business and his father's collecting activities.

The possessions of the Walters Art Museum are extremely varied. Both father and son liked glamorous objects: Byzantine and Hellenistic jewelry, golden objects from ancient Egypt, Limoges enamels, ivory croziers, illuminated medieval manuscripts, silver-gilt reliquaries, René Lalique's Tiger necklace, Fabergé eggs, a golden snuff box by the French master goldsmith Jean George, Japanese and Chinese porcelains. A floor-to-ceiling stained glass window (mid-thirteenth century) from Saint-Germain-des-Près near Paris is displayed next to a colorful tapestry.

Henry's biggest coup was the purchase of the entire contents of the Palazzo Accoramboni in Rome assembled by Don Marcello Massarenti, an official of the Holy See. The loot included seven magnificent Roman sarcophagi and a then-misattributed *St. Francis Receiving the Stigmata* by El Greco. The Massarenti collection also yielded a treasure trove of Greek and Roman art and artifacts including 180 black-figured and red-figured Greek pottery amphoras, as well as monumental sculptures, mirrors, and jewelry. At the suggestion of Bernard Berenson (see Isabella Stewart Gardner Museum, p. 202), called in to evaluate the Walters's varied treasures, Henry also bought a rare, intact altarpiece by Bicci di Lorenzo and Stefano di Antonio that has delighted visitors ever since.

Henry was partial to intimate, emotion-laden Renaissance works. The collection includes four panels from the predella (base section of an altarpiece) by Giovanni di Paolo, a remarkable Sienese painter of the fifteenth century. Flemish and Dutch painters are also represented. *Donor with St. John the Baptist* is a sensitive Hugo van der Goes. Later works include Raphael's *Madonna of the Candelabra.*

The museum soon needed more space and in 1905 Henry Walters commissioned a building modeled on Genoa's seventeenth-century Palazzo Babbi. He also continued to shop. Among the few twentieth-century French works we find Edouard Manet's introspective *At the Café* from 1879. The faces of a top-hatted older man and two women bespeak humankind's loneliness even in crowded public places.

The Walters' Egyptian collection of 1,000 pieces is considered to be among the most important in America. Henry Walters also carefully filled in his father's collections of Asian and Islamic art.

Most everybody responds to jewelry, the exquisite small decorative objects men and women use for personal adornment. The thousand pieces owned by the Walters include Phoenician gold crowns, a precious-stone-encrusted Hellenistic bracelet, and—perhaps best-beloved —a Tiffany sapphire iris brooch and the intricately carved *Rubens Vase,* created in Byzantium during the fourth century from agate owned three centuries earlier by the financially successful Peter Paul Rubens.

By 1974 the museum had again outgrown its quarters, and another building, in what the museum describes as the "1970s Brutalist" style, was added. Though attractive, it turned out to be difficult to climate-control and it was revamped in 2000. Its new four-story glass atrium features dramatic circular stairs connecting all the floors.

Massachusetts

BOSTON

Isabella Stewart Gardner Museum

Address: 280 The Fenway, Boston, MA 02115

Telephone: (617) 566-1401

Web: www.boston.com/gardner

Hours: Tues–Sun 11–5. Closed Mon and Thanksgiving and Christmas days. Open other holidays. Tours Fri at 2:30.

Strengths: Great European art displayed in an informal, accessible manner, tapestries, furniture, mosaics, and manuscripts.

Special Events: Concert series. Temporary shows related to the collection.

Other: Courtyard talks Tues–Fri at 11:30 and 1. Café with outdoor seating in summer. Museum shop.

Activities for Children: This small museum is suitable for children provided they don't touch.

Parking: Limited on street; paid, available at the Museum of Fine Arts garage or lot on Museum Road, two blocks away.

The inconspicuous door of the Isabella Stewart Gardner Museum (The Gardner) in Boston does not prepare the visitor for the imposing four-story-high skylit atrium—the courtyard of a Venetian palazzo—that forms the core of the building. Orange and yellow nasturtiums cascade from upper balconies. A Roman mosaic is the center of an interior garden, in which antique sculptures emerge from a carpet of flowering plants and greenery. Water trickles from a fountain.

The Gardner is much like its founder left it when she died in 1924. Like the Frick Collection in New York (p. 278) and the Norton Simon Museum in Pasadena (p. 68), the museum is the creation of one individual, only more so. Isabella Stewart Gardner not only picked the art but she also designed the building and hung the objects. Her will dictated that nothing could ever change.

Isabella Stewart was born in New York in 1840. When she was

Isabella Stewart Gardner was a legend in her own time. Here, Anders Zorn shows an enthusiastic *Mrs. Gardner in Venice.*

twenty she married financier John (Jack) Gardner and moved to Boston, where she is said to have felt like a foreigner. In 1865 the Gardners lost their only child and it took time before Isabella regained her balance.

An 1867 trip to Europe seemed to give her life new meaning. Upon her return she avidly entered Boston's staid social life, always treading the thin line between scandal and acceptability. She was flamboyant, willful, and eccentric. She craved attention and her exploits were fodder for the press. But she was also studious and determined, and left all of us a wonderful legacy.

In 1878, Isabella started to attend the lectures of Charles Eliot Norton, Harvard's first professor of art history. Here she met Bernard Berenson, a gifted, penniless young student. He impressed his elders with his taste and erudition and they provided funds for him to continue studying in Europe. Eventually "Mrs. Jack" alone renewed the stipend. It turned out to be a wise investment. Berenson, who became the ultimate authority on Italian art, faithfully advised his patron as she formed her collection. Isabella had a limited budget and Berenson searched for masterpieces that she could afford. According to Aline B.

Saarinen in *The Proud Possessors,* "the Gardner collection is essentially of Berenson's making."

In 1884, a round-the-world trip took the Gardners to Venice. For Isabella it was love at first sight. A portrait by Swedish painter Anders Zorn, now hanging in her museum, shows Isabella, arms outstretched, rushing into the room from a balcony overlooking the Grand Canal.

Isabella's father died in 1891, leaving her $1.6 million, and she started collecting art in earnest. An early, important acquisition was Sandro Botticelli's *Tragedy of Lucretia,* still one of America's best Renaissance paintings. Other Italian masterpieces followed—Titian's *Rape of Europa,* Raphael, Giovanni Bellini, Lippo Memmi, Giovanni di Paolo, Fra Angelico, Simone Martini, Piero della Francesca—all the leading names of the Italian Renaissance. She also collected works by Dutch, Flemish, German, and Spanish painters—Rembrandt, Jan Vermeer, Albrecht Dürer, El Greco—and paintings by more modern artists—Edgar Degas, Edouard Manet, and Henri Matisse.

Mrs. Gardner was a personal friend of James Whistler and John Singer Sargeant, and the museum owns a number of their works. Sargent's early painting of a Spanish flamenco dancer, entitled *El Jalero,* occupies a specially lit place in the Spanish Cloisters. The painting is illuminated from below, and is so evocative of the performance that one can almost hear the strumming of the guitars.

By 1896 the Gardners had agreed to build an art museum on The Fenway to house their collection. When her husband died, Mrs. Jack continued on her own. She went to Europe to collect architectural fragments, cornices, arches, stairs, wood paneling, brocades, damasks, and silks. With the assistance of Willard T. Sears, her long-suffering architect, she built the museum we see today, in the style of a Venetian palace. Her extraordinary memory enabled her to assemble the hundreds of fragments she had collected exactly as she had envisioned. Her interior decorating was equally fastidious. The Blue Room, for instance, was covered in five different eighteenth-century silk fabrics. Other walls were covered in damask or leather.

"Fenway Court" is a splendid work of art in itself. During her lifetime Mrs. Jack lived in the personal quarters she created on the fourth floor. She frequently entertained in the galleries, and occasionally opened her home to the public. As she intended, the museum fosters the love of art. Indeed, as you wander up and down the stairs you may forget to concentrate on the museum's special treasures and simply bathe in the atmosphere. You may wish to linger in the Gothic chapel, with its magnificent stained glass window from St. Denis near Paris, examine a Roman sarcophagus, read some of Isabella's correspondence, or look into the atrium from the third floor balcony. Or you may gaze at Sargent's painting of a young Isabella. The portrait shows her clad in a demure black dress, a double row of pearls encircling her waist, her hands clasped in front of her. She is silhouetted against a paisley fabric, whose design acts like a halo. She almost seems to make eye contact with her viewer, and if you listen carefully you may hear her enunciate her motto: "C'est mon Plaisir."

Museum of Fine Arts, Boston

Address: 465 Huntington Avenue, Boston, MA 02115

Telephone: (617) 267-9300

Web: www.mfa.org

Hours: Mon–Tues 10–4:45; Wed–Fri 10–9:45; Sat–Sun 10–5:45. Closed Thanksgiving and Christmas days. Tours Mon–Fri: General tour at 10:30 and 1:30; Asian, Egyptian, and Classical at 2:30; American art at 12:30; European art at 11:30. Sat: General at 10:30 and 1.

Strengths: Encyclopedic, with many special collections: American paintings (Copley, Stuart) and decorative arts, including silver. Comprehensive European collection including many French Impressionists (Monet, others) and Post-Impressionists. Egyptian, Nubian, and Near Eastern art; Asian art, especially of Japan. Textile and costume collection. Contemporary art.

Special Events: Many high-profile temporary exhibits. Open house (music and dance performances) and free admission on Martin Luther King, Memorial, and Columbus days.

Other: Three enchanting gardens featuring European, American, and Japanese designs. Restaurants. Museum shops.

Activities for Children: Family Place: Guided activity led by museum instructors (Sat, Sun 11–4, October–June) for age 4 and older accompanied by an adult. This program is also available during School Vacation Week Adventures (Feb, April, and Dec). At other times, self-guiding Family Place activity booklets are available free of charge at Sharf Information Center. A drop-in workshop (ages 6–12) is available most weekdays 3:30–4:45 in Children's Room.

Parking: Paid, in museum lot and garage; very limited metered on street.

On February 4, 1870, the Massachusetts legislature established a board of trustees "for the purpose of erecting a museum for the preservation and exhibition of works of art. . . ." Thus one of the nation's finest museums was created. The Museum of Fine Arts (MFA) moved to its present granite neoclassical building on Huntington Avenue in 1909.

Like the city of Boston itself, the MFA is both grand and restrained. The eyes of a visitor entering from Huntington Avenue invariably travel up the rotunda that crowns the museum's second floor. Mythological gods and goddesses cavort on the ceiling and in bas-reliefs that fill panels in an elegant colonnade. Both are the work of John Singer Sargent, the European-educated American who made Boston his spiritual home. Sargent died in 1925 before the installation of his murals was complete, and they were unveiled in the rotunda during his memorial service.

The MFA is an encyclopedic museum arranged chronologically. Its 1905 participation in archeological expeditions netted it the beginning of a superior Egyptian collection. The MFA owns the largest collection of Nubian art outside the Sudan (part of it is on permanent loan to the National Museum of African Art in Washington, D.C.—see p. 138). The museum also acquired Greek and Roman collections in which large, glistening works of marble contrast with delicately wrought gold objects.

Entire galleries are filled with emotion-laden Byzantine and Italian Renaissance art. Most moving is a frescoed chapel from Catalonia, Spain. The earthy and religious paintings, dating from a time when ordinary people could not read and learned about life and death, heaven and hell, from the art displayed in churches, still inspire a feeling of reverence. The MFA is especially proud of Donatello's relief *Madonna of the Clouds,* one of the few works in America by the great Florentine Renaissance sculptor.

Other treasures include *Fray Hortenso Felix Paravincino,* an early El Greco masterpiece acquired upon Sargent's recommendation and the first El Greco purchased by an American museum. The Dutch occupy

The Daughters of Edward D. Boit by John Singer Sargent, at the Museum of Fine Arts, Boston.

an entire gallery. The burghers painted by Rembrandt and Frans Hals look as staid and respectable as those who forged America during our Revolutionary War.

The MFA owns thirty-six paintings by Claude Monet, the largest collection of works by the painter outside France. His contemporaries—Edouard Manet, Edgar Degas, Auguste Renoir, Paul Cézanne, Camille Pissarro—are also well represented. Of note is Manet's *Execution of the Emperor Maximilian* (in Mexico), a reminder that international politics were always fraught with controversy. Other galleries are filled with prime examples of European art: English portraits, landscapes, and seascapes; German Expressionists, and more. The MFA owns Pablo Picasso's *Rape of the Sabine Women*, whose horses, ravaged women, and children are reminiscent of his *Guernica*, painted thirty years earlier.

Given Boston's patriotism, one expects an excellent American collection, and visitors will not be disappointed. Paintings by John Singleton Copley (over sixty) and Gilbert Stuart (fifty) fill a large gallery. Most relevant to Boston is the portrait of *Paul Revere*. The future Revolutionary hero, shown in shirtsleeves with a five-o'clock shadow, is working away at a silver teapot. His silver *Liberty Bowl*, engraved with the names of the ninety-two brave members of the Massachusetts House of Representatives who resisted the British, stands before the portrait.

Approaching our own times we come across paintings that celebrate the beauty of America: a misty *Niagara Falls* by George Inness, and explorations of the West by Hudson River School painters. *The Daughters of Edward D. Boit* by John Singer Sargent is one of the museum's best-loved pictures. The MFA has kept up with the times. Its collection of modern and contemporary American art is a joy to behold.

As befits a great, encyclopedic museum, the MFA overflows with excellent decorative arts, silver, ceramics, ancient and modern glass, musical instruments, and textiles—too much to see in one day.

CAMBRIDGE

Harvard University Art Museums

Fogg Art Museum,
Busch-Reisinger Museum
Arthur M. Sackler Museum

Harvard University has played a major role in the development of the American art museum. Charles Eliot Norton was the United States's first professor of fine art, as well as the first director of Harvard's Fogg Art Museum. Norton's special interest was the art of the Italian Renaissance, and his course at Harvard inspired Bernard Berenson, the future art expert, as well as collectors Isabella Stewart Gardner and Louis Fiske Hyde, of Glens Falls. Later the stewardship of the museum passed to Edward Forbes, who pioneered art conservation, and to Paul Sachs, who trained many of America's future museum directors (see Introduction and below).

In time, Harvard University also assembled excellent art collections, numbering more than 150,000 objects. Today a careful selection of these is neatly distributed among three eminently manageable and delightful museums: The Fogg Art Museum, the Busch-Reisinger Museum, and the Arthur M. Sackler Museum. The first two are located on Quincy Street, while the Sackler is around the corner on Broadway. One admission fee covers the three museums.

Fogg Art Museum

Address: 32 Quincy Street, Cambridge, MA 02138

Telephone: (617) 495-9400

Web: www.artmuseums.harvard.edu

Hours: Mon–Sat 10–5; Sun 1–5. Closed major holidays. Tours Mon–Fri at 11.

Strengths: Italian and French art. Impressionists and Post-Impressionists.

Other: Outstanding tours conducted by thoroughly trained docents. Museum shop.

Parking: Limited on street; pay garages.

In 1891 Harvard University founded a small museum housed in Hunt Hall. It did not amount to much until it received a major, surprise gift from Mrs. William Hayes Fogg, with instructions to build a museum in her husband's memory. The Fogg Art Museum (the Fogg) opened to the public in 1895. The building and its large interior court is modeled on a sixteenth-century Italian Renaissance palace in Montepulciano, Italy.

The Fogg's collections grew under the combined leadership of director Edward Forbes (appointed in 1909 and serving until 1944) and professor Paul Sachs (appointed in 1915 and serving until 1948). According to Nathaniel Burt, author of *Palaces for the People,* when Forbes took up his post, he "found a building with a lecture hall in which you could not hear, a gallery in which you could not see, . . . and a roof that leaked like a sieve." Forbes was to change all that.

The galleries of the Fogg are small and paintings are hung at eye level, a practice attributed to Sachs's short stature. French and Spanish Romanesque capitals line the ambulatory of the ground floor. Luscious Italian Renaissance paintings by Fra Angelico, Simone Martini, and others are displayed in adjoining galleries. The face of one Madonna from Botticelli's workshop looks so much like his Venus that it seems as if the master himself had painted it. Many of these are the gift of Edward Forbes. There are also magnificent works by Lucas Cranach the Elder, Rembrandt, Peter Paul Rubens, Albrecht Dürer, and Jusepe de Ribera.

On the second floor are several paintings by Jean-Auguste Dominique Ingres, one belonging to the series *Raphael and the Fornarina,* which is reminiscent of Ingres's great *The Marriage of Raphael* at

Claude Monet, *Red Boats, Argenteuil*, at Harvard University's Fogg Art Museum.

the Walters Art Museum in Baltimore (see p. 198). Perhaps most famil-iar are the paintings assembled in a remarkably short fourteen years by Harvard alumnus Maurice Wertheim. His gift includes Pablo Picasso's "Blue Period" *Maternity*, the heartrending figure of an emaciated, elon-gated, barefooted woman cradling her child. Though distanced by four centuries, it is as moving as the Sienese Madonnas from an earlier time. Equally moving is one of Vincent van Gogh's twenty-seven self-portraits. Writing to brother Theo, Vincent describes the picture as being: "all ashen gray against pale malachite. . . . The clothes are this brown coat with a blue border. . . . I have made the eyes slightly slant-ing like the Japanese. . . ." The painting, originally owned by Gauguin, ended up in a Munich museum. It was considered "degenerate" by the Nazis, deaccessioned, and sold in Switzerland at a "fire sale." The Wertheim legacy also includes other masterpieces by Claude Monet, Edouard Manet, Paul Cézanne, Henri de Toulouse-Lautrec, and others.

Busch-Reisinger Museum

Address: 32 Quincy Street, Cambridge, MA 02138

Telephone: (617) 495-9400

Web: www.artmuseums.harvard.edu

Hours: See Fogg Art Museum, p. 209, Tours Mon–Fri at 1.

Strength: German Expressionists.

Special Events: Moholy-Nagy's Light Space Modulator is turned on once a week (Wed at 1:30).

Other: Outstanding tours by thoroughly trained docents.

Parking: See the Fogg.

A glass door separates the Busch-Reisinger Museum (B-R), which is the only American museum devoted to the art of Central and Northern Europe, from the Fogg (previous entry). Though it owns German late medieval, Renaissance, and Baroque sculptures and paintings, the B-R's major strength is German Expressionist art. As with the Van Gogh self-portrait, the Nazis considered the art degenerate, purged it from major German museums, and sold it in Switzerland. Harvard acquired some of its treasures there. Only a very small fraction of the collection is on exhibit.

The B-R was founded in 1906 as an adjunct to the university's German department and even received gifts from Kaiser Wilhelm II himself. Because of anti-German sentiments the museum had to close during World War One, and then again during World War Two. Today the wildly colored and distorted paintings produced by the German Expressionists assault our consciousness. Key works include Max Beckmann's *Self-Portrait in a Tuxedo,* a cigarette dangling from his fingers (acquired for $400), Erich Heckel's triptych of *The Convalescent Woman,* Emil Nolde's Madonna-like *Mulatto,* and Franz Marc's *Grazing (Red) Horses,* so reminiscent of the artist's beloved *The Large Blue Horses,* at the Walker Art Center in Minneapolis (see p. 238). Ernst Barlach's seven-foot sculpture *Crippled Beggar* again illustrates the spirituality of the German Expressionists. The B-R also owns László Moholy-Nagy's *Light-Space Modulator,* an amazing electrically powered machine that scatters light.

Arthur M. Sackler Museum

Address: 485 Broadway, Cambridge, MA 02138

Telephone: (617) 495-9400

Web: www.artmuseums.harvard.edu

Hours: See Fogg Art Museum, p. 209. Tours Mon–Fri at 2.

Strengths: Chinese, Japanese, Korean, Islamic, and Indian art. Ancient Roman and Greek art and coins. Egyptian and Near Eastern art.

Other: Outstanding tours by thoroughly trained docents.

Parking: See the Fogg.

Harvard's newest museum is the Arthur M. Sackler, the gift of Arthur M. Sackler, a physician and medical publisher who became fascinated with Eastern and Oriental art. (Part of his collection is now at the Smithsonian in Washington, D.C.—see Freer Gallery of Art and Arthur M. Sackler Gallery, p. 134.) Harvard's Sackler is around the corner from the Fogg Art Museum and the Busch-Reisinger.

The building, designed by James Stirling, houses Greek and Roman antiquities, Chinese jades, Chinese cave paintings and sculpture, Korean ceramics, Indian and Persian miniatures, and decorative art from Persia. Again, only a small part of these exquisite collections are on view. The web site tells us that some of these collections are "the world's finest." Indeed, Harvard University was one of the earliest collectors of these treasures, since during the early part of the twentieth century it was the only university in America offering a course in Oriental art (also see the Nelson-Atkins Museum of Art, p. 242). Many of the Sackler's galleries emanate the peace characteristic of Asian art. In one, called Nature as Metaphor, we come across a vase decorated with blooming and fruiting branches of a peach tree. Nearby is a folding Japanese fan painted with *Blue and White Iris in Mist*.

Greek, Roman, and Indian art is displayed on the top floor. These exhibits can be reached via narrow, skylit stairs that resemble those found in Mexican pyramids. Here, as in the Fogg, objects are displayed at eye level. It is extremely satisfying to examine closely the black-on-red and red-on black paintings on Greek vases, the abstract-looking lines of Cycladic figures dating from 2300 B.C.E., and the sensuous curves of Indian sculptures.

NORTH ADAMS

Massachusetts Museum of Contemporary Art (MASS MoCA)

Address: 87 Marshall Street, North Adams, MA 01247

Telephone: (413) 664-4481

Web: www.massmoca.org

Hours: Daily 11–5. Summer (June–Oct) 10–6. Closed Tues and Thanksgiving, Christmas, and New Year's days. Open all other holidays.

Strengths: Contemporary and experimental art. Sound and art installations. Digital art.

Special Events: Temporary exhibitions.

Other: Theater and dance performances. Concerts. Films.

Activities for Children: The museum is child-friendly.

Parking: On site.

It may come as a surprise that America's newest—and so far largest—museum of contemporary art is located in a textile mill dating from 1890. The project was the brainchild of Thomas Krens, at the time director of the nearby Williams College Museum of Art (p. 226). Krens was frustrated by the lack of exhibition space for large works of contemporary art that did not fit into conventional museum galleries.

Locating the project in North Adams was killing two birds with one stone. During the nineteenth and early twentieth centuries North Adams was a thriving mill town. When the textile industry moved south, the town's largest industrial complex—consisting of twenty-seven buildings—was taken over by the Sprague Electric Company, which at one time employed 4,000 people. In 1986, Sprague too left North Adams, abandoning dozens of picturesque but useless buildings and leaving the community impoverished. P.S.1, the Contemporary Art Center in New York City (p. 306) had pioneered recycling useless buildings, and Massachusetts wanted to follow suit.

After making a few initial contacts for the project, Krens left Williamstown to assume the directorship of the Solomon Guggenheim Museum in New York, and his associate, Joseph C. Thomson, continued the project. Against incredible odds Thomson succeeded in creating a remarkable museum. MASS MoCA—the Massachusetts Museum of Contemporary Art—opened in May 1999 with nineteen galleries in several interconnected structures. Additional buildings are expected to be reclaimed in the future. MASS MoCA is not only a museum but also a cross-disciplinary center for other visual and performing arts.

MASS MoCA obviously thrives on an element of shock. As you approach the entrance you encounter half a dozen trees suspended upside down from poles. The reception desk—a massive construction of steel and wood balancing on a small cylinder—also looks upside down.

The architects have made excellent use of the 1890 factory buildings. They exposed some of the old brick walls and refinished others. Interior columns were removed and replaced by steel truss beams that are reminiscent of the buttresses of old cathedrals. New hardwood floors endow the place with light and grace. Bridges and walkways connect spaces at various levels. The galleries themselves vary in size. Some are enormous—one is the size of a football field, another is forty feet high.

The alternations in space, size, and height, and the juxtaposition of the old and the new, work well. From anywhere in the building one has interesting vistas of the artworks and the outside world. Through the old factory windows one glimpses a branch of the Hoosick River, the town's old Victorian tenements, the clock tower, other factory buildings, a gigantic outdoor performance area, or the green hills of the Berkshires.

MASS MoCA's aim is to remain on the cutting edge of art. To quote Thomson: "The institution is focused on the future. . . . We hope to be a lively cross-disciplinary laboratory for artists to create new work, a venue for visitors to experience works in progress."

Indeed, the museum has no permanent collection. Some of the works are ephemeral installations, some are long-term loans. The center emphasizes Pop Art, Minimalism, Conceptual Art, and Arte Povera. The museum is especially interested in developing sound art. One such work emanates every fifteen minutes from the clock tower of the old factory.

Some of the works on exhibit are by well-known artists of the twentieth century. Robert Rauschenberg's *1/4 Mile or Two Furlong* is an autobiographical "work in progress" on which the artist has been concentrating since 1981. James Rosenquist's enormous triptych, commissioned by the Deutsche Guggenheim, Berlin, explores Germany's recovery from its Nazi past, and John Chamberlain's *Doomsday Flotilla* is appropriately doomsday-like.

The center holds film, music, and dance festivals and hopes to develop a provocative performance program—one that would complement and enhance those offered at Tanglewood, Jacobs Pillow, and elsewhere in the Berkshires.

NORTHAMPTON

Smith College Museum of Art

Address: Elm Street at Bedford Terrace, Smith College, Northampton, MA 01063

Telephone: (413) 585-2760

Web: www.smith.edu/artmuseum

Hours: *Sept–June*: Tues, Fri–Sat 9:30–4; Wed, Sun 12–4; Thurs 12–8. *July and Aug*: Tues–Sun 10–4. Closed Mon and New Year's, Independence, Thanksgiving, and Christmas days.

Strengths: Eclectic. 19th- and 20th-century European and American art. Dutch and English landscape. Sculpture. Works on paper.

Special Events: Excellent temporary shows.

Activities for Children: Puzzles, postcard matching games, materials to copy paintings, and other games makes this a good place to visit with children.

Parking: Limited on street. Evenings and weekends use any campus parking lot.

Entire museum closed until 2002

"In high summer, when pleasure is at the prow, people who love looking at pictures, often remember the art museum at Smith College in Northampton . . ." writes art critic John Russell in the *New York Times* of August 4, 2000. Russell describes Smith's possessions as "a rhapsodic and quirky collection, lovingly tended by Smith College."

The college was founded in 1870, when few young women pursued higher education. In his inaugural address, L. Clark Seelye, the school's first president, stated that he wanted his students to "be made familiar with the famous masterpieces." Indeed, the first building of the college sported an art gallery. At first it was filled with plaster casts, but as early as 1879 Seelye began buying contemporary American art. Since then, astute purchases and loving gifts from educated alumnae have enriched a collection that numbered 24,000 works in 2000.

The physical plant of the Smith College Museum of Art (SCMA) has changed frequently. Its first building was the gift of Northampton druggist Winthrop Hillyer in 1881. Dwight W. Tryon, art teacher, gallery director (1886–1920), and an American Impressionist painter, donated money for an additional building in 1925. Tryon's work was much beloved by railroad-tycoon-turned-collector Charles Freer before the latter turned to Oriental art (see the Freer-Sackler Gallery of Art, p. 134). In 1972, Tryon Hall, a lovely, innovative building whose elegant, light-filled galleries, suitable for small-scale works originally bought for private homes, replaced both buildings. Another renovation and enlargement was started in 2000, and the museum is closed until 2002.

Seelye purchased works by his contemporaries, including Thomas Eakins (his first purchase was In Grandmother's Time) and Albert Pinkham Ryder, both of whom are now considered to be American Old Masters. Eakins, fired from his teaching post at the Pennsylvania Academy of the Fine Arts because he insisted on teaching drawing from nude models, was much neglected in his own time. Smith owns his poignant, unsentimental portrait of Mrs. Edith Mahon, painted toward the end of his career.

The museum is proud of John Singleton Copley's especially fine Seated Portrait of John Erving. A surprising possession is the deeply stirring work Mourning Picture, 1890, acquired in 1950 from a descendant of Edwin Romanzo Elmer, a little-known painter. The work depicts his deceased young daughter hugging her pet sheep, her doll carriage standing nearby. Her formally dressed parents sit in front of a solid clapboard house. There is a certain kinship between that house and Pretty Penny, Edward Hopper's rendition of actress Helen Hayes's abode. Both lovingly detailed houses illustrate the pride of their owners. Along very different lines we encounter Rolling Power, an almost Surrealist work by Charles Sheeler which alludes to the artist's work as an industrial photographer. The museum also owns a fine selection of American Impressionists.

Smith's European collection, emphasizing nineteenth- and twentieth-century French art, is rather wonderful. There are paintings by Henri Fantin-Latour, Puvis de Chavannes, Claude Monet, Edouard Manet, Edgar Degas, and Paul Cézanne, and many others. Major possessions include: Gustave Courbet's *La Toilette de La Morte;* a very large Degas, *Jephtha's Daughter;* and Cézanne's *La Route Tournante a La Roche Guyon.*

Smith is perhaps best known for the image of a lady with a bustle and a parasol promenading a monkey in a Paris park—a Georges Seurat sketch for his masterpiece *A Sunday on La Grande Jatte—1884,* owned by the Art Institute of Chicago (see p. 163). Seurat's work contrasts with the museum's well-known *Dodo and her Brother* by Ernst Kirchner. This pair is also dressed up in finery, Dodo wearing a yellow dress, long black gloves, and carrying a pink fan. The smirking expression of the faces and the violent colors used by the German Expressionists, however, makes the couple look almost sleazy.

No New England college museum would be complete without a selection of antiquities, Old Masters, sculptures, or contemporary art. Smith's collections of these are all fine and interesting.

PITTSFIELD

The Berkshire Museum

Address: 39 South Street (Route 7), Pittsfield, MA 01201

Telephone: (413) 443-7171

Web: www.berkshiremuseum.org

Hours: Tues–Sat 10–5; Sun 12–5. Closed Mon, except during July and Aug. Free tours Fri at 11 from middle of July through Aug.

Strengths: Hudson River School, portraits, genre paintings.

Special Events: Temporary exhibits.

Other: Interactive natural science exhibits, including aquarium with live animals. Music, movie, and theater programs. Snack bar (see Activities for Children). Museum shop.

Activities for Children: The museum is child-friendly. Children will also enjoy the Vend-O-Mat snack bar, a mechanical montage of recycled boilers and other "junk" that dispenses snacks.

Parking: On street, sometimes difficult.

A stegosaurus, or "hooded lizard," greets you as you approach the small Berkshire Museum in Pittsfield. The fiberglass dinosaur actually is a latecomer, having arrived during the 1940s. The Renaissance Revival building of the museum has been in the center of town since 1903. It is the gift of Zenas Crane, whose family still manufactures fine stationery and the paper for U.S. currency nearby. Crane wanted to "open a window" for his fellow humans. He decided to locate his museum in what was then a mill town, rather than in more sophisticated neighboring towns of Lee or Lenox.

Like Andrew Mellon, the donor of the National Gallery in Washington, D.C., Zenas Crane went shopping to fill his "Art and Science" museum. He must have had excellent taste, or else good advice. Many of the pictures on display are gems. The largest gallery of the museum is filled with paintings of the Hudson River School. They reinforce one another: A wild churning ocean is juxtaposed with a view of New York harbor as seen from the Brooklyn side. The massive Brooklyn Bridge, so beloved by later painters, including Georgia O'Keeffe and Joseph Stella, is already in place. The Manhattan skyline and the sailboat-filled harbor are very different from the way they appear today.

There are choice portraits by Ammi Phillips, John Singleton Copley, and John Singer Sargent. There is a good selection of genre paintings, a beloved form of anecdotal painting. The crowds that gather at the nearby Norman Rockwell Museum in Stockbridge are an indication that many of us still cherish this style. The European collection includes *The Adoration of the Magi* from 1477 by the Spanish painter Juan Pons and *The Flight to Egypt* by the Flemish painter Joachim Patinir.

The small collection of ancient art (glass, jewelry, pottery, a sarcophagus) is excellent. The huge plaster casts of the *Venus de Milo* and the *Nikke of Samothrace* are a reminder of what all museums used to be like. It turns out that the Calder family vacationed in the Berkshires, and the Cranes gave young Alexander his first commission. The Calder construction mobile is now in the theater of the museum, which has a lively performance program.

As its founder would have wished, the Berkshire Museum caters to families. Each winter it mounts a show with kids in mind. One featuring toys of the 1950s pleased both parents and kids and toured widely.

The museum also has a constantly revolving "refrigerator art" gallery in which art by children is displayed on thirteen colored refrigerator doors.

Kids especially will enjoy the aquarium, which features a New England tide pool and the cross section of a Berkshire lake in which the fish are watched over by a huge bullfrog.

SPRINGFIELD

Springfield Museums

Address: 220 State Street, Springfield, MA 01103

Telephone: (413) 263-8600

Web: www.quadrangle.org

Hours: Wed–Fri 12–5; Sat–Sun 11–4. Closed Mon, Tues, and major holidays. Extended hours during school vacations.

Strengths: Small, encyclopedic collection. American art. Prime examples of all major schools. Large collection of paintings by Erastus Salisbury Field. Comprehensive European collection with examples of Renaissance, Impressionist, and Post-Impressionist art. Large collection of cloisonné work.

Other: Restaurant. Museum shop.

Special Events: Temporary exhibits. Sept–May: Series of Sun family programs featuring live performances, art-making workshops, gallery games, appearance of special guests, and more. Events include: Dr. Seuss's birthday party; Meet Your Neighbors days with storytelling, and music and dance performances.

Activities for Children: See Special Events. The arts museums are small enough to appeal to children. When they get bored they can go to the Science Museum. A "stargazing" event is held at 7:30 p.m. at the Science Museum every first Fri. Other planetarium shows weekdays at 2:45.

Parking: Free, in museum lots; also on street.

Springfield developed a Center for the Arts long before it became fashionable to do so. Various civic groups formed a literary association in 1857, which endeavored to serve the entire population of the region. Today, four small museums (the George Walter Vincent Smith Art Museum, the Springfield Science Museum, the Springfield Museum of Fine Arts, and the Connecticut Valley Historical Museum) and a library surround a quadrangle watched over by Augustus Saint-

Gaudens's *The Puritan,* representing Deacon Samuel Chapin one of the founders of Springfield.

Springfield's art collection is distributed between two buildings: the George Walter Vincent Smith Art Museum (GWVS), a Victorian building dating from 1896, and the neoclassical Museum of Fine Arts (MFA), built in 1933.

The MFA, a gift from Dr. and Mrs. James Philip Gray, is an elegant structure filled with good art, especially American paintings. Upon entering the visitor is greeted by *Historical Monument of the American Republic, 1867–1888* by Erastus Salisbury Field, one of the museum's thirty works by this American folk painter best known for portraits. The enormous canvas depicts our nation's history in a series of ten almost surrealist towers. There are works by John Singleton Copley, Gilbert Stuart, Frederick Church, Albert Bierstadt, George Inness, Norman Rockwell, Georgia O'Keeffe, Frank Stella, and Childe Hassam, as well as by lesser-known artists. Some paintings have a curious history. When considering the acquisition of Winslow Homer's *Promenade on the Beach* (1880) the prospective buyer was shocked by the fact that the two fully clad young women were not chaperoned. Fortunately, a letter from Homer about the romantic scene was reassuring enough to clinch the sale.

Also at the MFA is Springfield's small and choice European collection. One gallery is filled with Italian Renaissance works, another provides examples of French Impressionists. An atypical seascape by Paul Gauguin is particularly appealing.

Springfield's GWVS Art Museum demonstrates what museums were like at the turn of the last century. Smith (1832–1925), a rich industrialist, and his wife, Belle Townsley, were passionate collectors. He retired at age thirty-five and assembled 6,000 objects including paintings, sculptures, snuff boxes, textiles, Japanese Shinto shrines, weapons, and other art objects. The Victorian structure he erected for these treasures still has a large gallery filled with plaster casts. Examining copies of the world's most beloved masterpieces—the frieze of the Parthenon or Michelangelo's *Moses* or his tomb for the Medicis in Florence—one becomes aware of the sheer size of these works. The museum's antiquated style may obscure the GWVS's real treasures such as America's largest collection of cloisonné work. The ashes of the Smiths, who visited "their" museum daily, are discretely buried in one of its walls.

STOCKBRIDGE

The Norman Rockwell Museum

Address: Route 183, Stockbridge, MA 01262

Telephone: (413) 298-4100

Web: www.nrm.org

Hours: *May–Oct:* Daily 10–5. *Nov–April:* Weekdays 1–4, weekends 10–5. Closed New Year's, Thanksgiving, and Christmas days.

Strength: Illustrations.

Special Events: Temporary exhibits showcasing aspects of Norman Rockwell's work, as well as that of other American illustrators.

Other: Museum shop. Extensive grounds. Rockwell's studio is open from May–Oct.

Parking: Free, on site.

Norman Rockwell's museum looks like his paintings: a pleasant New England town hall sitting on a well-manicured lawn. Visitors are encouraged to use the spacious grounds to picnic, stroll, and play. There are trails to explore the thirty-six scenic acres overlooking the Housatonic River and the Berkshire Hills.

Few artists have generated as much controversy as Norman Rockwell. His illustrations, many of them covers for the *Saturday Evening Post*—322 in all—depict idyllic scenes of what Rockwell himself called "the commonplaces of America . . . boys batting flies on vacant lots; little girls playing jacks on the front steps, old men plodding home at twilight, umbrella in hand." Rockwell was a true patriot, supporting Franklin D. Roosevelt and the nation's war effort. More than four million posters of the *Four Freedoms* were sold during World War Two, putting $132 million into America's war chest.

Norman Rockwell was born in New York City in 1894. From early on he knew that he wanted to become an illustrator. He had a special gift for reproducing what he saw and his classmates described him as

In his *Triple Self-Portrait*, part of the permanent collection of The Norman Rockwell Museum in Stockbridge, Massachusetts, the artist pokes fun at himself.

"the kid with the camera eyes." He quit high school and studied at the National Academy of Design and the Art Student's League. Success came early. When he was twenty-two he did his first cover for the *Saturday Evening Post*. In 1953, he moved to Stockbridge, where he died in 1978.

There was never any doubt that Norman Rockwell was a superior illustrator, on a par with Howard Pyle (see the Delaware Art Museum, p. 118, and the Brandywine River Museum, p. 348). The realistic details of his pictures—the texture of the clothes, the reflections in a mirror, the views through the window—are amazing. Rockwell, however, was never beloved by the art world. The criticism was directed at his cloying, idealized, overly sweet style. Rockwell himself characterized it as his "sledgehammer sentimentality." His pictures lack conflict, controversy, and bite. Real life is not the way Rockwell depicted it. Even the illustration showing an African American child going off to school protected by U.S. marshals does not give a hint of the turmoil that accompanied integration. The man illustrating free speech in the *Four Freedoms* series looks like a film star.

Rockwell's many fans are proof that escapism, in art and elsewhere, is also a necessity. His admirers include not only the humble folks he liked to paint, but also prominent people like writer John Updike and movie-maker Steven Spielberg.

And the crowds that visit his museum do not complain. Visitors by the thousands enjoy looking at the pleasures of simple life: *Saying Grace, Girl With a Black Eye, Home for Thanksgiving* (showing a soldier, on leave, peeling potatoes with his apron-clad mom), *Girl at the Mirror,* and, best of all, Rockwell's *Triple Self-Portrait.* The museum itself was created by popular demand when visitors to the Stockbridge Historical Society, which showed a few Rockwell paintings, swelled beyond that museum's small capacity.

At long last the art establishment too may revise its view of the painter. In the new millennium, 70 of his paintings and 322 covers for the *Saturday Evening Post* will go on Norman Rockwell's first national tour, stopping in seven major museums.

WILLIAMSTOWN

Sterling and Francine Clark Art Institute

Address: 225 South Street, Williamstown, MA 01267

Telephone: (413) 458-2303

Web: www.clarkart.edu

Hours: Tues–Sun 10–5. Open Presidents', Memorial, Labor, and Columbus days. *July–Aug:* also open Mon. Closed New Year's, Thanksgiving, and Christmas days.

Strengths: French Impressionists, especially Renoir. Old Masters. Homer, Sargent, Cassat, and Remington. Vast collection of silver, porcelain, prints, and photographs.

Special Events: Indoor and outdoor concerts. Special lectures. Intriguing temporary shows.

Other: Free gallery talks July and Aug at 3. Recorded tour. Extensive library open to the public without prior arrangement. Extensive grounds and parklike lawns available for hikes and picnics; trail map available at information desk. Café all year, restaurant in summer. Museum shop with good selection of art books.

Activities for Children: Family guide at information desk, and special audiotape.

Parking: On site.

Irises and peonies surround the broad marble steps that lead up to a gleaming Greek temple that houses the Sterling and Francine Clark Art Institute (the Clark) in Williamstown. The serene surroundings are appropriate to the collection, which was assembled to provide visual pleasure. The original building of the Clark dates from the 1950s. Access today is via the more modern (1973, 1998) granite addition.

The Clarks were childless. When the time came to donate their art they chose Williamstown because they felt that a small rural community was a safer place than a big city. They also liked the proximity of Williams College and its strong art department, which in turn was strengthened by the arrival of the Clark. Today the two institutions are a major force in the art world. The Clark has an extensive art library (150,000 books, many of them rare and illustrated, and 135,000 slides). The library, which also subscribes to art magazines and newspapers, is open to the public.

Sterling Clark was one of the heirs to the Singer Sewing Machine fortune. He had two major passions: collecting art and racing horses. He owned Never Say Die, the first American horse ever to win the Epsom Derby in England.

He started to collect around 1900 when he was twenty-three years old. He had strong opinions and, like Henry Clay Frick, only collected for his own pleasure. In the beginning that meant Old Masters. On a trip to France he met Francine, an actress at the Comédie Françise, and they married in 1919. After that the couple most often bought French nineteenth-century paintings. According to David S. Brooke (in *Antiques*, October 1997), "Clark valued his wife's opinion highly and bought nothing without her approval." The Clarks' collection is a very personal statement of their taste. Throughout their life the Clarks had a strong preference for certain painters: Auguste Renoir, Edgar Degas, Winslow Homer, and John Singer Sargent.

Visitors enter the Granite Building—as opposed to the older Marble Building—via the Court, a large bookstore cum café. They are greeted by a huge mural by Mexican artist Rufino Tamayo that seems at odds with the Clark's well-mannered collection. Indeed, the *Reclining Nude* was commissioned by Smith College, but somehow outgrew its allotted space and is now is on permanent loan to the Clark.

American nineteenth-century paintings occupy the galleries on the ground floor of the Granite Building. Clark bought his first Winslow Homer in 1916, and his last in 1955, the year the museum opened. The Homer collection, considered one of the finest in existence, represents all of Homer's many moods. There are representational pictures of the West, the lyrical *An October Day*, depicting the sun setting over a churning surf sea in Maine, and *Playing a Fish*, an introspective scene of a fisherman waiting for his prey.

More treasures await us in the Marble Building. Paintings are carefully arranged in galleries of varying sizes. Fireplaces, Oriental rugs, and exquisite furniture provide a homelike atmosphere. Old Masters, including portraits by Hans Memling and Jan Gossaert, are in a room that overlooks a Matisse-like water-lily pond. Piero della Francesca's *Virgin and Child Enthroned, with Four Angels* (one of only three examples of the painter in America), Domenico Ghirlandaio's saucy young lady painted against a formal Italian landscape, and a golden Sienese altarpiece by Ugolino da Siena, make you long for Italy. The estate of Herbert H. Lehman, a former governor of New York and graduate of Williams College, donated some of these Old Masters to the Clark, and the museum continues to acquire works that strengthen the collection and conform to the spirit of the donors.

The Clarks were partial to the Impressionists. A large gallery is filled with paintings by Renoir (more than thirty), about whom Sterling Clark wrote in his diary: "What a great master!!!! Perhaps the greatest that ever lived." Other nineteenth-century French painters were not neglected. There are marvelous examples of Edgar Degas, Claude Monet, Pierre Bonnard, Camille Pissaro, Paul Gauguin, Henri de Toulouse-Lautrec, and many others. Some of these works, such as Degas's sculpture of the *Little Dancer Aged Fourteen*, are particularly beloved. Most recently the Clark acquired the Jacques-Louis David *Portrait of Count Henri-Amédée de Tourenne*, painted in Brussels in 1816 when both count and painter were in exile. The Clark has an extensive collection of prints and drawings (2,000). Because photography started to become an important art form during the nineteenth century, the Clark is acquiring early photographs; a selection of the silvery and gold early prints is on view.

The Clark also owns many whimsical objects. There are two enormous concert grand pianos. The first, made by Lawrence Alma-Tadema during the 1880s, is an overornate affair standing on legs decorated by sphinx; the second a Steinway commissioned from the Hamburg factory in 1912 by Francine Clark for her own use. There is an extensive, excellent collection of silver from the 1930s and 1940s—Sterling Clark seems to have spent from forty to fifty thousand dollars on it annually. There also is an eclectic collection of porcelain.

The Clarks were mindful of the close interrelationship of the pleasures offered by nature and by art. The institute is located on 130 acres of Berkshire land, one of the East's prime recreational areas. There are cows, ponds, hills, and trees to be explored on well-maintained nature trails.

Williams College Museum of Art

Address: 15 Lawrence Hall Drive (Route 2), Williamstown, MA 01267

Telephone: (413) 597-2429

Web: www.williams.edu/WCMA

Hours: Tues–Sat 10–5; Sun 1–5. Closed Mon (except Memorial, Labor, and Columbus days) and New Year's, Thanksgiving, and Christmas days.

Strengths: Small encyclopedic museum. Modern and contemporary art. Prendergast estate.

Special Events: Excellent temporary shows.

Activities for Children: Excellent activity booklets for children (5–10) to explore the museum. Annual Family Day with hands-on activities throughout entire museum. Also frequent after-school programs (3:30–4:30) for children 4–11 accompanied by an adult.

Parking: Limited, in front of museum. Additional in campus lots, e.g., behind Thompson Memorial Chapel.

The Williams College Museum of Art (WCMA) has two faces. The first, fronting Main Street, consists of Lawrence Hall, a two-story octagon designed in 1846 by Thomas S. Tefft; the other, a three-story contemporary structure designed by Charles Moore, faces the back. On the inside the two halves mesh perfectly, each dramatic in its own way. The new building features a soaring three-story atrium with sleek columns, open stairs, and a flying bridge. The older portion retains its grand stairs. They ascend to a stunning, perfectly round, Greek Revival rotunda whose dome is supported with ionic columns. From these windows one has a view of Thompson Memorial Chapel and the stately trees of this typical New England campus.

The museum has been in existence since 1926. It has been lovingly endowed by the college alumni and by now owns good collections and a mix of eclectic treasures. Its collections of Ancient, Asian, Romanesque, and Gothic art are helpful since these subjects are mostly missing from its neighbor, the Clark Art Institute (p. 223). While Thomas Krens was a curator of the WCMA, he was instrumental in founding MASS MoCA (see p. 213), seven miles down the road, as a showplace for the large-scale contemporary art that could not be accommodated in Williamstown.

Among WCMA's older American paintings, note William Morris Hunt's large view of Niagara Falls, whose shimmering waters so entranced the Hudson River School painters, portraits by Thomas Eakins, and works by George Inness, Winslow Homer, and George Bellows. It may be of interest to compare the traditional view of Niagara Falls with Rube Goldberg's cartoon entitled *Professor Butts Goes Over Niagara Falls in a Collapsible Ash-Can.*

Many of the museum's American paintings and sculptures were the gift of Lawrence H. Bloedel, who divided his collection between the Whitney Museum of American Art and WCMA. Among many excellent works given by Bloedel you will find Lyonel Feininger's *Mill in Autumn,* characterized by the artist's Cubist buildings fractured by light, and Edward Hopper's *Morning in a City,* considered one of the artist's major works. The image of the naked woman dressing in a spartan room while contemplating the shuttered windows across the street spell loneliness and despair. Grant Wood's painting *Death on the Road,* in which a car races toward a lonely house amid cross-shaped telephone poles, is a chilling reminder of one of America's leading causes of death.

The museum's unique possession is the estate (379 works) of Maurice (1858–1924) and Charles (1863–1948) Prendergast, given to WCMA by Eugénie Van Kemmel Prendergast, Charles's widow. Born in Newfoundland and educated in Boston, Maurice went to Paris in 1886. Back in New York he exhibited with the future "Eight" or Ashcan School in 1908 and at the 1913 show at the Armory. Maurice Prendergast is considered a member of this group in name but not in style. The artist's joyous view of a happy humanity, frolicking during an eternal summer on beaches, and at festivals, or walking about with umbrellas and baby carriages, is unique and unmistakable. Prendergast used short strokes of pure color like the Pointillists. Charles was an artist too, making elaborate carved and painted frames and furniture. He was a staunch supporter of his deaf and sensitive brother. (Also see The Terra Museum of American Art, in Chicago p. 167.)

After its repeated expansion the WCMA is now spacious. However, it devotes many of its new galleries to excellent temporary shows, so many of its treasures, even the Prendergasts, may be in storage.

WORCESTER

Worcester Art Museum

Address: 55 Salisbury Street, Worcester, MA 01609

Telephone: (508) 799-4406

Web: www.worcesterart.org

Hours: Wed–Fri 11–5; Sat 10–5; Sun 11–5. Closed Mon, Tues, and New Year's, Easter, Independence, Thanksgiving, and Christmas days.

Strengths: Encyclopedic. Roman mosaics. American art. American decorative art, including more than 100 silver objects made by Paul Revere.

Other: Audio tours. Lectures. Garden court with tables, some sculpture, grass, and trees is ideal for relaxing, reading, or running around. Restaurant. Museum shop.

Activities for Children: Activity/treasure hunt booklets available at the front desk. Excellent Art Discovery Gallery.

Parking: On site.

As you enter the Worcester Art Museum (WAM), you almost step onto one of its most precious possessions, *The Hunt Mosaic* (ca. 559 C.E.), which, according to the museum, is the largest Roman mosaic floor in North America. Bears, lions, tigers, antelopes, goats, and wolves are hunted by handsome youths amid fruit trees. Even though it represents a hunt, the mosaic, with its muted colors, is cheerful and warm like a carpet. It endows the large Renaissance Court of the museum with a palatial atmosphere. Indeed, the Hunt mosaic once adorned a private house in Daphne, a suburb of Antioch, a large city in Asia Minor. The mosaic is in Worcester because the museum cosponsored archeological digs there during the 1930s.

Worcester, the second largest city in Massachusetts, has had a museum since 1896, when Stephen Salisbury III and fifty of his friends decided that their burgeoning industrial town needed one. A modest collection was exhibited in a small Classic Revival style building. Within five years the museum was bequeathed 3,000 Japanese prints and paintings. Other gifts arrived. Stephen Salisbury III died in 1905, leaving the museum a treasure trove of American portraits, silver, and furniture, as well as an endowment of $3 million—an enormous sum at the time—which enabled the museum to assemble small but high-quality encyclopedic collections.

Wandering through the invariably intimate, well-lit galleries you encounter a twelfth-century medieval chapter house from Le Bas-Nueil in France, and exquisite Romanesque and Gothic sculpture and stained glass panels from about 1205. There are excellent small collections of Egyptian, Sumerian, Assyrian, Greek, Persian, Japanese, and Indian art.

The collections of European and American art are comprehensive. Here as elsewhere in the museum, labels are very informative. Note *The Last Supper and the Agony in the Garden,* from about 1300, which is a rare fresco from an Italian church. Quentin Massys's *The Rest on the Flight into Egypt* combines detailed Flemish techniques with a typical Italian landscape. Andrea del Sarto's *Saint John the Baptist* is one of the few examples of works by this artist in America. Judith Leyster's *A Game of Tric-Trac* is a work by the only woman artist recognized as a professional in Holland during the seventeenth century. The *Portrait of the Artist's Daughters* is a charming work by Thomas Gainsborough, best known for his portraits of high society.

As do most New England museums, the WAM owns excellent early American portraits. *Mrs. Elizabeth Freake and Baby Mary* (1671–1674) and *John Freake,* painted around 1671 by an anonymous artist, are much beloved. Mr. Freake's lace collar, ruffled sleeves, and long white gloves contrast with his wife's demure clothing. Thomas Smith's *Self-Portrait* (1680) is America's earliest known self-portrait. A view of prosperous looking fields, trees, and two almost imperceptible church spires is a panorama of Worcester in 1800 by Ralph Earl, a native of the city. Earl's full-size portrait of an English gentlemen and his two hunting dogs hangs in the same gallery. Of it the painter wrote to John Trumbell (see the Yale University Art Gallery, p. 116, and the Wadsworth Atheneum, p. 108), "It is the best I ever painted."

The collection moves with the times. There are paintings by John Singer Sargent, Winslow Homer, George Inness, Thomas Eakins, Childe Hassam, Mary Cassatt, Paul Gauguin, and even two works by Claude Monet.

Early-twentieth-century American artists are well represented and well exhibited. A gallery with small paintings by Georgia O'Keeffe, Milton Avery, Arthur Dove, and Jacob Lawrence is a gem. There is a Campbell's soup can by Andy Warhol, a black and white abstraction by Franz Kline, the *Great American Nude #36* by Tom Wesselman, and a construction by Louise Nevelson.

The decorative arts display was redesigned and expanded in 1999. A deep red background highlights over a hundred silver objects made by Paul Revere. The display includes thirty of the forty-five pieces of the graceful Rococo-style *Paine Service,* crafted in 1773. The service, Revere's largest commission ever, was ordered by Worcester resident Dr. William Paine for his bride, Lois Orne. Luck would have it that a painting of the future Mrs. Paine, aged two, hangs nearby. The fact that both portrait and wedding gift have come down to us through the generations is a reassuring token of permanence in our mobile society.

Michigan

BLOOMFIELD HILLS

Cranbrook Art Museum

Address: 39221 Woodward Avenue, Bloomfield Hills, MI 48303

Telephone: (248) 645-3323

Web: www.cranbrookart.edu/museum

Hours: *Sept–May:* Tue–Sun 11–5, Thurs until 8; *June–Aug:* Tues–Sun 11–5, Fri until 10. Closed Mon and major holidays.

Strength: 20th-century art and design, including Art Deco, Modernism, and the avant-garde.

Special Events: 5 annual temporary exhibitions of cutting-edge work by contemporary art and design frontrunners in all media.

Other: Saarinen House. Network Gallery, showcasing the work of the Academy's graduate students, alumni, and faculty. Lectures, films, and concerts stressing contemporary works.

Activities for Children: The museum is child-friendly.

Parking: On site.

In 1904, George G. Booth, publisher of the *Detroit News,* and his wife, Ellen Scripps Booth, purchased a huge tract of land in Bloomfield Hills, twenty miles outside the city. Four years later, Albert Kahn, Detroit's up-and-coming architect (see The Detroit Institute of Arts, p. 233) built them a house. Much attention was lavished on the park surrounding the house. A scion of English craftsmen, Booth named the estate Cranbrook after his father's birthplace in England. Booth was an avid supporter of the arts, including the Detroit Institute of Arts. In particular he was captivated by America's Arts and Crafts Movement and its European counterparts, William Morris, the Bauhaus, and the Wiener Werkstätte. He conceived the idea of creating a planned art and design community in Michigan after visiting the American Academy in Rome in 1922. To this end he contacted Eliel Saarinen, the well-known Finnish architect, who conveniently was then working in the Midwest. Saarinen and his wife, Loja, a weaver, arrived in Cranbrook in 1925 to develop a tripartite institution that was to include a school (kindergarten through graduate school), atelier space, and an art colony. Certain items were manufactured for commercial distribution. The concept was a success. Today the products of the Cranbrook Academy of Art's faculty and students are renowned in the design world, particularly the *Eames Lounge Chair and Ottoman* created by Charles and Ray Eames, who met and married at Cranbrook.

Eliel Saarinen headed the Cranbrook Educational Community for twenty-five years. During that time he built four of the institution's major buildings, including, in 1942, its museum. Today the museum is filled with furniture, prints, metalwork, contemporary art, sculpture, and Saarinen's drawings, displayed in the tasteful manner for which Cranbrook is known.

Most satisfying, however, is the land that surrounds the edifices. Landscaping it was Booth's priority and it blossomed under Saarinen's reign. In *Design in America—the Cranbrook Vision*, Neil Harris compares the landscape of Saarinen's native Finland with that of the Midwest, "[both] dominated by the presence of nature, harsh winters, the abundance of summer sunlight." Today the park consists of extensive formal gardens, natural woods, lakes, fields, and waterways.

Cranbrook's first sculptor in residence was Carl Milles, a Swede. Milles was a student of Auguste Renoir, whose fluidity he transformed and translated into sinuous, playful figures. The academy owns the largest collection of his work outside Sweden, most notably *Europa and the Bull, Dancing Girls*, and the *Orpheus Fountain*, a circle of faunlike figures standing just outside the museum. There are other significant works, including *Sculptured Ape, The Thinker* by Marshall Fredericks, a Michigan resident; Mark DiSuvero's *La Petite Clef*; and works by Michael Hall and Alice Aycock.

Most telling of Cranbrook's overwhelming influence on American architecture and decorative art is the lovingly restored Saarinen House, designed and built by Saarinen in 1930. Eliel and Loja paid attention to every minute detail. Her rug, a geometric masterwork woven in beige, orange, and brick, fills the center of the large living room. The curtains and a wall hanging over the fireplace are also hers; he designed the torchières, the peacock andirons, and the tiles that face the fireplace. Like Frank Lloyd Wright, Saarinen took care to utilize readily available industrial materials.

The Saarinen contribution did not stop with Cranbrook. Eliel Saarinen also designed the Des Moines Art Center (p. 174). His son Eero became an influential architect as well (the Milwaukee Art Museum—p. 413, the St. Louis Arch, the TWA Terminal at Kennedy Airport). Together father and son designed the music shed at Tanglewood. Eero's wife, Aline, is the author of *The Proud Possessors*, so often quoted in this guide.

DETROIT

The Detroit Institute of Arts

Address: 5200 Woodward Avenue, Detroit, MI 48202

Telephone: (313) 833-7900

Web: www.dia.org

Hours: Wed–Fri 11–4, Sat–Sun 11–5; first Fri 11–9. Closed Mon, Tues, and some holidays.

Strengths: Encyclopedic. Excellent European, American, ancient Middle-Eastern, and decorative arts collections. Diego Rivera murals. Gothic chapel. Period rooms.

Special Events: Films. Lectures. Temporary exhibits.

Other: Restaurants. Museum shop.

Activities for Children: Extensive materials including self-guided tours to various collections of the museum and the Rivera court. A game entitled Mystery of the Five Fragments, which prompts children to find works of art throughout the museum. Interactive computer guides.

Parking: Cultural Center Garage (Woodward and Farnsworth); lot on Frederick Douglass between John R and Bush Streets. On weekends, parking is also available in John R Lot, adjacent to the museum.

The Detroit Institute of Arts (DIA) was founded in 1885, a short eleven years before the commercial production of the first automobile. In 1889, the year the DIA's original fortress-like building went up, the museum received its first major gift: eight Old Master paintings from newspaperman James A. Scripps. Another early gift was General Custer's Cheyenne shield, presaging the DIA's multi-ethnic approach to art.

The manufacture of cars became the mainstay of Detroit's economy and a symbol of American culture. By 1911, Ford produced 1,000 cars per day. The Dodges, the Fords, the tire-making Firestones, Charles Freer, and other captains of industry enriched the DIA while the city assumed operating costs, financed construction, and established an acquisition fund. Education was always a crucial component of the DIA. In 1893, director Armand Griffith initiated Sunday lectures that attracted a thousand listeners. Visits by classes of school children started in 1905.

During the Depression, Edsel Ford commissioned murals from Diego Rivera now in the Garden Court of The Detroit Institute of Arts. A detail shows a cameo of the donor and the museum's director William R. Valentiner.

Detroit's wealth continued to grow. During the 1920s an entirely new Art Deco–type building designed by Paul Cret and the well-known Detroit architect Albert Kahn was erected. By then the trustees of the DIA had appointed a professionally trained director. William R. Valentiner arrived in Detroit in time to have an impact on the design of the new galleries, installing authentic period rooms and a French Gothic chapel with stained glass windows. The influence of the German-born art historian and scholar was to extend to other American museums as well, notably in Los Angeles (see Los Angeles County Museum of Art, p. 60) and Raleigh, North Carolina (see The North Carolina Museum of Art, p. 320).

Many of the museum's choice possessions date from the 1920s. A self-portrait became the first Vincent van Gogh to enter a public collection in the United States. Paintings by Claude Monet, Henri Matisse, Paul Cézanne, Eugène Boudin, Edgar Degas, and John Singer Sargent, as well as etchings, lithographs, and woodcuts by artists ranging from Albrecht Dürer to James Whistler, entered the collection. The museum enlarged its holdings of Old Masters, acquiring among other works, *St. Jerome in His Study* by Jan Van Eyck, *The Wedding Dance* by Breugel the Elder, and a Madonna and Child by Giovanni Bellini. The DIA is also an important repository of African, especially Benin, art, and the proud possessor of the *Dragon of Babylon*, a tiled panel of the Ishtar Gate (Assyrian).

The Depression was particularly hard on Detroit, and the city had to curtail its support for the museum. Fortunately, many private donors came to the rescue. In 1930, Valentiner met Diego Rivera, the Mexican muralist, who happened to be interested in Detroit and its industry. Edsel Ford commissioned murals for the museum, to be painted on site. The murals, which now fill the museum's Garden Court, depict American industry, the assembly line, the generation of electricity, women, and even the birth of a child. A small cartoon shows the "donors," Edsel Ford and William Valentiner. Furor greeted the unveiling of this masterpiece. Some considered the murals pornographic, others objected to Rivera's Communist leanings, most were offended by the fact that U.S. dollars went to a foreigner while artists "at home" starved. Fortunately the work survived and did not meet the fate of the mural at Rockefeller Center in New York, which was destroyed because of conflict between patron and painter.

Robert H. Tannahill, the wealthy scion of Detroit's J. L. Hudson's department store fortune, was another one of the charismatic Valentiner's friends. Tannahill built a superior collection of Post-Impressionists (Cézanne, van Gogh, Paul Gauguin, Matisse, Constantin Brancusi, Pablo Picasso, and others) and—under the guidance of Valentiner—German Expressionists. Tannahill donated 450 art objects to the DIA during his lifetime and left the museum most of his worldly goods, including another 400 works of art.

Eventually, Detroit's middle class abandoned the inner city, and the museum fell upon hard times, from which it is now slowly recovering. The DIA is the United States's sixth largest museum. I would give it three stars, meaning that it deserves a trip of its own.

Minnesota

MINNEAPOLIS

The Minneapolis Institute of Arts

Address: 2400 Third Avenue South, Minneapolis, MN 55404

Telephone: (612) 870-3200

Web: www.artsMIA.org

Hours: Tues–Wed, Sat 10–5; Thurs–Fri 10–9; Sun 12–5. Closed Mon and Independence, Thanksgiving, and Christmas days. Public tours Tues, Wed, Fri at 2; Thurs at 2 and 7; Sat, Sun at 1 and 2.

Strengths: Encyclopedic museum with excellent European, American, Asian, African, and Judaica collections. Period rooms including a Chinese scholar's study and the hallway of Frank Lloyd Wright's Francis W. Little House.

Special Events: Temporary exhibits.

Other: Interactive computers in the museum's front lobby help visitors locate special galleries. Interactive learning stations provide information about specific works of art and other pertinent information. Restaurants. Museum shop.

Activities for Children: Family day one Sun a month 12–5, with activities related to specific themes. Family Center, with child-friendly computers that teach children about art and allow them to create their own pictures, educational computer games, and play area with soft sculptures, tables, chairs, games, and books. Nursing room. Snack area.

Parking: On site.

At the time of America's great westward expansion, Minneapolis became an important industrial center. In 1883, the transplanted Easterners who built its flour mills and railroads decided that their new home needed fine art, and so the Society of Fine Arts was founded. At first the fledgling museum was housed in the public library. In 1908, financier Clinton Morrison donated his ten-acre homestead, Villa Rosa, to the museum. Other benefactors provided superior works of art and funds to erect a building. The New York firm of McKim, Mead & White was asked to build a splendid marble-clad museum reminiscent of Europe's great palaces. The museum opened its doors in 1915, and still shares in the vision of its forebears. The building underwent a major renovation in 1998, and visitors now not only enjoy the grandeur of the past but also today's increased art expertise and technological know-how. The "rebirth" restored some of the gracious features of the building that had been lost over the years, especially the ceiling of the old rotunda.

A healthy endowment and the good taste of its benefactors yielded a superior collection of European and American art. Significant works include some Old Masters, Jean Clouet's portrait *Princess Charlotte of France*, Rembrandt's *Lucretia*, Courbet's *Deer in the Forest*, Nicholas Poussin's *Death of Germanicus*, van Gogh's *Olive Trees*, Monet's *Grainstack: Sun in the Mist*, and prime examples of all major European and American schools of painting.

The MIA takes pride in its Department of Asian Art, which occupies twenty-two galleries. According to museum literature, "Nowhere out-side Asia itself—will you find a collection of Asian treasures as varied, vast and valuable as at the MIA." Among other treasures it features the T. B. Walker Memorial Collection of Chinese jades, the largest in North America, which includes the *Jade Mountain*, a gigantic 640-pound jade sculpture. There are also three Chinese period rooms: a reception hall, a scholar's study, and a garden.

Among the other period rooms, the most touching is a hallway of Frank Lloyd Wright's Francis W. Little House, whose large living room can be seen in New York's Metropolitan Museum of Art (see p. 293). The house was built in 1908 on Minnesota's Lake Minnetonka, which is evoked in a trompe l'oeil mural glimpsed through Wright's leaded windows.

The MIA also features ancient art. There is a wonderful old mosaic from Turkey featuring an elephant attacking a feline. There are excellent examples of art from Africa, the Americas, the Pacific Islands, and Native America as well as textiles, decorative arts, and Judaica.

Since its early days the MIA has been considered avant-garde. Even though the works were deemed to be "monstrosities" at the time, in 1923 the museum organized an exhibition of Post-Impressionist paint-ings featuring works by Henri Matisse, Pablo Picasso, Georges Braque, and André Derain. Today the MIA owns representative samples of twentieth-century art. Max Beckmann's monumental triptych *Blind Man's Buff* dominates a gallery devoted to German Expressionists.

Walker Art Center

Address: Vineland Place, Minneapolis, MN 55403

Telephone: (612) 375-7600

Web: www.walkerart.org

Hours: Tues–Wed, Fri–Sat 10–5; Thurs 10–9; Sun 11–5. Closed Mon and major holidays.

Strengths: Seminal paintings of the early 20th-century; Pop Art.

Special Events: A very active performance program, presenting dance, music, theater, films, and video events.

Other: Classes, lectures, tours, and workshops for people of all ages. Minneapolis Sculpture Garden adjacent to the museum. Restaurant: Pleasant indoor cafeteria and outdoor roof garden, with spectacular views of downtown skyline and sculpture garden. Museum shop.

Parking: Pay, on site.

The Walker Art Center, like many American museums, began as the collection of a single man: Thomas Barlow Walker, a successful Minnesotan lumberman. At the turn of the century he assembled a collection of Old Masters, paintings of the French Barbizon School, and American landscapes as well as art from Asia, Syrian glass, Greek vases, and American Indian pottery. His eye was not always discerning. When he offered to donate his collection to the Minneapolis Society of Fine Arts, it was refused.

Hurt, T. B. Walker opened his own museum first in his home, then in a specially erected Moorish-style palace—the Walker Art Gallery. The patriarch died in 1927, but his son and grandchildren continued to operate the museum, which managed to squeak through the Depression and was rescued by the Federal Arts Project, which appointed Daniel Defenbacher as director.

Fortunately for the museum, Hudson Walker remained fascinated by his grandfather's gallery. Together with Defenbacher, Hudson Walker built a contemporary collection now housed in a modern brick building designed by architect Edward Larrabee Barnes. The museum adjoins the Guthrie Theater, with which it shares a huge lobby partially occupied by a large Alexander Calder stabile. The flexible space of the Walker easily accommodates the large contemporary works the museum favors. The galleries flow into one another via shallow stairs, which allows for pleasant ambling.

The Walker mostly displays twentieth-century art, with major emphasis on Pop Art. Andy Warhol's *Sixteen Jackies* greets visitors with their frozen expression, and Donald Duck tells Mickey Mouse about his fishing exploits in Roy Lichtenstein's *Artist's Studio No. 1.* Huge canvases by Robert Rauschenberg, Barnett Newman, and Jasper Johns are displayed throughout.

The most beloved and best-known possession of the museum, however, is Franz Marc's *The Large Blue Horses*, dating from 1911. Unlike many other German Expressionists, Marc did not depict depraved, corrupt society but mostly painted animals. His work swirls with the primary colors. Some other, older works of the Walker include Lyonel Feininger's *Church of the Minorities II*, a version of Joseph Stella's *Brooklyn Bridge*, John Sloan's *South Beach Bathers*, George Luks's *Breaker Boy of Shenandoah, Pa.*, and Edward Hopper's *Office at Night.*

The top floor of the museum houses a restaurant that offers views of downtown Minneapolis. You can sit on a terrace and admire Claes Oldenburg's sculpture of a giant yellow Mickey Mouse in contrast to the many surrounding churches, one of which is reminiscent of the Sacré Coeur in Paris's Montmartre, making you reflect on the variability of human taste.

The Walker's eleven-acre urban sculpture garden, one of Minneapolis's most beloved attractions, has a collection as important as that of the museum. Green hedges frame familiar sculptures by Henry Moore, Isamu Noguchi, Georg Kolbe, Marino Marini, and others. Claes Oldenburg and Coosje van Bruggen's joyful *Spoonbridge and Cherry* sit in an open meadow.

The garden's greenhouse looks as if it dates from Victorian times, but it was built only ten years ago. The Cowles Conservatory is filled with plants, palms, and flowers. Live birds chirp among the leaves, and a huge sculpted fish with glistening, translucent scales and fins sits in a pool surrounded by aquatic plants. Architect/sculptor Frank Gehry constructed the fish in 1986. On a small plaque affixed to the rim of the pool he explains: "In Toronto, when I was very young, my grandmother and I went to a Jewish market to buy carp." The carp was stored in the bathtub until, to young Gehry's great sadness, it was made into gefillte fish.

The Frederick R. Weisman Art Museum

Address: 333 E. River Road, Minneapolis, MN 55455

Telephone: (612) 625-9494

Web: hudson.acad.UMN.edu

Hours: Tues–Wed, Fri 10–5; Thurs 10–8; Sat–Sun 11–5. Closed Mon and major holidays.

Strengths: American art from the first half of the 20th century. Murals from the 1939 New York World's Fair.

Special Events: Special exhibits often stressing the history of architecture.

Other: Museum shop. Lectures, films, and special performances.

Activities for Children: Stimulating self-guided-tour response forms intended to help young people articulate their response to specific artworks.

Parking: Pay garage, under museum.

"Baby Bilbao," as Frank Gehry's building for the University of Minnesota's Frederick R. Weisman Art Museum (WAM) has been called, sits on the banks of the Mississippi. The bays, turrets, curves, angles, overhangs, and windows of this fantastic steel-clad structure reflect the light from the water and the sky. Gehry, as one learns while visiting Minneapolis, is also a sculptor, a fact that may account for his extraordinary architectural creations.

The astonishment engendered by the WAM continues as you enter the building. Trusses and large beams crisscross the open space and from the windows you never tire of looking at the skyline of downtown Minneapolis, America's fabled Mississippi River, and the massive Washington Bridge. In 1934, University of Minnesota president Lotus Coffman founded a teaching museum. Hudson D. Walker, grandson of Thomas Barlow Walker (see previous entry) became the first director

"Baby Bilbao" is the affectionate name of The Frederick R. Weisman Art Museum at the University of Minnesota in Minneapolis, designed by Frank Gehry.

and a major donor to the teaching museum. Frederick (Fred) R. Weisman, a Minneapolis native whose business interests included mining, banking, a race track, canning, foods, and the distribution of Toyotas in the Midwest, adopted the institution and commissioned the new building. The new building opened in 1993.

The WAM's collection is small and select, mostly devoted to modern American art. On the first floor hang two huge Pop Art canvases painted for the 1964 New York World's Fair, one by Minnesota native James Rosenquist and the other by Roy Lichtenstein. Other examples of the permanent collection include works by Milton Avery, Keith Haring, Frank Stella, Arthur Dove, Lyonel Feininger, and Georgia O'Keeffe.

Andy Warhol immortalizes the donor of the museum in a portrait. Duane Hanson represented Weisman's parents in two lifelike figures that are so realistic that one is taken aback when one realizes that they are statues. Papa William sits at a desk phoning and Mom Mary, with her pocketbook, seems ready to go out shopping. There is no picture of Martha Weisman, Fred's former wife. One can see her, along with Fred, in a nasty double portrait now owned by the Art Institute of Chicago (see p. 163), entitled *American Collectors*. It is a 1960s critique of American consumerism, particularly the art-buying business, by David

Hockney. Mrs. Weisman, the sister of Norton Simon, founder of the Norton Simon Museum in Pasadena (see p. 68), obviously did not like the portrait and stored it in her brother's museum in California; eventually the Art Institute of Chicago acquired it.

Children and adults may enjoy the Pedicord Apartments by Edward and Nancy Kienholz, an audio-visual reconstruction of a tenement in which visitors can listen to the sounds and conversation that take place behind the closed door.

The museum stresses architecture. Resources include the estate of Ralph Rapson, a major American architect who built Minneapolis's world-renowned Guthrie Theater.

Relationships among Minneapolis's three museums were always close. Like the Walkers before him, Weisman contributed art and funds to the other two museums in addition to his own.

Missouri

KANSAS CITY

Nelson-Atkins Museum of Art

Address: 4525 Oak Street, Kansas City, MO 64111

Telephone: (816) 561-4000

Web: www.nelson-atkins.org

Hours: Tues–Thurs 10–4; Fri 10–9; Sat 10–5; Sun 12–5. Closed Mon, New Year's, Independence, and Thanksgiving days, and Dec 24 and 25.

Strengths: Comprehensive collection of American, European, and Asian art. Largest collection of George Caleb Bingham and Thomas Hart Benton in the world, and largest collection of Henry Moore sculptures outside England.

Special Events: Temporary exhibitions.

Others: 17-acre sculpture park subdivided into 4 areas. Restaurant. Shops.

Activities for Children: Occasional family days.

Parking: In lots on north side of building.

The Nelson-Atkins Museum of Art is a neoclassical limestone and marble palace located on a hill on the outskirts of Kansas City. In spite of the fact that it opened at the height of the Depression in 1933, it is lavish. It was the gift of William Rockhill Nelson, the publisher of the *Kansas City Star* and a real estate developer. Nelson left the bulk of his estate, twelve million dollars, to Kansas City for a museum. Kansas City, however, had another donor: Mary Mcfee Atkins, a retiring school teacher. She also left her estate to Kansas City, for the same purpose. To everybody's surprise the estate consisted of one million dollars.

Neither Atkins nor Nelson had collected art, but their gifts were so sizable that, according to contemporary reports, "only the Metropolitan Museum in New York had more money." In a way the situation of the Nelson-Atkins was comparable to that of the Getty Trust in 1986: lots of cash, but no building or art. The difference is that there was more great art available during the 1920s and 1930s than during the 1990s.

At first the trustees of the Nelson-Atkins considered acquiring reproductions. Fortunately, they quickly abandoned this approach in favor of "art of all people and all times." European Old Masters they acquired include Titian, El Greco, Peter Paul Rubens, Rembrandt, and others; noteworthy are *The Holy Family in a Domestic Interior* by Petrus Christus, a masterpiece of the Northern Renaissance, and *St. John the Baptist in the Wilderness,* one of America's rare works by Michelangelo da Caravaggio, the seminal Italian painter whose style bridged the Renaissance and more realistic art. The collection of later and contemporary European works is comprehensive.

The museum's American collection ranges from Colonial times to the present. Of note are works by Missouri-born artist George Caleb Bingham. His much beloved *Canvassing for a Vote, 1852* alludes to the painter's political involvement in the campaigns of W. H. Harrison and Henry Clay. The Nelson-Atkins also owns the largest collection of Thomas Hart Benton, another native son, in the world.

Chance would have it that the Nelson-Atkins also owns one of America's leading Chinese art collections. Among the experts consulted by the museum during its buying sprees was Langdon Warner, a Chinese art expert working at Harvard's Fogg (see p. 209). In 1930, while in China, Warner acquired Asian art for the Nelson-Atkins.

Before returning home, Warner suggested that his former student, Laurence Sickman, continue his task. A native of Colorado, Sickman had been fascinated by Oriental art from the time he was seventeen years old. He enrolled at Harvard in 1926, then the only American university teaching Oriental art. Endowed with taste, scholarship, and decisiveness, Sickman bought Chinese masterpieces for Kansas City before China was cut off from the West. His proudest achievement was the rescue of pieces from the Lung Man cave, a Buddhist chapel in the Honan Province. Sickman had observed vandals destroying the cave. Since his warning to Chinese officials went unheeded, Sickman himself acquired a stone lion and a relief of *The Empress as Donor with Attendants.* Upon his return from China in 1935, Sickman joined the Nelson-Atkins, eventually becoming its second director in 1953.

Another strength of the museum is its sculpture collection. The Henry Moore Sculpture Garden is a gift of the Hall family, reminding the visitor of another great American enterprise, Hallmark Greeting Cards of Kansas City. Giant *Shuttlecocks* by Claes Oldenburg and Coosje Van Bruggen sitting on the front lawn add a note of irreverence to the museum's stately facade.

ST. LOUIS

Saint Louis Art Museum

Address: 1 Fine Arts Drive, St. Louis, MO 63110

Telephone: (314) 721-0072

Web: www.slam.org

Hours: Tues 1:30–8:30; Wed–Sun 10–5. Closed Mon and New Year's, Thanksgiving, and Christmas days. Tours Wed–Fri at 1:30 (30 min); Sat–Sun at 1:30 (60 min).

Strengths: Encyclopedic. German Expressionism; largest collection of Max Beckmann in the world. Good collections of American, European, African, Oceanic, and Asian art. Extensive decorative art collection with 6 period rooms.

Other: Extensive audiotour (230 objects) designed to allow visitors to explore the museum at their own pace. Café overlooking sculpture terrace. Museum shop.

Activities for Children: 10 stops on the audiotour (see Other) especially designed for children and families.

Parking: Free, on site.

At the close of the nineteenth century, World's Fairs were the plum the Olympics are today. In 1904, St. Louis was allowed to host the exhibition celebrating the centenary of the Louisiana Purchase. Halsey C. Ives (also see next entry), who had served as chairman of the art department of the 1893 Chicago Columbia Exhibition, convinced the city of St. Louis to erect a "Palace of the Arts" that would survive the fair.

Cass Gilbert—the future architect of Manhattan's beloved Woolworth Building—was selected as the architect. This in itself was a milestone because Gilbert was a graduate of MIT, America's first school of architecture. Gilbert modeled the central unit of the museum on the Baths of Caracalla in Rome. Daniel Chester French and Augustus Saint-Gaudens sculpted giant figures representing *Sculpture* and *Painting* for the facade. A huge bas-relief representing the great artists of the world ran across the front and sides of the building. The motto of the museum, DEDICATED TO ART AND FREE TO ALL, chiseled into the museum's lintel, expressed Ives's democratic, anti-elitist views. A large equestrian statue, *The Deification of Saint Louis*, guards the entrance. So much of the one-million-dollar building budget was spent on the outside of the museum that its interior had to be kept rather plain.

The building has served the city well and it remains one of America's best-loved Beaux Arts edifices. Visitors still enter through the seventy-eight-foot-high sculpture hall and enjoy the museum's top-lit galleries. Time, however, aged the original structure and throughout the years it has had to undergo several major renovations.

Since it started collecting so long ago, the Saint Louis Art Museum (SLAM) managed to assemble a wonderful encyclopedic collection. As early as 1919 the W. K. Bixby Oriental Art Trust Fund allowed it to assemble Chinese, Japanese, Indian, and Islamic collections. The museum also has extensive textile, decorative arts, Mesopotamian, Greek, and Roman collections. The institution's Pre-Columbian (more than 3,000 pieces) and Oceanic (900-plus pieces) are especially noteworthy, as is its collection of African art. The collections of Western art (European and American) are strong; most major artists are represented. Highlights of the European collection include seventeenth-century Dutch art, landscapes, portraits, and genre scenes. Since the museum dates its beginnings to an American World's Fair, American art is covered in depth with examples of Colonial portraits, Hudson

River School landscapes, and scenes highlighting the American frontier (George Caleb Bingham and Charles Wimar). American Impressionism, Abstract Expressionism, and Pop Art are well represented.

Teaching remains a SLAM priority. The museum's crosscultural approach to its possessions is emphasized in the excellent guides. One, entitled "Myth and Stories," takes us to Giorgio Vasari's (1511–1574) *Judith and Holofernes*, to a *Sioux Pipe* made by an unknown artist of the Great Plains, and to *Xolotl*, a ninth-century clay vessel in the shape of the canine monster-creator from Oaxaca, Mexico.

Most surprising, perhaps, is that a museum founded twelve decades ago on the then American frontier owns an extensive German Expressionist collection. Max Beckmann, an important German painter of the twentieth century, came to the U.S. soon after Hitler branded his art "degenerate." One would have expected him to settle in cosmopolitan New York, but after some trial and error he started teaching at Washington University, and remained in St. Louis for the rest of his life. Today, SLAM's collection of forty-one paintings, one sculpture, and fifty-eight works on paper is the largest Beckmann collection in the world. According to museum literature, "Beckmann depicted the realities of modern life and the human emotions that accompanied them: despair, loneliness, confusion and disorder. . . ." The message rings as true today as when the works were created more than half a century ago.

Washington University Gallery of Art

Address: 1 Brookings Drive, St. Louis, MO 63130

Telephone: (314) 935-4523

Web: www.wustl.edu/galleryofart

Hours: Mon–Fri 10–4:30; Sat–Sun 1–4:30. Closed holidays and summer.

Strengths: Selected art of the late 19th and early 20th centuries. Complete survey of modern art.

Special Events: Temporary exhibits.

Other: Personalized gallery talks and viewing of objects not on display can be arranged at no charge by calling (314) 935-5490. The John Max Wulfing Numismatic Collection of 14,000 Greek, Roman, and Byzantine coins.

Parking: On site.

In 2000, Washington University's Gallery of Art (WUGA) mounted an exhibit entitled *Beginnings: The Taste of the Founders*. It included sixty-five works that illustrated the institution's early collecting history. The museum was founded in 1881, during one of America's museum-building booms, when major and minor cities built temples devoted to culture. The moving force behind the St. Louis effort was Halsey C. Ives, a devoted teacher and art expert. Wayne Crow, a state senator and founder as well as benefactor of what was to be Washington University, donated a museum building in memory of his son. Built in Ruskin-approved Italianate style, the two-story structure was luxurious and impressive.

At the opening exhibit, 200 casts of the world's great sculptures occupied the first floor galleries and 143 loan paintings occupied the second. Many of the latter were eventually bequeathed to the museum. Over and above their artistic value—many of the donations did not weather the test of time—the gifts of the founders provide invaluable historical insights. Wayne Crow was a strong supporter of Harriet Hosmer. According to the WUGA Illustrated Checklist of 1981: "St. Louisans were proud of the diminutive, energetic sculptor. . . ." Today the museum still cherishes Hosmer's grieving *Oenoné*—the spurned wife of Paris—and her bust of *Wayne Crow*.

The story of the museum's small version of Thomas Ball's *Freedom Memorial, 1875* is moving and astonishing. A museum publication relates that "In 1865, shortly after Lincoln's assassination, a local former slave, Charlotte Marietta . . . offered five dollars, 'her first earning in freedom,' towards the erection of a monument of the colored people[s'] . . . best friend on earth. . . ." More money was raised from black infantry regiments and eventually, through the mediation of Reverend W. G. Eliot, Washington University's founder and chancellor, the statue was commissioned from Ball and now stands in Washington, D.C.'s Lincoln Park.

The WUGA also owns Joaquín Sorolla y Bastida's prize-winning *Another Margarita!*, which shows Goethe's ill-fated Faustian heroine in prison guarded by an armed soldier. The realistic style of the work is unusual for Sorolla, best known for his impressionistic views of Spain (see The Hispanic Society of America, p. 285). Frederick Church's *Twilight, Mount Desert Island, Maine*, whose orange sunset and blue sky, peeking out from between dark clouds, is as fresh today as when painted toward the end of the Civil War. As contemporary critic William M. Bryant wrote in the *Spectator* (May 28, 1881): "It is the very picture of the world in which all differences are vanishing. . . . There has been a struggle; but it is ended."

The development of the Washington University Gallery of Art came to a halt in 1904 when its collections were transferred to the Saint Louis Art Museum, where its works were simply identified as "On loan from the University Museum." More and more pictures migrated into storage and by the mid-1940s they had been forgotton.

However, a rebirth was at hand. During the 1940s, H. W. Janson, author of the popular *History of Art,* was professor of art history at Washington University and curator of the collection. He established a small art gallery on campus, deaccessioned some works, raised funds, and built a strong collection of postwar American abstract painting, including works by Jackson Pollock, Willem de Kooning, and Arshile Gorky. By the 1960s, W. N. Eisendrath, the museum's first director, continued to promote public awareness and the collection grew to include European masterpieces by Edvard Munch, Paul Klee, Ludwig Meidner, Fernand Léger, Max Beckmann, James Ensor, and Yves Tanguy, to name only a very few. He also persuaded the Steinberg Charitable Trust to fund the building of a new museum—Steinberg Hall—that, in its own way, is as memorable as the museum's first gallery. It was built by Fumihiko Maki, then a young Japanese architect-in-residence, who went on to win the prestigious Pritzker Prize. The museum, which opened in 1960, has small windows and a characteristically "folded" roofline that admits indirect light. Alexander Calder's stabile *Five Rudders* guards the entrance. By 2000 WUGA owned 3,000 art objects, a delightful mix of old and new. Maki will enlarge the structure in the near future.

Nebraska

OMAHA

Joslyn Art Museum

Address: 2200 Dodge Street, Omaha, NE 68102

Telephone: (402) 342-3300

Web: www.joslyn.org

Hours: Tues–Sat 10–4; Sun 12–4. Closed Mon and major holidays. Tours Wed at 1; Sat at 11.

Strengths: General survey museum with emphasis on European and American art. Works related to the exploration of the West, Native American art, 20th-century art, ancient Greek pottery, and small collection of Asian art.

Special Events: About 12 special exhibitions a year, often complementing the permanent collections.

Other: Every first Sun, Bagels and Bach in café. Oct–May: Every first Fri music by local and regional bands. During the summer: Free Jazz on the Green concerts on six consecutive Thurs. Restaurant. Museum shop.

Activities for Children: All age groups can explore art in the Mind's Eye Gallery. There also is a hands-on room.

Parking: Free, east and north of the museum.

Omaha is squarely located in America's Corn Belt. Like Kansas City, Missouri, one would hardly expect it to be an art center, especially an older one. And yet, it has a treasure of a museum, the gift of George A. and Sarah Joslyn, originally from Vermont. The Joslyns moved to Des Moines, Iowa, where George made $1.25 a day unloading papers from freight cars. He was promoted to an office position and in 1880 the couple arrived in Omaha, Nebraska. Eventually he created the Western Newspaper Union, which at his death operated printing plants in thirty-two prominent cities.

George died in 1916 and his wife embarked upon creating a memorial to him. The Joslyns loved music and art and at first his wife wanted to build a concert hall; eventually her gift would also encompass a museum. In 1931 a splendid establishment opened, which had cost three million dollars. It featured a large auditorium and art galleries. With its clear Art Deco lines and luxurious marbles—chiseled from thirty-eight different quarries around the world—the building is magnificent. At the opening a visitor was overheard describing it "better than St. Louis' [museum]." At her death in 1940, Mrs. Joslyn left the bulk of her fortune to the museum, enabling it to become a major player in the American art world.

At first the museum concentrated on buying European art. Prize possessions of the European collection include Titian's *Man with a Falcon*, Francisco Goya's *Portrait of the Marquesa de Fontana*, Rembrandt's *Dirk van Os*, Paolo Veronese's *Venus at her Toilet*, El Greco's *St. Francis in Prayer*, Jusepe de Ribera's *St. Jerome*, and a polychrome sculpture of *St. Petronius*, as well as a number of Impressionist paintings by Claude Monet, Mary Cassatt, and Auguste Renoir.

When the collection focus was widened, the museum acquired works dating from antiquity and expanded its American collection. A wonderful painting by Missouri native Thomas Hart Benton, *The Hailstorm*, shows the struggle of a farmer with both unpredictable weather and a stubborn mule. There are works by Thomas Eakins, Albert Bierstadt, John Sloan, Grant Wood, Stuart Davis, Jackson Pollack, and many other famous and less famous artists.

The Joslyn, however, was always faithful to its Midwestern roots. The decorative motif throughout the building is the wings of the thunderbird, found on the capitals of the columns, some ceilings, a fountain, and even lamps. The museum is the repository of the work of Karl Bodmer (1809–1865) a Paris-trained Swiss illustrator who accompanied botanist Prince Maximilian of Wied-Neuwiede to America in 1833–1834. On his return to Paris, Bodmer translated his watercolors into superb engravings of Indian life on the upper Missouri River. The Joslyn owns 427 of Bodmer's original sketches as well as the original plates for Prince Maximilian's book *Travels in the Interior of North America*.

The Joslyn also is the repository of the work of Alfred Jacob Miller, another artist who in those pre-camera days was part of an expedition exploring the West. Miller was born in Baltimore in 1809 and trained in America and Europe. At age twenty-seven he accompanied William

Drummond Stewart, a Scotsman, to the Wind River of Wyoming. His 109 watercolors, as well as his painting of *The Trapper's Bride,* now hang in Omaha, a reminder of the romanticism that existed when America was young (also see The Walters Art Museum, p. 240.)

By 1990 the Joslyn had outgrown its space. A large addition, costing more than five times as much as the original "extravagant" building, was added. Its exterior was constructed in Georgia Pink Marble mined from the same quarry as the main building. The space, lit by hidden skylights, is mostly used for special exhibitions.

New Hampshire

HANOVER

Hood Museum of Art, Dartmouth College

Address: Wheelock Street, Hanover, NH 03755
Telephone: (603) 646-2808
Web: www.dartmouth.edu/~hood/
Hours: Tues–Sat 10–5, Wed until 9; Sun 12–5. Closed Mon and major holidays.
Strengths: Orozco murals (in the Baker Library of the college). Assyrian bas-reliefs. A comprehensive collection of Oceanic art.
Other: Temporary exhibits.
Activities for Children: About 5 Family Sundays (12–5) a year, providing a variety of guided activities centering on a particular theme for children age 6–12. Artventures, a monthly guided interactive tour for children 8 and older.
Parking: Limited metered, on Wheelock Street and behind the museum on Lebanon Street.

The Reverend Eleazar Wheelock founded Dartmouth College in 1769 under a charter issued by John Wentworth, New Hampshire's last royal governor. To improve the education of its students the college was given or purchased art and natural science objects, as well as curiosities. One of the first gifts so received were "some curious elephant bones found about 600 miles down the Ohio River" sent to the "young museum" by Reverend David McClure, a young tutor. A much beloved and joked about stuffed zebra arrived in 1798.

Today's audience is more appreciative of the Colonial portraits that entered the collection in these early days. Of these, Copley's pastel portrait of Wentworth is considered particularly fine. In 1856, Sir Henry Rawlinson managed to acquire six highly prized Assyrian reliefs from the Northwest Palace of Ashurnasirpal II at Nimrud, for Dartmouth. These artworks were so treasured because it was believed that they provided evidence that the Bible was historically truthful. Even though one encounters these finely chiseled granite images of winged kings, soldiers, lions, horses, and chariots in many museums throughout the world—the United States was able to acquire close to a hundred shipments—one cannot fail to be impressed every time by their pictorial strength.

Dartmouth's first official museum building dates from 1929. Nelson Rockefeller attended Dartmouth College as part of the class of 1930. Unsurprisingly, the art collection would benefit from Rockefeller benevolence. Mrs. Abby Aldrich Rockefeller's gift of over 100 examples of mostly modern paintings, drawings, prints, and folk art drew attention to the museum, and today the Hood owns a nice mix of American and European works: Thomas Eakins, William Merritt Chase, George Inness, Ernest Lawson, Georges Rouault, Alfred Maurer, Jacques Lipchitz, and others. The museum owns a painting of *Santa Barbara* by Lavinia Fontana (Italian, 1552–1614; also see the National Museum of Women in the Arts, p. 128); also Pablo Picasso's *Guitar on a Table*, a seminal Cubist work donated by Nelson Rockefeller, which at one time belonged to Gertrude Stein. The present-day American collection is also comprehensive.

Dartmouth's greatest and most unique possession is *The Epic of American Civilization*, a large mural by José Clemente Orozco consisting of twenty-four independent compositions. From 1932–1934 the Mexican painter held a faculty appointment at Dartmouth. (Note that during that same time interval Diego Rivera painted a mural at the Detroit Institute of Arts—see p. 233.) Orozco was trained as an architect and had drawn political cartoons for a Mexican newspaper. His murals, like those of other Mexican muralists, are highly politicized, depicting his outrage at the destruction of Mexico's native culture by the Spanish Conquistadores. One panel at Dartmouth, entitled *The Departure of Quetzalcoatl,* shows the mystical feathered serpent god observing the skull-headed conquerors. In the end the human spirit triumphantly destroys religious, cultural, and militaristic oppression.

In 1985 a new building, the Hood Museum of Art, opened its doors. It includes collections of African and Native North American Art, nineteenth- and twentieth-century American paintings, contemporary art, and a large print collection. Among these, the early American silver and the Melanesian (Oceanic) art collection (1,300 objects) are particularly noteworthy.

The museum also owns a major collection of nineteenth- and early-twentieth-century landscape paintings of New Hampshire and the White Mountains.

New Jersey

MONTCLAIR

Montclair Art Museum

Address: 3 S. Mountain Avenue, Montclair, NJ 07042
Telephone: (973) 746-5555
Web: www.montclair-art.com
Hours: Tues–Wed, Fri–Sat 11–5; Thurs, Sun 1–5. Summer: Wed–Sun 12–5. Closed Mon and most major holidays.
Strengths: American art, George Inness. Extensive Native American collection.
Other: Interesting temporary shows. Museum store.
Parking: On site.

Smack in the middle of downtown Montclair, amid imposing clapboard houses and contemporary stores, stands a stately neoclassical building whose four ionic columns face a small park. The Montclair Art

Delaware Water Gap, 1859 by George Inness is part of the treasure trove of American masterpieces at the Montclair Art Museum.

Museum (MAM), which houses one of the nation's superior, though small, comprehensive collections of American art, has been standing on this site since 1914.

Montclair, a small town within easy reach of New York City, always had an artistic bent. It is most closely associated with George Inness—a long-time resident—but also played an important role in the life of other American artists. In 1908 a group of citizens established the Montclair Art Commission. A year later, William T. Evans, a patron of George Inness and other contemporary artists, offered the commission fifty-four paintings provided it built a suitable museum to showcase the nascent American School.

The challenge was met, and the collection of the museum now numbers more than 600 works by major American painters of the eighteenth to the twentieth centuries. Curators, directors, and patrons have exercised excellent taste in what they acquired for, or donated to, the museum. In his foreword to the book *300 Years of American Painting* [at the MAM], J. Carter Brown, then director of the National Gallery of Art, described the collection as "studded with masterpieces [including] a superb pair of portraits by Joseph Blackburn; a serene and beautiful landscape by Asher B. Durand; three great Innesses: *Winter Morning,*

Montclair; Early Autumn, Montclair; and *Delaware Water Gap; Queensborough Bridge* by Elsie Driggs; *A Tambourine Player* by William Merritt Chase . . . and *White Music* by Robert Motherwell."

Other favorite works include *Snake River* by Thomas Moran, *Tools* by Jacob Lawrence, *After the Bath* by Raphael Soyer, and *Ridgefield Landscape,* a very early, atypical painting by Man Ray.

Unfortunately, the MAM is so small that most of its permanent collection is rarely on view. To alleviate the disappointment of its visitors the museum has mounted an extensive web site featuring 200 images.

The MAM also collects Native American art, enlarging a major collection donated by founding member Florence Rand Lang. Today, this collection numbers 4,000 objects, including baskets, textiles, and jewelry.

The MAM mounts approximately eight temporary shows per year, some of them highlighting works from the permanent collection, others featuring emerging artists or historic art events. A recent show recreated the exhibit of the "American School" from the Universal Exhibition in Paris in 1900.

NEWARK

The Newark Museum

Address: 49 Washington Street, Newark, NJ 07101

Telephone: (973) 596-6550

Web: www.newarkmuseum.org

Hours: Wed, Fri–Sun 12–5; Thurs 12–8:30. Closed Mon, Tues, and major holidays.

Strengths: Asian art, especially of Tibet and the Himalayas. American paintings from Colonial times to the present. African art. Decorative arts of the 18th and 19th centuries. American folk art, including sculpture made by leading black artists. Craft collection highlighting local artists.

Special Events: Temporary exhibits. Garden Jazz Concerts in summer. Lectures, symposia. Black Film Festival.

Other: Ballantine House, a completely restored late Victorian mansion. Restaurant. Museum shop.

Activities for Children: Family festivals. Special exhibits in the Junior Gallery teach children about art, museums in general, and the collections at hand. A mini zoo displays primates and other small animals in their natural environments.

Parking: Low-cost public garage on site.

Like Detroit, Newark was abandoned by its middle class and beset by inner-city problems. Then the 1960s riots tarnished its image. The Newark Museum (NM) triumphed over these events and remains a "must-see" institution.

From its inception, the NM was part of the downtown urban fabric and not an esoteric palace on a hill. Yet when you pass through the gates of the museum you are in a gentler world, epitomized by the Tibetan altar, which celebrates one of the world's most forgiving and peace-loving religions.

The institution consists of four disparate buildings, three of which were built for other purposes. The 1989 renovation by Michael Graves is a stunning example of the successful reuse of such older structures. Today the buildings are linked by the Engelhard Court, which immediately conjures up the centerpiece of the American Wing of New York's Metropolitan Museum of Art. Both are gifts of Charles W. Engelhard, a Newark-based precious-metal magnate.

Since its founding in 1909 the NM has charted a distinctive course. Then as now, its aim was to teach and to be non-elitist. Good taste and good luck turned its collections into a priceless repository of great art. The museum grew from a collection of art that librarian John Cotton Dana exhibited at the Newark Free Library. In 1926, department store owner Louis Bamberger funded a separate Beaux Arts–style museum building.

Dana was determined to avoid mimicking the powerful, well-endowed museums of New York and Philadelphia. He concentrated on collecting contemporary American art, American folk art, furniture, and crafts. There are works by African American artists, including sculptures by William Edmondson and David Butler, two prominent twentieth-century folk artists. The holdings of Newark's African art collection—sculptures, ceramics, textiles, baskets, and metal arts—and its Native American art collection—baskets, jewelry, wood carvings, and beadwork—are extensive.

As is so often the case, chance influenced the character of the institution. In 1910, Edward Crane, an early museum trustee, met Dr. Albert L.

Shelton, an American missionary physician, aboard a ship coming back from Shanghai. Dr. Shelton had assembled a remarkable collection of art objects from the Sino-Tibetan border region, which he intended to sell to fund his medical mission. Crane arranged for their exhibition in Dana's library space. When Crane died unexpectedly, his family bought the entire collection and donated it to the NM in his memory. Eventually, four additional missionary collections were acquired as well as objects from the neighboring Himalayas, India, Korea, and China. Herman A. E. Jaehne and Paul C. Jaehne donated their enormous Japanese and Chinese collection to the museum. A complete Tibetan altar—the first in America—was erected in 1935 and consecrated by the Dalai Lama in 1988. Today the NM owns one of the finest Tibetan collections in the world, numbering more than 2,000 objects, including paintings, sculpture, costumes, and ritual implements.

A major possession of the NM's American art collection is Joseph Stella's *The Voice of the City of New York Interpreted*, dating from 1920–1922. The five panels include an exuberant view of the artist's favorite subject, the Brooklyn Bridge, which he considered a metaphor for modern life. In Stella's words: "Many nights I stood on the bridge . . . [feeling] deeply moved, as if on the threshold of a new religion or in the presence of a new divinity."

The museum's acquisition of the Ballantine House, the luxurious late-Victorian home of Newark's leading beer brewer, was another lucky accident. The home dates from 1885 and was located at what was then Newark's best address. The museum planned to demolish the house, but World War Two delayed the wrecker's ball and in 1976 the house, with its stained glass windows and carved woodwork, was restored to its previous splendor. The Ballantine House now is the centerpiece of the NM's extensive decorative arts collection. The blend of eighteenth- and nineteenth-century furniture, glass, ceramics, silver, and older and contemporary crafts is exciting.

John Cotton Dana headed the museum until his death in 1929. His belief that "beauty has no relation to price, rarity, or age" has been adhered to by his successors. The museum teaches visitors to see beauty in ordinary objects. It is a place for children, sophisticated art-lovers, serious students of African, American, and Asian art, admirers of late Victorian houses, and many, many others.

New Mexico

SANTA FE

Georgia O'Keeffe Museum

Address: 217 Johnson Street, Santa Fe, NM 87501

Telephone: (505) 946-1000

Web: www.okeeffemuseum.org

Hours: *Nov–June*: Mon–Tues, Thurs–Sun 10–5; Fri 10–8. Closed Wed, and New Year's, Easter, Thanksgiving, and Christmas days. *July–Oct*: Also open Wed 10–5. Tours Tues, Sat, Sun at 2.

Strength: Works by Georgia O'Keeffe.

Other: Temporary exhibits. Café. Museum shop. O'Keeffe's Home and Studio in Abiquiu are open seasonally Mon, Thurs, Fri. For reservations for the one-hour tour, call (505) 685-4539. Ghost Ranch, now a Presbyterian Church conference center and retreat, can be reached at (877) 804-4678. The Ghost Ranch Living Museum (3 miles from conference center; telephone: 505-685-4312) is part of the Carson National Forest with 330 miles of nature trails.

Parking: On street.

Anyone celebrating the world's artistic heritage is saddened by the fact that throughout history women painters were a rarity. It is thus with great pleasure that we welcome the Georgia O'Keeffe Museum, one of the few institutions devoted to a single artist, and the only one devoted to a major woman painter.

The museum opened its doors in 1997, eleven years after O'Keeffe died in Santa Fe at the age of ninety-eight. The art and funds for construction were mostly the gift of the Burnett Foundation, whose founders had collected works by the painter for many decades. The collection of more than 130 works is comprehensive, ranging from 1916 to 1980.

Compared to most artists, Georgia O'Keeffe led an enchanted life. She was born in Wisconsin in 1887. Her talents were recognized early and she received art lessons at home. She studied art at various places, including the Art Institute of Chicago and Teachers College in New York, and taught art in Amarillo, Texas. Early in life she developed a personal style that appealed to many. Alfred Stieglitz, the photographer who also ran Studio 291 and other avant-garde galleries, sponsored—and later married—her. By the time she was thirty, O'Keeffe had her first solo show and thereafter retrospectives at major museums.

Stylistically, O'Keeffe was an abstract painter, uniquely translating what she saw. She painted fruits and flowers, bones and buildings, the sun and the sky. Her canvases are filled with jewel-like colors. Typically she might only paint a fraction of an object, one blossom occupying a whole canvas, the image reduced to increasingly simple, sensuous shapes.

O'Keeffe visited New Mexico for the first time in 1929, and fell in love with the stark landscape and the rugged mountains. From then on, her art included paintings of adobe huts and churches, Penitente crosses, red mountains, and bare winter trees.

In 1949, after Alfred Stieglitz's death, O'Keeffe moved permanently to New Mexico, dividing her time between Abiquiu and Ghost Ranch. O'Keeffe's house and studio in Abiquiu—fifty-five miles north of Santa Fe—can be visited by special arrangement. Visitors can also visit the New Mexican landscape so closely associated with O'Keeffe at the Ghost Ranch Living Museum and the Ghost Ranch Conference center. Here you can hike the hills and experience the otherworldly landscape, the red rocks, the brilliant sun, and the clear skies and recognize much of what inspired O'Keeffe's pictures.

Museum of New Mexico

Museum of Indian Arts and Culture
Museum of International Folk Art
Museum of Fine Arts, Santa Fe

The Museum of New Mexico in Santa Fe is an umbrella organization for three small art museums and a history museum. Together the museums present a unique overview of the Southwest's past and present. The art museums are the Museum of Indian Arts and Culture and the Museum of International Folk Art, both on Museum

Plaza at the outskirts of town, and the Museum of Fine Arts, Santa Fe, in the center of the old town. The fourth museum is the Palace of the Governors, which most specifically explores the history of New Mexico and the Southwest. All four museums can be visited on a single four-day pass. A shuttle bus runs between Museum Plaza and the Santa Fe Trails bus stop in old Santa Fe. Merchandise purchased in any of the particularly nice gift shops is tax-exempt. This is helpful since some of the American Indian crafts (pottery, rugs, and jewelry) cost thousands of dollars.

The private Wheelwright Museum (508-982-4636) founded in 1932, is also located on Museum Plaza. The Wheelwright, the inside of which is shaped like a Navajo hogan (house), exhibits American Indian art and ethnographic material of the Southwestern Navajo, Apache, and Pueblo people. It is open Mon–Sat 10–5, Sun 1–5.

Museum of Indian Arts and Culture

Address: Museum Plaza, 710 Camino Lejo off Old Santa Fe Trail, Santa Fe, NM 87505

Telephone: (505) 827-6344

Web: www.miaclab.org

Hours: Tues–Sun 10–5. Closed Mon, and New Year's, Easter, Thanksgiving, and Christmas days. Tours at 10:30, 12:30, 2, and 3:30.

Strengths: Southwestern pottery spanning 2,000 years of Pueblo culture. Interactive exhibit, *Here, Now and Always,* celebrating Native American life in many different ways including arts, language, and song.

Special Events: Monthly: Breakfast with the Curators, consisting of a lecture by a guest speaker. Annual: Fiber Arts, a juried invitational show featuring traditional fiber art of the Southwest (quilts, baskets, rugs, and textiles). Winterfest: Exploration and preparation of traditional foods of the Southwest.

Other: Temporary exhibits of contemporary Native American painters. Museum shop: Objects in this high-end shop are made by Native Americans, including classic pottery made by 7 major New Mexican pueblos (Acoma, Cochiti, Hopi, Jemez, San Ildefonso, San Juan, and Santa Clara), Hopi kachina dolls, handwoven, hand-dyed Navajo rugs, spectacular jewelry. Restaurant.

Activities for Children: The entire museum will fascinate children of all ages. Also: Scavenger hunt maps and hands-on gallery and discovery area.

Parking: On site, plentiful.

The Museum of Indian Arts and Culture is a hybrid museum and research institution. This is not surprising; it is an outgrowth of two older institutions—the American Indian Arts Fund and the Laboratory of Anthropology (the Lab). In 1924, John D. Rockefeller visited the American Indian cave dwellings at Mesa Verde and other sites with vestiges of Native American life. He was so impressed by what he saw that he proposed founding a research institution that would attempt to uncover the history of the native population. Leading anthropologists shared Rockefeller's view and in 1927 the Laboratory of Anthropology opened its beautifully carved doors on a fifty-acre tract of land outside Santa Fe. For a while the Lab was a mecca for scholars, but soon it ran into financial difficulties resulting from the Depression, the end of Rockefeller's seed money, and World War Two.

Though the primary goal of the institution was research and education, it immediately attracted many who wished to admire its treasure troves: textiles, Navajo rugs, katsina dolls, jewelry, and especially pottery. In 1947 the Lab and its art treasures became a unit of the Museum of New Mexico.

Today the Lab remains an active research institution. A separate museum opened its doors in 1987 and is still growing. Exhibits concentrate on the legacy of the Navajo, Apache, Hopi, Tohono O'odham, and the nineteen Pueblo peoples of the Southwest.

A big interactive exhibit entitled *Here, Now and Always* explores these gifts in eight overlapping themes. "Ancestors" supplies a time scale. In "Cycles" we become acquainted with the rhythms of the Native world. In "Architecture" we explore human habitations. "Language and Song" is alive with the sounds of the Southwest, including Indian rock and roll and the Navajo "code-talkers" of World War Two. We learn about native plants and animals, agriculture, baking bread, trading posts, and "Indian Affairs" classrooms. Finally we enter the "Art" gallery that displays paintings, pottery, basketry, rugs, and jewelry, each piece speaking with its own voice of the Southwest.

More pottery, selected from among 10,000 Native American pots owned by the museum, can be found in the Buchsbaum Gallery of South-western Pottery. The display of black, red, ocher, and painted pottery is a feast for the eyes. Docents are on hand to explain the firing and other processes involved in making the festive and utilitarian vessels. Some pots are old, other masterpieces were made recently by artists who adhere to the traditional ways of building pots by hand from coils of clay.

Throughout the museum the bond between yesterday and today is highlighted. "There is no single Indian way," museum literature states, "but a web of interdependence woven around a core of Indian traditions." The museum also presents changing exhibitions of contemporary Native American art.

Museum of International Folk Art

Address: Museum Plaza, 706 Camino Lejo off Old Santa Fe Trail, Santa Fe, NM 87507.

Telephone: (505) 476-1200

Web: www.moifa.org; also www.statenm.us/moifa/

Hours: Tues–Sun 10–5. Closed Mon and New Year's, Easter, Thanksgiving, and Christmas days. Tours at 10:15, 12, 2, and 3.

Strengths: New Mexican Spanish Colonial art, folk art, outsider art.

Special Events: Holiday events, temporary shows.

Other: The "Lloyd's Treasure Chest" gallery provides a glimpse of museum restoration and other behind-the-scene functions of a museum. Teaching guides.

Activities for Children: The entire museum will fascinate children of all ages. Hands-on activities like mask-making, book-making, doll-making, etc.

Parking: On site, plentiful.

Folk art defies definition. Objects include paintings and sculptures, religious objects, clothing, quiltings, carvings, and toys created and decorated by ordinary folks or anonymous artists with the purpose of elevating utilitarian, everyday objects above the ordinary. The works often are fun and humorous and folk art never elicits the same reverence as fine art. There is a strong bond among the folk arts created by various cultures throughout history.

Collectors of folk art are a passionate lot and their possessions can be varied in the extreme. This is the case with the objects displayed at the Museum of International Folk Art (MOIFA). The museum was founded by Florence Dibell Bartlett (1881–1954), who felt that everywhere mass manufacture was displacing folk art. Miss Bartlett managed to assemble costumes, pottery, metalwork, everyday objects, and pieces of great value from thirty-seven different countries. In 1952 she founded and built the MOIFA and she witnessed its dedication in 1953, shortly before her death. Since then the museum has grown, and today it houses several major collections.

The MOIFA also houses a Hispanic Heritage wing. Culturally, New Mexico is part of Mexico and Spain. Cortez landed in Mexico in 1519 and within two decades the Spanish had explored and colonized northward. In 1610, Santa Fe became the capital of the Spanish colony of New Mexico. It is therefore the oldest continuously functioning state capital in the United States.

As elsewhere in the New World, Franciscan and Jesuit missionaries accompanied the colonists and successfully converted the native population. At first, church equipment and religious objects came from Mexico, but for more than a hundred years after 1700 New Mexicans created their own very characteristic art. Today the MOIFA is the repository of more than 70,000 objects of New Mexican Spanish Colonial Art.

The works of art (paintings, figures, altar screens) were made by artists known as santeros, so-called because they engaged in producing religious art. Their creations are joyous even though the artists did not stray from traditional Christian iconography and were guided by art created in Mexico and even in Northern Europe. Crucifixion scenes, Madonnas, saints, and archangels are painted on gesso-covered wood with water-soluble paints that even after all these years look fresh. As impressive as the paintings are the many bultos or santos—wooden sculptures of saints, often made for home use. The Hispanic wing of the MOIFA is also filled with altar screens, retables, straw-decorated crosses and chests, furniture, weavings mirroring native American patterns, characteristic tin frames and boxes, and genealogies of families going back to 1729.

The experience of the Hispanic wing is amplified in a comfortably furnished court filled with the sounds of "Spanish New Mexico," consisting of recordings of the sounds of "people living their lives against wind and water, animals and birds, talking and working." Nearby maps explain New Mexico's complicated past.

In 1978 the designer Alexander Girard and his wife, Susan, donated their enormous collection (106,000 objects) of crosscultural folk art to to the State of New Mexico. Their gift quintupled the size of Miss Bartlett's museum. "Sandro" Girard himself has a crosscultural American-Italian background. He was always fascinated by toys and miniatures and his collection appeals to children and the child in all of us. The large selection on exhibit in the Girard Wing is a contender for being the most whimsical display in a major museum. The 10,000 objects on view include miniature villages and buildings, toys, dolls, miniature trains, wall hangings, tin retables, and much, much more, all displayed in an imaginative fashion.

The newest addition to the museum, the Neutrogena Wing, is a vast collection of folk art (3,000 objects and textiles) assembled by Lloyd Cotsen, who explained that "the objects struck an emotional bell . . . appealed to my curiosity, to the thrill of discovery, the extraordinary in the ordinary, to my sense of humor . . . and to my search for the beauty in simplicity." The exhibitions in this part of the museum change every eighteen months or so.

Museum of Fine Arts, Santa Fe

Address: 107 W. Palace Avenue, Santa Fe, NM 87501

Telephone: (505) 476-5072

Web: www.nmculture.org

Hours: Tues–Sun 10–5; Fri 10–8. Closed Mon and New Year's, Easter, Thanksgiving, and Christmas days. Tours at 10:30, 1:30.

Strength: New Mexican and Southwestern art, including Native American and Spanish colonial art, and interpretations of the state's rugged landscape by 19th- and 20th-century American artists working in Taos and other parts of New Mexico.

Parking: On street.

Nothing indicates that the solid Spanish Colonial building in the center of Santa Fe is a museum. Its identity, however, can be deduced from bronze plaques embedded in the sidewalk that fronts the museum. The plaques, dedicated to local painters, were installed in 1992, when the museum celebrated its seventy-fifth birthday. The start of New Mexico's artist colony dates back to 1898. Legend has it that in that year two New York artists, Ernest Blumenschein and Bert Phillips, set out from Denver, Colorado, planning to paint in Mexico. Early in September their horse-drawn wagon broke down near Taos, New Mexico. Mexico was forgotten and the two friends set up shop, or rather a studio, in Taos. Other painters joined them and in 1915 the group formed the Taos Society of Artists, hoping that the move would improve sales. At its height the Taos Society had twenty-one members.

Gradually, Taos and Santa Fe became a center for artists and writers. In 1917 a number of their patrons founded the Museum of Fine Arts, Santa Fe. Its permanent collection concentrates on painters of the region. The museum is proud that it owns examples of the work of all the members of the Taos Society, including Georgia O'Keeffe. A very few selections from these large holdings are usually displayed in the galleries of the second floor. The ground floor houses excellent temporary exhibits.

New York

BUFFALO

Albright-Knox Art Gallery

Address: 1285 Elmwood Avenue, Buffalo, NY 14222
Telephone: (716) 882-8700
Web: www.albrightknox.org
Hours: Tues–Sat 11–5, Sun 12–5. Closed Mon and New Year's, Thanksgiving, and Christmas days.
Strengths: 20th-century art, especially works produced after 1945. Survey of world art including ancient art, Renaissance paintings and sculptures to American and European art of the 19th century. Large Clyfford Still collection.

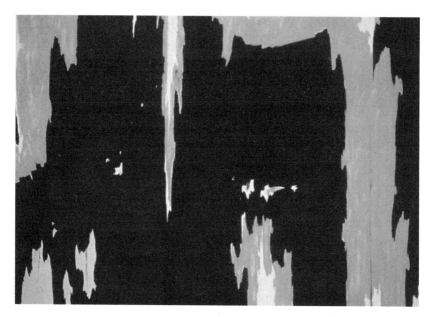

The Albright-Knox Gallery owns the largest collection of works by Clyfford Still in the world. Here is his *1957-D No. 1.*

Special Events: 6–8 temporary exhibits annually.

Other: G. Robert Strauss, Jr. Memorial Library, open to the public. New room of contemporary art featuring up-and-coming American and European artists. Restaurant. Museum shop. Especially informative education guides about the collections.

Activities for Children: Family day on selected Sun. Occasional hands-on activities for children.

Parking: Low-cost garage on site.

"One day before Christmas, 1861, [the organization] held the first public art exhibition in Buffalo. American Hall was engaged . . . portraits were borrowed, artists . . . were asked to contribute. . . . Men of influence . . . were requested to say a few kind words . . . ladies of taste were asked to lend the light of their countenance." (J. B. Townsend, 1962, speaking on the occasion of the Albright-Knox Art Gallery's 100th anniversary, quoted in a museum publication on the occasion.) The affair netted $835 and a year later the Buffalo Fine Arts Academy came into being. The academy and the public art gallery it opened that very year were among America's first half dozen, the others being in

Philadelphia, Boston, New Haven, Hartford, and Washington, D.C. To begin its exhibition program the academy had to borrow works of art from art dealers, private citizens, and artists. A small purchase fund was used to buy two landscapes by Albert Bierstadt: *Laramie Peak, Rocky Mountains* and *Marina Grande, Capri.* The academy's finances, however, were shaky and the institution almost foundered during its initial decade. Salvation came in 1900 when J. J. Albright funded a $750,000 Greek Revival–style building designed by E. B. Greene of Buffalo, the architect of the Toledo Museum of Art (see p. 332). The Buffalo Parks Department donated a spectacular site overlooking Delaware Lake.

The Albright-Knox Art Gallery (AKAG) was never bequeathed large collections, but relied on the taste and expertise of its staff to buy art and organize exhibitions. According to an AKAG publication, "firsts" or notable events included: major exhibitions of photography in 1910 and contemporary American sculpture in 1916; the appointment of Cornelia B. S. Quinton, America's first female museum director, in 1910; performances by Anna Pavlova, the dancer (1914), and Sarah Bernhardt, the "divine" actress (1916). It is interesting that at the time the American Association of Museum Directors had only three women members—Quinton, Gertrude Herdle (of the Memorial Art Gallery in nearby Rochester, see p. 315), and Juliana Force (of the Whitney Museum of American Art, see p. 310)—all of whom worked in New York State.

Gordon Smith assumed the directorship of the museum in 1955. He was creative, had a great sense of humor, and, like the Museum of Modern Art's Alfred Barr (see p. 297), was a graduate of Paul Sachs's museum course at Harvard (see Harvard University Art Museums, p. 208). Smith was determined to build a great collection. Fortunately for all concerned, he joined forces with Seymour Knox II, an art lover with very deep pockets. According to John Russell (*Smithsonian*, December 1979), "Knox and Smith were made for each other . . . They were on to the fundamental fact about buying for a museum . . . [which involves acquiring] the biggest, strongest, most uncompromising statement that the artist in question has made." In a relatively short time they acquired masterpieces by Adolph Gottlieb, Frank Stella, Jasper Johns, Arshile Gorky, Jackson Pollock, Franz Kline, Robert Motherwell, and

Mark Rothko. They went to Europe and bought major pieces by Francis Bacon, Ben Nicholson, and other contemporary artists. Their biggest coup was to buy two paintings from the reclusive American Abstract Expressionist Clyfford Still. The painter was so impressed by the pair and the smoothness of the transaction that he agreed to a rare retrospective exhibition and eventually gave the museum thirty-one works, making the AKAG the largest public repository of his oeuvre. Still stipulated that his work be exhibited as a whole, stating that ". . . it is like a symphony in which each painting has its part."

The original museum building could not absorb the result of these shopping sprees. In 1955 the Knox family funded a major addition, an architectural masterpiece designed by Gordon Bunshaft. The new wing has plenty of glass, white floors, and an inner court covered with white pebbles—a year-round reminder of Buffalo's legendary snow. The building was dedicated in 1962, exactly 100 years after the founding of the museum, which on that occasion was renamed the Albright-Knox Art Gallery.

Today the museum owns more than 6,000 art objects, over half of which date from after 1945. In addition to its Abstract Expressionist masterpieces the collection includes earlier American works (Edward Hicks, Winslow Homer, George Bellows, George Inness), eighteenth- and nineteenth-century European paintings, especially Impressionists and Post-Impressionists (Claude Monet, Paul Cézanne, Edgar Degas, Vincent van Gogh, Paul Gauguin, Georges Seurat). Chaim Soutine's *Page Boy at Maxim's,* Joan Miró's *Carnival of Harlequin,* Henri Matisse's *La Musique,* and Pablo Picasso's *La Tonette* are among the public favorites.

Sculpture, displayed in the 1905 Sculpture Court, the 1962 Sculpture Garden, and the West Corridor, has always played a major role at the AKAG. Gaston Lachaise's hefty *Standing Woman,* Wilhelm Lehmbruck's emaciated *Kneeling Woman,* Auguste Rodin's *Eve,* a Benin bronze head, and a mask from the coast of West Africa are among the favorites. Other pioneering sculptors of the twentieth century included in the collection: Ernst Barlach, Constantin Brancusi, Jean Arp, Naum Gabo, Seymour Lipton, Louise Bourgeois, Alexander Calder, and Henry Moore. The museum was the first American institution to buy a Moore (1939).

GLENS FALLS

The Hyde Collection Art Museum

Address: 161 Warren Street, Glens Falls, NY 12801

Telephone: (518) 792-1761

Web: www.hydeartmuseum.org

Hours: Tues–Sat 10–5; Sun 12–5. Thurs until 7. Closed Mon and all major holidays. Tours daily 1–4.

Strengths: Western European art with emphasis on Italian Renaissance, Dutch, and Flemish (17th century), French (18th to early 20th century) works. Selected works by American artists. Italian and French decorative arts.

Special Events: Temporary exhibits, some of which feature the work of established regional artists, others that of promising high school students.

Other: Museum shop.

Activities for Children: Monthly family days.

Parking: On Warren Street and behind museum.

One would not suspect that Glens Falls, New York, shelters a jewel of an art museum, especially one conceived ninety years ago, when lumber was the small town's principal industry. And yet here, in what was once a private home, hang pictures by Sandro Botticelli, Rembrandt, Raphael, Jean-Auguste-Dominique Ingres, Winslow Homer, Peter Paul Rubens, El Greco, and Thomas Eakins. The works are of such high caliber that their presence is often requested at shows organized by major museums here and abroad.

Charlotte Pruyn and Louis Fiske Hyde met in Boston in 1888, when he studied law and she attended a finishing school. They were married thirteen years later. At Harvard, Louis took Charles Eliot Norton's Italian Renaissance art class. His fellow students included Bernard Berenson and Isabella Stewart Gardner. Louis and Charlotte were deeply impressed by the flamboyant Mrs. Gardner and the museum she created on The Fenway. They were to follow in her footsteps.

In 1907, Charlotte's father persuaded Louis to come home to Glens Falls and head the family's paper business. By 1912 the Hydes had built a large house modeled after a Florentine Renaissance villa. In the two-and-a-half story structure the rooms are grouped around a large glass-covered, plant-filled court. Outside, the manicured grounds slope toward the Hudson. The rooms awaited antique furniture; a picture gallery, located on the upper floor, awaited great art.

Little is known about how the Hydes went about assembling their art. They were private, retiring, publicity-shy people, collecting for their own pleasure. They were partial to works of the Italian Renaissance and northern Europe. Most of their possessions are small-scale, fitting the space of a private residence. Most often they bought on their own, though Bernard Berenson was involved in the acquisition of Botticelli's *Annunciation,* an exquisite panel that was once the predella of an altar.

Another friend, William R. Valentiner, the longtime director of the Detroit Institute of Arts (see p. 233 and Introduction), was instrumental in the acquisition of Rembrandt's powerful *Portrait of Christ.* Like some of the treasures of the National Gallery, the Rembrandt was bought during the 1930s from the financially strapped Soviet Union. Equally strong are Peter Paul Rubens's *Head of a Negro* and Raphael's *Portrait of a Young Man.*

Art critic John Russell has written that for him a successful visit to a museum must strike an emotional chord. In Glens Falls the trigger may be Ingres's *Paolo and Francesca,* Dante's star-crossed lovers. The painting is disarmingly simple, exuding such passion and intimacy that the viewer feels like an intruder. The book the two were reading has dropped to the floor. Clad in a red dress, with down-cast eyes, Francesca looks Madonna-like. Paolo embraces her, unaware that this first kiss will be their last.

Louis Hyde died in 1934. Assisted by Otto Wittman, a graduate of Paul Sachs's museum course in Boston (see Harvard University Art Museums, p. 208), Charlotte continued collecting, broadening, filling in, and expanding the collection by two-thirds. Today the Hyde owns over 2,500 works, including some Impressionists, Post-Impressionists, and American painters including James Whistler, Childe Hassam, and Albert Pinkham Ryder.

As the fame of her possessions spread, Harvard and New York's Metropolitan approached Mrs. Hyde, trying to convince her to will the collection to their larger museums. She refused. Today the works are still housed in Glens Falls. Like The Frick Collection in New York (see p. 278), the Hyde is more than an art museum. It looks as if the house were still lived in, waiting for someone to sit in the library reading a book and glancing from time to time at a portrait, an Oriental rug, a tapestry, or a piece of sculpture.

NEW YORK CITY

The Asia Society

Address: 725 Park Avenue, New York, NY 10021

Telephone: (212) 517-2742

Web: www.asiasociety.org

Hours: Tues–Sat 10–6; Sun 12–5. Closed Mon and major holidays. Tours Tues–Sat at 12:30, Sun at 2:30.

Strength: Art of South, Southeast, and East Asia.

Special Events: Temporary shows. Lectures, discussion with artists. Performances.

Other: Interactive computer. Café. Museum store.

Activities for Children: Semi-annual family days.

Parking: Metered and scarce; pay garages.

In 1956, as part of his interest in rebuilding a democratic Japan, John D. Rockefeller III founded the Asia Society. The goal of the institution was and is the fostering of improved understanding between Asia and the United States. From early on, Mr. Rockefeller and his wife, Blanchette, decided that art would play an important role in the society. Given the Rockefeller tradition—Blanchette was heavily involved in her mother-in-law Abby's Museum of Modern Art in New York and John had grown up with the Chinese porcelains his father had acquired in 1915 from the estate of J. P. Morgan—the couple started to collect with discernment. At first they mostly acquired ceramics, and these remain the heart of the collection.

In 1963 the Rockefellers felt they needed professional advice and contacted Sherman E. Lee. He clearly was their man. Lee, an Asian art expert, had been instrumental in forming the outstanding Asian art collections of both the Seattle (p. 407) and Cleveland (p. 327) museums of art. In his introduction to a catalog of the Asia Society collection Lee writes: "It was soon evident that both Rockefellers were more interested in objects than in oriental paintings." Under Lee's guidance the collection, however, became comprehensive and grew to include scrolls, paintings, tomb figurines, bronzes, sculptures, and other artworks from South, Southeast, and East Asia—dating from 2000 B.C.E. to the nineteenth century.

Eventually the collection included 285 objects, which is modest when compared to those assembled by Charles L. Freer (see the Freer Gallery of Art in Washington, D.C., p. 134) and Avery Brundage (see the Asian Art Museum in San Francisco, p. 85), but is universally described as "gemlike." As Vishaka N. Desai, director of the gallery, wrote in 1994: "It is one of the most notable collections of Asian art in the United States, primarily because of the high proportion of acclaimed masterpieces." Sculptures are especially heavily represented. A stylized, many-armed Shiva as Lord of the Dance inside a flaming mandorla (semicircle) is especially impressive, as are the male and female sandstone figures from the eleventh century. The museum is particularly proud of a hanging scroll from the late thirteenth century attributed to Lou Guan that depicts a towering mountain.

The collection was first exhibited at Asia House, a townhouse on East Sixty-fourth Street in New York City. In 1981, three years after John D. Rockefeller's death, it became the property of the Asia Society and moved with it to 725 Park Avenue. Edward Larrabee Barnes designed its new red granite headquarters. Colorful banners announcing current exhibits usually garland the building, lending a festive air to sedate Park Avenue.

The Asia Society is a very active institution. It slowly increases its permanent collection and also hosts relevant temporary shows and offers discussions, performances, readings, and other special events. By 2000, more space was needed and a renovation was in order. This refiguration allows the Rockefeller collection to be on permanent display. A new glass-enclosed, skylit garden court with sculpture, plantings, and a café has been added. The architect for the successful renovation is Bartholomew Voorsanger, who also designed the Pierport Morgan Library's delightful garden court in New York (see p. 303).

Brooklyn Museum of Art

Address: 200 Eastern Parkway, Brooklyn, NY 11238

Telephone: (718) 638-5000

Web: www.brooklynart.org

Hours: Wed–Fri 10–5; Sat 11–6; Sun 11–6. First Sat 11–11. Closed Mon, Tues, and New Year's, Thanksgiving, and Christmas days. Tours.

Strengths: Encyclopedic. Comprehensive collections of European and American paintings and sculpture. Excellent Egyptian collection. Extensive collections of African, Oceanic, Inuit, and Native American art. 27 period rooms. Rodin collection. Sculpture garden filled with architectural fragments from demolished buildings.

Special Events: Temporary exhibits. First Sat evenings until 11: Special programs (dancing to live music, films, other). Daily gallery talks on a variety of subjects such as Ancient Egypt, Animals in Art, American Paintings, 20th-Century Decorative Art.

Other: Restaurants: Buffet service in Museum Café and Sculpture Garden Café. Extensive shop with imports from around the world. Special shop for children.

Activities for Children: The BMA has always catered to children. Sun tours for parents and children, sporadic. As always, children are fascinated by the Egyptian collection. Special web site for children: www.brooklynexpedition.org).

Parking: On site, pay lot.

Manhattan and *Brooklyn,* two allegorical figures by Daniel Chester French, flank the entrance of the Brooklyn Museum of Art (BMA). The large statues, which once guarded the approach to the Manhattan Bridge, symbolize the sometimes strained relationship between New York City's oldest boroughs.

The BMA is almost as large as Manhattan's Metropolitan Museum of Art, and almost as old. It owns great art, yet during entire decades the museum seemed almost forgotten. Fortunately, at long last, this wonderful treasure trove shows new vigor. People flock there to significant temporary shows, such as *Monet and the Mediterranean* or *Impressionists in Winter,* and return to view the extraordinary permanent collections.

Concerned citizens of the Village of Brooklyn founded the Brooklyn Apprentices' Association in 1823. At one time Walt Whitman, a Brook-

The Moorish Smoking Room from the John D. Rockefeller townhouse in Manhattan is one of the Brooklyn Museum of Art's twenty-seven period rooms.

lyn resident, served as acting librarian of the institution. Eventually the original Association split into the BMA, the Brooklyn Academy of Music, the Brooklyn Botanic Garden, and the Brooklyn Children's Museum, all of which still flourish. In 1893, McKim, Mead & White developed plans for a new museum. The first wing of the building opened in 1907. Like the Met, the BMA adjoins its borough's big park, Prospect Park, which was developed by Frederick Law Olmsted, designer of Central Park, and also adjoins the magnificent Brooklyn Botanic Garden. When it opened, the BMA's collection numbered 532 art objects; by 2000 that number had grown to over 1.5 million.

The BMA has always been forward-looking. It was the first museum in America to have a department of photography. In 1923, it held a precedent-setting exhibition of its African collection, billing the works as fine art rather than ethnographic objects. In 1926, it organized a large and comprehensive *International Exhibition of Modern Art,* also controversial. This adventurous spirit is evident in the museum's possessions.

The staff of the museum participated in archaeological excavations and expeditions. In 1902 the museum received its first gift of Egyptian antiquities. Participation in excavations as well as gifts and purchases of several major collections has yielded one of the world's finest Egyptian collections. The fine works that Dr. Henry Abbott, an Englishman, had assembled in Egypt during the nineteenth century were a major acquisition. This collection was shipped to New York and acquired by the New York Historical Society in 1860. It was loaned to the BMA in 1937, and acquired in 1948. Much of the museum's exclusive collection is now presented in a major reinstallation in the recently renovated Morris A. and Meyer Schapiro Wing.

Art from other non-Western cultures—China, India, Nepal, Japan— is equally satisfying. Most impressive are objects gathered from the "New World." There are totem poles from Haida, kachina dolls, Pre-Columbian pottery, and golden objects from Panama. Selections from more extensive holdings are beautifully displayed. Free brochures make the viewing meaningful.

The painting and sculpture departments are housed on the fourth floor. The chronologically arranged European paintings range from the fourteenth to the twentieth century. Among Italian Renaissance works, the *Annunciation* by Nichola di Maestro Antonio D'Ancoma and the *Portrait of a Young Man as St. Sebastian* by Jacometto Veneziano are particularly noteworthy. There are also representative examples of the Dutch school. And given the BMA's early interest in "modern" art, the museum owns excellent paintings by the Impressionists as well as work by artists who preceded and followed them. There are paintings by Camille Corot, Gustave Courbet, Claude Monet, Auguste Renoir, Camille Pissaro, Edgar Degas, Vincent van Gogh, Paul Cézanne, Henri Matisse, André Derain, Kees van Dongen, Pierre Bonnard, Odillon Redon, Henri de Toulouse-Lautrec, Edvard Munch, Georges Braque, and Paul Klee, to cite only a few.

Iris and B. Gerald Cantor (also see the Cantor Center for Visual Arts, p. 102) donated fifty-eight works by Auguste Rodin, including twelve studies and figures from *The Burghers of Calais*. These are beautifully displayed in the museum's rotunda.

The BMA has an excellent collection of American paintings. Highlights from the eighteenth century include famous portraits of George Washington by Gilbert Stuart and by Charles Willson Peale, and a version of Edward Hicks's *A Peaceable Kingdom*. The Hudson River School is represented by Thomas Cole, Frederick Church, and Albert

Bierstadt. There are paintings by George Inness, John Singer Sargent, Winslow Homer, Mary Cassatt, and other American Impressionists as well as by more recent American artists including Georgia O'Keeffe, Marsden Hartley, Stuart Davis, Alex Katz, Mark Rothko, Richard Diebenkorn, and Louise Bourgeois.

The oldest of twenty-eight period rooms comes from the Flatlands section of Brooklyn and dates from 1675. The Moorish Smoking Room from John D. Rockefeller, Sr.'s house in Manhattan is also of interest. The decorative arts section of the museum is magnificent. There are entire galleries displaying glass, silver, and porcelain—elegant and plain as well as utilitarian objects. There are wonderful stained glass windows by John La Farge and Tiffany, as well as murals funded by the WPA.

Architectural fragments from demolished buildings are cleverly assembled in the Frieda Schiff Warburg Memorial Sculpture Garden. Works include capitals from a building on Bleecker Street designed by Louis Sullivan, pieces of Coney Island's Steeplechase, and fragments and keystones from ordinary houses. This display of our own recent urban ruins suits a museum that is so devoted to the heritage of past civilizations. (Warburg donated her extravagant Renaissance mansion on Fifth Avenue to The Jewish Museum—see p. 289.)

In 2001, the Landmarks Preservation Commission of the City of New York approved a plan to redesign and renovate the museum's main entrance with a glass entrance pavilion and public plaza, doubling the space of the existing lobby.

The Cloisters

Address: Fort Tryon Park, New York, NY 10040

Telephone: (212) 923-3700

Web: www.metmuseum.org (under Collections)

Hours: *March–Oct*: Tues–Sun 9:30–5:15; *Nov–Feb*: 9:30–4:45. Closed Mon, New Year's, Thanksgiving, and Christmas days. Daily tours and lectures.

Strength: Medieval art: Reconstructed cloisters, chapels, and charter house; outdoor gardens; Unicorn tapestries; Bury St. Edmunds cross; paintings, sculptures, artifacts.

Special Events: Medieval festivals. Gregorian chant. Concerts.

Other: Museum shop.

Activities for Children: An ideal place to introduce children to life in medieval Europe. Even very young children may appreciate and enjoy the cloisters themselves, the Unicorn tapestries, the ceremonial objects, the period room, and the gardens.

Parking: On site.

You don't have to like medieval art to love The Cloisters, the only outpost of New York's Metropolitan Museum of Art (Met). According to Germain Bazin, a former director of the Louvre, The Cloisters is "the crowning achievement of American museology." As soon as you climb up a long set of stone steps you are transported to a time far removed from today. You may wander through old cloisters—four in all—two small chapels, and a chapter house, or simply gaze at treasures of long ago. On most days you can step outside onto a terrace, or into the open Trie or Bonnefont cloisters. Far below you'll see the mighty Hudson River and the Palisades, the rocky outcropping across the river in New Jersey. Then you glimpse the steel girders of the George Wash-ington Bridge, and you realize that you are not in thirteenth-century France.

The Cloisters is the realization of the dream of three men: George Grey Barnard, a sculptor, John D. Rockefeller, Jr., the patron, and James J. Rorimer, curator of medieval art of the Met and later its director. Barnard lived and worked in France before World War One. As a sideline he collected abandoned church art in Europe and shipped architectural fragments home to America, eventually opening a small museum in Washington Heights. In 1922, Rockefeller, with Rorimer's enthusiastic approval, bought Barnard's entire collection for the Met. Mr. Rockefeller envisioned it housed in a structure of its own and, together with Rorimer and architect Charles Collens, developed a setting that evokes the serenity of ecclesiastic structures.

Many original elements (columns, capitals, stained glass windows) were incorporated into the building itself; others were freely displayed in intimate galleries. Compared to the mammoth collections of its mother institution, the collections of The Cloisters are small and manageable. They are also exquisite. The treasures include the fifteenth-century *Hunt of the Unicorn* series of tapestries, considered to be among the greatest in the world; the twelfth-century Bury St. Edmunds ivory cross, a large altarpiece by Jan van Eyck, rare illuminated manuscripts, enameled reliquary caskets made in Limoges, France, and gorgeous stained glass windows displayed at eye level. Our medieval forebears were fond of animals—elaborately carved dogs and lions support the feet of the stone effigies of the Spanish noblemen transplanted to New York. There is even part of a medieval house, whose door is a reminder that people used to be much shorter than they are today.

It is, however, the ambience that remains the heart of The Cloisters. Gregorian chants waft through the chapter house and the cloisters. The landscaping is simple. There are potted orange trees, paper narcissus, and lilies of the valleys. The garden of the Trie cloister is filled with plants shown in the Unicorn tapestries. Medicinal and kitchen herbs fill the brick-enclosed beds of the Bonnefont cloister. Special gallery displays mark the seasons. At Eastertime Christ enters Jerusalem on a small wooden donkey, which, like a child's pull-toy, is equipped with wheels. At Christmas we are welcomed by brightly painted wooden sculptures of the Three Kings.

The Frick Collection

Address: One E. 70th Street, New York, NY 10021

Telephone: (212) 288-0700

Web: www.frick.org

Hours: Tues–Sat 10–6; Sun and Feb. 12, Nov. 2, Nov. 11, 1:00–6:00. Closed Mon and New Year's, Independence, Thanksgiving, Christmas Eve, and Christmas days.

Strengths: Portraits, landscapes, art of Western Europe (Dutch, English, French) with emphasis on the 17th to 19th centuries. Portraits by Gainsborough, Rembrandt, Reynolds, Romney, Sargent, Ingres. Bronze sculptures. Decorative art: Porcelain, enamels, furniture. Rooms paneled with murals by Fragonard and Boucher.

Special Events: Free chamber music concerts on selected Sun at 5:00 (written requests accepted on the third Mon before the concert). Lectures. Exhibition of single relevant portraits from other collections.

Other: Free acoustiguide in six languages. Interesting 20-min audiovisual introduction to the collection. Museum bookstore specializing in art books related to the collections. Research library open to the public.

Activities for Children: Children under 10 not admitted.

Parking: Scarce on street; pay garages in the neighborhood.

At One East Seventieth Street, the Frick Collection is the downtown anchor of New York's "Museum Mile," the strip of a dozen or so museums lining Fifth Avenue. With its manicured front lawn, now surrounded by tall apartment houses, the sleek three-story Italianate palazzo of the Frick clearly dates from another era. Carrère and Hastings built it in 1913–1914 as a home for Henry Clay Frick. The firm had just completed the New York Public Library at Forty-second Street. Both buildings are timeless and elegant. At the time, Fifth Avenue was lined with mansions. Cars were few and life's pace was slower. Even today a feeling of calm and pleasant anticipation engulfs those who enter the house that clearly belongs to America's Gilded Age. It is no wonder that The Frick Collection is one of New York's most beloved museums.

Compared to the Metropolitan Museum of Art, located a mere ten blocks to the North, the Frick is a boutique museum. The building and its collection were originally shaped by the taste of one man and by the

A view of the charming Garden Court at the Frick, designed by John Russell Pope, architect of the National Gallery of Art in the nation's capital.

availability of the art he craved. Frick collected at the end of the nineteenth century. To the delight of art dealers, he competed for quality works with J. P. Morgan, the Havemeyers, and others whose possessions we enjoy today. Like Boston's Isabella Stewart Gardner, Frick planned to leave his house as well as his collection to the public.

The feeling of "time out" from the stresses of everyday life heightens as we amble through the house, which is luxurious but not overwhelming. Walls are paneled or covered in fine fabric. The floors are wood or marble, the windows overlooking Central Park are draped with brocade.

When asked about Frick's approach to art, Helen Clay Frick used to say: "My father collected paintings that were pleasant to live with." Indeed, the paintings of the collection avoid violence, poverty, and even religious martyrdom. It is a very personal collection.

Henry Clay Frick was born in 1849 in rural Pennsylvania and moved to Pittsburgh in 1867, where he made his fortune in coke (a form of coal) and steel, eventually becoming an associate of Andrew Carnegie. When he was thirty-one years old, and a millionaire, Frick traveled to Europe in the company of Andrew Mellon, to whom we owe the National Gallery of Art in Washington, D.C. (see p. 125). Even before he was wealthy Frick bought art, but now he could acquire masterpieces, portraits and landscapes created by artists of Western Europe: England, France, Holland, and Italy. He was partial to glamorous women (English, eighteenth century), but he also liked the more modest burghers painted by Frans Hals and the deeply emotional paintings of Rembrandt.

Sculptures, enamels, precious porcelains, tapestries, and exquisite furniture are scattered throughout the galleries. Everything is on a human scale. The list of treasures owned by The Frick is imposing, but it is the manner in which the possessions are displayed that makes the collection unique. Objects are organized for aesthetic effect rather than by theme or chronology. Even the large West Gallery is broken up by Oriental rugs, a big library table, small statuary, and comfortable sofas on which visitors can relax. The paintings by Rembrandt, Frans Hals, Georges de La Tour, Jan Vermeer, Anthony Van Dyck, Camille Corot, and many more are lit by natural light.

Most rooms still reflect their original function. Some of the museum's special treasures are in "The Living Hall," which fronts

Fifth Avenue. A stern El Greco *St. Jerome* looks down from above the fireplace. The saint is flanked by two portraits by Hans Holbein the Younger: *Sir Thomas Moore* and *Thomas Cromwell*. The Frick owns two of Vermeer's rare interiors, and works by William Turner, Thomas Gainsborough, Titian, and so many more. Some of the Frick's art is playful. *The Progress of Love*, eleven panels painted by Jean Honoré Fragonard, line a small parlor again facing Fifth Avenue. Four of the Fragonard panels were commissioned and then refused by Madame Du Barry, mistress of Louis XV. At one time the entire set decorated J. P. Morgan's house in London. After Morgan's death they were sold by Belle da Costa Greene, Director of the Pierpont Morgan Library, in New York (see p. 303). Frick was also able to acquire other master-pieces from the Morgan estate.

Mr. Frick derived peace from the contemplation of his treasures. Nights when he could not sleep after a tumultuous day at work, he would spend an hour communing with his possessions. His three favorite paintings were Hans Holbein, the Younger's *Sir Thomas Moore*, Giovanni Bellini's *St. Francis in the Desert*, and Rembrandt's last self-portrait, a moving image of the great painter's careworn face.

After Mrs. Frick's death the house was adapted for use as a public museum by John Russell Pope, who also built the National Gallery of Art. To him we owe the Garden Court, which is the most peaceful spot of the Frick. Palms and ferns as well as orchids and other blooming plants surround a pool beneath a vaulted glass ceiling. Water spouted by two resident bronze frogs falls gently, and sometimes the Frick's magnificent Aeolian pipe organ is played. With luck, on Sundays you may also be able to attend a chamber music concert in the cut-velvet-lined music room.

The Solomon R. Guggenheim Museum

Address: 1071 Fifth Avenue, New York, NY 10128

Telephone: (212) 423-3500

Web: www.guggenheim.org

Hours: Sun–Wed 9–6; Fri–Sat 9–8. Closed Thurs and Christmas Day. Tours daily.

Strengths: 20th-century non-objective art. Tannhauser Collection of late-19th-

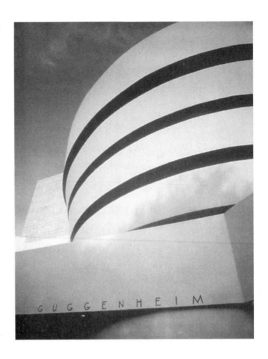

The Solomon R. Guggenheim Museum, New York City.

and early-20th-century art. The collection includes concentrated holdings of Kandinsky, Picasso, Brancusi, and Chagall.

Special Events: Temporary exhibits.

Other: Restaurant. Museum shop. Guggenheim Soho (575 Broadway at Prince Street, New York, NY 10012; phone same as main museum): a satellite in an interesting space with good temporary exhibits. Hours: Thurs–Mon 11–6; closed Tues and Wed.

Activities for Children: Films, tours, and workshops throughout the year.

Parking: Very limited on street; pay garages.

At Eighty-seventh Street the staid buff-colored buildings of Fifth Avenue are interrupted by a strange-looking stark-white circular structure. The Solomon R. Guggenheim Museum, variously described by architecture critics as the most beautiful building in America, an inverted cup and saucer, a turnip, a giant snail, and a cement mixer, is now one of New York City's easily recognized landmarks.

Upon entering the building through an almost hidden door, your eyes will soar six stories upward to a huge skylight. At first the edifice seems empty, then you'll notice a ramp that coils around inside its perimeter. Take the small elevator up to the seventh floor. Descend the ramp slowly, looking down onto the crowd that mills on the ground floor, the small elliptical pool, and a tree or two. As you concentrate on the current exhibition, glance across to the other side of the building, and also look at the works from afar. It is a unique and exhilarating way to view art.

In 1927, when Solomon R. Guggenheim was sixty-six years old, rich, and bored, he met the Baroness Hilla Rebay von Ehrenweiss, a painter and passionate crusader for abstract and non-objective art. Miss Rebay convinced Solomon to buy art by the carload: Marc Chagall, Wassily Kandinsky (170 works), Rudolph Bauer, Paul Klee (140 works), László Moholy-Nagy, Lyonel Feininger, Amedeo Modigliani, Pablo Picasso, and many others. At the time, this avant-garde art was still rather unknown in America and rather inexpensive.

As the paintings accumulated, they were shown in private quarters in the Plaza Hotel, but in 1939, two years after Solomon established the Solomon R. Guggenheim Foundation, the small Museum of Non-Objective Painting was opened in a Manhattan townhouse, with the baroness as director.

By all accounts, Miss Rebay was eccentric, opinionated, and rather unpleasant, and ruffled many feathers, including those of Solomon's wife and daughters, but she was a visionary. As Vivian Endicott Barnett wrote in the *Handbook of the Guggenheim Collection*, "The collection [of the museum] today still derives its main strength from the purchases made in the era of the Museum of Non-Objective Painting."

By 1944 the museum had outgrown its townhouse and Frank Lloyd Wright was contacted. According to John L. Davis, Guggenheim's biographer, in *The Guggenheims*, when Solomon examined Wright's first plans "there were tears in his eyes. 'Mr. Wright,' he said, 'I knew you would do it, this is it.'" Unfortunately, the museum was not completed until sixteen years later and by then both Guggenheim and Wright were dead. It took forever to find a site for the museum and to iron out the thirty-two violations of New York's Department of Housing Building Code, but finally, on October 21, 1959, the museum opened its doors. There has always been controversy about how well the building, with its curved, slightly slanting walls, functions as a museum and it clearly suits some works of art better than others. But most of the exceptional temporary shows and retrospectives are a match for the extraordinary galleries.

In time the Guggenheim was given four other complementary collections. The most important of these is the Justin K. Thannhäuser Collection of Impressionist, Post-Impressionist, and early modern masterpieces. Thannhäuser, an art dealer, was forced to leave Germany because he was Jewish. The museum now also owns Karl Nierendorf's collection of German Expressionists, part of Katherine S. Dreier's collection of paintings and sculptures of the historic avant-garde (also see Yale University Art Gallery, p. 116), and Count Giuseppe Panza di Biumo's collection of American Minimal Art of the 1960s and 1970s. The museum's holdings also include purchases and individual gifts.

Selections from the permanent collection are on view in the museum's post-Wright Thannhäuser Wing of more conventional galleries. Here we can admire Marc Chagall's zany, green-faced violin player, the original *Fiddler on the Roof*; Lyonel Feininger's crazily broken-up church *Gelmeroda IV*, Kandinsky's *Compositions,* Klee's *Red Ballon,* and many other familiar favorites. The letters Vincent van Gogh wrote to his brother Theo discussing the genesis of many of his paintings are often displayed.

The Guggenheim is ideally suited to holding events. On Friday evenings visitors can listen to jazz, sip wine, and amble up and down the great ramp. Children love the Guggenheim. Its collection is not overwhelming, and the art encourages openness and freedom.

Unlike most museums, the Guggenheim has satellites. The closest by far is its Soho branch, which has temporary shows featuring post-World War Two and contemporary art. Others are in Bilbao, Spain; Berlin, and Venice. Like her uncle, Peggy Guggenheim collected and even dealt in non-objective, abstract, and Surrealist art. She assembled a superior, very personal collection, which since 1949 has been exhibited in the Palazzo Venier dei Leoni in Venice. Even though she had not always gotten along with the other Guggenheims, Peggy left her collection to her uncle's museum, provided it would remain in Venice. The new Guggenheim in Bilbao, Spain, was built by the American architect Frank Gehry (also see the Frederick R. Weisman Art Museum, p. 240).

The Hispanic Society of America

Address: 613 W. 155th Street, New York, NY, 10032

Telephone: (212) 926-2234

Web: www.hispanicsociety.org

Hours: Tues–Sat 10–4:30, Sun 1–4. Modern paintings, including Sorolla, on Sat only. Closed: Mon, Jan 1, Feb 12, Feb 22, May 30, Good Friday, Easter Sunday, and Independence, Thanksgiving, and Christmas days.

Strengths: Art and artifacts of Spain, Latin America, and the Philippines. Superior survey of paintings of the Spanish Golden Age (1550–1700) and of the work of Joaquín Sorolla y Bastida. Hispano-Moresque lusterware and other decorative arts.

Other: Courtyard with sculptures by Anna Hyatt Huntington.

Parking: On street.

The Museum of the Hispanic Society of America is Manhattan's best-kept secret. It owns half a dozen El Grecos, as many Goyas, paintings by Francisco de Zurbarán and Diego Velázquez, and the largest collection of Joaquín Sorolla y Bastida in the United States. Yet it counts visitors by the dozens rather than by the hundreds or thousands.

Archer Milton Huntington (1870–1955) inherited a railroad fortune (also see Introduction and Huntington Library, Art Collections, and Botanical Gardens, p. 96). Early in life, Huntington fell in love with Spain. In 1904, to increase America's awareness of its Spanish heritage, he founded the Hispanic Society. He built his museum on what was to become "Audubon Terrace," a court accessible from Broadway, so named because the land was once part of the ornithologist's Manhattan farm, called Minnie's Land. At one time five small museums, including the Museum of the American Indian, were located here.

The main portion of the small museum consists of a covered court surrounded by a balcony. No expense was spared in the decoration of the arches and stuccoed walls, which indeed feel like an old Spanish castle. Your eyes immediately meet two large portraits by Francisco Goya, one of the Duchess of Alba standing in the landscape of her estate. The duchess's head and shoulders are swathed in filmy black lace and her gold-shod feet are firmly planted on the ground. Romantics have suggested that sitter and painter were lovers because the duchess points at Goya's signature with her index finger. She also wears two rings, one spelling Alba, the other Goya.

The smaller galleries radiating from the central court are filled with marble paintings of the Spanish Renaissance. Retables and other works attest to the fierce religiosity and crusading spirit of Spain. One gallery is filled with tombs from the monastery of San Francisco de Cuellar, dating from the early sixteenth century. The marble effigies are among the most spectacular ones in America. Cabinets are filled with the intricate work of gold- and silversmiths and rare examples of Hispano-Moresque lusterware decorated with a combination of Islamic and local themes. Spain's Arab tradition is also evident in textiles exhibited behind glass.

Most of the paintings of Spain's Golden Age are on the second floor. The paintings are deeply affecting, even though one wishes that they were better hung. Saint Lucy and Saint Rufina by Francisco de Zurbarán face each other. Jusepe de Ribera's *The Ecstasy of Mary Magdalen* shows the saint floating in the sky carried by putti. An early El Greco Pietà shows the painter's training in Byzantine art. His later picture of St. Jerome is in his more typical ascetic sytle. Three paintings by Diego Velázquez, including the grandiose portrait of Count Duke of Olivares and the introspective *Portrait of a Little Girl*, as well as some smaller Goyas, illustrate Spain's secular art.

The Hispanic Society had a special relationship with Joaquín Sorolla y Bastida (1863–1923), no doubt Spain's most famous painter of the early twentieth century. Huntington commissioned thirteen murals of the *Provinces of Spain* for the west wing of the museum. Sevilla is represented by a bullfight, Navara by a procession, Aragon by dances. Other scenes depict cattle and cacti, oranges, and fishermen with their catch. Other paintings by Sorolla, more closely related to Impressionism, are in the museum's north wing (only open Saturday). Most moving is Sorolla's portrait of Louis Comfort Tiffany. Sitting in a sea of white and yellow flowers in the garden of his Oyster Bay estate, Tiffany, in a white suit, a shaggy dog at his side, is painting. The sun is shining and the sea is glistening in the background. This idyllic picture of the magician of stained glass makes you forget that at his death he was embittered, poor, and out of fashion.

One of the charms of the museum is that it is located on a terrace graced by the sculptures of Anna Hyatt Huntington, wife of Archer. The sculptor's prize-winning equestrian statue of Joan of Arc can be seen at New York's Riverside Drive and One-hundredth Street. A cast of her statue of El Cid, made for Sevilla, Spain, stand in front of her husband's museum. Other casts of Huntington's El Cid stand in front of the California Palace of the Legion of Honor in San Francisco (see p. 87), and on the Prado in San Diego. In New York the warrior is surrounded by four imposing bronze figures. Groups of animals, jaguars, wild boars, brown bears, and vultures guard two additional equestrian bas-reliefs, one of Don Quixote, Spain's beloved antihero, the other of Boabdil. A poem by Archer Huntington, engraved on another wall, attests to the couple's love for España: *"Land of the Winds of Promise and Desire / Land of the Ethereal Distances and Dreams / Land of the Song of Battles and Love / High, high above each silvered Height in moonlight gleam / Oh haunted land of history and fire."*

The Isamu Noguchi Garden Museum

Address: 32-37 Vernon Boulevard, Long Island City, NY 11106

Telephone: (718) 721-1932

Web: www.noguchi.org

Hours: *Summer only.* Wed–Fri 10–5; Sat–Sun 11–6. Closed Mon, Tues. Free guided tours at 2.

Strength: Overview of a single artist's oeuvre, emphasizing his desire to link the spirit of Eastern and Western art.

Special Events: Films on the life and work of Noguchi.

Other: Museum shop which carries a full line of Akari lamps (mail/phone order 718-721-2308), books, postcards.

Parking: On street.

"Art is everywhere," Isamu Noguchi said. "The whole world is art . . . some people see it and some people don't." The Japanese-American sculptor spent his life helping people experience the beauty of sculpture, rocks, plants, gardens, and deceptively simple public spaces. Serenity surrounds visitors the minute they step into the garden of his former studio in Long Island City in the borough of Queens.

Isamu Noguchi himself planned the museum, one of a growing number devoted to a single artist. He oversaw the placement of every single sculpture and planting. After he died in 1988, half his ashes were buried here, the other half resting in his garden museum in Japan.

The museum houses over 300 works by Noguchi. Large stone sculptures fill the garden. Like Stonehenge, England's well-known prehistoric (2000 B.C.E.) circle of monoliths, Noguchi's sculptures instill respect. The partly polished, partly rough works are interspersed among plants and trees: white birches, weeping cherry, black pine, ivy, bamboo, and others. A fountain dispenses water. Planes taking off or landing at nearby La Guardia Airport may roar overhead or you may hear the siren of an ambulance screeching by on the busy street of this industrial neighborhood, but chances are that you won't pay too much attention because of the peace that prevails in the museum.

Like its neighbor, P.S.1 Contemporary Art Center (p. 306), the Noguchi museum occupies a triangular space, but whereas the school is one of America's biggest exhibition spaces, Noguchi's museum must be one of the smallest. Both, however, reuse old spaces. Noguchi's served as a photoengraving plant before it became a studio, then a museum.

Noguchi was born in Los Angeles in 1904. His father was a Japanese poet, his mother a writer. During his youth, and later in life, Noguchi divided his time between Asia and the West. Early in his career he saw the polished-marble sculpture of Constantin Brancusi and apprenticed himself to the artist in Paris. His horizon broadened and today his garden-landscapes form the entryways to important buildings throughout the world: The UNESCO headquarters in Paris, the IBM headquarters in Armonk, New York, a sculpture garden for the Israel Museum in Jerusalem.

He was fastidious about the thirteen museum galleries. Works spanning the sculptor's career are arranged chronologically and/or by the material he employed. There are the bronze sculptures created in Paris during the 1920s, the interlocking sculptures of the 1940s, and the smaller works made from marble, wood, and stone.

To the public at large the sculptor may be best known for his Akari light sculptures that were inspired by traditional lanterns used for night fishing in Japan. The lamps are both whimsical and elegant.

Noguchi created over 100 different designs—some standing on the floor, some standing on tables, some hanging from the ceiling, some perching on thin stalks of bamboo. About twenty are on view. Most of the original designs can be ordered at the museum.

The museum pays tribute to the Japanese American sculptor's other contributions: the sets he designed for Martha Graham's dance company, his (projected) playgrounds, outdoor plazas, landscapes, and sculpture gardens (see The Museum of Fine Arts, Houston, p. 388).

The Jewish Museum

Address: 1109 Fifth Avenue, New York, NY 10128

Telephone: (212) 423-3200

Web: www.jewishmuseum.org

Hours: Sun–Mon, Wed–Thurs 11–5:45; Tues 11–8. Closed Fri, Sat, and major Jewish and other holidays.

Strengths: Jewish ceremonial art objects, significant artwork by Jewish artists or featuring Jewish subjects, and multimedia installations. Videos, audios, films related to Jewish life and rituals.

Special Events: Many films, lectures, concerts, discussions.

Other: Small sculpture court. Café with kosher food. Museum shop with distinctive gifts, Jewish ceremonial objects, jewelry, and children's items. Unique collectible works created by contemporary artists are available in the Jewish Museum Design Shop next door.

Activities for Children: Exhibits celebrating Jewish life are extremely suitable. Also family days (some free) highlighting Purim, Passover, and other festivals and topics.

Parking: Limited on street; pay garages.

Students devoted to the study of New York's Gilded Age, or readers of Stephen Birmingham's *Our Crowd*, will be delighted to visit the famous Warburg 1908 French Gothic chateau at Fifth Avenue and Ninety-second Street. Even though it has been necessary to remove the grand stairs and other details during expansion, some of the glamour of the former home, with its parquet floors, wood paneling, stonework, and views of Central Park remains.

Moritz Daniel Oppenheim, *The Return of the Jewish Volunteer from the Wars of Liberation to His Family Still Living in Accordance with Old Customs*, at The Jewish Museum, New York City.

The Jewish Theological Seminary founded The Jewish Museum in 1904. The collection "lived" in the library of the Seminary until 1944, when Frieda Schiff Warburg donated her mansion, located toward the northern end of the "Museum Mile," in memory of her father, Jacob Schiff, her brother, Mortimer, and her husband, Felix Warburg. As expected, the museum owns a very fine collection of Jewish ceremonial art. Some of the objects come from Danzig, which once upon a time had a flourishing Jewish community. As the specter of the Nazis rose in Eastern Europe, the Danzig Jews decided to send their treasures to safety in America, where today they are a poignant reminder of a destroyed civilization.

The museum's mission is "to preserve, study, and interpret Jewish Cultural History throughout the world." Its approach to any subject is ecumenical. As stated by Stephen Kayser in 1947, the aim of the institution is to give "the American community . . . insight into the traditions, history, legends and aspirations of the Jewish people."

From an initial gift of twenty-six objects in 1904, the collection of paintings, sculpture, works on paper, photographs, ethnographic material, archeological artifacts, numismatics, ceremonial objects, and broadcast media of the museum has grown to 28,000 objects. The centerpiece of the museum is a two-floor permanent exhibit entitled *Culture and Continuity: The Jewish Journey,* which explores the essence of Jewish identity—the basic ideas, values, and culture developed by this ancient people over 4,000 years. Vivid illustration of this continuity is the display of excavated artifacts from the first century B.C.E., the recreation of an ancient synagogue, an etching by Rembrandt of *The Great Jewish Bride,* and George Segal's haunting figure of a *Holocaust Survivor* (also see The California Palace of the Legion of Honor, p. 87).

Given the richness of Jewish culture and the fact that Jews have participated in so many areas of life as artists or patrons, the museum is never at a loss for topics for stimulating temporary exhibitions. Shows range from small retrospective one-man shows to broad topics such as the exploration of the artistic life of Jews in Germany before Hitler. The museum regularly mounts exhibitions featuring contemporary artists exploring Jewish themes and issues.

Jacques Marchais Museum of Tibetan Art

Address: 338 Lighthouse Avenue, Staten Island, NY 10306
Telephone: (718) 987-3500
Web: www.tibetanmuseum.com
Hours: *April–Nov*: Wed–Sun 1–5; *Dec–March*: Wed–Fri 1–5. Call for more details.
Strength: Tibetan Art displayed in a setting resembling a Tibetan temple in a monastery.
Special Events: Lectures, films, concerts, dance performances, and other events intended to familiarize visitors with the intricate, compassionate culture of Tibet.
Other: Museum shop with items from Himalayan region and Japan.
Parking: On street.

The minute you enter the gate of this tiny museum you are in a magic world. The terraced, hillside garden is crowded with trees, benches, and statuary. There is a friendly bronze elephant, two ceramic monkeys, and a white marble Buddha holding fresh flowers. From the edge of the terrace you look down onto a pool. The tops of old trees hide the suburban surroundings and you indeed feel as if the museum were in a remote place.

Everything is surprising about the Museum of Tibetan Art, including the person and name of its founder. Jacques Marchais is the adopted name of Edna Klauber. Marchais was born in Cincinatti in 1887. By all accounts she had a horrible childhood, then worked as an actress, and eventually married Harry Klauber. In 1921 the couple bought a house and land on the crest of Lighthouse Hill in Staten Island.

Nobody knows how and why Jacques Marchais became interested in, and knowledgeable about, Tibetan art. Legend has it that as a child she played with small temple figures her grandfather brought back from India; she, herself, never visited Tibet. In an excerpt from an unfinished autobiography, she wrote: "I hope to build on our hill adjoining the garden, [a temple] . . . large enough to house 300 people at a time. . . . It will be of fieldstone, the interior done in the color conducive to peace and quiet meditation—with a huge Buddha smiling down . . . in benevolent benediction."

During the 1930s, to raise money for the venture and to build a collection of her own, Marchais opened the Gallery of Tibetan Art in Manhattan. She was a well-respected dealer. In time her collection numbered 1,200 objects, originating in Tibet, China, Mongolia, Japan, and Nepal.

In 1945, Marchais started to build the library building, then the temple. She had designed both buildings and was infuriated when New York State required approval of the plans by a licensed architect. Marchais, a stone mason, his assistant, and a carpenter did the construction work and landscaping. When construction was completed, her choice possessions were moved into place: statues of Buddha in many incarnations, many-armed, many-faced Hayagrivas, Bodhisattvas, mandalas, altar tables, ritual objects and shrines, and paintings. Work was completed in 1947, and the museum opened. According to her biographer, Barbara Lipton, during the festive dedication ceremony: "Jacques Marchais was seated by the altar in a long blue gown, surrounded by incense burners, a lion, flowers and buddhas."

Her pleasure in her life's achievement was extremely brief. Jacques Marchais died four months after the opening. From 1953 on the museum was only open sporadically and fell into disrepair. Financial support and professional stewardship rescued it during the 1970s and it is now an evocative Tibetan oasis for those who never will be able to visit the country.

The one very large room that comprises the museum is still very much like its creator left it. Well-educated docents explain the function of the objects with reverence and show a twenty-minute videotape about Buddhism and the museum.

His Holiness the Fourteenth Dalai Lama visited and blessed the museum in 1991. He was truly impressed by this miniature copy of the Potala of Lhasa, sending the following message: "I feel that the unique Tibetan culture and way of life strongly influenced by the compassionate and peaceful teachings of Buddhism, does not belong to Tibetans alone, but to the entire human community."

The Metropolitan Museum of Art

Address: 1000 Fifth Avenue, New York, NY 10028

Telephone: (212) 535-7710

Web: www.metmuseum.org

Hours: Tues–Thurs, Sun 9:30–5:15; Fri–Sat 9:30–8:45. Closed Mon and New Year's, Thanksgiving, and Christmas days. Tours in English, French, German, Italian, Japanese, and Spanish.

Strengths: Encyclopedic. Excellent Egyptian, Ancient, Near Eastern, and Asian art collections. Art from Africa, Oceania, and the Americas. Superior survey of Western (European and American) art. Highlights include: Havemeyer and Lehman Collections, Impressionism, Old Masters, works of the Italian and Northern European Renaissance, Astor Court, Michael C. Rockefeller Wing, Temple of Dendur, period rooms, the American Wing, and the Petrie European Sculpture Court.

Special Events: Temporary blockbuster shows.

Other: Excellent audiotapes highlighting various sections of the museum. Maps and brochures in Chinese, French, German, Italian, and Spanish at International

Visitors Desk. Restaurants, snack bars. Wine bars and music Fri and Sat after-
noons and on 20th-Century Sculpture Roof Garden (May–Oct). Museum shops.

Activities for Children: Treasure hunt maps are occasionally available.

Parking: On site in pay garage.

No matter what the weather, the steps in front of New York's Metropolitan Museum of Art (the Met) are crowded. More people are milling
inside the Great Hall of the undisputedly greatest museum in America.
The Great Hall has little charm except for five enormous vases always
filled with the most exquisite and exotic fresh flowers. Lila Acheson
Wallace, co-founder of the *Reader's Digest* and a great friend of the
museum, endowed these fresh flowers in perpetuity.

First-time visitors will be in a quandary about their destination.
Should they look at the great European paintings or go to the superior
American Wing? The excellent Egyptian collection? The art of Africa,
Oceania, and the Americas in the Michael C. Rockefeller Wing? The
period rooms? Should they look at the collections of musical instruments, or arms and armor? The Robert Lehman Collection in its own
pavillion? The newly renovated Greek and Roman Galleries? The Costume Institute developed by the legendary Diane Vreeland?

Indeed, at one point critics of the Met claimed that it was growing
too large and should be separated into smaller, more specialized museums. This did not come to pass; the Met is a wonderful jumble of
excellent parts and repeated visits always result in exciting new discoveries.

The idea for a national art museum to be located in New York City
was proposed by John Jay, the grandson of our first chief justice, during
a Fourth of July celebration at the Pré Catalan, an outdoor café in Paris,
in 1863. Deliberations were continued at the Union Club in New York,
and the first board of trustees was elected in 1870, but progress was
slow. Initially the Met received little support from the general public.
A collection was started and some of the works collected then, like
William Turner's *The Slave Ship*, Frans Hals's *Malle Babbe*, and Frederick Church's huge *Heart of the Andes*, are still important today. At the
time of its founding, American museums were keenly interested in
antiquities, and the Met formed a lasting relationship with "General"
Luigi Palma Conte di Cesnola, an amateur archeologist, from whom

the museum bought its huge Greek-Cypriot collection. Cesnola became the museum's first paid director. In 1882 the Met moved to its new quarters on Fifth Avenue. According to Calvin Tomkins, who chronicled the history of the museum in *Merchants and Masterpieces,* "its Ruskin Gothic red brick building, by Calvert Vaux [was] generally considered ugly inside and out." (Today an archway of the original building can be glimpsed through an opening in a second floor gallery.) The museum continued to grow, and it became fashionable for New York Society to leave it their treasures. These ran from superior works of art to things better forgotten.

In 1901, the Met received an unexpected five-million-dollar endowment fund—yielding $200,000 annually—from Jacob S. Rogers, an eccentric locomotive manufacturer from Patterson, New Jersey. Overnight the museum became a very rich institution. Many of its prize possessions bear a small label indicating that they were bought with money from the Rogers Fund.

A new era for the Met started in 1904 with the death of Cesnola and the election of J. P. Morgan to the presidency. Morgan was an inveterate and extremely knowledgeable collector (also see The Pierpont Morgan Library, p. 303, and the Wadsworth Atheneum, p. 108), and many of his treasures can be seen at the Met. Under his stewardship the museum became more professional. Edward Robinson came from the Museum of Fine Arts in Boston (p. 205) to assume the Met's directorship. Other experts joined the staff, one being William R. Valentiner. This European-trained art scholar would play a decisive role in the development of several U.S. museums (see Introduction). At the Met, Valentiner turned the amorphous possessions of the Department of Decorative Art into superb, highly specialized departments (Far Eastern, Near Eastern, Medieval Art, the American Wing, etc.).

Not only did the collections grow, but the building kept sprouting new wings. The construction cost was borne by the City of New York, which also covers part of the maintenance. New north, south, and west wings were built onto the original red brick structure. In 1902, Morris Hunt added a neoclassic limestone wing on Fifth Avenue which could properly be described as a suitable "Palace for the Arts," and the Met had acquired its familiar look, though a new and even grander facade was added in 1970 and the rebuilding continues.

The first three decades of the twentieth century were a turning point for the Met. It absorbed a number of great collections including the mostly Old Master collection assembled by Bernard Altman (approximately 1,000 objects, then valued at $15 million). Altman died in 1913, the same year as Morgan. The Met had assumed that it would be the chief beneficiary of Morgan's art. In the end, however, some of Morgan's art was sold to pay inheritance taxes and some of it ended up in other museums (see The Frick Collection, p. 278). In the end, mostly through the generosity of J. Pierpont Morgan, Jr., approximately 40 percent of his father's collection went to the Met.

In 1929 the Met received an extraordinary collection—numbering 1,972 works—assembled by Horace O. Havemeyer, the sugar king, and his wife, Louisine. Horace was the more conservative partner and initially preferred Old Masters such as Rembrandt and other Dutch painters, but under the guidance of Mary Cassatt—a close friend of his wife—they bought El Grecos, including the powerful *View of Toledo,* Francisco Goya's *Majas on a Balcony,* Camille Corots, and Courbet's *Woman with a Parrot.* As important, they collected French Impressionists, especially Edgar Degas, Edouard Manet, and Paul Cézanne. The Havemeyers also championed Louis Comfort Tiffany, donating his earliest vases to the museum.

As the decades passed the Met acquired other masterpieces, some by gift and some bought at auction—the acquisition of Rembrandt's *Aristotle Contemplating the Bust of Homer* made history when the Met paid $2,300,000 for it in 1961. Robert Lehman left the Met his collection, now housed in a separated pavillion. During the 1990s—when it would seem that all the great picture collections had been spoken for—Walter and Louise Annenberg promised the museum their choice Impressionists and Post-Impressionists.

You cannot see the Met's possessions all at once, especially since in addition to its own possessions, there usually are several exciting temporary exhibitions. Most first-time visitors want to see the paintings. How did so many end up in America? The art not only chronicles humanity's taste throughout the ages and continents, but retells history. Near the top of the grand stairs you'll see Jacques-Louis David's great portrait of Louis Antoine Lavoisier, the father of chemistry, and his wife, Marie, working in their laboratory. A few years later this genius would have his head cut off by the guillotine during the French Revolution. A bit further on you come to paintings of the Italian Renaissance, Altman's treasures, then those contributed by Havemeyers and Annenbergs. Quit when you are tired and find less taxing exhibits. Where else in America can you actually wander through a genuine Egyptian temple (Dendur)? Go to the American Wing, and look into Central Park from the elegant Englehard Court. While there, peek into the living room of the house Frank Lloyd Wright built for the Little family (also see Minneapolis Institute of Arts, p. 236, and The Allentown Art Museum, p. 346). Get lost among the exquisite enamels made by European craftsmen during the Middle Ages. Take your children to see the Riggs armor collection or feast your eyes on the Tiffany glass first popularized by the Havemeyers. There is an overornate Tiffany fountain and windows, lamps, and columns saved from the artist's house in Oyster Bay, Long Island (also see the Charles Hosner Morse Museum of Art, p. 156). Before you go, have a cup of coffee in the European Sculpture Court, which incorporates an early south wall of the museum.

The Museum of Modern Art

Address: 11 West 53rd Street, New York, NY 10019

Telephone: (212) 708-9400

Web: www.moma.org

Hours: Sat–Tues, Thurs 10:30–5:45; Fri 10:30–8:15. Closed Wed and Thanksgiving and Christmas days.

Strengths: Survey of modern art from 1880 to present. Abby Aldrich Rockefeller Sculpture Garden. Design collection. Photography, film, and video archives.

Special Events: Retrospectives of major modern and contemporary artists and special smaller exhibits of works by less well established artists. *Artist's Choice* exhibits are selections from the museum's permanent collection made by prominent artists.

Other: Two or more screenings daily selected from the museum's 13,000-film library (free with admission). Free daily gallery talks on a variety of topics. Conversation with contemporary artists (on Fridays). Audio guides, called MoMA Informs, allow visitors to access 3 hours of commentary and information about

60 works of art. Restaurants. Extensive museum shops with books and contemporary design objects.

Activities for Children: Family programs for children 5–10 and their adult companions including: Tours for Tots, gallery talks, family films, and family workshops.

Parking: Pay garages.

Museum will close in spring of 2002 for a major renovation. Operations will shift to MoMA Queens (45-20 33rd Street at Queens Boulevard) until the project is completed in late 2004/early 2005.

Even if you have never visited the Museum of Modern Art (MoMA) before, the building and its art are so well-known that they seem familiar. The museum's sleek facade does not stand out from the other buildings on Fifty-third Street. The lobby is large and functional. From the escalators, now located in the glass-enclosed garden wing, one glimpses the sculpture garden—the model for numerous sculpture gardens throughout America.

The impression of déjà vu increases as one reaches the second floor and sees Vincent van Gogh's *Starry Night,* Paul Cézanne's *Bather,* Pablo Picasso's *Boy Leading a Horse* and *Les Demoiselles d'Avignon,* Henri Matisse's *The Red Studio* and his *Swimming Pool,* one of the cutouts he made late in life. There is more: Marc Chagall's *Floating Bride,* Ben Shahn's *Three Judges,* Jackson Pollock's *The She-Wolf.* On a higher floor one may encounter "ordinary" Breuer chairs, familiar china, and even the ubiquitous-looking beetle Volkswagen.

As in the case of many other American museums, women—Mrs. John D. (Abby Aldrich) Rockefeller, Jr., Miss Lillie P. Bliss, and Mrs. Cornelius J. Sullivan—founded MoMA. During the mid-1920s, all three had become very interested in "modern" art. Miss Bliss had bought artworks at the famous 1913 Armory Show. Mrs. Rockefeller had constructed a small art gallery in her private house on Fifty-fourth Street. It was located on an upper floor so that displays would not irritate her husband, who abhorred modern art, but it influenced the young Rockefellers.

In 1929, a month after the stock market crash, the three ladies, now assisted by twenty-six-year-old Alfred H. Barr, Jr., opened their museum in six rented rooms at 730 Fifth Avenue, an office building.

During the first month, 47,000 visitors came to see their inaugural show. New York was ready for modern art. Barr vowed to provide New York with the "greatest museum of modern art in the world."

In 1931, two years after the opening, Lillie Bliss died. She left her collection to the infant museum on condition that money could be raised to care for it. Within months $600,000 was on hand.

Alfred Barr was a graduate of Paul Sachs's museum course at Harvard (see Harvard University Art Museums, p. 208). Thereafter, during a year-long European study trip, he had been captivated by the Bauhaus in Dessau, Germany. This integrated design community, which was closed by the Nazis during the 1930s, had developed a unified concept pertaining to all arts: fine arts, architecture, photography, typography, dance, theater, furniture design, film, and decorative arts. Well-known members of the Bauhaus included Walter Gropius, Paul Klee, Wassily Kandinsky, Lyonel Feininger, and László Moholy-Nagy.

Barr was fortunate in his patrons. Mrs. Rockefeller was instrumental in founding the museum. In 1939, thirty-year old Nelson succeeded his mother as president; later, her daughter-in-law Blanchette held the post. Nelson was an inveterate art collector and, like Barr, an astute businessman. The two managed to make MoMA self-supporting. The museum developed a loyal following. Katherine S. Dreier, one of the few early advocates of modern art, gave MoMA part of her stunning private collection. The gift included 102 works by Constantin Brancusi, Fernand Léger, Wassily Kandinsky, Paul Klee, Marcel Duchamp, and others. (See Yale University Art Gallery, p. 116, for further details.) James Thrall Soby donated an in-depth collection of neoromantic and Surrealist art (Giorgio De Chirico, Balthus, Joan Miró, and others). William Paley, the founder of CBS, donated some early Picassos and other seminal modern works, which at one time had belonged to Gertrude Stein, to the museum.

The museum moved into its permanent Fifty-third Street quarters in 1939, where it has been ever since. The Rockefellers provided the land and much of the funds for the original structure. The museum was enlarged in 1964 and again in 1976. Wings were added to the north, east, and west. By now it is difficult to identify the original small museum—and the major renovation of 2002 will change things even further. Escalators located in a huge glass-enclosed structure ferry thousands of visitors between floors. The permanent collection is on the second and third floors. The galleries are still small and intimate, and the works are neatly arranged according to school: Post-Impressionism, Fauvism, Cubism, Futurism, Constructivism, Surrealism, Dadaism. Works by American artists—Edward Hopper, Andrew Wyeth, Georgia O'Keeffe, Robert Motherwell, Mark Rothko, Willem de Kooning, and Jackson Pollock—are on the third floor.

Before museum fatigue sets in, visitors should take advantage of Barr's concept that a museum is for far more than simply looking at art. Thanks to his vision, a visit to MoMA is always fulfilling. Nostalgia-evoking movie posters set the mood for viewing vintage films selected from the museum's collection of 13,000, or for evaluating this year's new crop of experimental or foreign films. There are selections from the departments of photography, works on paper, and design. There are always exciting temporary shows and when you are tired of looking at these, you may repair to the Abby Aldrich Rockefeller Sculpture Garden, one of the most beautiful urban spaces in the world. Here, Auguste Rodin's *Balzac* proudly gathers his cloak around his ample body, Aristide Maillol's *River* carefully balances on her hip, and Elie Nadelman's humorous *Soldier* forever stands at attention. Trees and reflecting pools separate the art objects.

Today, modern art is everywhere, and the concept that museums are more than a picture gallery is not unique, but when MoMA opened its doors it was revolutionary. As Aline Saarinen, the author of *The Proud Possessors*, wrote: "The museum's arteries have hardened slightly with age. . . . yet MoMA has been the most ardent champion of modern art and the most important taste-making institution in the world."

During the spring of 2002 the Museum of Modern Art will close for a major, $650 million renovation. The project, expected to be completed in late 2004/early 2005, will enlarge the exhibition space, add new facilities, and restore historic elements of the existing building, including the sculpture garden. Yoshio Taniguchi is the architect. While the renovation is underway, MoMA will move its operations and exhibitions to its new facility in Queens, the remodeled former Swingline factory building. Michael Maltzan, a California architect, masterminded the adaptation of the Queens building. MoMA Queens is projected to open during the summer of 2002. In addition to hosting temporary shows, the Queens site will exhibit highlights of the museum's permanent collection.

The New-York Historical Society

Address: 2 W. 77th Street (at Central Park West), New York, NY 10024

Telephone: (212) 873-3400

Web: www.nyhistory.org

Hours: Tues–Sun 11–5. Closed Mon and New Year's, Thanksgiving, and Christmas days. Often open on Indpendence Day.

Strengths: 19th-century American paintings, especially Thomas Cole. Original Audubon watercolors. Tiffany lamps. The history of New York.

Special Events: Temporary exhibits featuring such topics as New York's role as the nation's premier entertainment center (theater, dance, musicals), specific events in New York's history such as the famous sale of Manhattan by the Native Americans, New York's new immigrants, and the like.

Other: Luce Center for the Study of American Culture: 650,000-volume library, two million manuscripts, 30,000 maps, 500 letters to and from George Washington.

Activities for Children: Kid City with reproductions of old shops, dress-up clothes, and other displays.

Parking: Limited metered on street. Pay lots on 77th, 76th, and 75th streets.

The New-York Historical Society (N-Y Historical) sits in a marble palace across the street from the American Museum of Natural History and across Central Park from New York's Metropolitan Museum of Art. Whereas the latter two are must-see tourist stops, the N-Y Historical is practically unknown, though it had an art collection long before the Met existed.

The N-Y Historical dates from 1804, when New York was a prosperous city of 70,000 inhabitants. By 1807 the Society owned a library and in 1809 it celebrated the bicentennial of Henry Hudson's North American discoveries. At first the N-Y Historical occupied makeshift quarters, but in 1857 it could afford fireproof quarters on Eleventh Street and Second Avenue, then a very fashionable neighborhood.

One enthusiastic supporter was Lumen Reed, a self-made grocer from upstate New York and a passionate art collector. At first he

John J. Audubon's *Snowy Owl*, at
The New-York Historical Society.

bought European art, then he developed a taste for American landscape
and genre paintings. Lumen supported the fledgling American art community and commissioned a five-part series, *The Course of the Empire*,
from Thomas Cole. Once a week the public was invited to view the art
on the top floor of his mansion on Greenwich Street. When Reed died
suddenly in 1836, his family, other art-minded grocers, and other business associates managed to transfer his collection to the newly created
New York Gallery of Fine Arts. In 1858, when the latter failed because
of lack of attendance, the works were given to the N-Y Historical, by
then a catchall for orphaned collections. In 1860, it had absorbed Henri
Abbott's Egyptian collection, which eventually ended up at the Brooklyn Museum (see p. 273). In 1864, it received the artworks carefully
assembled by Thomas Jefferson Bryan. In order to educate his compatriots Bryan bought paintings in Europe and exhibited them privately in
New York. When his museum, the Gallery of Christian Art, failed, the
paintings—many misattributed—were given to the N-Y Historical

Society. Bryan's experience is reminiscent of that of James Jackson Jarvis, who tried to share his love of Italian Renaissance works with his compatriots (see Yale University Art Gallery, p. 116). In 1863 N-Y Historical bought 431 of the original watercolors of Audubon's *Birds of America*, still one of its most precious possessions.

The Eleventh Street building became too small for all these possessions. In 1908 the Society moved to its present site and started to concentrate on its dual mission of exhibiting art and documenting the history of New York. Financially the museum continued to have its ups and downs. During the 1990s it was again about to close, but now it seems to be out of the woods and it is a fun place to visit.

Its permanent art holdings are located on the second floor, which includes the Lumen Reed Gallery. Here we may come across Thomas Cole's *Empire Series*, genre paintings by William Sidney Mount, and—most moving—Charles Willson Peale's rendition of *The Peale Family*, which Bryan acquired from the failed Peale museum in Philadelphia. There are other wonderful paintings, many with a New York theme: *Interior of the Park Theater, N.Y.C* (1882) by John Searle; *Flags, 57th Street* (1918) by Childe Hassam; *The Spirit of '46*, by N. C. Wyeth.

The museum has a superior decorative arts collection, most importantly 113 Tiffany lamps and shades and much New York–made silver. There are mementos: George Washington's inaugural chair and the American flag that flew over Federal Hall when New York was the nation's capital. There is an extensive collection of photographs (500,000), the architectural records of McKim, Mead & White and Cass Gilbert, a collection of street signs, reconstructed shops, and more. By 2000 the N-Y Historical owned five million objects spanning more than three centuries of American life—too many to comfortably access. A new Henry Luce III Center for the Study of American Culture now occupies the museum's fourth floor and is open to the public.

The Pierpont Morgan Library

Address: 29 E. 36th Street, New York, NY 10016
Telephone: (212) 685-0008
Web: www.morganlibrary.org

Hours: Tues–Thurs 10:30–5; Fri 10:30–8; Sat 10:30–6; Sun 12–6. Closed Mon and holidays. Guided tours for special exhibitions.

Strength: Illuminated manuscripts, rare books, first editions, music manuscrips. Seals. Drawings and prints (10,000) from the 14th to the 20th century, including works by Blake, Degas, Dürer, Gainsborough, Pontormo, Rubens, and Watteau.

Special Events: Temporary exhibits of drawings and manuscripts.

Other: Charming garden restaurant. Excellent museum shop. Lectures, concerts, films.

Parking: Pay garages.

Stepping into The Pierpont Morgan Library from busy Madison Avenue at Thirty-sixth Street is like entering a private European Renaissance palazzo. Indeed part of the building, dating from 1906, was the private retreat of the great financier who twice saved the United States from bankruptcy.

J. Pierpont Morgan was not a modest man, nor did he rise from poverty. His family, five generations of solid Connecticut burghers, were well off. Young Morgan was educated in Europe. He was a financial genius and soon had the means of embarking on a life-long shopping spree, buying tons of fine and decorative art.

The *Biblia Latina*, published by Johann Gutenberg and Johann Fust about 1455, at The Pierpont Morgan Library in New York City.

Eventually most of his possessions found their way into America's great museums. New York's Metropolitan Museum of Art, of which Morgan was a long-time president, clearly was the winner, eventually receiving six to eight thousand objects. Morgan also donated major collections to the Wadsworth Atheneum (see p. 108) in Hartford—his father's birthplace—the Bodleian Library in England, and a number of other institutions.

Morgan's appetite for art was wide-ranging, but his personal passion was books and manuscripts. For a long time he enjoyed these in his comfortable but unremarkable brownstone in New York City. By 1900 the mass of illuminated manuscripts, rare bibles, and first editions began overflowing the bookcases and even the storage room in the cellar. Morgan contacted Charles McKim, the fashionable architect, and asked him to construct a freestanding building, separated from the family quarters by a garden. Eventually a large gallery and offices serving the museum replaced the family quarters.

Many experts consider this exquisite building McKim's masterpiece. It was an expensive extravaganza. The pink marble used for the walls was set without mortar; other costly stones were used in the inlaid floors, columns, and ceilings; and gold leaf was applied lavishly. But the effect is elegant and restrained, matching the jewel-like colors of the illuminated manuscripts. The original building consisted only of the East Room (Morgan's study) and the West Room (Morgan's private library), separated by a small rotunda. Three tiers of bookshelves line the East Room. A Flemish sixteenth-century tapestry, ironically representing *The Triumph of Avarice*, hangs over a fireplace. Exhibition cases, filled with illuminated manuscripts, one of three Gutenberg Bibles, and other selections from the collection of nearly 1,300 manuscripts line the walls and fill the center.

Morgan himself looks down on us from the walls of his red-brocade-lined study. The ceiling of the room came from a palace in Lucca, Italy. Medieval stained glass is embedded in the walls. The room is filled with precious objects. One can imagine the financier sitting at his big desk, resting his eyes on Hans Memling's *A Man with a Pink*, the portrait of *Giovanna Tornabuoni* by Domenico Ghirlandaio, or the marble bust of a Florentine lady.

Morgan's collaborator in assembling his stupendous collection was

Belle da Costa Greene, whose passion for literary possessions equaled his own. Originally a library clerk in Princeton, Ms. Greene was Mr. Morgan's private librarian, and became a formidable scholar. When the library opened to the public in 1924, she became its first director, serving until 1948. Ms. Greene's hand can be seen in many of the collection's treasures, which include the manuscript of *Alice's Adventures in Wonderland*, a rare edition of Malory's *Morte d'Arthur*, and the exquisite collection of master drawings.

Morgan died in 1913, and his son, J. P. Morgan, Jr., known as Jack, took over the West Room. At first, to Belle Greene's disgust, he refrained from adding new treasures, but eventually he relented. In 1924, Mr. Jack gave the library to the public. Today the East and West Room are an oasis in Midtown Manhattan. Small shows of drawings or book illustrations are held in the large gallery. The enormous resources of the permanent collection permit it to "trade" possessions with other institutions.

In 1996 the library expanded into Mr. Jack's Thirty-seventh Street brownstone. The two parts of the library are joined by a charming, enclosed garden. Here, sitting under trees, you can have lunch or tea, feeling as if you were a millionaire.

P.S.1 Contemporary Art Center

Address: 22-25 Jackson Avenue (at 46th Avenue and 21st Street), Long Island City, NY 11101

Telephone: (718) 784-2084

Web: www.ps1.org

Hours: Wed–Sun 12–6:00. Closed Mon, Tues. Call for changeable holiday schedule.

Strength: Contemporary art.

Special Events: During summer, performances in sculpture court.

Other: Café with snacks, sandwiches, pastries. Bookstore in café; T-shirts.

Parking: On street; pay lots.

To the unprepared, P.S.1 may come as a shock. The museum occupies a large, triangular urban block. A red-brick Romanesque Revival former school building dating from 1890 occupies half the space; the other half is a sculpture court enclosed by high concrete walls. A disembodied voice, emitted by what is described as a "surveillance piece" mounted on the huge entrance gate, informs all who enter about the museum's café. Space-age robots that currently occupy the sculpture court emphasize the feeling of other-worldliness.

Art is about passion, and so it was that in 1972 Alanna Heiss began creating a museum for contemporary art in Long Island City. From the beginning, the mission of her institution was championing "new (contemporary) art." In addition, she wanted to provide exposure for young and mid-career artists from the U.S. and abroad.

Contemporary art is inevitably displaced by the creations of the next generation. "Art Nouveau" was created around the turn of the last century. "Modern Art" dates back to the 1920s. Like wine, art "ages" and later generations will decide who and what will remain part of our permanent artistic heritage. Some of Rembrandt's paintings were considered revolutionary in his own time and the now-treasured Impressionists were banned when first exhibited. Not owning any of the works it exhibits may indeed enable museums like P.S.1 to remain truly contemporary.

In addition to contemporary art, Alanna Heiss champions the recycling of abandoned buildings. She convinced the city to let her have a disused public school building for a museum. When the institution opened, some art critics described it as "delightfully funky," "cheerfully unorganized," "remarkably open to the off-beat." Over the next twenty-one years the museum held 2,000 different exhibitions. Some of the artists like Robert Mapplethorpe and Richard Serra, who first exhibited at P.S.1, became major figures in the art world.

Old buildings need tender, loving care. By 1995 the roof of the old school was caving in and a major renovation was in order. Frederick Fisher, a California architect who specializes in transforming old buildings into art galleries, masterminded the work. (Fisher also built Colby College's new art gallery—see Colby College Museum of Art, p. 193.) P.S.1 reopened to the public in 1998.

The rebuilding matured the art center. Some galleries and the hallways still evoke old classrooms; others are smooth and almost traditionally museum-like. Some of the double-height galleries are suited to the gargantuan size of selected contemporary art pieces.

On the day of our visit, work by 125 emerging and established artists filled much of the enormous space (125,000 square feet) of the old school. The exhibits featured paintings, drawings, photographs, intricately stacked loose bricks, sleek sculptures, colossal industrial-looking constructions, artful assemblages of the "discards" of everyday life, and objects trouvés. A light sculpture, displayed in an old skylit chimney, seemed tailor-made for its space. None of the art was ponderous and a feeling of fun prevailed. Both the building and the school are vibrant, and visitors, many of them young, were smiling.

The renovated school has rent-free studio space for twenty artists, and is a major educational force for neighborhood schools. In addition to art galleries there are several spaces for concerts and dance and theater performances. The pleasant café doubles as a bookstore and exhibition space.

In 1999 P.S.1 signed an agreement of cooperation with New York's venerable Museum of Modern Art (MoMA). By 2001 this had resulted in one jointly organized exhibition.

The Studio Museum in Harlem

Address: 144 W. 125th Street, New York, NY 10027

Telephone: (212) 864-4500

Web: www.studiomuseuminharlem.org

Hours: Wed–Thurs 12–6; Fri 12–8; Sat–Sun 10–6. Closed Mon, Tues, and major holidays.

Strengths: 19th- and 20th-century African American art. 20th-century Caribbean and African art. Photo archive of James Van der Zee.

Special Events: 5–10 temporary exhibits annually.

Activities for Children: Extensive activities on first Sat: Special guided tours, treasure hunts, gallery activities, hands-on workshops.

Parking: Municipal garage at 126th Street between Lenox and Adam Clayton Powell Boulevard. Also commercial garages.

In the middle of the block of a broad urban street, across from a stern-looking office tower, stands a five-story cast-iron building. Upon closer inspection its lower floors house a museum. The entrance is low-key, the galleries are spacious and pleasant, and there is a small sculpture garden. You have arrived at The Studio Museum in Harlem. It is located on Manhattan's 125th Street in the center of Harlem.

Eighty years ago Langston Hughes wrote that "Harlem was in vogue. It was a magnet for black artists and writers" and it became the capital of Black culture. That was in the 1920s, during the Harlem Renaissance. But, "as soon as the Renaissance announced itself, the artistic merits of Black America's great cultural awakening came under sharp criticism because [it smacked] of isolationism and hopeless conventionalism" (From the *Harlem Renaissance* exhibition catalog by Mary Schmidt Campbell).

Like other inner-city ghettos, Harlem went into decline. Nevertheless, in 1968 The Studio Museum in Harlem was founded. At the time, the work of many black artists was still excluded from mainstream galleries and museums. The mission of the new museum was to supply studio space for and support the careers of African American artists, to preserve and exhibit art of Black America and of the African Diaspora, and to illuminate the impact of these on American culture. The museum closely adheres to this mission.

It built an impressive collection of 1,600 objects centering on nineteenth- and twentieth-century African American paintings, twentieth-century Caribbean art, and traditional and contemporary African art and artifacts. A sampling of these includes work by such major African American artists as Romare Bearden, Elizabeth Catlett, Sam Gilliam, Jr., William H. Johnson, Jacob Lawrence, Valerie Maynard, and Norman Lewis. The museum also owns the archive of James Van Der Zee, a photographer who chronicled the Harlem Renaissance.

Like artists of other ethnic groups in the U.S., African American artists belong to two worlds: the generally prevailing culture and that defined by their specific background. Today, work by African American artists is widely distributed throughout America's museums. This is just as well—because of space limitations, work from The Studio Museum's permanent collection is rarely on view. This, however, will soon be remedied.

By 2000, New Yorkers—black and white—were rediscovering Harlem. As part of its thirtieth anniversary celebration The Studio Museum will be renovated and expanded. Its modest exterior is being replaced by what the museum describes as a "striking, translucent facade that will emphasize the Museum's role as the cultural cornerstone and economic gateway to Harlem." The sculpture garden will be enlarged and there will be galleries to exhibit some of the permanent collection, an auditorium, and other amenities.

The five to ten annual temporary shows organized by the museum document important aspects of African American art. Memorable shows include *Harlem Renaissance; Art of Black America; African-American Artists in Paris 1945–1965; Memory and Metaphor: The Art of Romare Bearden; To Conserve a Legacy: American Art from Historically Black Colleges and Universities;* and *Forever Free: Emancipation Visualized.* Each year, work created during the museum's Artist-in-Residence Program introduces the work of emerging artists of African descent.

Whitney Museum of American Art

Address: 945 Madison Avenue (at 75th Street), New York, NY 10021

Telephone: (212) 570-3600

Web: www.whitney.org

Hours: Tues–Thurs 11–6; Fri 1–9; Sat–Sun 11–6. Closed Mon and on major holidays.

Strength: 20th-century American art.

Special Events: Temporary shows.

Other: Library open by appointment. Restaurant. Museum shop. Branch Museums: *At Philip Morris:* 120 Park Avenue New York, NY 10017. Phone: (917) 663-2453. Hours: Mon–Fri 11–6; Thurs 11–7:30. Closed Sat, Sun, and holidays. *At Champion:* One Champion Plaza (Atlantic Street at Tresser Boulevard), Stamford, CT 06921. Phone: (203) 358-7630. Hours: Tues–Sat 11–5. Closed Sun, Mon, and holidays.

Activities for Children: Family activity guides geared to special exhibits. Sketchbooks. Free family audioguides. Family days.

Parking: On street, mostly metered, scarce. Pay garages abound.

At the Whitney Museum of Art, everything seems big, sleek, and matter-of-fact: the height of the entrance hall, the industrial lamps embedded in the coffered ceilings, the rough concrete walls, the enormous sales desk, the stone floors, the large elevators designed to transport huge works of art, the large stairs.

The building, designed by Marcel Breuer, a leading Bauhaus architect, was a sensation when it opened in 1966 on genteel Madison Avenue and it still is impressive today. The fortress-like granite facade is shaped like an inverted ziggurat. The entrance, protected by what could be a drawbridge, is a few steps below street level. The facade is practically windowless except for a small one that watchfully juts out from an upper level. The museum, as well as the art it shelters, is very much part of our industrialized, urban fabric.

At the beginning of the twentieth century, newly minted American millionaires chased after great European masters, ignoring works created by contemporary American artists. Gertrude Vanderbilt Whitney, herself a sculptor, proceeded to remedy the situation. In 1908, Gertrude Whitney bought four of the seven works exhibited by the renegade artists known as The Eight, or Ashcan School artists. In 1914, she created the Whitney Studio in Greenwich Village where artists could exhibit and sell their work regardless of whether it met the aesthetic or artistic standards of the day. Whitney bought many works and in 1929 she offered a collection of 500 works and an endowment to the Metropolitan Museum of Art. When it was refused, Whitney set up her own museum. Juliana Force, who eventually became the first director of the Whitney, assisted her. In her book *The Whitney Women*, Flora Miller Biddle, Gertrude's granddaughter, writes that Force "made up for her lack of training in art history with her intelligence, informed opinions, steely will, and wit." Force, together with Gertrude Herdle (see Memorial Art Gallery of the University of Rochester, p. 315) and Cornelia B. S. Quinton (see Albright-Knox Art Gallery, p. 265), were, during the early part of the nineteenth century, the only female members of the American Association of Museum Directors.

It is of interest that two wealthy New York women championed art considered "modern" during the first quarter of the twentieth century. The Whitney and the Museum of Modern Art were founded within a year of one another. To begin with, however, Abby Rockefeller concentrated on "modern" European art, whereas Gertrude Whitney focused on American art. As America became increasingly industrialized, American artists no longer painted portraits of beautiful landscapes, but depicted urban and industrial scenes, dockers, steamships, smoke-stacks, skyscrapers, bridges. These were the days of the Ashcan artists, so-called because they included the poor as subjects of their paintings.

Being in the right place at the right time enabled the Whitney to acquire a fantastic collection of American art—11,000 works by 1,700 artists. The once avant-garde names are now icons: Milton Avery, Thomas Hart Benton, George Bellows, Alexander Calder, Stuart Davis, Arshile Gorky, Edward Hopper (the museum received the entire artistic estate of the painter, 2,000 objects), Jasper Johns, Gaston Lachaise, Reginald Marsh (850 works in all), Louise Nevelson, Ben Shahn, and many more.

Being the repository of so much great art is a problem for a museum, especially if its mission is to exhibit living artists. It is fortunate that the Whitney now exhibits part of its permanent collection in a gallery devoted to that purpose. If you are lucky you may see Alexander Calder's famous *Circus*, Ben Shahn's *Three Judges* from the series *The Passion of Sacco and Vanzetti*, Joseph Stella's *Brooklyn Bridge*, Edward Hopper's *Early Sunday Morning*, or Robert Henri's seductive portrait of a reclining Gertrude Vanderbilt Whitney, reminiscent of Francisco Goya's *Majas*.

The museum has always championed more than art for art's sake. It has always examined the interaction of fine art with America's currently prevailing political, social, economic, and other forces. Its temporary shows are thought-provoking, instructive, and sometimes controversial.

PURCHASE

The Donald M. Kendall Sculpture Gardens

Address: At PepsiCo, 7000 Anderson Road, Purchase, NY 10577
Telephone: (914) 253-2900
Hours: Daily 9–dusk.
Strengths: Large outdoor sculpture garden and park.
Other: Obtain map for self-guided tour at entrance kiosk.
Activities for Children: Suitable for the entire family.
Parking: On site.

Within a mile of the Neuberger Museum of Art (see next entry) are the Donald M. Kendall Sculpture Gardens. The gardens surround PepsiCo's World Headquarters, which were designed by Edward Durrell Stone. Forty-five large sculptures, identified in the free self-guided brochure, are displayed on 168 acres of formally landscaped grounds designed by Russell Page. As you wander through the Grass Garden, Oak Grove, Stream Garden, or Fall and Spring Gardens, you encounter works by major twentieth-century artists. You will come across *Hats Off,* a huge orange stabile by Alexander Calder; Claes Oldenburg's *Giant Trowel II,* several Henry Moores, Isamu Noguchi's *Energy Void,* and Louise Nevelson's *Celebration II.* Barbara Hepworth supplied several figures entitled *The Family of Man,* and you can share a bench with George Segal's *Three People on Four Benches.*

The park is magical, especially in spring when the dogwoods and azaleas are in bloom. You can bring a picnic, the children, and even your dog, provided you have a leash and a pick-up bag.

The Neuberger Museum of Art

Address: Purchase College, SUNY, 735 Anderson Hill Road, Purchase, NY 10577

Telephone: (914) 251-6100

Web: www.neuberger.org

Hours: Tues–Fri 10–4; Sat, Sun 11–5. Closed Mon and major holidays. Tours weekdays at 1, Sun at 2 and 3.

Strengths: American art of the 20th century. Ancient art. African art. Constructivist, Dada, and Surrealist works.

Special Events: Annual festivals: Fall, Harvest Festival; Winter, Voices; Spring, Take Part in Art.

Other: Temporary exhibits, lectures, workshops, outdoor concerts. Café. Museum store.

Activities for Children: Excellent games designed to help children enjoy various forms of art. Also family festivals.

Parking: On site, free.

Early in life Roy R. Neuberger hoped to become an artist. He soon decided that he was not gifted enough and he became an art afficionado instead. When he was young, during the 1920s, he visited Paris and was saddened by the fact that most artists are only discovered after their deaths. Then and there he vowed that if he ever had the means he would support and collect living artists.

Fortunately for all concerned, Neuberger did make it big and collected contemporary American art. He supported many of these artists before they were well known. In 1970, his friend Nelson A. Rockefeller, governor of New York, convinced him to build a museum on the newly emerging campus of the State University of New York at Purchase. Selections of Neuberger's permanent collection provide a wonderful overview of American art, with emphasis on artists working from 1920 to 1960. It is a very personal collection. Neuberger preferred small, "living-room-size" paintings and sculptures. *Transparent Sculpture VII* by Louise Nevelson, constructed from small Plexiglas panels, even fits on a tabletop.

Neuberger had a wonderful eye, and selected peaceful, cheerful, often humorous works. His collection includes most well-known twentieth-century American artists: Georgia O'Keeffe, John Marin, Jackson Pollock, Ben Shahn, Jacob Lawrence, Alexander Calder, Romare Bearden, and Alexei Jawlensky. Neuberger's selections are often surprisingly novel. He also collected less well known artists. There is Philip Evergood's (1901–1948) unworried *Little Captain*, sitting in a row boat struggling against enormous waves rendered with Van Gogh–like fury, and Jack Levine's *Banquet,* at which four swarthy men feast. Neuberger is probably best known for his support of Milton Avery, whose intimate, almost watercolor-like paintings with their delicate colors are in a category of their own. The museum owns forty of his works and Neuberger donated another sixty to other museums throughout America.

Most often, selections from Neuberger's collection of ancient art are also on view. Here again the objects are small: a perfect ibis from Egypt, a single Cycladic figure, or Hittite bronze objects.

The museum also has two excellent African collections, one concentrating on works from the Western Sudan and Guinea, the other on works from Central Africa, especially from Gabon and the Democratic Republic of the Congo. The latter was assembled by Laurence Gussman, a one-time president of the Albert Schweitzer Fellowship in New York.

ROCHESTER

Memorial Art Gallery of the University of Rochester

Address: 500 University Avenue, Rochester, NY 14607

Telephone: (716) 473-7720

Web: www.rochester.edu/MAG/

Hours: Tues 12–9; Wed–Fri 10–4; Sat 10–5; Sun 12–5. Closed Mon and New Year's, Independence, Thanksgiving, and Christmas days.

Strengths: Small encyclopedic museum, with excellent ancient art and American and European collections and a great sculpture garden.

Special Events: Weekend after Labor Day: Large arts and crafts festival at which work of 600 artists is for sale; also live entertainment and food.

Other: Shop. Restaurant.

Activities for Children: Fri at 10:15, preschool family workshop.

Parking: Free, in Goodman or Prince Street lots.

In 1872, Rochester artists founded an informal sketching club, whose reputation attracted even painters from New York City. Landscape painting was at its height and the club sketched Rochester's spectacular surroundings. Finding exhibition space for the club's output was more difficult. Shows were held in banks, schools, and various other places. Matters changed in 1902 when Rush Rhees, an ordained Baptist minister, became head of the University of Rochester. According to Elizabeth Brayer—whose book *MAGnum Opus* examines the history of the museum—calling the school a university was a misnomer because its student body totaled 157 souls. Rees, however, was both ambitious and efficient. By 1905 he had developed a building plan that included a site for an art museum. A few years later, Rees convinced his neighbor, Mrs. Emily Sibley (Averell) Watson, to donate a building in memory of her son James George Averell, who had died of cholera at the age of twenty-two. Like the museum Jane Stanford built in memory of her son Leland Jr. (now the Cantor Center for Visual Arts—see p. 102), the University of Rochester's Memorial Art Gallery (MAG) is the gift of a grieving mother.

The building, designed by Foster and Gade of New York, was modeled after the mausoleum of the Malatesta family in Rimini, Italy, which young Averell had greatly admired. The Pierpont Morgan

Library in New York was another inspiration. The finished Renaissance-style building has been compared to a "jewelbox" ever since.

Reese appointed George Herdle, a painter and the president of the aforementioned Rochester Arts Club, director of the museum. It was a wise choice. Herdle became totally immersed in his new job. Initially he presided over an empty building, but he was a master at organizing loan shows, with many of the works borrowed from Rochester's leading citizens.

Rochester's patrons had the good fortune of being connected with several burgeoning industries. Both Emily Sibley Watson and her second husband, James Watson, were descendants of the founders of Western Union. Lensmakers Bausch and Lomb were located in Rochester, as was George Eastman, the founder of Eastman Kodak. In 1914, the year after MAG opened, the museum premiered the world's first exhibition of Kodachrome color prints.

George Herdle died in 1922, nine years after the opening of the gallery. Fortunately for MAG, Gertrude, his elder daughter and loyal assistant, became the new director, remaining at the museum's helm for forty years. At twenty-six, she was the American Association of Museum Director's youngest member and one of only three women, the Albright-Knox Art Gallery's Cornelia Quinton (see p. 265) and the Whitney's Juliana Force (see p. 310) being the other two. Aware of her youth, Gertrude sported a pince-nez to look older. A few years later, Isabel, George Herdle's younger daughter, studied art history and took Paul Sachs's famous classes for museum administrators at Harvard (see Harvard University Art Museums, p. 209). Isabel too spent her professional life at the MAG. The Herdle sisters worked incessantly, studied, cultivated dealers and patrons, and never missed an auction or an opportunity to enrich their beloved museum. Their pockets were not very deep, but they often bought before a particular type of art became fashionable.

The medieval collection, the Herdles' favorite, is one example of their perseverance, luck, and thrift. Through a combination of circumstances, MAG acquired fifty-four pieces (for $14,000 instead of an estimated $180,000 value) from the estate of Joseph Brummer, the art scholar and dealer who was instrumental in forming several major medieval collections. Their acquisition included *The Legend of St.*

Thomas, a French column capital of the late twelfth century. At one point a scholar doubted the sculpture's authenticity, but upon close investigation it turned out that MAG has the original, while the French church has a replacement. MAG's other medieval works include a lindenwood sculpture of *St. John the Evangelist* (School of Veit Stoss), a large three-piece grouping of a twelfth-century Spanish crucifix, and a thirteenth-century mourning *Virgin and St. John*. The Renaissance collection, with its Florentine altarpiece and other works, is equally delightful.

The Herdles created and completed other collections. The MAG's small collection of antiquities—Egyptian, Greek, Roman—is superior. Brayer points out that chance again played an important role. Frederic Ginnell Morgan, at one time vice-consul in Cairo, had assembled a collection of antiquities. For a variety of reasons Gertrude was asked to evaluate it and her "ridiculously low" offer of $1,500 was accepted. MAG acquired more than 200 objects including Roman glass (100 objects), column capitals, textiles, and, most important, a pair of rare Mycenian kraters.

The Herdles were not the only ones shaping MAG. George Eastman's collection of Old Masters, including paintings by Rembrandt, Anthony Van Dyck, Frans Hals, and Tintoretto, as well as English portraits by Henry Raeburn, Thomas Gainsborough, and George Romney, came to the museum. Other devoted patrons provided endowments and purchased or bequeathed major works. European Impressionists and their predecessors and followers arrived one at a time and the museum has a respectable American collection, covering this country's entire artistic history. The *Portrait of Colonel Nathaniel Rochester*, the city's founding father, attributed to John James Audubon, is particularly appropriate.

The mounting treasures rapidly outgrew the "jewelbox" and the museum was enlarged in 1925 and again in 1968, when a large sculpture court—called the Gertrude Herdle Moore Sculpture Garden—was added. More space was needed in 1987 and there was much discussion involving a move to the then-fashionable outskirts of the city, but the museum decided to stay put. All three additions to the museum were carefully planned and today the complex is an attractive whole and MAG is one of America's most delicious small museums.

UTICA

Munson-Williams-Proctor Institute Museum of Art

Address: 310 Genesee Street, Utica, NY 13502

Telephone: (315) 797-0000

Web: www.mwpi.edu

Hours: Tue–Sat 10–5; Sun 1–5. Tours by appointment.

Strengths: 19th- and 20th-century American art. European paintings and sculptures. American decorative arts.

Other: Dance and music performances.

Activities for Children: Children's Room equipped with creative toys, games, and books (open Tues–Fri 11–2 and Sun 1–4).

Parking: On site.

As museum names go the Munson-Williams-Proctor Institute (MWPI) is a jaw-breaker; however, it explains how this wonderful museum came into being. In 1850, James Watson Williams, a comfortable merchant, and his wife, Helen Elizabeth Munson Williams, built Fountain Elms, an imposing Italianate-style house in Utica. The Williamses' daughters, Maria and Rachel, married two brothers: Thomas and Frederick Proctor. Since neither couple had children, they decided, in 1919, to bequeath their earthly possessions to create a tripartite institution: a school of art, a center for performing arts, and a museum that would bear their names. The gift included an art collection started by the elder Williamses in 1860, whose taste ran mostly to ancestral American portraits by Ralph Earl, John Trumbull, and Ezra Ames, but also included Frederick Church's *Sunset,* which had cost a whopping $2,000 in 1879.

The institute remained dormant until after World War Two when the MWPI hired its first director, Harris K. Prior, who proceeded to expand the collection. In 1949, Prior invited Edward W. Root to join his effort. Root taught art at Utica's Hamilton College. According to Aline Saarinen, who chronicled the life of great American collectors in her book *The Proud Possessors,* he was one of the few Americans who was then genuinely interested in American art. He was a personal friend of many of the Ashcan School artists, so-called because they painted realistic pictures of back street and slum life in New York. Slowly, Root assembled a fabulous collection of works by Edward Hopper, Maurice Prendergast, George Luks, Ernest Lawson, William Glackens, and dozens of other then-unknown American painters. Prior and Root developed a list of "must-have paintings." In time, Root's own collection became well known. According to Saarinen: "In 1953 the Metropolitan Museum of Art in New York [invited] Edward Root to show his collection [at the museum]. . . . It was the first private collection of contemporary art [so honored and was a testimonial to] its quality and its revelation of a sensitive personal taste." In 1956 the collection was willed to the MWPI and combined with its own holdings. The museum now is an important stop for those studying the history of twentieth-century American art.

During the first forty years of its existence the MWPI mostly used the various buildings left by its founders, but in 1960 it commissioned an International-style building from Philip Johnson. The new museum has a severe exterior, but the top-lit galleries are ideal for the institute's collections. As you wander around the twenty galleries you will encounter Church's aforementioned Maine landscape, *Sunset*. The lonely pine, the lake, the mountains, the clouds, and the orange and pink hues of the sky reflected on the water look as fresh and peaceful as they did the day they were painted. Elsewhere you will encounter Charles Burchfield's colorful, anthropomorphic *Childhood's Garden*, with its fantastic houses, flowers, and trees, and Milton Avery's lyrical *Pink Tablecloth*, a gift of Roy Neuberger (see The Neuberger Museum of Art, p. 313).

In time the institute restored Fountain Elms and connected it to the main building with a new education wing. Fountain Elms now serves as a delightful decorative arts center furnished with nineteenth-century American furniture, silver, rugs, and toys. The institute also owns an extraordinary collection of historical timepieces.

The museum's new buildings as well as its superior collections have served as a magnet for other donations. The MWPI now owns a respectable collection of nineteenth- and twentieth-century European art, including works by Jean Arp, Salvador Dali, Lyonel Feininger, Wassily Kandinsky, Pablo Picasso, and others.

North Carolina

The North Carolina Museum of Art

Address: 2110 Blue Ridge Road, Raleigh, NC 27607

Telephone: (919) 839-6262

Web: www.ncartmuseum.org

Hours: Tues–Sat 9–5; Fri 9–9; Sun 11–6. Closed Mon and New Year's, Independence, and Thanksgiving days, and Christmas Eve and Day. Tours Tues–Sun at 1:30. Special tours for the visually impaired.

Strengths: Encyclopedic. Kress collection. German Expressionist art.

Other: Mary Duke Biddle's Educational Gallery, an interactive computer center for art education. Restaurant. Museum shop.

Activities for Children: A variety of art-related programs, workshops, hands-on activities, and performing arts are offered on most Sat.

Parking: On site.

In 1917, according to the acerbic essayist H. L. Mencken, the South was "the Sahara of the Bozarts." Depressed by the aftermath of the Civil War, it took the region a while to recover. Today, however, it is marked by an increasing number of fine museums. One of these is the North Carolina Museum of Art (NCMA). In 1920 a group of North Carolinians formed a Fine Arts Society for the purpose of collecting money and works of art. The Depression and World War Two hindered progress until the 1940s, when attorney Robert Lee Humber renewed the quest for a museum.

Humber went to New York and approached Samuel H. Kress (see p. 31), who promised a major gift. Before documents were drawn up Kress became ill, and the verbal promise was in jeopardy. Eventually, however, North Carolina secured a major Kress collection as well as a million-dollar appropriation from a reluctant state legislature.

The museum, which opened in 1956 in a renovated state office building, had additional good luck. William R. Valentiner, the director

of the fabulous Detroit Institute of Arts from 1924 to 1945 (see p. 233),
co-director of the Los Angeles County Museum of Art from 1946 to
1949 (see p. 60), and founding director of The Getty Villa from 1954 to
1955 (see p. 37), agreed to advise and head the NCMA. Though his
tenure was short (he died in 1958), the contribution of this ebullient
and scholarly man cannot be underestimated. The overall quality of the
core collection he helped assemble is excellent.

Valentiner affirmed the NCMA's statewide mandate by advertising
its first international loan exhibition, *Rembrandt and His Pupils*, on
billboards throughout the state. The show, celebrating the painter's
350th birthday, was a wild success.

From the outset it was known that the museum would eventually
require new quarters. Edward Durrell Stone, who built New York's
Museum of Modern Art, was hired. The building, located on a 140-acre
site, opened its doors in 1983. By then the NCMA had acquired another
set of benefactors, most notably textile magnate Gordon Hanes and his
wife. The Haneses enabled the museum to form Egyptian, Greek,
Roman, African, New World, and Oceanic collections and expand its
twentieth-century art collection.

Today, temporary exhibits of European and American twentieth-
century art occupy the entrance level of the museum. We encounter
paintings by Georgia O'Keeffe, Thomas Hart Benton, Jacob Lawrence, Franz Kline, Frank Stella, and by other familiar and unfamiliar
artists. Here we also find Ernst Ludwig Kirchner's *Panama Girls*,
Karl Schmidt-Rottluff's *Portrait of Emy*, Emil Nolde's *Still Life,
Tulips*, and other brilliant and violent German Expressionist art
bequeathed to the museum by Valentiner. This floor also houses a
Judaica collection.

The seventy-one works donated by the Kress Foundation are exhibited on the mezzanine level. Most remarkable among these is the
Peruzzi Altarpiece by Giotto di Bondone and assistants. The five-panel
work, painted in Florence between 1310 and 1315, is one of the rare
complete altars by the master, a fortunate accident: The central panel,
showing Christ, had been separated from the others until Samuel H.
Kress reunited them. Another early work is the lindenwood figure of a
Female Saint by Tilman Riemenschneider, a German master sculptor
working during the transition period between the "statuesque" late

Gothic and "more natural" Renaissance. Though sculpted 400 years ago, the expression of the saint and her stance look modern.

All other European schools of painting—Spanish, Dutch, French, and British—are represented. We come across *Count Shuvalov* by Elisabeth Vigée Lebrun (see the Kimbell Art Museum, p. 380, and the New Orleans Museum of Art, p. 183), a portraitist active between 1770 and 1835. There are examples of American art from the Colonial days, including portraits by John Singleton Copley; landscapes by Albert Bierstadt, Thomas Moran, George Inness, and Winslow Homer; genre paintings, and a small cast version of *The Puritan* by Augustus Saint-Gaudens, the original of which stands on the quadrangle in front of the Springfield Museums (see p. 219).

Currently the museum is concentrating on the development of its vast outdoor space, in which two large sculptures by Henry Moore are displayed. The institution is proud of its new outdoor stage, set amid a novel design-sculpture-cum-message by Barbara Kruger spelling PICTURE US.

Ohio

CINCINNATI

Cincinnati Art Museum

Address: 953 Eden Park Drive, Cincinnati, OH 45202

Telephone: (513) 639-2995

Web: www.cincinnatiartmuseum.org

Hours: Tues–Sat 10–5; Sun 12–6. Closed Mon and major holidays. Tours Tues–Fri at 1; Sat–Sun at 2.

Strengths: Encyclopedic. European and American 17th- to 20th-century art. Nabatean art. American and European portrait miniatures. Rookwood Pottery. Decorative arts.

Special Events: Fall, winter, spring: First Fri 6–9: "Thank Van Gogh's Fridays," with music, dance, cocktails, and limited museum access. Summer: Free Sun concert series.

Other: Café. Museum shop. Mary R. Schiff Library open to the public.

Activities for Children: Family Fun Tours Sat at 1, Sun at 2.

Parking: Free, in lot adjacent to museum.

During the first part of the nineteenth century, Cincinnati, a major shipping and agricultural center, was America's gateway to the West. Located on the cusp between the North and the South, the town was an important stop along the Underground Railroad. It also was the home of the Beecher family, whose scions, Henry Ward Beecher, the fiery minister, and Harriet Beecher Stowe, the writer, played such an important role during Emancipation.

In 1876, Cincinnati resident Maria Longworth Nichols, an amateur china painter, attended the Centennial Exhibition in Philadelphia. The visit convinced her to make pottery. Her creations were so successful that Rookwood, her trademark, became the most successful American Arts and Crafts pottery, regularly winning prizes at World's Fairs here and abroad. In 1899 it garnered the gold medal at the Paris World Exposition.

Back home in Cincinnati, Nichols and her friends formed the Women's Art Museum Association with the intent of establishing a museum. A short three years later, Charles West offered a matching grant of $150,000. In 1886 the Cincinnati Art Museum (CAM) opened atop Mount Adams in Eden Park. Its Romanesque-style building was heralded as "The Art Palace of the West." Within two decades the original building had sprouted two wings and a classic entrance, whose temple-like portico has become a familiar landmark.

Behind this facade the museum has been enlarged and modernized. Today its 80,000 works of art are housed in eighty-eight galleries. Given the length of its history, as well as the devotion and wealth of the town citizenry, one would expect the museum's collection to be grand. Visitors won't be disappointed. The museum is encyclopedic, covering 6,000 years of human creativity. Among many excellent examples of ancient art the museum owns the largest collection of Nabatean art outside Jordan. This was the gift of Nelson Glueck, president of Cincinnati's Hebrew Union College, who as a young archeologist supervised excavations at Khirbet Tannur in southern Jordan.

In 1927, Mrs. Thomas Emery bequeathed the museum a fabulous

collection of Old Masters including Andreo Mantegna's *Mordecai and Esther*, Titian's portrait of *Philip II*, showing the young king at the height of his power, and Sandro Botticelli's *Judith with the Head of Holofernes*. Other important European works include a smaller version of Francisco de Zurbarán's *Saint Francis* (at the Milwaukee Art Museum, see p. 413) and Hans Memling's *Saint Christopher* and *Saint Stephen*. Skipping through the centuries we come to a collection of Impressionists and Post-Impressionists including Vincent van Gogh's *Undergrowth with Two Figures* and Amedeo Modigliani's cheerful portrait of Max Jacob, a French poet.

The American collection includes portraits by John Singleton Copley and Charles Willson Peale, and landscapes by John Singer Sargent, William Merritt Chase, and George Inness.

CAM's special asset, however, is its unmistakable local flavor. There is a whole room full of Frank Duveneck paintings, including his much beloved *Whistling Boy*. Duveneck, who studied in Munich when that city was an important art center (see Frye Art Museum, p. 404), helped plan his hometown museum. There is Robert S. Duncanson's romantic *Blue Hole, Little Miami*—a view of a neighboring pool beloved by landscape painters. In 1861 the *Cincinnati Gazette* hailed Duncanson "the best painter in the West," a remarkable achievement for the son of a Scottish Canadian father and an African mother, who succeeded despite many obstacles in becoming a member of the Hudson River School. There is Grant Wood's acerbic *Daughters of the Revolution*—nobody can help being amused by the three self-righteous matrons standing in front of a painting of George Washington Crossing the Delaware.

The CAM has a wonderful decorative arts collection including examples of the amazingly contemporary looking Rookwood Pottery. Its clean shapes, dark glazes, and naturalistic, simple decorations show a definite Japanese influence. The CAM also owns the panels made by the Rookwood Pottery for David Sinton's downtown hotel (see The Taft Museum of Art, next entry). There are two more artworks commissioned by local hotels: one by Saul Steinberg, the other by Joan Miró. More recently, Proctor and Gamble, makers of Folger's coffee, donated ninety-six quite marvelous pieces of silver related to the history of this addictive brew, most of them coffee pots.

The Taft Museum of Art

Address: 316 Pike Street, Cincinnati, OH 45202

Telephone: (513) 241-0343

Web: www.taftmuseum.org

Hours: Mon–Sat 10–5; Sun and holidays 1–5. Closed New Year's, Thanksgiving, and Christmas days.

Strengths: 17th-century Dutch, 18th- and 19th-century French, Dutch, and Spanish paintings. Quing dynasty. Chinese porcelains. French Limoges enamels. Period furniture.

Other: Sensory tours can be scheduled for visitors with visual, auditory, or mental disabilities. Museum shop.

Activities for Children: Treasure hunt maps

Parking: Limited, free, in rear of museum.

The Baum-Longworth-Taft House, the home of the Taft Museum of Art (the Taft), would be remarkable even if it were not filled with treasures. In 1812, Martin Baum, a Cincinnati merchant, bought nine acres "this side of Deer Creek" in what is now downtown Cincinnati. Eight years later a local architect was commissioned to build a stunning American Palladian house, whose imposing, column-flanked entrance is now dwarfed by skyscrapers. Within the year, in the bank panic of 1820, Baum lost his fortune. Nicholas Longworth, an art patron and father of Maria Longworth Nichols (see Cincinnati Art Museum, previous entry), acquired the house. He added plasterwork, fan windows, and other details. Most importantly, he commissioned Robert Scott Duncanson, a self-trained African American artist (also see previous entry) to paint eight murals and three over-door decorations.

After Longworth's death, David Sinton, an industrialist, acquired the house. His daughter Anna married Charles Phelps Taft, the older half-brother of William Howard Taft, the future twenty-seventh president of the United States. (William Howard's political career was launched in the garden of the house and the dress his niece wore to his Inaugural Ball was found in a closet of the house.) David Sinton died in 1900, leaving Anna $15 million, thereby making her the richest woman in Ohio.

According to one of Charles's letters the couple had decided that it "would be just as well to invest [money] in pictures as to pile it up in bonds or real estate." Between 1902 and 1927 the Tafts assembled an impressive collection centered around European paintings—especially portraits, landscapes, and Dutch genre scenes—Chinese porcelains, and Limoges enamels. The Tafts relied on the advice of dealers but used their own taste. Contrary to the collecting habits of some of their fellow American collectors, they did not acquire Renaissance art or Impressionists.

In 1932, after the deaths of the Tafts, the house became a museum. The collection includes a number of masterpieces. *Portrait of a Young Man Rising from His Chair* is one of several Rembrandts. (The companion of this picture is at New York's Metropolitan Museum of Art—see p. 293.) The Taft also owns portraits by Frans Hals and Anthony Van Dyck, landscapes by Camille Corot and Jean-François Millet, and genre paintings by Jan Steen and Jozef Israëls. We come across John Singer Sargent's portrait of *Robert Louis Stevenson* showing the author relaxing in a wicker chair, and James Whistler's half-sister and her young daughter sitting *At the Piano*. Both paintings are particularly intimate. The Tafts themselves can be seen in portraits by Spanish painter Raimundo de Madrazo. Anna is wearing the pearl necklace she bought at Tiffany in Paris. There also is a likeness of William Howard Taft by Joaquín Sorolla y Bastida (see The Hispanic Society of America, p. 285). Unusual among the museum's possessions are ten watercolors by William Turner. His unfinished *Europa and the Bull* clearly heralds the Impressionists.

The museum's most precious possession is the foot-high ivory statue of the *Virgin and Child* from the Abbey Church in Saint-Denis, near Paris. The work, dating from 1269–1280, is one of only three from the historic edifice to have survived the French Revolution. The Taft's Limoges enamel collection is very fine, as are its Chinese porcelains.

In spite of their European taste, the Tafts were loyal to Cincinnati. Frank Duveneck's *The Cobbler's Apprentice* is much beloved. Only luck preserved the Duncanson murals of which the museum is so proud. They had been plastered over with wallpaper in the late 1800s, and were uncovered intact when the house became a museum.

Viewing artistic treasures in a home has its special attraction. Like New York's Frick Collection (p. 278) and Boston's Isabella Stewart

Gardner (p. 202), the Taft lets us appreciate what domestic life was like for a fortunate few at the beginning of the last century.

CLEVELAND

Cleveland Museum of Art

Address: 11150 East Boulevard, Cleveland, OH 44106

Telephone: (888) 269-7829

Web: www.clemusart.com

Hours: Tues, Thurs, Sat–Sun 10–5; Wed, Fri 10–9. Closed Mon and New Year's, Independence, Thanksgiving, and Christmas days.

Strengths: Encyclopedic, from ancient Egypt to present. Comprehensive Asian collection. Medieval and Pre-Columbian art collections. European art including masterpieces by Caravaggio, El Greco, Poussin, Rubens, Goya, and Turner, and Impressionists and Post-Impressionists. Strong American art collection, contemporary art. Also arms and armor, and textiles.

Special Events: 13–17 temporary exhibits annually. Summer: Wed and Fri 7–9, free concerts; low-cost movies; lectures and gallery tours. 4 community festivals (see Activities for Children).

Other: Restaurant. Museum shop.

Activities for Children: Annual family festivals. April: Mask Festival and Performance; June: Parade; Sept: Chalk Festival, drawing on sidewalk around museum; Dec: Holiday CircleFest and Winter Lights. All festivals involve workshops at which participants make items to be used/worn at festivals.

Parking: On site.

On July 8, 1999, Frans Hals's portrait of *Tieleman Roosterman* went on the block at Christie's auction house in London. The winning bid— $12.8 million—was made by the Cleveland Museum of Art (CMA). Now the ruddy-cheeked Dutch merchant, in his black suit, white ruff, and lace-edged cuffs, hangs next to the painter's *Portrait of a Woman*. The Roosterman portrait, painted in 1634, itself has a fascinating history. It was acquired by a Rothschild during the nineteenth century, confiscated by the Nazis, and stored in a salt mine. Eventually it was restored to Rothschild heirs and sold. Now it is one of countless treasures of Cleveland's remarkable museum.

Frans Hals's portrait of *Tieleman Roosterman* is only one of the Cleveland Museum of Art's many Old Masters.

In 1825, Cleveland was a small pioneer village. By 1900, thanks to the Erie and Ohio canals and the burgeoning steel industry, it was the United States's seventh largest city. Like other Midwestern towns, the community felt Cleveland needed an art museum. Fortunately, three leading citizens had already earmarked large portions of their estates for this purpose. By 1913 a marble-clad Beaux Arts building with grand galleries was under construction. To begin with, the museum owned 119 paintings. Today it owns nearly 40,000.

From its very beginning the leadership of the CMA was guided by an extremely knowledgeable staff and consultants who built a superior, encyclopedic collection using the sizable endowments of loyal patrons. Among several such gifts the $342 million provided by Leonard Hanna "for the purchase of pictures of outstanding importance" is the most remarkable. The Hanna fund permitted the acquisition of Michelangelo de Caravaggio's *Crucifixion of Saint Andrew,* El Greco's *Christ on the Cross with Landscape,* Georges de La Tour's *The Repentant Saint Peter,* Jacques-Louis David's *Cupid and Psyche,* Claude Monet's *La Capeline Rouge—Madame Monet,* Paul Gauguin's *L'Appel,* Pablo Picasso's *La Vie,* Vincent van Gogh's *The Road Menders at Arles,* and

Paul Cézanne's *La Montagne Sainte Victoire*. Almost sixty years after it first became operational, the fund paid for the abovementioned Frans Hals. It is of note that some of the CMA's Italian Renaissance works were the gift of Liberty E. Holden. This early benefactor of the CMA had acquired them from James Jackson Jarves, who had acquired a second collection of Italian works after he sold the first to Yale (see Yale University Art Gallery, p. 116).

Revenues from other funds enabled the museum to buy more treasures. During the 1930s it bought the *Portable Altar* and two crosses from the Guelph Treasure. These jewel-encrusted gold objects, crafted in 1038–1040, are among the most famous treasures of the Middle Ages.

The CMA has a strong and comprehensive American collection. Frederick Church's *Twilight in the Wilderness* glows with the rays of the setting sun, and one hears the waves crash in Winslow Homer's *Early Morning After a Storm*.

F. A. Whiting, the inaugural director of the museum, was much interested in Asian art. The CMA thus acquired a world-renowned Oriental art collection. From 1958 to 1982, Sherman E. Lee, one of America's greatest experts on Oriental art, headed the museum (also see The Asia Society, p. 271). The CMA's 48,000 objects include exceptional statues of Buddha, bronzes, ritual vessels, porcelains, ceramics, scrolls, screen paintings, drawings, and illuminated manuscripts.

Being encyclopedic, the CMA has also developed collections of art from Africa and the Americas. Its outstanding collection of contemporary European and American art is growing steadily.

COLUMBUS

Columbus Museum of Art

Address: 480 E. Broad Street, Columbus, OH 43215

Telephone: (614) 221-6801

Web: www.columbusart.mus.oh.us

Hours: Tues–Sun 10–5:30; Thurs 10–8:30. Closed Mon and major holidays. Tours most Fri and Sat at 2.

Strengths: American art, George Bellows, Charles Burchfield. Sculpture, including a sculpture garden.

George Wesley Bellows, *Blue Snow, The Battery*, at the Columbus Museum of Art.

Special Events: First Thurs 5–9: Art, music, and a cash bar. First Sat 10–1: Family programs on varying topics with hands-on workshops.

Other: Temporary exhibitions. Café. Museum shop.

Activities for Children: The museum is geared to children and has many changing activities such as: W.O.W. Art! (Wed 1:30–2:30), Doodles! (Sat 1 and 3), Eye Spy computer games, etc.

Parking: On site.

Among Ohio's many museums, the Columbus Museum of Art (CMA) was the first to register its charter with the State, in 1878. The museum, however, only hit its stride in 1928 when a handsome Renaissance Revival style building was erected in downtown Columbus, five blocks from Ohio's capitol. The opening exhibit included many paintings by the late Columbus native George Bellows. Eventually the museum would own the largest collection of George Bellows in the world.

Since then, some of Columbus's wealthier citizens have showered the museum with gifts, and today it owns an eclectic collection of 3,000 art objects. The first exhibition in the new building also celebrated the gift of the Ferdinald Howald Collection. The 280 items included American art (Maurice Prendergast, Charles Demuth, and Charles Sheeler) and European modernists (Pablo Picasso, Edgar Degas, André Derain, Georges Braque, and Henri Matisse). The 167 works the museum received from F. W. Schumacher in 1957 stressed Dutch Flemish, English, French, and Italian artists (Jean-Auguste Dominique Ingres, Jacob Jordaens, Jacob van Ruysdael, Peter Lely, Thomas Gainsborough, William Turner, James Whistler) as well as paintings by early American artists. The 1990 gift of 76 Impressionists and Post-Impressionists by Howard and Babette Sirak allowed the museum to complete its survey of Western art.

In 1977, sensing that sculpture was a neglected medium, the museum concentrated on the acquisition of post-1870 European and American sculpture. Today the entrance to the CMA is illuminated by a large neon sculpture by Stephen Antonakos. Other possessions included works by Henry Moore, Alexander Archipenko, Aristide Maillol, Arnaldo Pomodoro, George Rickey, Giacomo Manzú, Gaston Lachaise, Degas, and others. These are displayed in a stunning sculpture garden designed by the English garden designer Russell Page.

It is the special collections that often define a museum. At the CMA this may very well be the fantastic work of Charles Burchfield (also see the Munson-Williams-Proctor Institute Museum of Art, p. 318). Burchfield was born in nearby Salem in 1893 and studied at the Cleveland School of Art. At one time he lived in Buffalo, where he supported his family by designing wallpapers. This experience may account for the patterning in some of his work. Burchfield did not like Buffalo. In his diaries he wrote: "I long for the old half-forgotten moods—for endless summer days spent in the Ohio hills . . . for the joy of God's newly created earth. . . ." Like Thomas Hart Benton and Grant Wood, his fellow Midwesterners, Burchfield is a Regionalist, but he has a mystery and quirkiness all of his own. The CMA owns many of his works, including *Daybreak* from 1920. The painting, in which a strip of silhouetted trees occupies the lower edge of a canvas otherwise filled with an illuminated sky, conjures up Monet's *Lever de Soleil* (Sunrise), the painting that first generated the term Impressionism. Burchfield's *The Visit*, with its decrepit clapboard farmhouse, deformed trees, and emaciated horse harnessed to an unoccupied carriage, is both spooky and humorous.

Other special collections include the estate of Columbus folk artist Elijah Pierce; the Stuck Collection of 352 woven coverlets, one of the largest in the United States; Pre-Columbian and Asian collections, and a growing collection of photographs.

TOLEDO

Toledo Museum of Art

Address: 2445 Monroe Street at Scottwood Avenue, Toledo, OH 43697

Telephone: (800) 644-6862

Web: www.toledomuseum.org

Hours: Tues–Sat 10–5; Fri 10–10; Sunday 11–5. Closed Mon and New Year's, Independence, Thanksgiving, and Christmas days.

Strengths: Encyclopedic. High-quality European and American art. Comprehensive collection of glass ranging from antiquity to contemporary studio glass.

Special Events: "It's Friday": Live music, lectures, public tours, and other entertainment Fri eves.

Other: Daily: Trips down the Nile, and other interactive museum experiences. Café. Museum shop.

Activities for Children: Family center (ages 3–10): Costumes, games, books, and puppets. Gallery hunts which encourage children to explore special exhibits and permanent collections. First Sun: Demonstrations by visiting artists.

Parking: Well-lit, guarded lot.

At important temporary exhibitions throughout the United States a surprising number of quality paintings are loaned by the Toledo Museum of Art. How, one may wonder, did this pleasant but rather unremarkable Ohio town come by such treasures?

By the 1870s, large American cities like Boston, New York, and Philadelphia had established major cultural institutions. Toledo, then home to a mere 150,000 or so souls, was not in that league, but Edward Drummond and Florence Scott Libbey had a dream. They believed that "art has the power to ignite imagination, stimulate thought, and provide enjoyment," and they felt that Toledo needed a museum.

Fortunately, the Libbeys had the means to make their dream come true. In 1888, Edward had moved his family's New England Glass Company from Boston to Toledo. It prospered and by 1920 a dozen Libbey (later Owens-Illinois) factories employed tens of thousands of workers to mass-produce glass products (tableware, bottles, light bulbs, sheet glass).

In 1901, Toledo incorporated its fledgling art institution as a museum, though it owned neither building nor art. Edward Libbey engaged George W. Stevens, a poet, art lover, and Renaissance man, and his wife, Nina, an artist, to help him convince the general population that art was an essential part of life. The Toledo citizenry responded with enthusiasm. In 1912 the residents, including 10,000 schoolchildren, contributed money toward the museum's first permanent building. This original space was expanded in 1926, 1933, 1982, and 1987. The building has withstood the test of time. It is a pleasure to amble through the generously proportioned, airy galleries.

With a museum in mind, the Libbeys began collecting art. They went to Egypt in 1905 and sent back hundreds of objects. Then they bought works by Rembrandt, Hans Holbein the Younger, Jusepe de Ribera, Edouard Manet, John Constable, and William Turner. Florence Libbey concentrated on assembling an outstanding collection of American art, including Winslow Homer, George Bellows, and Childe Hassam as well as more modern works.

Since he was a professional glassmaker, Libbey assembled a comprehensive glass collection that would "show the complete development of the art from antiquity to the present." This collection, which continues to grow, fulfills his intention.

Edward Libbey died in 1925; Florence outlived him by thirteen years. Both left their huge estates to the museum in two separate trust funds to be used, in large part, for the acquisition of works of art.

The collections of the Toledo Museum of Art are surprising in both quality and variety. There are imposing Old Masters, seventeenth- and eighteenth-century Italian art, light-infused Impressionists, forceful Expressionists, early and late Picassos. There are sculptures by Louise Nevelson, Augustus Saint-Gaudens, Constantin Brancusi, and Aristide Maillol. Whenever you are tired of contemplating great art, you can immerse yourself in the sensuous delight of decorative objects—silver tureens, Renaissance tapestries, inlaid furniture, and glass—or meditate in the reconstructed Gothic cloisters. The museum also has excellent Egyptian, Islamic, and African collections. As befits the name of the town, the museum owns *Agony in the Garden,* a painting by El Greco, who created his ascetic canvases in Toledo, Spain.

YOUNGSTOWN

The Butler Institute of American Art

Address: 524 Wick Avenue, Youngstown, OH 44502

Telephone: (330) 743-1711

Web: www.butlerart.com

Hours: Tues, Thurs–Sat 11–4; Wed 11–8; Sun 12–4. Closed Mon and major holidays.

Strengths: American art from early works created by folk artists to masterworks of the 19th and 20th centuries. Free tours upon request.

Special Events: Midyear (summer) juried painting exhibition. First week of December: Fine arts and crafts fair.

Other: Sculpture garden. Branches in Salem (Tel: 330-332-8213) and Howland (Tel: 330-609-9000). The new Beecher Center for the creation and display of electronic and digital fine art. Extensive web site with mini-shows. About 38 temporary shows annually at the museum's 3 sites. Museum shops.

Activities for Children: Children's Gallery featuring interactive exhibits.

Parking: On site.

"How the vagrant shower of artworks, perennially produced," writes Barbara Novak in *Master Paintings from the Butler Institute of American Art,* "eventually come to settle in a formal museum setting is as antic, contradictory and full of colorful eccentricities as human nature itself. But settle they do, some energetically, captured and purchased, some politely accepted, some coveted and generously bestowed through bequests and gifts."

The Butler Institute of American Art is the gift of Joseph G. Butler (1860–1927). The comprehensive collection he had carefully selected over three dozen years to give to his hometown was destroyed by fire. When he started all over again, he assembled a collection of American art in a short two years (1917–1919). Butler commissioned a building from McKim, Mead & White. The architects patterned the Renaissance Revival building on the Casino at Villa Farnese at Caprato, Italy (ca. 1555). No expense was spared. Georgian marble was used inside and out and the facade was adorned with Roman deities. The entrance consisted of a Romanesque triple archway flanked by Ionic columns and brass doors. As always, the work of the architectural firm was exquisitely detailed.

Devoting an entire museum to American art was a first. Butler selected over 200 works, many of which have stood the test of time. In what was to be characteristic of the museum, Butler chose works by famous and less-well-known artists. The initial possessions of the museum included Winslow Homer's *Snap the Whip,* one of the artist's quintessential America genre paintings, and the dramatic *In Flanders Field—Where Soldiers Sleep and Poppies Grow* by Robert Vonnoh, a lesser-known American Impressionist. The founder, his son, and his grandson directed the museum until 1981, after which the directorship passed to Louis A. Zona.

The 10,000 works assembled by the museum since 1919 are astounding in their breadth and quality. It is hard to identify an unrepresented American artist. The museum owns works by Fitz Hugh Lane, Frederick Church, John Singer Sargent, Thomas Hill, Thomas Moran, Arthur Dove, Andrew Wyeth, Philip Pearlstein, Andy Warhol, Jacob Lawrence, and Romare Bearden, to cite a few at random. The museum does have its favorites: Winslow Homer (more than 100 works including works on paper), Ohio native Charles Burchfield (more than ten, including samples of wallpaper he designed in Buffalo), and William Gropper, whose silently screaming *Youngstown Strike* (1937) vividly recalls the bloody struggle between labor and proprietors that characterized the early twentieth century. Of great interest is the work of Elbridge Ayer Burbank (1858–1949), who spent his life sketching and befriending Native Americans. The Butler owns hundreds of his drawings and oils, including a version of his *Snake Dance,* a nine-day long prayer for rain which outsiders were rarely allowed to witness.

Joseph Butler's small museum has been repeatedly enlarged. Fortunately the additions respected the delicacy of the initial building. The museum grew wings and second floors, and in 1987 added the Post-Modern west wing which, with its enormous glass walls, is as dramatic as the original building. A sculpture garden and terrace were added in 1992.

The year 2000 opening of the Beecher Center for high-tech art enabled the Butler to achieve another first. The ground floor is reserved for technology-oriented exhibits and installations. The remainder is mostly lab space for the creation of electronic and digital fine art. The center's vauditorium (visual/audio auditorium) also offers a high-powered interactive computer program.

Along the same lines, the Butler has an extensive web site. Since only 2 percent of its collection is on view at any one time, the museum mounts exhibits entitled "For the Web Only." For one viewing it showed marine paintings, a gentlemanly collection assembled by the three generations of Butlers.

Recently the Butler also opened two branches in nearby Salem and Howland. These small museums offer temporary exhibits and art instruction.

Oklahoma

NORMAN

Fred Jones Jr. Museum of Art

Address: 410 W. Boyd Street, Norman, OK 73019

Telephone: (405) 325-3272

Web: www.ou.edu/fjjma

Hours: Tues–Fri 10–4:30; Thurs 10–9; Sat, Sun 12–4:30. Home football game days: 10–4:40.

Strengths: French Impressionism. New Deal and State Department collections (American art of the second quarter of the 20th century). East Asian art. Native American art.

Claude Monet's *La Berge à Lavacourt* from the Aaron M. and Clara Weitzenhoffer Collection at the Fred Jones Jr. Museum of Art at the University of Oklahoma.

Activities for Children: Family packs with sketchbooks, gallery guides, and other items of interest to help families look at art together.

Parking: On site.

In 1915, when Oscar B. Jacobson was appointed director of the School of Art at the University of Oklahoma, the curriculum offered a single art class. In addition, according to museum literature, "supplies for drawing and painting were scarce and sculpture materials were non-existent. . . . The nearest art center was in St. Louis," some 750 miles to the northeast. Jacobson was about to change that state of affairs. By 1936, when the university's museum was officially founded, Jacobson, the founding director of the new institution, had assembled 2,500 works of art.

Fate, which always shapes a museum's possessions, would have it that the museum ended up with two collections and that each included a survey of works produced by American artists in the second quarter of the twentieth century. The first of these, described as The New Deal Collection, consisted of works produced under the auspices of the Public Works Art Project (PWAP) from 1933 to 1934. The collection came to OU because Jacobson was a regional director of the federally funded art project. The collection includes works by Stuart Davis, Joseph Hirsch, Aaron Bohrod, and Julian Levi, and also works by Native American painters.

In another rare involvement of government with the arts, in 1946 the State Department acquired seventy-nine oils and thirty-eight watercolors created by Ben Shahn, Romare Bearden, Max Weber, Adolph Gottlieb, Edward Hopper, Georgia O'Keeffe, and others. The paintings were to be shown abroad in exhibitions entitled *Advancing American Art*. The venture was criticized from the beginning for a variety of reasons and in 1988 the works, for which the government had paid about $60,000, were auctioned off as war surplus and ended up in Oklahoma.

In 1971, Mr. and Mrs. Fred Jones donated a fine arts building in memory of their son who had died in a plane crash during his senior year at the university. The galleries in the handsome two-story building are light and airy.

In 1996 the Fred Jones Jr. Museum of Art (FJJMA) acquired the Richard H. and Adeline J. Fleischaker Collection of mostly Native American and Southwestern art. This, together with the collection of the nearby Thomas Gilcrease Museum in Tulsa (see p. 341), makes Oklahoma an important repository of the art of the region.

The productivity of the Impressionists and Post-Impressionists is truly astounding. Each time one believes that all works of these painters have been accounted for, a new collection surfaces. In 2000, the FJJMA was the recipient of the Clara Rosenthal Weitzenhoffer bequest of thirty-three works of art which, according to OU president David L. Boren, literally overnight turned the Fred Jones Jr. Museum into one of the preeminent repositories of Impressionist art in the Great Plains.

Both the Rosenthals and the Weitzenhoffers profited from Oklahoma's oil. But whereas Clara's father had arrived from Illinois at the beginning of the boom, her husband Aaron was a native whose family had moved to Oklahoma in 1881 when the state was still a territory. During their lifetimes the Weitzenhoffers were strong supporters of the arts in Oklahoma City. During the 1950s and 1960s, Clara quietly and lovingly assembled a large collection of paintings and also seventeenth-

and eighteenth-century decorative arts, the existence of which was relatively unknown and which was virtually unexhibited.

Soon after the museum received the gift, the paintings by Camille Pissarro, Claude Monet, Edgar Degas, Edouard Vuillard, Maurice Utrillo, Paul Signac, Auguste Renoir, Childe Hassam, Henri de Toulouse-Lautrec, and other familiar names spread their cheer on the walls of the FJJMA. Among them Vincent van Gogh's portrait of Alexander Reid, the British art dealer and painter who befriended him during his London stay, was particularly noteworthy. After the exhibit the paintings went into storage awaiting the building of a new wing, designed by Hugh Newell Jacobsen, a Washington-based architect. In addition to the pictures it will house some of the furniture, carpets, silver, and porcelain in a setting evocative of an elegant family home. Until the wing is ready the Weitzenhoffer Collection will not be on view.

TULSA

The Philbrook Museum of Art

Address: 2727 S. Rockford Road, Tulsa, OK 74114

Telephone: (800) 324-7941

Web: www.philbrook.org

Hours: Tues–Sat 10–5; Thurs until 8; Sun 11–5. Closed Mon and major holidays. Guided tours Sun at 2. Wed at 12, 15-min talks about a piece in the collection.

Strengths: Kress collection of Italian Renaissance and Baroque works. 19th-century American landscape painting. Native American pottery and baskets.

Special Events: Family day once a month on weekend.

Other: Restaurant overlooking sculpture garden and grounds. Museum shop.

Parking: On site.

Imagine a Tuscan Renaissance villa, with a large loggia opening up on a verdant garden, cypresses, statuary, and reflecting pools, in arid Oklahoma! The Philbrook Museum of Art (PMA) is the former private residence of oil magnate Waite Phillips and his wife, Genevieve. Edward Buehler Delk of Kansas City built the villa during the 1920s. According to David Dillon (*Southern Accents*, November–December 1992), Delk

The Philbrook Museum of Art.

"deftly blended French and Italian influences with a dusting of frontier bravura. . . . Fauns and maidens cavort across walls and ceilings; elfin creatures inhabit the hallway; and the grand staircase is framed by swirling columns in pure cowboy Bernini." It is the twenty-three-acre grounds that are most surprising in their lushness.

The Phillipses assembled a modest collection of Taos painting, Native American pottery and baskets, and nineteenth-century American and European paintings. Before they moved away in 1938, they donated the villa and collection to the Tulsa Art Association, for the benefit of the citizens of what was sometimes called the "Oil Capital of the World."

The Philbrook's more than 8,600 works come from many sources. The Samuel H. Kress Foundation donated thirty-five Italian Renaissance and Baroque Old Masters dating from the fourteenth to the sixteenth century. Laura A. Cobb, a teacher and rancher's wife whose lands spouted eight million dollars worth of oil, gave the museum about eighty paintings. They include Thomas Moran's *Spirit of the Indian, Upper Falls Yellowstone,* and *Slaves Escaping in the Swamp.* Other prize possessions include portraits by John Singleton Copley and Benjamin West, Adolphe William Bouguereau's *The Shepherdess,* for long the museum's signature work, as well as American nineteenth-century landscapes by Worthington Whittredge, George Inness, Albert Bierstadt, and Childe Hassam.

Mindful of being part of the American frontier, the museum and its benefactors assembled superior Native American art and artifacts. The Philbrook owns 521 ceramic pieces and 1,110 baskets, representing 172 tribes. Most of these are the gift of Clark Field, who was a newspaper reporter in the Oklahoma Territory from 1900 to 1903, and then became a salesman. He used his modest means to assemble this magnificent collection. From 1946 to 1979 the museum also organized the "Indian Annual" at which it regularly purchased works. Over time the style of these paintings slowly evolved from art favored by "the White Man," to freer, contemporary works. The Philbrook also has excellent, small collections of African and Asian art.

By the mid-eighties the museum had outgrown its by then deteriorated villa. The Philbrook undertook a major capital campaign ($28 million), restored the villa and garden, and built a new wing. The old and the new blend remarkably well. The addition includes an auditorium and a luxurious rotunda whose splendor and elegant lines would have pleased the original builders. Today, much of the permanent collection is housed in the villa, while the new wing is used for temporary shows. As before, the formal and informal gardens with their hedges, fountains, little temple, and nooks and crannies is reminiscent of seventeenth-century Italy—an ideal place for dreaming about the past, present, and future.

Thomas Gilcrease Museum

Address: 1400 Gilcrease Museum Road, Tulsa, OK 74127

Telephone: (918) 596-2700

Web: www.gilcrease.org

Hours: Tues–Sat 9–5; Sun and federal holidays 11–5. Also Mon 9–5 from Memorial to Labor Day. Closed Christmas Day. Tours daily at 2.

Strengths: World's largest, most comprehensive collection of art of the American West. Native American art and artifacts. A major collection of historical manuscripts, documents, and maps.

Other: Restaurant. Museum shop.

Activities for Children: Ideal place for children to explore the history of the West.

Parking: On site.

"Saving a Vanishing Frontier, Part-Creek Oilman Spends Millions on Art of Indian Days." With this *Life* magazine headline of March 8, 1954, Thomas Gilcrease became a legend in his own time. He was born in Louisiana in 1890. When he was a baby, his Scotch-Irish father and his one-fourth Creek mother moved to Oklahoma where he grew up as an Indian child and was entered in the Creek Tribal Rolls. He planned to farm and teach school, but in 1899, as part of an Indian land deal, the U.S. government gave him a 160-acre tract of land. According to the *Life* magazine article the land sat "on a pool of oil" and Gilcrease made a fortune.

Fortunately for us, Gilcrease also became a passionate collector, assembling more than 400,000 objects. It is said he had the idea of creating a museum devoted to Native Americans when he noted that European museums mirror their countries' history. Gilcrease purchased his first painting—a sentimental work entitled *Rural Courtship,* by a long-forgotten painter—in 1912. Thereafter he became more discriminating. In addition to artworks by Frederic Remington (18 of his 22 bronzes), George Catlin (60-plus paintings and manuscripts), Alfred Jacob Miller (many works from his estate; also see the Joslyn Art Museum, p. 249), Karl Bodmer, and the Taos painters (including 350 works by Henry Sharp), Gilcrease also acquired 100,000 books, manuscripts, documents, and maps. The maps range from 1494 to the present and the archival material pertains to the discovery of the Americas, the formative years of the United States, the West, Mexico, and Mesoamerica.

Thomas Gilcrease opened his first exhibition space in 1941, in San Antonio, Texas, at the headquarters of his oil company. In 1945 the collection was relocated to Tulsa. As a consequence of dropping oil prices and overambitious purchases, the founder temporarily ran into financial difficulties and was about to sell the collection to an interested group in nearby Claremont. The citizens of Tulsa would not let the collection go, and floated a bond issue, so the Gilcrease, like the very different Philbrook (see previous entry), stayed in Tulsa.

The museum's original Native American Indian loghouse building from 1949 was enlarged in 1987. Only 6 percent of the entire collection can be shown at one time. It is subdivided into themes such as Warfare on the Plains; Western Commerce; and Western, Eastern, and Natural Landscape. Among many treasures are *The Blackmore Watercolors* by Thomas Moran. These particularly Turner-like paintings of the Yellowstone region were commissioned by Sir William Blackmore in 1872. Moran's field sketches helped convince the U.S. Congress to create Yellowstone National Park—the first area so protected.

The Gilcrease is full of surprises. There is a prehistoric Beaver Effigy Platform Pipe created by the Hopewell people in about 200 C.E.; *A Good Treaty*, a painting by Edward Hicks of *Peaceable Kingdom* fame, depicting William Penn giving the Delaware Indians a fair price for land; and a certified copy of the Declaration of Independence.

Twenty-three of the Gilcrease's 430 acres have been developed into gardens that mirror styles used throughout the American West. There are gardens resembling those in fashion during Pre-Columbian, pioneering, Colonial, and Victorian times. Meandering through these little worlds one can but think of Thomas Gilcrease's wish to "leave a track of some sort." Glancing at the distant towers of modern Tulsa and the Osage Hills, Gilcrease's home for almost half a century, one realizes the aptness of the museum's motto: "Where the story of the American West unfolds."

Oregon

PORTLAND

Portland Art Museum

Address: 1219 S.W. Park Avenue, Portland, OR 97205

Telephone: (503) 226-2811

Web: www.portlandartmuseum.org

Hours: Tues–Sat 10–5; Sun 12–5; first Thurs 10–8. Closed Mon and major holidays.

George Segal's *Helen with Apples,* at the Portland Art Museum.

Strengths: Native American art of the Northwest. American and European paintings and sculptures. Asian, African, Pre-Columbian art. Photography. Works on paper. English silver.

Special Events: Temporary exhibits.

Other: Museum After Hours: Usually Oct–April, Wed eves 5:30–7:30. Elegant café overlooking the sculpture court. Museum shop.

Activities for Children: Family Drop-In Days. Room equipped with simple art activities, books, and puzzles, usually open Tues–Fri 10–12; Sat, Sun 1–3.

Parking: Limited on street; pay lots.

The entrance to the Portland Art Museum (PAM), filled by Henry Moore's *Woman* standing on a pedestal surrounded by white flowers and greenery, is understated. As one passes through glass doors into a double-height, skylit sculpture court, one's eyes are immediately drawn to George Segal's *Helen with Apples.* The blue-tinted woman is sitting at a rickety blue table in front of a blue window, staring at red and yellow apples spread out on a dirty cloth. Like other Segal works, this one is oozing emotions; those who have visited FDR's memorial in Washington, D.C., are reminded of the sculptor's *Bread Line,* whose desperate, unemployed men are a poignant reminder of the Great Depression. Sculpture does play a major role at the PAM. Small works are scattered throughout the museum and larger works by Auguste Renoir, Emile Bourdelle, Wilhelm Lehmbruck, and Alexander Archipenko are in an outdoor sculpture garden. There, Gwynn Murrill's realistic *Coyote VI* reminds us that we are out West.

The PAM, the oldest museum in the Pacific Northwest, was founded in 1892. At first the collection grew slowly. Today the museum owns 32,000 works and, with the addition of several wings, ranks among the twenty-five largest museums in North America.

To begin with, the impressive American collection was the special interest of C. E. S. Wood, described as "the Easterner" in accounts of the museum's history. Wood, a gifted amateur artist, moved to Portland in 1884. He maintained his friendships with J. Alden Weir, Albert Pinkham Ryder, Childe Hassam, and other East Coast artists and induced them to come and paint in Oregon. In spite of initial opposition by the trustees, the PAM now has a stunning American collection. The earlier landscapes include a view of nearby *Mount Hood* by Albert Bierstadt with the Columbia River in the foreground. Thanks to Wood, American Impressionists are well represented. There is another view of snow-capped *Mount Hood*, this one by Childe Hassam. There are works by more recent painters: Joseph Stella, Max Weber, Marsden Hartley, Milton Avery, Jack Levine, and Jacob Lawrence.

The PAM's European collection is satisfying. The Kress Foundation supplied thirty-two early Renaissance works, including a painting of Saint Michael and Saint Dominic attributed to Domenico Ghirlandaio. Recently the PAM acquired Anthony Van Dyck's imposing portrait of *Cardinal Domenico Rivarola*. There is a sprinkling of Pre-, actual, and Post-Impressionists; Gustave Courbet's *Autumn*, with its snow-capped mountains, is very appropriate to this part of the country. The museum is particularly proud of Chaim Soutine's fluid *Le Petit Patissier* (the little pastry maker), whose white smock and toque contrast with the red background.

The museum's East Asian collections (Japan, China, Korea) are particularly fine. In addition to traditional work they feature the work of contemporary artists. Among several large screens, one from 1600–1618 depicting the arrival of the Europeans in Japan, is particularly instructive.

The PAM also has a small, well-displayed African collection and a growing Center for Graphic Arts, part of which is on exhibit. Contemporary art is on display in large, well-lit galleries adjacent to the sculpture court.

In 2000, the PAM opened the Confederated Tribes of Grand Ronde Center for Native American Art. According to museum literature the eight galleries permit visitors to appreciate the enormous scope of PAM's holdings. Four hundred works of art, drawn from virtually every major cultural group in North America, are on view.

Paralleling these displays is the Center for Northwest Art, devoted to works produced by artists from this part of the country. A two-story-tall work by glass artist William Morris was commissioned for the opening.

Pennsylvania

ALLENTOWN

Allentown Art Museum

Address: Fifth and Court Streets, Allentown, PA 18105

Telephone: (610) 432-4333

Web: www.allentownartmuseum.org

Hours: Tues–Sat 11–5; Sun 12–5. Closed Mon and major holidays. Informal tours Wed at 12, on varying subjects related to collections or exhibitions (see web site or phone for details).

Strengths: Regional art of Lehigh Valley and New Hope. Kress collection. Library of Francis E. Little House by F. L. Wright. Collection of textile art.

Special Events: Third Thurs 11–1: Art Identification Day. Annual family festival: First Sun in May, Creativity Festival on Fifth—a large outdoor activity organized by several Allentown cultural institutions. Winter Carnival (indoors). 3–4 special free lectures; more.

Other: Store. Small café.

Activities for Children: ARTime: drop in hands-on activities for ages 4–12 accompanied by an adult, in summer, Tues, Thurs, Sun 12–3. (Also see Special Events.)

Parking: On street; public pay lots.

In 1926, Walter Emerson Baum, a local artist, organized an outdoor painting class for twenty-two art teachers working in Allentown and the surrounding Lehigh Valley. At the end of the season the students wished to exhibit the results of their labor and eventually a museum was incorporated. At first the city of Allentown did not provide any funds, but in 1934 the city gave the museum a building in which to mount exhibitions. Early activities of the museum included art classes—Baum's school still exists today—exhibitions of the work of regional artists, and a circulating picture club. In 1956 the city provided larger quarters.

Samuel H. Kress, American art's Santa Claus, had been born in nearby Cherryville and the Kress Foundation offered the museum a regional collection provided it would be housed properly. In searching for new quarters the museum found a deconsecrated church. The Allentown Art Museum may very well be the only museum located in a neo-Romanesque ecclesiastic edifice.

In 1970 the museum needed additional space. Edgar Tafel, a New York-based architect, gutted, refigured, and expanded the former church. In the process he discovered, under the roof, a 3,000-foot hidden plenum which space was transformed into much needed-additional galleries. Tafel, a former associate of Frank Lloyd Wright, was aware that Wright's Francis E. Little House in Wisconsin was being dismantled. The library of the epoch-making structure ended up in Allentown, The reconstructed living room of the house is now an important part of the American Wing in New York's Metropolitan Museum of Art.

Allentown's collections—a mixture of gifts and purchases—grew along with its building. The museum actively collected regional American painters, including those working in nearby New Hope. Well-known representatives include Gilbert Stuart, Gustavus Grunewald, Edward Redfield, Daniel Garber, William Lathrop, and Keith Haring. The Gilbert Stuart *Portrait of Ann Penn Allen* (1795), is of special interest. The elegant, blue-eyed blonde, dressed in contemporary finery, shown in the half bust, was the granddaughter of William Allen

(1704–1780), chief justice of the Province of Pennsylvania and founder of Allentown. The surrounding columns, drapery, and windows endow the young woman with a regal air.

Grunewald, born and educated in Europe, is represented by an almost mystical view of Niagara Falls. The museum also owns a version of Augustus Saint-Gaudens's *The Puritan*, which guards the village green in Springfield, Massachusetts (see Springfield Museums, p. 219).

Since the region was settled by German and Dutch immigrants, the Kress gift concentrates on works of Northern Europeans, including Hans Maler's *Portrait of Anton Fogger*, a banker and art patron; Jan Steen's amusing genre painting *As the Old Sing, So the Young Pipe* (1668), and *The Adoration of the Magi* by a contemporary of Albrecht Dürer.

The acquisition of the Francis E. Little Library initiated Allentown's decorative arts collection. According to the museum literature, "the [size of the] library [the culminating work of Wright's Prairie Style] is ideally suited to Allentown . . . it contains many typical features, variable ceiling height, light decks, natural materials, and stained glass windows." The decorative arts holdings were enhanced by Kate Fowler Merle-Smith's gift of her large collection of textiles, French silver, and Arts and Crafts Movement ceramics.

The museum keeps up with contemporary artists, including local photographers, and holds a nationwide juried biennale.

CHADDS FORD

Brandywine River Museum

Address: U.S. Route 1, Chadds Ford, PA 19317

Telephone: (610) 388-2700

Web: www.brandywinemuseum.org

Hours: Daily 9:30–4:30. Closed Christmas Day.

Strengths: Illustrations and cartoons by American artists. Paintings by members of the Brandywine School and its followers, including Howard Pyle and the Wyeth family.

Special Events: Native plant and seed sale. Steeple chases. Antiques show. A

James Wyeth, *Portrait of Pig,* at the Brandywine River Museum.

Brandywine Christmas featuring children's book illustrations, dolls, and doll houses.

Other: Tours of N. C. Wyeth Studio, owned by the museum (summer only). Temporary exhibits related to American illustrators. Spectacular restaurant overlooking river. Museum shop with signed prints. Wildflower gardens.

Activities for Children: This indoor-outdoor museum is highly suitable for children, who are allowed to climb on the outdoor sculptures.

Parking: On site.

The Brandywine River Museum is one of those institutions one would be happy to visit even if not a single artwork were on display. We owe this gem to a group of quick-witted, quick-acting local residents who in 1967 bought the land at auction when it was threatened by industrial development. A few years later, Hoffman's mill—a former gristmill—was bought and lovingly transformed into a museum.

The land on which the museum stands originally belonged to the Lenni Lenape Indians. During the American Revolution it was the site of a major battle. The Brandywine River supplies southeastern Pennsylvania and northern Delaware with water; the land is good to farm and beautiful enough to inspire painters. By accident it also became the cradle of American book and magazine illustration.

The original gristmill is a tall brick structure, which architect James R. Grieves paired with an ultramodern circular building. A tower, pierced by giant windows, unites the two buildings. As visitors progress from floor to floor they are never far from the river, the walkways, the bridges, and the gentle, tree-studded landscape.

As befits a museum that wants to celebrate the farmland on which it grew, artworks featuring animals play an important role at the Brandywine. From most vantage points one can see the life-size bronze statues of a cow—*Miss Gratz*—(by J. Clayton Bright) and a pig (by André Harvey), lazing on the banks of the Brandywine. Old millstones, the museum's insignia, are distributed throughout the grounds, and in summer acres of wildflowers contribute to the feeling of enchantment.

About half the paintings are displayed in the galleries of the old mill, with its original wooden beams and wide floor boards. The other half is located in the light-filled modern galleries.

It is no surprise that the three generations of Wyeths (N. C., Andrew, and Jamie) are represented at the museum, since their family home was in Chadds Ford. There are oils by N. C. that relate to his book illustrations, notably Robert Louis Stevenson's *Treasure Island* and James Fenimore Cooper's *The Last of the Mohicans*. There are deeply personal portraits and landscapes by Andrew, and everybody loves Jamie's rendition of a contented, happy pig. Other Jamie Wyeth works are his portraits of Rudolph Nureyev and Andy Warhol. (For more information about the Wyeths, see The Farnsworth Art Museum, p. 190) There are oils by N.C.'s teacher, Howard Pyle, whose dramatic style made a lasting impact on his students. There are wonderful landscapes and still lifes by other important painters of the period: Jasper Cropsey, John Haberle, Thomas Doughty, Frank Schoonover, and Horace Pippen, the self-taught African American primitive painter.

As is the case with its close neighbor the Delaware Art Museum (p. 118), it is the history of American illustration that forms the backbone of the Brandywine River Museum collection. Examples of illustrations by the Brandywine School artists mentioned above as well as by Charles Dana Gibson, Thomas Nast (the political cartoonist), Harrison Cady, Frederic Remington, Maxfield Parrish, Rockwell Kent, Winslow Homer, Al Hirschfeld, and others are displayed.

The Brandywine River Museum owns N. C. Wyeth's restored studio in which many of the everyday artifacts that sustained the artist in his work are displayed. The studio is reached by special shuttle bus departing from the museum.

MERION

The Barnes Foundation

Address: 300 N. Latch's Lane, Merion, PA 19066

Telephone: (610) 667-0290

Web: www.barnesfoundation.org

Hours: Fri–Sun 9:30–5. *July and Aug:* Wed–Fri: 9:30–5:00 Reservations are required for all visitors; call (610) 664-7917. The Foundation recommends making reservations 60 days in advance. No walk-ins accepted.

Strength: French Impressionism and Post-Impressionism: Renoir, Cézanne, Matisse, Picasso, Seurat, Rousseau, Modigliani, Soutine, Manet, Monet, Degas, and others.

Other: Arboretum. Museum shop.

Parking: Pay, on site.

With some perseverance and planning you may visit The Barnes Foundation, a small museum in a wealthy suburb of Philadelphia. There, in an elegant cream-colored limestone building set in a twelve-acre arboretum, you will be surrounded by a treasure trove of mostly French paintings: 180 Renoirs, 69 Cézannes, 60 Matisses, 30 rare early Picassos, and works by Georges Seurat, Honoré Daumier, Vincent van Gogh, Edouard Manet, Claude Monet, "Le Douanier" Rousseau, Maurice Utrillo, Amedeo Modigliani, and Chaim Soutine. William Glackens, Maurice Prendergast, Charles Demuth, and others represent American painters. There is a bit of African sculpture, a few Old Masters, and a handful of selected antiquities. It is, in the words of Dr. Albert Barnes's biographer, Howard Greenfeld, "a remarkable collection, all the more so because it is the result of one man's taste, passion, and eccentricities."

Barnes attended Central High in Philadelphia, a magnet school for talented students. From there he went on to medical school. He interned at the State Hospital for the Insane in Warren, Pennsylvania, "to enable him to gain greater insight into human behavior," a skill he deemed valuable. After graduation he became a clinical pharmacologist. To further his education he worked and studied at universities in Berlin and Heidelberg in Germany. In 1902, together with Hermann Hille, he developed Argyrol, effective antiseptic, silver-nitrate-based drops which, in pre-antibiotic days, prevented serious eye and ear infections. Within a decade Barnes became a wealthy man.

Art had always been important to Barnes. At first he tried his hand at painting. Dissatisfied with the result, he became a collector. He asked his friend and former classmate William "Butts" Glackens—a member of The Eight, or Ashean School—to teach him about art. In 1912, Glackens went to Paris and, on Barnes's behalf, bought twenty "modern masters" including works by Renoir, van Gogh's *Postman*, and Picasso's *Girl with a Cigarette*. That same year, Barnes started to buy art on his own. The quality of his possessions—which include, among many others, Matisse's *The Dance* and *Joy of Life*, Cézanne's *Card Players and Girl*, Monet's *House Boat*, and Giorgio de Chirico's portrait *Dr. Albert C. Barnes*—is a tribute to his taste.

By Greenfeld's account, Barnes was "bizarre, colorful, paranoid, and acid tongued." His relationship with other art institutions in America was troubled. In 1923 the Pennsylvania Academy of Fine Arts exhibited seventy-five of his paintings. The reaction of the public was such that Barnes felt snubbed and decided to go it alone. In 1923 he and his wife constructed the twenty-four-room gallery we know today. The complex was designed in French Renaissance style by Paul Cret, who also built Philadelphia's Rodin Museum. Bas-reliefs for the exterior of the buildings were commissioned from sculptor Jacques Lipchitz. The floor was tiled in a pattern based on designs from the Ivory Coast. Attention was lavished on the gardens and arboretum.

From the beginning, however, Barnes wanted to do more than just own excellent art. A teacher at heart, he published his first article about art education, entitled "How to Judge a Painting," in 1915. In 1922 he created the Barnes Foundation, whose goal was to "promote the advancement of education and the appreciation of fine arts." The foundation was given an endowment of $65 million and 710 paintings.

Barnes had strong beliefs about how his art should be viewed. According to the brochure distributed by the foundation, "Barnes had no qualms about mixing media and intermingling traditions—East and West, experimental and classical. His dynamic grouping of old and new masters form juxtapositions that challenge students to see connections and draw relationships among often seemingly disparate traditions and among works by the same artist." These groupings, which have been carefully preserved, may seem unusual today. Paintings are hung three deep and are surrounded by wrought-iron decorations. Sometimes it is difficult to get close to a particular chef-d'oeuvre, but the overall experience is overwhelming. Where else can one see the work of specific artists in such depth?

PHILADELPHIA

Pennsylvania Academy of the Fine Arts

Address: Broad and Cherry Streets, Philadelphia, PA 19102

Telephone: (215) 972-7600

Web: www.pafa.org

Hours: Tues–Sat 10–5; Sun 11–5. Closed Mon and New Year's, Easter, Independence, Thanksgiving, and Christmas days. Various docent-led tours: weekdays at 11:30 and 1:30, weekends at 12 and 2.

Strength: Encyclopedic overview of American art. Building is best example of flamboyant Gothic architecture in U.S.

Special Events: Temporary exhibits.

Other: Restaurant. Museum shop.

Parking: Discounted, at several adjacent Parkway Corporation lots.

Busy Broad Street vanishes as soon as you enter the Pennsylvania Academy of the Fine Arts (PaFA), the nation's first and oldest art museum and school of fine arts. Charles Willson Peale, a preeminent painter, along with seventy other Philadelphians, founded it in 1805, and it has functioned as a small museum ever since.

In preparation for America's Centennial Exhibition, held in Philadelphia in 1876, the Institute built a flamboyant Victorian Gothic building, so lavishly decorated that it puts Disneyland and Hearst Castle to shame. The burgundy-colored walls are encrusted with a pattern of gilded roses. More roses are chiseled in the buff-colored stone. Big five-domed torchères crown the newel posts of the grand stairs. A royal-blue star-studded sky surrounds the skylight. There are marble columns and broken gothic arches, gilded railings, and stained glass windows. The floors are covered with intricately patterned tiles. There are palms and important marble statues. Somehow, this overabundance of ornament works, and for an hour or two you are transported into another world.

Few institutions provide such a clear overview of the development of art in America. Each of the museum's thirteen galleries is devoted to a specific aspect of art, such as the grand manner tradition, art during the Colonial and Federal periods, genre art, portraits, "national" subjects, landscapes, war, and history, to name a few. Gallery 9, the largest, is devoted to American Impressionism. Galleries 10 and 13 present examples of early modernism and social realism, including the harsher views of city life represented by the Ashcan artists as well as diverse expressions of post World War Two art. Only a small portion of the museum's large collection is on view.

Peale's *The Artist in His Museum* is fortunately on permanent display. This large self-portrait shows a formally clad Peale lifting a heavy red velvet curtain revealing glass cabinets filled with stuffed birds, gold-framed portraits, and other curiosities. The painting is reminiscent of the cabinets of curiosities so typical of seventeenth-century Europe. We come across a portrait attributed to Joshua Johnson, an early African American painter (active 1796–1824). Johnson was a self-taught portraitist who advertised his skills in a Baltimore newspaper (also see Bowdoin College Museum of Art, p. 186, and The Baltimore Museum of Art, p. 195). There is a version of Pennsylvania-born Edward Hicks's charming *The Peaceable Kingdom,* and *Death on the Pale Horse,* a violent battle scene by Benjamin West, sometimes called "the father of American painting." A painting by John Sloan shows the Sixth Avenue el running in front of New York's Jefferson Market building, built in a style reminiscent of the PaFA. *John Brown Going to His Hanging* by Horace Pippin, the primitive African American artist, is shocking. There are examples of the work of the academy's many illustrious alumni, among them Mary Cassatt, Thomas Eakins, Stuart Davis, Robert Henri, and Alexander Calder. Louis Kahn—the architect of The Yale Center for British Art (p. 113) the Yale University

Art gallery (p. 116), and the Kimbell Art Museum (p. 380)—also studied at PaFA.

Philadelphia Museum of Art

Address: 26th Street and Benjamin Franklin Parkway, Philadelphia, PA 19130

Telephone: (215) 684-7500

Web: www.philamuseum.org

Hours: Tues–Sun 10–5; Wed 10–8:45. Closed Mon and major holidays. A variety of tours.

Strengths: Encyclopedic, with many unusual collections: European art, Old Masters, Renaissance, Impressionist and Post-Impressionist, Cubist, Dadaist, and Surrealist art, American art, and American decorative art. Reconstructed cloisters and temples. Largest collection of Thomas Eakins in the world.

Special Events: Large, sometimes groundbreaking, exhibitions.

Other: Rodin Museum (22nd Street and Benjamin Franklin Parkway; phone: 215-763-8100; web: www.rodinmuseum.org). Restaurants. Museum shops. Concerts and performances. Second Sat: Free music in galleries.

Activities for Children: Award-winning Family Programs and special performances.

Parking: Limited free space available around the museum. Paid parking at Eakins Oval and, Sat–Sun, on Upper Terrace in the Azalea Gardens.

The origins of the Philadelphia Museum of Art (PMA) go back to 1876, when the City of Brotherly Love was the site of the United States Centennial Exposition—the first World's Fair held in America (also see Pennsylvania Academy of the Fine Arts, previous entry). Paintings were borrowed for the occasion and exhibited in Memorial Hall. The following year a private museum was chartered. The museum remained at Memorial Hall, but by 1919 plans for a larger museum were afoot.

Eventually an imposing structure, affectionately called the "Greek Garage," was constructed. The building was lavishly inlaid with colored and glazed terra cotta tiles and winged mythological beasts. Ionic and Doric columns flank the entrance. Four acres of roof protect ten acres of space, nearly 200 galleries, and 500,000 works of art—too many to see in one afternoon.

As you ascend the stairs of this modern temple, you will notice a statue of Chief Justice John Marshall by Jacob Epstein entitled *Social Consciousness*. In the near distance a gilded equestrian statue of Joan of Arc reminds you that Philadelphia always stood for our country's sense of liberty and fair play.

A museum building is only an envelope for its art. The encyclopedic PMA has been extremely fortunate in the support and gifts it has received. As you amble through the halls, you are reminded of people and industries forever associated with Philadelphia: the Franklin Mint, Tyson, Smith Kline, and Johnson. Lawyer John G. Johnson pleaded a still unsurpassed record of 168 cases before the Supreme Court. His clients included the mighty—Frick, Rockefeller, Widener, Havemayer—as well as humble female teachers fighting for equal rights. Johnson represented Standard Oil in its celebrated antitrust suit.

Johnson's avocation was art. He formed his collection relying on the qualities that made him a great lawyer: thoroughness, ingenuity, and creativity. He could not spend as much money as his well-heeled clients, but when he started collecting during the 1890s, early Italian (Sienese and Florentine) and Lowland (Flemish and Dutch) art was comparatively inexpensive. Johnson thus acquired paintings by Jan van Eyck, Hieronymus Bosch, Quentin Massys, Sandro Botticelli, Masolino, Roger van der Weyden, Dieric Bouts, Sassetta, and Titian, eventually acquiring 1,279 works. Johnson loved small, intimate paintings and his treasures radiate a sense of peace rarely achieved on such a scale by other schools of art. Johnson was also a board member of New York's Metropolitan Museum and advised fellow collectors Louisine Havemayer and P. A. B. Widener.

The PMA is a treasure trove of early American paintings. It has the world's largest collection of works by native son Thomas Eakins. Other notable paintings are by John Singleton Copley, John Trumbull, Gilbert Stuart, Edward Hicks, and George Inness. The works of Pennsylvania craftsmen dominate the extensive decorative art collections. Most of the furniture, glass, porcelain, and silver—from solid Shaker furniture to a whimsical figure of a lacquered pig from a carousel—is exquisite.

The reconstruction of entire edifices is one of the nice surprises of the PMA. An immense Romanesque portal from the Abbey Church of Saint Laurent is placed near a cloister reassembled from fragments of the

Abbey Saint Genis-des-Fontaines in the Pyrenees. The walls of the PMA are high enough to accommodate the outer walls of the cloisters, including the tiled roof covering the ambulatory (covered walk) of the structure. The soothing sound of water flowing from the central fountain fills the space.

A different spirit animates the mandapam, or pillared hall, of a sixteenth-century temple complex from India. The temple, dedicated to the worship of Vishnu, is the centerpiece of the PMA's important Indian art collection. Tall, sensuous figures enclose a dimly lit court that shelters a bronze sculpture of Rama. The architectural elements of the temple, the only Indian stone temple existing in the United States, were given to the PMA by the Gibson and Pepper families. This gift stimulated the museum to strengthen its collection of Indian art.

Other arts of Asia (China, Japan, Tibet) are also well represented. There are outstanding examples of Chinese ceramics (more than 3,000), porcelain, rockcrystal, textiles, costumes, jade, and Ming furniture. There is a Japanese temple and teahouse, a Chinese scholar's study, and a reconstructed hall from a large Chinese Buddhist temple complex built during the fifteenth century. It is interesting to note that the Nelson-Atkins Museum (p. 242) has a ceiling from this same temple complex.

The PMA's holdings of nineteenth and twentieth-century art are outstanding. The museum owns many Impressionist and Post-Impressionist masters, including several by Edouard Manet, Claude Monet, Auguste Renoir, Henri ("Le Douanier") Rousseau, Henri de Toulouse-Lautrec, Paul Cézanne, and Vincent van Gogh. Most of these works are so familiar that the common reaction is one of recognition.

The gift of the Walter C. and Mary Louise Stevens Arensberg Collection made the PMA into an important center of Cubist, Abstract, Surrealist, and related art. During the 1930s the Arensbergs hosted many of the painters of the Dada movement in New York City. According to Suzanne Muchnic (the author of *Odd Man In*, Norton Simon's biography), "the star of the frequently wild and drunken scene was the French expatriate artist Marcel Duchamp, but on any given night the cast might include the artists Man Ray, Francis Picabia, and dancer Isadora Duncan." In time the Arensbergs acquired 1,500 objects, including epoch-making works by Marcel Duchamp and Salvador Dali, numerous sculptures by Constantin Brancusi, Pablo

Picasso, Georges Braque, Fernand Léger, Joan Miró, and others, as well as Pre-Columbian works they felt were spiritually related to the above. The Arensbergs considered donating their holdings to the then-embryonic Los Angeles County Museum of Art (p. 60), but eventually decided that the PMA was a safer place. The PMA owns many of Marcel Duchamp's best-known works, including *Nude Descending the Staircase, The Bride Stripped Bare by Her Bachelors, Box in a Valise,* and his various *Ready Made Objects.* The Arensbergs' Brancusi collection fills an entire room. The gift of the large Gallatin Collection added key Cubist paintings including works by Braque, Juan Gris, Jean Arp, and Picasso.

In 1923, Jules E. Mastbaum, a Philadelphia movie mogul, began collecting works by Auguste Rodin. Eventually this very excellent collection was housed in a stunning building designed by Paul de Cret. The small museum and its sculpture garden are administered by the PMA and are located within an easy walk of it. Here we encounter many of Rodin's familiar and unfamiliar works including casts of *The Thinker* and the *Gates of Hell.* (Also see Iris & B. Gerald Cantor Center for Visual Arts, p. 102)

PITTSBURGH

Carnegie Museum of Art

Address: 4400 Forbes Avenue, Pittsburgh, PA 15213

Telephone: (412) 622-3131

Web: www.cmoa.org

Hours: Tues–Sat 10–5; Sun 1–5. Closed Mon, except from Independence to Labor days, and on major holidays. Daily tours.

Strengths: European and American art from the mid-19th century to the present. Decorative arts, including architect-designed objects (Robert Adam, Frank Lloyd Wright, H. H. Richardson). Hall of Architecture.

Other: Ongoing film series showing selections from the film and video archive. In summer, free concerts in the sculpture court. Restaurant. Museum shop.

Activities for Children: Sat 12:30–3:30: ARTventures, Family Art Activities. Last Sat 1–2: Storytelling with puppets. Treasure hunt maps.

Parking: Ample low-cost, in six-level garage.

Andrew Carnegie was born in Scotland and raised in the U.S. He created Pittsburgh's steel industry. When he died in 1919, at age eighty-four, he had made and given away $350 million. His gifts were earmarked for education and the arts and include countless libraries, Carnegie Hall in New York, the Carnegie Foundation, and of course the Carnegie Institute in Pittsburgh. The latter, multifaceted organization includes the Carnegie Museum of Art (the Carnegie) and its twin, the Carnegie Museum of Natural History.

The Carnegie Institute opened its doors in 1895, but two years later it was already deemed too small. By 1907 the enlarged, magnificent edifice reopened. It looked, and looks, very much like other neoclassical museums of its time. Large bronze figures representing Music, Art, Science, and Literature adorn the roof, and those of Shakespeare, Michelangelo, Bach, and Galileo flank the entrances. The interior is luxuriously appointed with grand stairs, an inlaid marble floor, and an elaborately carved, gilded ceiling.

Pittsburgh had a Palace for the People, but at first it was devoid of art. Carnegie planned to fill it with the masterpieces of tomorrow. In 1896 he organized a yearly International Exhibition—the first such venture in America. In addition to putting unlikely Pittsburgh on the art map, these competitions enriched the museum's collections. Of the museum's 1,200 paintings and 200 sculptures, a third were bought at these Carnegie Internationals. The works include Winslow Homer's *The Wreck*, James Whistler's *Arrangement in Black*, John Singer Sargent's *Venetian Interior*, Mary Cassatt's *Young Women Picking Fruit*, Georges Rouault's *The Old King*, Childe Hassam's *Fifth Avenue in Winter*, and more recently Anselm Kiefer's *The Unknown Painter*.

To represent the architectural marvels of Europe, Carnegie commissioned architectural casts. The works were of particularly high quality and today the Hall of Architecture—based on the Mausoleum at Halicarnassus—is one of three such collections in the world.

Eventually the museum acquired other major benefactors, most notably Sarah Mellon Scaife. After her death her family donated a new wing, the Sarah Scaife Gallery, built by Edward Larrabee Barnes. The museum also owns the ivory collection assembled by Henry J. Heinz, whose ketchup and fifty-seven flavors of soup hail from Pittsburgh, and the Ailsa Mellon Bruce Collection of decorative art.

Many of the paintings of the Carnegie are both heart-warming and familiar. We come across Edgar Degas's top-hatted *Portrait of Henri Rouart* standing in a railroad yard leading to a large New Orleans ice-making factory the painter had seen during his 1871–1872 visit to that city. Rouart, Degas's boyhood friend, had invented part of the ice-making process. There is James Ensor's *Tribulations of Saint Anthony,* clearly related to the painter's Belgian compatriot Hieronymus Bosch. There is an 1883–1887 self-portrait by Paul Cézanne; Eastman Johnson's *My Jew Boy,* now considered one of America's finest portraits, which was acquired from the painter's widow for $75; Vincent van Gogh's *The Plain of Auvers;* Willem de Kooning's *Woman IV;* and David Hockney's *Divine.* Finally, there is the founder's portrait by Anders Zorn. The latter also immortalized two other American collectors, Isabella Stewart Gardner and Berthe Potter Palmer, whose portraits are now the property of, respectively, the Isabella Stewart Gardner Museum (p. 202) and the Art Institute of Chicago (p. 163).

The Andy Warhol Museum

Address: 117 Sandusky Street, Pittsburgh, PA 15212

Telephone: (412) 237-8300

Web: www.warhol.org

Hours: Wed–Sun 10–5; Fri 10–10. Closed Mon, Tues, and major holidays.

Strength: Complete survey of the many aspects of Andy Warhol's work

Special Events: Good Friday: Every Fri 5–10, a "happening" with dance, lecture, concerts, and a cash bar.

Other: Daily screenings from extensive Warhol film archives. Café.

Activities for Children: Every Sat and Sun 12–4 a hands-on art project using some of the innovative techniques Warhol used to create his works.

Parking: Museum pay lot one block north on Sandusky Street. Additional pay lot in vicinity.

The artist, his face framed by "electrified" yellow hair, stares at you from a portrait as you enter The Andy Warhol Museum in downtown Pittsburgh. The building, an eight-story warehouse, is not, as Richard Gluckman, the Warhol's architect, points out, "your ordinary

The entrance to The Andy Warhol Museum.

museum," but it enabled him to create spaces for typical works in the collection. As Warhol would have appreciated, the industrial feeling of the old warehouse has been preserved. Care was taken to utilize familiar Warhol materials: an aluminum-leaf ceiling in the entrance hall, window sills made of galvanized steel, cowhide banquettes in the coffee shop, and luxurious woods.

As you wander through the museum and its extension, you'll encounter most of the artist's famous works—in particular a larger-than-life-size *Elvis* brandishing a gun; the *Brillo, Heinz Tomato Ketchup,* and *Campbell's Soup* paintings, the Oxidation paintings; multiples of *Jackie, Marilyn,* and *Chairman Mao;* selections from the *Death and Disaster* series; and the *Last Supper.* There are also many less-well-known works.

Since Andy Warhol was a filmmaker you may end up in the small theater, viewing one or more of his films. The museum owns a complete set of his productions.

The existence of The Andy Warhol Museum in Pittsburgh, his native town, is fortuitous, resulting from the cooperation of three institutions: the Andy Warhol Foundation for the Visual Arts, Inc., the Carnegie Foundation, and the Dia Foundation. The latter had been a major collector of Warhol during the 1970s, and was willing to transfer eighty or so works to the new museum.

Warhol, a pack rat, never discarded anything. When he died unexpectedly in 1987, his Manhattan brownstone and his studio, "the Factory," were stuffed with his possessions. Sotheby listed their contents in a six-volume catalog. The ten-day auction yielded $25.3 million, most of it going to the Andy Warhol Foundation. These riches, and the fact that Warhol produced his work in multiples, suggested a museum. Frederick Hughes, the director of the Andy Warhol Foundation, approached the Carnegie Museum and received a warm welcome. The Carnegie was interested in having the museum in Pittsburgh, especially since Frick and Mellon had bestowed their art on New York and Washington.

Andrew Warhola was born in Pittsburgh in 1928 to Slovakian immigrants. He was not yet ten when he started to collect comic books, take photographs and art classes, and use a kiddie film camera. He attended Carnegie Tech (now Carnegie Mellon University), and moved to New York in 1949. He worked as a commercial artist, winning prizes for his shoe ads for I Miller. Shoes always remained important to Warhol. In 1960 he started to use comics and advertisements in his artwork. He employed large photo-silkscreen techniques. In addition to pictures, films, and tapes, Warhol also produced Interview, a monthly film journal.

The creation of many of his best-known works was triggered by tragedy. His *Jackie* was done after the assassination of John F. Kennedy. The portraits of his mother and of Marilyn Monroe were done after their deaths. The silkscreen of the *Electric Chair* was inspired by the execution of Ethel and Julius Rosenberg.

Warhol's life and his art were very public and loud, encompassing celebrities, irreverence, and fun. Warhol became well known for his multiple paintings of America's idols (Marilyn, Elvis, Jackie). For a while in the sixties and seventies his social life at Studio 54, Max's Kansas City restaurant, and his own "Factory," made headlines. Before AIDS decimated New York's gay community, Warhol's life seemed to consist of nonstop happenings. Much of his development is recorded in the memorabilia he collected during his entire life. There was, however, another side to Warhol. He was shy and secretive, a practicing

Catholic, and, until her death, lived quietly with his beloved mother, Julia Warhola.

It is as an artist that Warhol will be remembered. He developed new techniques, utilizing ready-made images, cartoons, and photographs made in photo booths. He changed the way we look at art. "Once you 'got' Pop," Warhol wrote, "you could never see America the same again."

Rhode Island

PROVIDENCE

The Rhode Island School of Design Museum

Address: 224 Benefit Street, Providence, RI 02903

Telephone: (401) 454-6500

Web: www.risd.edu

Hours: Tues–Sun 10–5; 3rd Thurs 10–9. Closed New Year's, Easter, Independence, Thanksgiving, and Christmas days. Free guided tours Sat and Sun at 2.

Strengths: Teaching museum with excellent collections of Etruscan, Greek, and Roman sculpture, Romanesque and Gothic works, American and European paintings, Asian art, and works on paper.

Other: The Pendleton House, featuring 18th-century American decorative art and furniture in period setting. Museum shop.

Special Events: Temporary exhibits, including display of students' work. Concerts, lectures.

Activities for Children: Free-for-All Saturdays, every last Sat: Games, treasure hunts, hands-on-activities, performances, refreshments. The intermediate size of this well-organized museum, however, makes it fun to visit with children at all times.

Parking: Very limited on street. Half-price parking in Metropark lot at the corner of N. Main and Steeple Streets.

It is hard to pick out the Rhode Island School of Design Museum (RISD) from among the other understated, red-brick buildings of this

Edouard Manet, *Le Repos* (Portrait of Berthe Morisot), at The Rhode Island School of Design Museum.

charming college-town-like section of the city of Providence. The interior of the museum, founded in 1877, is surprisingly spacious. A sizable sampling of its 85,000 works of art, displayed in attractive, intimate galleries, is spread over six floors. Small touches, such as a window "stained" with Art Nouveau tracery, tasteful railings, a sculpted doorway, remind visitors that the museum is part of one of the nation's top design schools. Indeed, RISD was the first to have an "American wing" (the Pendleton House). The addition of the 1993 Daphne Farago Wing, with its soaring atrium, permits the museum to display large works of contemporary art and to host temporary exhibitions. At selected times throughout the year the museum also displays works by its students. It is a rare treat to see the innovative fabrics, jewelry, art glass, metalwork, pottery, and other creations of America's future craft artists.

The museum's collections of ancient art are comprehensive and pleasant. The Egyptian collection, with its real mummy, is a favorite with children, the glazed brick *Lion Relief* from the Ishtar Gate in Babylon is awe-inspiring, and the Greek, Etruscan, and Roman collections are considered especially fine. The *Standing Bronze Warrior*, dating from 500 B.C.E. and the Hellenistic *Aphrodite* from about 100 B.C.E.

are impressive, as are the examples of Romanesque and Gothic art, including a typical doorway from a Romanesque church and a tiny diptych from a small portable ivory altar.

Providence was Abby Aldrich Rockefeller's hometown and the Asian galleries are dedicated to her memory. Here again, extreme care was lavished on details: walls covered in grass cloth or painted in colors harmonizing with the displays. One entire gallery is occupied by an immense twelfth-century wooden Buddha, and the Japanese print collection is noteworthy.

The RISD may have fewer "great" paintings than other beloved New England college museums, but it is full of pleasant surprises. Of note is Edouard Manet's *Le Repos*, a portrait of Berthe Morisot, the painter's future sister-in-law, reclining on a sofa, her small foot coquettishly protruding from below the hem of her filmy white dress. Another gem of the European collection is *Venus Africaine* by Charles-Henri-Joseph Cordier (1827–1905). The sculpted silvery head of this African beauty, with its corn-braided hair and big earrings, looks contemporary. RISD also owns Nicolas Poussin's *Landscape with a Mill*, several Claude Monets, a Paul Cézanne, and Edgar Degas's *Dancer with a Bouquet*.

Older American painters are well represented: John Singer Sargent's imposing portrait of *Manuel Garcia*, Fitz Hugh Lane's view of *Little Good Harbor Beach, Cape Anne*, Thomas Eakin's earnest *Baseball Players Practicing*, William Bradford's *Arctic Sunset*, showing the icebergs so beloved by landscape painters of the time, and Winslow Homer's *On a Lee Shore* (1900).

Spectacular examples of early- and mid-twentieth-century art are found on the lower floors: *Two Horses* by Franz Marc; a *Green Pumpkin* sitting on a windowsill by Henri Matisse; and *Rosy Light*, a dramatic, Expressionist-type landscape by Oscar Bluemner (American, 1867–1938). There are several playful sculptures by Elie Nadelman and Raymond Duchamp-Villon's *Seated Woman*, a sleek, gold-washed Art Deco work. Interesting objects include a *"Cubist" Coffee Set* designed in 1927 by Erik Magnusen for the Gorham Manufacturing Company, an enormous Art Nouveau fireplace, and flower-strewn wallpaper designed by French painter Raoul Dufy in 1912. Other decorative art displays include murals from Pompeii; tapestries and textiles, all particularly appropriate for a school that stresses weaving and design; and a large collection of porcelain figures donated by Lucy T. Aldrich, Abby Rockefeller's sister.

South Carolina

CHARLESTON

Gibbes Museum of Art

Address: 135 Meeting Street, Charleston, SC 29401

Telephone: (843) 722-2706

Web: www.gibbes.com

Hours: Tues–Sat 10–5; Sun 1–5. Closed Mon and major holidays. Tours of temporary exhibits Tues and Sat at 2:30 and 2nd Tues at 6.

Strengths: Miniature portraits. Portraits and landscapes of Charleston and the Colonial South. Japanese wood block prints of the Ukiyo-e period. 20th-century American art.

Special Events: Lectures, seminars, concerts, and films.

Other: Museum store.

Activities for Children: Sensational (Family Program) Saturdays are held six times a year. Also Open Studio days.

Parking: Garage on Queen and Cumberland Streets.

When one takes its antecedents into account, Charleston's Gibbes Museum of Art is among the nation's oldest. During the mid-1700s, Charleston was a prosperous and cultured city and its citizenry considered creating an art organization. Portraits were commissioned from Gilbert Stuart and John Trumbull. Samuel F. B. Morse, Raphaelle and Rembrandt Peale, and other well-known painters came for visits. There were art exhibits and even a museum, but eventually these efforts floundered. The Carolina Academy Art Association was founded one hundred years later in 1857. It has existed ever since, even though at times, especially during and after the Civil War, it was dormant.

In 1899, James S. Gibbes, a wealthy merchant, left a legacy jointly to

The elegant Beaux Arts Gibbes Museum of Art in Charleston, South Carolina, with its Tiffany-style dome, dates from 1905.

the Art Association and to the mayor of Charleston. The Gibbes Museum of Art, housed in an elegant Beaux Arts building, opened its doors in 1905. Expanded in 1977, it features a sumptuous entrance hall, large galleries, and a rotunda crowned by a green and yellow Tiffany stained glass dome.

During World War One, when transatlantic travel came to a standstill, artists including Edward Hopper and William Merritt Chase and collectors like Solomon R. Guggenheim and Samuel H. Kress spent their winters in Charleston. In 1934, Robert Whitelow, the Gibbes's first professional director, organized a Kress collection loan show, to be followed in 1936, by one featuring non-objective art from the Guggenheim's collection.

Throughout its history the Gibbes assembled 10,000 works of art. Its collection of over 500 miniatures is world-renowned. These little gems, used to serve the purpose of photographs, range from 1740 to the twentieth century. The museum's regular-size portraits include works painted in Charleston during Colonial times and shortly thereafter. One of these is the portrait of *Mrs. Francis Dallas Quash* by Samuel F. B. Morse (see The Terra Museum of American Art, p. 167). Of special interest are works of the Charleston Renaissance that flourished during the 1920s and 1930s particularly regional artists whose impressionistic views of Charleston and South Carolina landscapes, abloom with magnolias and wisteria, are most lyrical.

The Gibbes's collection has moved with the times and includes works by major nineteenth- and twentieth-century American artists and a photography collection. The Gibbes also owns over 400 Japanese wood-block prints of the Ukiyo-e period, given to his hometown museum by Harvard professor Motte Alston Read.

COLUMBIA

Columbia Museum of Art

Address: Main and Hampton Streets, Columbia, SC 29202

Telephone: (803) 799-2810

Web: www.colmusart.org

Hours: Tues–Sat 10–5; Wed 10–9; Sun 1–5. Closed Mon and major holidays.

Strengths: Kress collection featuring Medieval, Italian Renaissance, and Baroque works of art. Works on paper, a growing collection of post-1946 art. Tiffany glass collection and other decorative arts.

Other: Temporary exhibits. Museum store.

Activities for Children: Children's gallery with art produced by children or young adults.

Parking: On street, and low-cost pay garages.

Compared to its neighbor the Gibbes Museum of Art in Charleston (see previous entry), the Columbia Museum of Art is a youngster. It opened its doors in 1950 in the historic Taylor House, where it shared its quarters with a science and natural history museum and the newly established Gibbes Planetarium. During its initial decade the CMA received a Kress collection of Medieval, Renaissance, and Baroque art.

Museums tend to grow. Modest wings were added to the Taylor House in the 1960s. During the 1970s and 1980s the natural history collection was deaccessioned. Finally the museum decided to move. By then the city, which wanted to revitalize its sagging downtown, offered the CMA the vacant Macy's Department Store on Main Street. George Sexton Associates turned the old store into a stunning museum, another illustration of successful recycling of superfluous buildings. Features include an imposing entrance, high ceilings, hardwood floors, dramatic stairs, and an open atrium surrounded by galleries.

The museum's permanent collections are located on the second floor. The extremely large Kress collection (seventy-eight pieces) invites quiet contemplation. *Virgin and Child Enthroned between Saints Lawrence and Stephen* (1434) is a large triptych by Giovanni dal Ponte, who retained the gold background of the Sienese painters but transitions to the more earthy style of Giotto and Masaccio. Also remarkable is Sandro Botticelli's *Nativity*.

In South Carolina we are never far from the wounds inflicted by the Civil War and slavery. So it is that director Salvatore G. Cilella relates the symbolism of Mariotto Albertinelli's *Madonna and Child with Saints and Angels* (ca. 1510) to Michael Thomas Holman's *Symboli Innocentes Svnt* (Are Symbols Innocent; 1990). According to Cilella, symbols are only readily understood in their own time. We have long forgotten the meanings of those used during the Italian Renaissance, but quickly comprehend that of the Confederate flag that Holman, an African American, uses in his contemporary canvas.

The staff of the CMA delights in providing such unusual insights. To this end it has three small, intimate "focus" galleries in which it presents frequently changing artworks—prints, drawings, photographs, and small-scale decorative arts that provide a new understanding of the collection and increase the viewing pleasure of repeat visitors.

Other European and American schools of painting are well represented. The museum has arranged its treasures in seventeen individual galleries, including Mannerism, Dutch School, Eighteenth Century, Neoclassicism, European and American Nineteenth Century, Art Glass, and Modern and Contemporary. The museum is particularly proud of Thomas Sully's charming double portrait of his daughters, *Blanche and Rosalie*; native son William Harrison Scarborough's *Crossing the Ford*; William Merritt Chase's portraits of Columbians; Canaletto's *View of the Molo*; Claude Monet's *The Seine at Giverny*; and Raphael Soyer's *Entering the Studio*. In the latter there is something touching and intimate about the young woman, the artist's wife, clad in a simple striped blouse shyly peering into the room.

The CMA owns excellent decorative art including an extensive

Tiffany glass collection. Building on these possessions the museum continues to acquire art glass. Also noteworthy is some Art Nouveau style furniture. Acquisitions like Frank Gehry's *Cross Check Armchair* keep the furniture collection up to date.

Tennessee

MEMPHIS

The Dixon Galleries and Gardens

Address: 4339 Park Avenue, Memphis, TN 38117

Telephone: (901) 761-5250

Web: www.dixon.org

Hours: Tues–Sat 10–5; Sun 1–5. Mon: Gardens only, for half price.

Strengths: Impressionism and its antecedents and followers. 18th- and 19th-century British portraits and landscapes. Daumier drawings. Decorative arts; 18th-century German porcelain; French and English porcelain, pewter, and period furniture.

Special Events: Special exhibitions.

Other: Spectacular gardens patterned on grand English landscaping.

Activities for Children: The gardens and limited size of the museum make it a pleasant experience for children.

Parking: On site.

"Cotton was in both their backgrounds," states the introduction to a booklet about the Dixon Galleries and Gardens. Hugo Norton Dixon's grandfather owned a cotton mill in Lancashire, England, and Margaret Oates's family traded cotton in Memphis. In 1921, after working in Europe, Hugo relocated to Texas, married, and moved to Memphis in 1939. Soon thereafter, the couple bought seventeen acres of woodland and built the equivalent of an elegant English country home. They transformed the land into luscious gardens with vistas and brick walks, fountains, statuary, and formal flowerbeds. Clipped hedges sectioned the garden, and the native oaks and hickories formed a perfect background for the flowering dogwoods and azaleas. Monet and Renoir would have loved it.

In 1944 the Dixons bought their first painting—William James's *View of Venice*, a perfect fit for their English-style house. Buying paintings became a passion and, as they gravitated toward Impressionism, they relied on the advice of John Rewald, the noted art scholar. Works by Auguste Renoir, Claude Monet, Camille Pissarro, Mary Cassatt, Camille Corot, Henri Fantin-Latour, and others entered the collection.

Childless, the Dixons decided to donate their house, gardens, and art collection to Memphis. When they died in 1974—Margaret after a long illness and Hugo unexpectedly—friends had to execute their wishes. This was achieved within a short two years. Eric A. Catmur, a long-time family friend, added a museum-quality wing to the residence, changed the entrance, refurbished the gardens, and hired a professional staff. Michael Milkovich, formerly of the Museum at Binghamton University in New York, assumed the directorship on January 1, 1976. The Dixons had owned thirty-three important works, a lot for a private family but few for a full-fledged museum. Ten more had been willed to the Memphis Brooks Museum (see next entry) before Hugo had decided on creating his own museum. The collection had to be expanded. After some negotiations, Mrs. Wanda Stevens Stout agreed to leave her superior collection of German porcelain to the Dixon and other gifts followed. By now the Dixon owns more than 1,200 works, and another wing was added in 1986. Most important was the gift-purchase acquisition of the two dozen paintings, including French and American works from the nineteenth and early twentieth centuries, assembled by Montgomery H. W. Richie, a long-time friend of Hugo. Fans of Honoré Daumier will relish the collection of fifty of his drawings.

Visitors to the Dixon feel privileged as they wander through the well-appointed house. Most of the Dixons' original treasures—Edgar Degas's *Dancer Adjusting Her Shoe*, Mary Cassatt's *The Visitor*—hang in the house. An impressive assemblage of works by Pissarro, Pierre Bonnard, Maurice Prendergast, and Paul Cézanne can be found in the new galleries. The casual visitor will find many unfamiliar names as well: Romain Jarosz, Henri-Edmond Cross, Gaston De La Touche, Jean Charles Cazin. Indeed, the Dixon makes a deliberate attempt to acquire works by lesser Impressionists and Realists who exhibited in Paris between 1874 and 1886 at the Impressionist exhibitions.

The gardens, beautiful any time of the year, are especially magical in spring, when the blooming trees rival the colors of the art objects. Both the art and the gardens are "rose-colored," and for a few hours visitors can bask in the luxury that once existed for a privileged few.

Memphis Brooks Museum of Art

Address: 1934 Poplar Avenue, Memphis, TN 38104

Telephone: (901) 544-6200

Web: www.brooksmuseum.org

Hours: Tues–Fri 10–4; Sat 10–5; Sun 11:30–5. First Wed: 10–8. Closed Mon and New Year's, Independence, Thanksgiving, and Christmas days. Tours Sat at 10:30 and 1:30, Sun at 1:30.

Strengths: Encyclopedic. European and American paintings. Kress collection of Italian Renaissance, Baroque, and Northern European Old Master paintings.

Special Events: Lectures. Afternoon programs for seniors.

Other: Temporary exhibits. Restaurant. Shop.

Activities for Children: Free family guides.

Parking: On site, free.

In 1916, the Memphis Brooks Museum of Art (the Brooks) opened its doors on the highest point of the Frederick Law Olmsted-designed Overton Park. The Renaissance Revival building, based on Rome's Villa Guilia and New York's Morgan Library, was the gift of Mrs. Bessie Vance Brooks. Mrs. Brooks stipulated that the board of trustees include three prominent American artists: William Merritt Chase, Cecilia Beaux, and Kate Carl. Thus, unsurprisingly, the Brooks started to collect American art of the 1920s, including Childe Hassam, Robert Henri, Arthur B. Davies, Anna Hyatt Huntington, and others. Cecilia Beaux's pleasant portraits of Mr. and Mrs. Samuel Brooks also entered the collection.

Activity at the Brooks accelerated in 1942 when Memphis mayor Walter Chandler managed to buy W. S. McCall's collection of European art. All of a sudden Memphis owned works by Anthony Van Dyck and Peter

Paul Rubens, including the *Portrait of a Lady, Possibly Eleanora, Duchess of Mantua*. The work is an understated Rubens. Eleanora, wearing a grand black dress and a saucy hat, stands in front of a drawn-back velvet curtain; an Italian landscape can be glimpsed in the background.

Samuel Kress opened his first five-and-dime store in Memphis, and when his foundation bequeathed its twenty-one regional collections (see p. 31), the city headed the list of recipients. The Brooks's twenty-seven "Kresses" include Renaissance, Baroque, and Northern European works.

Today the Brooks is an encyclopedic museum. According to museum literature, its collection "spans time from 2700 B.C. to the present . . . and surveys artistic achievements from five continents." The museum features collections of African and Latin American art, antiquities from the Mediterranean, and Asian art. Its building, too, has grown, by the pairing of the original building with an ultra-modern wing.

The European and American art collections, however, remain the museum's biggest assets. According to a museum survey, a visitors' favorite is Adolphe William Bouguereau's *At the Foot of the Cliff*, purchased in 1953 for $2,800 from Armand Hammer, one of America's most colorful collectors. Hammer regretted the transaction and offered to buy it back for $500,000. Other favorites are Ralph Earl's *Portrait of Andrew Jackson*, Bartolomeo Manfredi's *Ecce Homo* (from 1610–1612), Anthony Van Dyck's *Portrait of Queen Henrietta Maria* (from 1638), and two landscapes by Camille Pissarro. The latter two were gifts from the Hugo Dixons (see The Dixon Galleries and Gardens, previous entry), who were major supporters of the Brooks. The museum also owns a large collection (5,000-plus works) of graphic art.

The Brooks has always supported local artists. It owns more than seventy works by Carl Gutherz (1844–1907), an American symbolist and at one time Memphis's most prominent painter. Since 1955 the museum has also collected the work of Carroll Cloar (1913–1994), a regional artist working in Tennessee. In his *My Father Was as Big as a Tree* the painter preserves the imagery and scale with which a child sees the world.

These paintings, like many of the museum's other possessions, manifest a sense of humor. Arthur Dove's *Car in Garage* is reminiscent of

Antoine de Saint Exupéry's Little Prince drawing a *Snake Who Swallowed an Elephant*. Thomas Hart Benton's *Engineer's Dream* shows a sleeping man in overalls threatened by an onrushing locomotive, and Marisol's Madonna-like construction of *The Family* contrasts with the many Virgin-and-Child paintings of the Kress collection.

Texas

DALLAS

Dallas Museum of Art

Address: 1717 N. Harwood Street, Dallas, TX 75201

Telephone: (214) 922-1200

Web: www.dm-art.org

Hours: Tues–Wed, Fri–Sun 11–5; Thurs 11–9. Closed Mon and New Year's, Thanksgiving, and Christmas days. Gallery talks Wed at 12:15.

Strengths: Encyclopedic. European art from antiquity to 20th century, including Impressionist and Post-Impressionist paintings and a group of early and late works by Piet Mondrian. American art, with masterworks of the Hudson River School, the 20th century, and contemporary art. Collections devoted to art of Asia (Buddhist and Hindu sculptures, China, and Japan), Africa, and the Pacific.

Other: A state-of-the-art computer system provides information on works in the collection. Sculpture garden. Gourmet restaurant and casual café. Museum shop.

Special Events: Live music, usually jazz, and Art Talk every Thurs 6–8.

Activities for Children: The Gateway Family Education Area features a three-dimensional version of Edward Hicks's *Peaceable Kingdom*, an African hut with a Senufo drum, and crayons, paper, plaques to rub, puzzles, and lots of books on open shelves.

Parking: Metered on street; underground pay garage.

As you progress along the main axis of the Dallas Museum of Art (DMA) you come across a lion, a fox, a tiger, a lamb, and even a mother holding her child. All these creatures evidently wandered out of Edward Hicks's *Peaceable Kingdom*, demonstrating to the young audience in the Family Room of the DMA that art is fun and accessible.

The DMA goes back to 1903, a time at which major towns in Texas decided that art was important. Initially located on the outskirts of the city, the institution moved downtown in 1983 when Dallas created an Arts District. It occupies a handsome minimalist-style building designed by Edward Larrabee Barnes.

The collections are comprehensive and well displayed. The Art of the Americas ranges from prime examples of Pre-Columbian art to work by noted twentieth-century artists such as John Singer Sargent, Edward Hopper, Thomas Hart Benton, and Andrew Wyeth. The museum is justly proud of Frederick Church's spectacular *The Icebergs*, based on sketches he made in 1859 during a trip along the coasts of Newfoundland and Labrador. Viewers in those pre-camera days must have been amazed by the massive mountains of ice rising out of a brown, yellow, and green sea. Dallas also owns many contemporary works. *Stake Hitch*, a large sculpture by Claes Oldenburg and Coosje Van Bruggen, fills a whole room and Chris Burden's huge mobile representing the entire fleet of U.S. submarines (625 in all) fills another.

Wendy and Emery Reves gave the DMA Impressionist and Post-Impressionist works by Auguste Renoir, Vincent van Gogh, Camille Pissarro, Paul Cézanne, and others, stipulating that they be displayed in galleries evoking their villa on the French Riviera. These period rooms, with a festively set table, rugs, and decorative objects, let us glimpse the life of the rich and glamorous in one of Europe's fabled playgrounds.

The museum's collection of early-twentieth-century art is famous and includes a group of works by Piet Mondrian, as well as works by Constantin Brancusi, Fernand Léger, Kazimir Malevich, Paul Gauguin, Georges Braque, Pablo Picasso, and Juan Gris. There is also a small collection of classical antiquities, works from Africa including a rare standing male figure from Zaire, Spanish Colonial art, Pre-Columbian art, and much more.

Much of the year Texas is hot and dry, and it is a pleasure to glimpse several outdoor spaces with their prominent trees, reflecting pools, geysers, and cascading water falls. Works by nineteenth- and twentieth-century artists are displayed in well-defined areas in the large sculpture garden. A monumental abstract sculpture by Ellsworth Kelly anchors a reflecting pool. In front of it is Scott Burton's *Granite Settee,* which was commissioned by the DMA. Burton died at the height of the AIDS epidemic; by installing his sculpture-cum-furniture on World AIDS Day in 1999, the DMA reminds us of this scourge and "emphasizes the importance of artistic creativity in our culture."

EL PASO

El Paso Museum of Art

Address: One Arts Festival Plaza, El Paso, TX 79901

Telephone: (915) 532-1707

Web: www.elpasoartmuseum.org

Hours: Tues–Sat 9–6; Thurs 9–9; Sun 12–5. Closed Mon and major holidays.

Strengths: Kress collection of Renaissance and Baroque paintings. Spanish Colonial art. Contemporary American art. Artists of the Southwest.

Special Events: 10–12 temporary exhibits, some focused on the museum's collections.

Other: Museum shop.

Activities for Children: Tours for children. Family days.

Parking: In Performing Arts and Convention Center garage.

The El Paso Museum of Art moved into a brand-new building in 1998, over fifty years after its founding. El Paso greeted its new museum with pride and enthusiasm. Old and young gathered for the party celebrating the museum's first birthday in 1999. The museum had had a slow start. Over time, citizens donated various art objects to the city, which for a while were housed in the basement of the city hall. Eventually the objects were exhibited in the neoclassical Turney Mansion and in 1947, the El Paso International Museum was incorporated. Several years later the Samuel H. Kress Foundation promised the museum a major gift provided that it would improve its quarters. The city of El Paso and its citizens came to the rescue. Two large wings were added to the original house and in 1961 the museum received fifty-nine Renaissance and

Baroque works of art from the foundation—and was renamed the El Paso Museum of Art.

The museum's collection continued to expand and by the 1990s it had outgrown the Turney Mansion. The City of El Paso once more helped the institution participate in the Texas museum-building boom. The downtown Greyhound station was purchased, taken down to its foundations, and a new state-of-the art building was erected. The area around the old bus terminal was transformed into the Arts Festival Plaza. The two-story building is fronted by a reflecting pool and a walkway with an accordion-pleated roof that invite lingering. *Vaquero*, a Mexican cowboy reinterpreted by Mexican American artist Luis Jiménez, marks the entrance to the museum. The exuberant rider, made of fiberglass and painted in vivid colors, contrasts with the museum's somber facade. (Another version of the statue stands in front of the Smithsonian American Art Museum, see p. 140). *Vaquero* emphasizes El Paso's multicultural population and the museum's commitment to feature contemporary artists of the Southwest and to stress its proximity to Mexico and New Mexico. Luis Jiménez is a native of El Paso; the museum also owns works by James Drake, James Surls, and other regional artists.

The museum's collections focus on European Old Masters, American art, Spanish Colonial art, and contemporary art of the Southwest. Highlights of the Kress collection include works by Lorenzo Lotto, Canaletto, Jusepe de Ribera, and Artemisia Gentileschi. *Christ with the Symbols of Passion* by Lavina Fontana (see the National Museum of Women in the Arts, p. 128) is notable, and the museum is particularly proud of Anthony Van Dyck's *Portrait of a Lady*.

Some of the museum's older possessions also reflect El Paso's ties to Hispanic culture. The Spanish Viceroyal and Mexican folk art collections include paintings from the seventeenth through the nineteenth century made on wood, canvas, copper, and tin. The museum owns 600 Mexican folk retables.

The American collection is quite inclusive, presenting an overview from the eighteenth and nineteenth centuries (Gilbert Stuart, Thomas Sully, and Rembrandt Peale) to the present, with an emphasis on American Impressionists.

El Paso has an extensive collection of works on paper ranging from the sixteenth to the twentieth century. Among the highlights are Old

Master prints by Rembrandt and Giambattista Piranesi, and American prints by Thomas Hart Benton and Romare Bearden.

FORT WORTH

Forth Worth's ambition is to become the art capital of the South, and it may very well be on its way. Its three principal art museums, two of which are in the throes of major construction, have agreed not to overlap. The Amon Carter collects American art principally from 1850–1960; the Modern Art Museum of Forth Worth collects world-wide art, dating principally from 1945 to the present; and The Kimbell Art Museum collects mostly European, Asian, and Pre-Columbian art. Since the museums are, or will soon be, within walking distance of one another (watch for opening dates of the new buildings), this makes for an intense art experience.

Amon Carter Museum

Address: 3501 Camp Bowie Boulevard, Fort Worth, TX 76107

Telephone: (817) 738-1933

Web: www.cartermuseum.org

Hours: Tues–Wed, Fri–Sat 10–5; Thurs 10–8; Sun 12–5. Closed Mon and major holidays. Highlights tours Fri at 12; Sat–Sun at 2.

Strengths: American art from 1850–1960. Western art. American photography, especially landscapes and Western subjects.

Other: Museum shop.

Activities for Children: Occasional story-telling programs. Lunchbox tours: Kits filled with games to help children interpret artworks.

Parking: Free, on site.

People who think that the Amon Carter Museum in Fort Worth is simply a museum of Western art are in for a surprise. True, Amon Carter, the founder, mostly collected works by the two most popular Western artists of his time: Frederic Remington and Charles Marion Russell. He hoped, however, to found a museum of American art. His children,

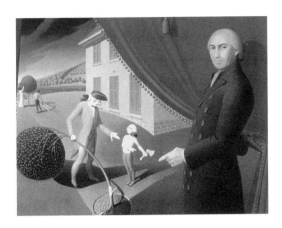

Grant Wood's *Parson Weems' Fable*, at the Amon Carter Museum, retells the legend of George Washington chopping down a cherry tree.

especially his daughter, Ruth Carter Stevenson, implemented his wishes. As she wrote so eloquently in a museum publication: "I was very fortunate to have seven or eight years of conversations [with my father] about his concepts and philosophy for a museum. . . . We [his children] thoroughly understood also that mediocrity in any undertaking was unacceptable." With the advice of friends, art historians, and a wise board, Mrs. Stevenson assembled important and stunning works, and today the museum is recognized the world over as one of the leading collections of American art.

Like many of those who enriched our cultural heritage, Amon Carter was born poor, and started waiting on tables at age eleven. Soon, however, he became a newspaperman, entrepreneur, and oil magnate. He spent his life giving some of his riches back to Fort Worth.

The collection of the Carter (now numbering more than 300,000 works) celebrates America. There are few emotionally disturbing pictures by artists who depict the cruel side of life. We admire the beauty of the land in paintings by Thomas Cole, Thomas Moran, Frederick Church, Albert Bierstadt, and Georgia O'Keeffe. The scene of the skinny-dipping boys in Thomas Eakins's *The Swimming Hole* harks back to simpler times. The museum has a slight preference for works with a Western theme, befitting a town that treasures memories of days when there were real cowboys and Indians—a National Cowgirl Hall of Fame is in the planning stage. Two American icons, a watercolor of *The Brooklyn Bridge* by John Marin and Fitz Hugh Lane's view of *Boston Harbor*, as well as many other works, however, remind us of the rest of America. Adults and children will be enchanted by Grant Wood's *Parson Weems' Fable*. Weems, one of George Washington's early biographers, invented the cherry tree story. In Wood's painting, Weems, as master showman, reveals a glimpse of our first president as a child, except that his head is a miniature version of Gilbert Stuart's official portrait. The work, painted in a mock folk style, is a reminder of the need for fantasy in life as in art.

Even non-Texans know of the flowering bluebonnets (lupines) that tint the Texas landscape in late March. These flowers are imortalized in Julian Onderdonk's *A Cloudy Day, Bluebonnets, near San Antonio*, an Impressionist painting fittingly dedicated to Lady Bird Johnson. Most recently the Carter has started to collect photography, rapidly becoming a force to be reckoned with.

Architect Philip Johnson designed the museum's first abode in 1961. Its five large bays overlook the skyscrapers of downtown Fort Worth. In time the collections outgrew its space and the eighty-year-old Johnson and his firm drew the plans for a greatly enlarged, remodeled structure which reopened in 2001.

Kimbell Art Museum

Address: 3333 Camp Bowie Boulevard, Fort Worth, TX 76107

Telephone: (817) 332-8451

Web: www.kimbellart.org

Hours: Tues–Thurs, Sat 10–5; Fri 12–8; Sun 12–5. Closed Mon and New Year's, Independence, Thanksgiving, and Christmas days.

Strengths: Superb-quality European art from antiquity through the middle of the 20th century. Art of Asia (China, Japan, Korea, Cambodia, India). Pre-Columbian and African art.

Special Events: Temporary shows thematically related to the museum's collection.

Other: Restaurant. Museum shop featuring excellent art books.

Activities for Children: The limited size of the collection and its variety make it a great teaching tool. An excellent treasure-hunt map is available at the front desk.

Parking: Free, on site.

Owning a version of Michaelangelo da Caravaggio's *The Cardsharps* (*a*) would be a feather in any museum's cap. The Kimbell Art Museum in Fort Worth also owns Georges de La Tour's *The Cheat with the Ace of Clubs* (*b*). The Louvre in Paris owns versions of these same two works.

Sitting on a lawn, the twelve linked barrel vaults that make up the Kimbell Art Museum in Fort Worth look like a piece of sculpture. The front of the museum is windowless. Except for Joan Miró's birdlike creature entitled *Woman Addressing the Public*, there is no hint of the treasures hidden within. One descends a few steps and enters a low-lit gallery lined with exquisite Japanese and Chinese scrolls from the fourteenth to the sixteenth century. A brick-red Japanese wine flask from the sixteenth century is displayed in the center. There is a reception desk surmounted by a blooming orchid. The bustle of the outside world dissipates.

Light floods the stairs that ascend to the main floor. It is this light that makes the museum so special. Natural light, intricately diffused through the barrel-vaulted ceilings, illuminates the art. Direct sunlight, streaming into an interior court, endows Aristide Maillol's floating nude *L'Air* with special glamour. The quality of the light, filtered through a group of spindly trees in the back of the museum, reminds this visitor of Paris and of Georges Seurat's painting *A Sunday on La Grande Jatte—1884.*

Many experts call the Kimbell America's best small museum. Not only is this magic building architect Louis Kahn's masterpiece, but its collection has been carefully assembled and nurtured. The museum is the gift of Kay and Velma Kimbell, and it became a reality after Kay's death in 1964. The couple had collected French and English portraits, which they donated without any strings attached. The board, headed by founding director Dr. Richard F. Brown, decreed that any work acquired or retained should define a particular artist by its quality, rarity, importance, suitability, and emotional appeal.

The European collection is arranged chronologically. As befits the scale of the museum, most works are small and intimate. One of the earliest works is Duccio's *The Raising of Lazarus.* Christ's golden halo shimmers, as the disbelieving crowd sees Lazarus emerging from his sepulcher. The small egg-tempera panel was created in 1308-1311 for an altar in Siena's Cathedral. It is lucky for us that the Italians were prone to redecorate their houses of worship. When they refurbished the Siena altar, they got rid of this panel, which ended up in Texas in 1975.

During the 1980s the museum acquired two of its signature possessions—Michelangelo da Caravaggio's *The Cardsharps* (about 1594) and its reinterpretation, thirty-five years later, by Georges de La Tour as *The Cheat With the Ace of Clubs.* Both paintings depict handsome cheats fleecing equally attractive, but naive, noble youths. Two other versions of these same paintings are owned by the Louvre, where they also hang side by side, their labels referring to their sister paintings in Fort Worth. The other European holdings are equally inspiring, such as Rembrandt's *Portrait of a Young Jew*, with its dark, expressive eyes, and Henri Matisse's *L'Asie*, a luscious woman playing with her pearls. An unusual find is a self-portrait of Elisabeth Vigée-Lebrun (French, 1755–1852), a successful woman painter who was summoned to Versailles by Marie Antoinette (also see New Orleans Museum of Art, p. 183).

The museum's Asian, African, and pre-Columbian artworks are select and visually pleasing. Buddhas—gilded and in stone—vie with Pre-Columbian rain gods, intricate Mayan stelae, and a few tribal African sculptures. Since the museums in Fort Worth are noncompetitive, the Kimbell does not collect American art and contemporary European art.

Modern Art Museum of Fort Worth

Address: 1309 Montgomery Street, Fort Worth, TX 76107

Telephone: (817) 738-9215

Web: www.mamfw.org

Hours: Tues–Thurs 11–6; Fri–Sat 11–10; Sun 1–5. Closed Mon and holidays. Tours Sat at 2.

Strengths: American and International art after 1945, especially from the New York School. Photography. New media works.

Special Events: Temporary shows. Day of the Dead Festival.

Other: Museum shop.

Activities for Children: Special tours by prearrangement.

Parking: Free, on site.

A new museum building, currently under construction, is scheduled to open in September 2002. The old museum will be open until shortly before that.

What is now called the Modern Art Museum of Fort Worth (MAMFW) was founded in 1892. Until 1954, it was physically part of Fort Worth's Carnegie Public Library; then it moved to its own building. By then, as Fort Worth's only art museum, it had a history of organizing great shows and owned a sizable collection.

The purchase of Pablo Picasso's *Femme Couchée Lisant* at the world's first televised art auction by the Modern Art Museum of Fort Worth made headline news.

It took a while for Fort Worth's three museums to sort out which would do what (see p. 378). With a few exceptions, such as Pablo Picasso's *Femme Couchée Lisant,* purchased during the world's first satellite-linked art auction, the MAMFW now collects art created after 1945. This definition includes American and International art and photography as well as works in new media.

By the time the museum celebrated its 100th birthday, its holdings were stupendous. Today its collection includes twenty-one works by Jackson Pollock, thirty-five by Robert Motherwell, thirteen by Milton Avery, sixteen by Morris Louis, as well as works by Ellsworth Kelly, Andy Warhol, Hans Hofmann, and Richard Diebenkorn.

Recently the museum developed a special relationship with several German painters including Anselm Kiefer, considered by many to be Germany's leading post–World War Two artist. The MAMFW owns his *Papst Alexander VI Die Goldene Bulle,* a powerful painting of a huge mountain of bricks that resembles a decaying Mexican pyramid. The stones in the painting look so real that it is hard to resist touching. Another unfamiliar experience is *The Greeting,* a video sound installation by Bill Viola. The work is based on a sixteenth-century painting by

Jacopo de Pontormo. Three women, clothed in red, blue, and yellow flowing garments, meet, chat, and separate. Viola captures their gestures and expressions, wind billows their clothes, and after watching the slow-speed presentation the images are long-lasting.

In a less serious mood is *Ruckus Rodeo* by Red Grooms. In 1975 the MAMFW commissioned eleven artists to create works celebrating the Great American rodeo. Grooms constructed a zany three-dimensional Texas-size work using wire, canvas, burlap, paint, and fiberglass. The beloved work—often in storage or on loan—features bulls and horses, a rodeo queen, and bronc riders, demonstrating to one and all that art can be good fun.

By the end of the century the MAMFW had outgrown its space and a new museum will be ready in late 2002. Museum officials proudly declare that as modern art museums go, "it will be second in size only to New York's MoMA." At the rate at which the U.S. is growing museums, however, it may not have that distinction for long.

HOUSTON

The Menil Collection

Address: 1515 Sul Ross, Houston, TX 77006

Telephone: (713) 525-9400

Web: www.menil.org

Hours: Wed–Sun 11–7. Closed Mon–Tues and New Year's, Presidents', Martin Luther King's, Easter, Memorial, Thanksgiving, and Christmas days.

Strengths: Antiquities from Paleolithic to pre-Christian eras. Byzantine art. African and Oceanic art. 20th-century art with special emphasis on Surrealism, especially Max Ernst and René Magritte, and works verging on the fantastic and allegorical. Also School of Paris Modernism, New York School, and Pop Art.

Other: Rothko Chapel. Byzantine Frescoe Chapel Museum. Cy Twombly Gallery. Bookstore.

Parking: At 1515 W. Alabama Street; also on street.

Dominique and John (Jean) de Menil, who inherited the Schlumberger oil fortune, were young, rich, and generous, and lived in Paris before World War Two. So, when a friend suggested that they support Max Ernst,

Max Ernst, *Portrait of Dominique*, 1934, at The Menil Collection.

a struggling Surrealist painter, they commissioned Dominique's portrait. For ten years the de Menils ignored the painting. When they finally did pay attention, the world had changed.

By then the headquarters of Schlumberger and the de Menils had moved to Houston. More crucial for the subject at hand, the couple had begun to collect art. Throughout their collecting years, both Dominique and John heavily relied on their emotional response to art, buying objects and images that appealed to their sensibilities. As Dominique writes in a Guide to the de Menil collection: "However well parenthood is planned, children are what *they* are, not what their parents decided. Like children, treasures of a collection are what *they* are. Complex sets of circumstances brought these treasures into the family: a chance encounter, a visit to an artist or a dealer, a glance at an auction catalogue, a successful bidding, a favorable moment for spending. This somehow unsystematic approach was our way of collecting. Nothing was excluded . . . yet deep inclinations existed."

As a consequence, the de Menil collection of approximately 10,000 objects is highly personal, concentrating on art of ancient cultures, Medieval and Byzantine art, European paintings, Colonial art in the New World, art of the Tribal Cultures, and twentieth-century art, especially Surrealism.

John de Menil died in 1973 and it was up to Dominique to build their museum. In her search for an architect she came across Renzo Piano, the co-designer of the Pompidou Center in Paris and of a museum in Ein Harod, an Israeli kibbutz. Dominique seems to have gone about the building process as determinedly and tastefully as Boston's Isabella Stewart Gardner (see the Isabella Stewart Gardner Museum, p. 202). She worried about the light, the grouping of figures, the texture of the floor, the juxtaposition of the old and the new, the supersophisticated and the primitive. She created a masterpiece.

Cases filled with small white Cycladic figures are contrasted by tall black and brown African and Oceanic works, both types of art presaging Cubism. The tribal works are surrounded by interior gardens filled with huge tropical plants. One small room holds only two festively dressed Spanish Colonial Madonnas; it is reminiscent of the white-washed chapels of New Mexico.

In another part of the museum we experience the mind-boggling world of the Surrealists. The museum has thirty-two works by Max Ernst, and scores of works by René Magritte, Marcel Duchamp, and Joseph Cornell. A recent exhibit entitled "A Surrealist Wunderkammer"—a pun on earlier assemblages of wondrous objects by German princes—combined eighty-nine objects into an impressive whole. Elsewhere there is American twentieth-century art by Mark Rothko, James Rosenquist, and other members of the New York School. In one room George Segal's cast figure of *A Seated Woman* stares as if in disbelief at three Warhol paintings. All objects on view are so perfect that one regrets that the museum is small, fulfilling Dominique's wish of avoiding "museum fatigue." A free-standing gallery, devoted to the works of Cy Twombly, is across the street.

Religion and spirituality were always important to the de Menils. It is not surprising that they asked Rothko to create paintings for a small chapel in 1971. Just outside the Rothko Chapel is Barnet Newman's *Broken Obelisk*, dedicated to the memory Dr. Martin Luther King, Jr. In 1992, Dominique ransomed thirteenth-century Byzantine frescoes, cut into thirty-eight pieces, from art robbers and built a replica of a diminutive Byzantine chapel near the museum. Sitting in the low-lit fresco museum, visitors cannot help experience the inner peace and reverence the art was meant to inspire.

The Museum of Fine Arts, Houston

Address: 1001 Bissonnet, Houston, TX, 77005

Telephone: (713) 639-7300

Web: www.mfah.org

Hours: Tues–Wed, Sat 10–7; Thurs–Fri 10–9; Sun 12:15–7. Closed Mon and Thanksgiving and Christmas days.

Strengths: Encyclopedic, with good collections covering 6,000 years of creativity from Asia, Central and South America, and Africa. European collections from antiquity to contemporary, including a Kress collection. Comprehensive American collections.

Special Events: Temporary exhibits.

Other: Sculpture gardens. Restaurant. Museum shop. Houston's new Contemporary Arts Museum, a noncollecting institution that organizes approximately 12 shows a year, is located next to the MFAH.

Activities for Children: Second Sun (1–4): Family day with discovery tours, performances, art workshops. Every Sun at 2:30: Storytime; also hands-on workshop.

Parking: On site.

At the turn of the current millennium, museums in Texas began a building spree. The Museum of Fine Arts, Houston (MFAH) completed and opened a new building on March 25, 2000, the centennial anniversary of the institution. Three major architects have worked on the museum complex during its hundred-year history. W. W. Watkin designed the first building, a Beaux Arts structure. It was enlarged twice by Mies van der Rohe in his signature International style. The newest addition, the Audrey Jones Beck building, is the work of Rafael Moneo, Spain's leading architect, responsible for several major European and U.S. museums. For the time being, this addition will make the MFAH the sixth largest museum in the U.S.

The Beck's grand entrance and the atrium that serves as an American sculpture gallery soar seventy-nine feet to a skylit roof. The American art galleries are on the first floor. European art is displayed on the second floor, where it is lit by diffused natural light. Pioneered by the Kimbell Art Museum in Forth Worth (see p. 380), this type of lighting is becoming a must for many new museums. At the Beck it is achieved by filtering sunlight through a unique system of "lantern and throat" combinations. The diffused light bathes the paintings in a spectacular fashion.

When the MFAH opened in 1924, it owned fifty works of art. An early gift came from Samuel H. Kress, long before his foundation became a major donor to America's art museums. Later, the Kress Foundation donated thirty paintings. By 1941 the museum had also attracted the attention of Macy's CEO Percy Straus and his wife, Edith Abraham, the daughter of the founder of Abraham and Straus. The Strauses had assembled a fabulous collection of Old Masters. Their pledge of eighty-two works of art to the MFAH was announced on December 7, 1941, Pearl Harbor Day. The spectacular art gift regrettably did not receive the attention it deserved.

By 1947, oil had been had been discovered in Texas and the MFAH acquired another set of benefactors, the Blaffers. The couple had the good fortune of being related to both the Humble Oil and Refining Company and Texaco. While studying in Boston, the future Sarah Blaffer had fallen in love with Isabella Stewart Gardner's museum (see p. 202). The young Texan became an inveterate art devotee and collector, with an innate sense of taste, always ranking quality above quantity. Her gifts to the MFAH comprised two dozen European works ranging from the Renaissance to the Post-Impressionists. Included was a rare work by Giovanni di Paolo, *Saint Clare Rescuing a Child Mutilated by a Wolf*. The almost childlike painting shows the wolf with the mangled hand of its victim, and a horrified mother calling out to a floating saint.

The third large contributor to the MFAH's European collections is Audrey Jones Beck. When she visited Paris at age sixteen, she fell in love with Impressionism and Post-Impressionism. Together with her husband, John, she largely assembled the MFAH's collection of nineteenth- and twentieth-century art, which includes paintings by Camille Pissarro, Auguste Renoir, Odilon Redon, Vincent van Gogh, and others. Kees van Dongen's painting of a young woman with a red turban, red lips, and immense black eyes has become the signature piece of the collection. Houston's excellent American collection was assembled over many years by a number of people and purchases.

There is something magic about gold; Houston's spectacular Glassell Collections of African, Indonesian, and Pre-Columbian gold are surprising in their depth. The Akan people of the Ivory Coast and

Ghana created large bracelets, ear ornaments, pectorals, and necklaces for their royal court. Even the typical carved wooden figures or drums look glamorous because they are gilded. The equally luscious Indonesian collection includes crowns, ritual objects, earrings, and a dagger.

The MFAH and the City of Houston are joint caretakers of a large sculpture garden designed by Isamu Noguchi (see The Isamu Noguchi Garden Museum, p. 287). This oasis contains over twenty-five masterpieces by leading artists including Robert Graham's elegant athletes, Emile Bourdelle's mournful *Adam*, Aristide Maillol's well-behaved *Flore*, Auguste Rodin's headless *Walking Man*, Giacomo Manzu's *Pilgrim on a Horse*, Alberto Giacometti's *Large Standing Woman*, and four of Henri Matisse's *Backs*. Water gurgles from a large fountain, grass surrounds each sculpture, and trees—pines, sycamores, mimosas, water oaks, magnolias—are planted throughout this wonderful refuge from the hot Texas sun.

SAN ANTONIO

Marion Koogler McNay Art Museum

Address: 6000 N. New Braunfels Avenue, San Antonio, TX 78209
Telephone: (210) 824-5368
Web: www.mcnayart.org
Hours: Tues–Sat 10–5; Sun 12–5. Closed New Year's, Independence, Thanksgiving, and Christmas days.
Strength: French Post-Impressionist and early-20th-century European and American art.
Special Events: Annual fairs.
Other: Museum shop.
Parking: Free, on site.

High on a hill overlooking downtown San Antonio sits a Spanish Mediterranean style mansion surrounded by landscaped gardens. It is the Marion Koogler McNay Art Museum (the McNay). Sunset Hill was grand when Marion Koogler McNay built it in 1927. During its construction she oversaw every detail. She personally stenciled ceilings; she included other dramatic details and decorations such as Spanish-style wrought iron grilles and torchères, painted tiles, stuccoed walls, huge earthenware jars filled with exotic plants, and tall trees. When Sunset Hill was finished, San Antonio was invited for a grand celebration.

Marion Koogler McNay belongs to a handful of determined ladies whose vision endowed America with some of its most charming museums, the Isabella Stewart Gardner in Boston (p. 202), the Menil Collection in Houston (p. 385), and the Museum of Fine Arts, St. Petersburg (p. 146) among them. Marion was the only daughter of Dr. Marion Koogler, who practiced medicine in El Dorado, Kansas, at the turn of the last century. A farmer at heart, Dr. Koogler amassed 3,248 acres of good grazing land. But, instead of fattening cattle, the acreage spouted oil during the Kansas oil boom.

Lois Burkhalter, Marion's biographer, described her as introverted, impulsive, generous, moody, shy, and easily discouraged. Fortunately, she also had a sense of humor. She certainly was artistically gifted. At age ten she visited the famous World's Columbian Exposition in Chicago and became enthralled by Mrs. Potter Palmer's French Impressionists at the Art Institute of Chicago (p. 163), where she later studied. In 1913 she went to New York to visit the Armory Show, where again she was captivated by the beauty of works by Cézanne, Picasso, Gauguin, Pissarro, van Gogh, Degas, and Renoir. Along the way she got married five times and very slowly began to buy art. She became a more systematic collector in 1933 after she met gallery owner Edith Gregor Halpert, who also advised Abby Aldrich Rockefeller. Later she relied on the advice of major Los Angeles art dealers Dalzell and Ruth Hatfield.

Marion was partial to watercolors, her own preferred medium, and her collection includes many sensitive works. Jules Pascin's oil of *Two Girls in an Armchair* is so soft that it could almost be a watercolor. Gauguin looks pensively at his visitors in his *Self-Portrait with the Idol*, and Cézanne's *Houses On the Hill* are strangely verdant in this Texas landscape. There are works by Georges Seurat, Chaim Soutine, Picasso, Amedeo Modigliani, Marc Chagall, van Gogh, Georges Braque, Henri Matisse, Maurice Utrillo, Pierre Bonnard, Paul Klee, Paul Signac, and Raoul Dufy.

Given the proximity of Texas to Taos, New Mexico, Marion Koogler started to visit the art colony there and acquired works by Robert

Henri, John Marin, and Winslow Homer. Eventually her collection included works by other American painters including Childe Hassam, Maurice Prendergast, and Mary Cassatt.

Early on, Mrs. McNay also collected works by Mexican artists. As a matter of fact, Diego Rivera's portrait of *Delfina Flores* was the first oil painting she purchased. Today the McNay also owns works by David Alfaro Siqueiros, José Orozco, and other Mexican artists.

Marion Koogler McNay always shared her home and possessions with others. In 1942, she decided that after her death her home would become a museum. Methodically she regulated the museum's fate in a carefully crafted will. All new purchases and gifts had to be approved unanimously by a seven-member board. In addition they had to be vetted by the director of the Art Institute of Chicago, the Art Institute of Santa Barbara, and the head of the Fine Arts Department of the University of Texas. The museum thus is very much as she left it—an oasis of pleasure. Her precious paintings are interspersed with antique French and Spanish furniture and decorative objects.

Museums, however, do grow. In 1955 the McNay received a major collection of Gothic and Medieval art from Dr. and Mrs. Frederic Oppenheimer. In 1975, Sivan and Mary Lang donated a collection of mostly American paintings and sculptures. Most recently the museum was given a large chunk of the L. B. Tobin Collection of Theater Arts which, according to museum literature, is considered to be "one of the finest in the world, encompassing thousands of rare books, stage designs, drawings, prints, and posters." Sunset Hill, which so heavily relies on make-believe, is an ideal location for a theater art collection.

San Antonio Museum of Fine Arts

Address: 200 W. Jones Avenue, San Antonio, TX 78215

Telephone: (210) 978-8100

Web: www.samuseum.org

Hours: Tues 10–9; Wed–Sat 10–5; Sun 12–5. Closed Thanksgiving and Christmas days.

Strengths: Encyclopedic. Antiquities. Asian art. Latin American art from Pre-Columbian to the 20th century. Glass collection.

Special Events: Annually: Asian Festival, Family art days, Bazar Sábado Art Market, Three Kings' Festival, June Celebration.

Other: Museum shop.

Activities for Children: Every Sun 1–4: Make-n-Take art class for kids. First Sun: Family day. Also self-guided tour for families.

Parking: On site.

On June 13, 1691, the feast day of Saint Anthony, the Spanish reached the Indian village of Yanaguana, which they renamed San Antonio. A mission called the Alamo was established there in 1718. A hundred years later, in 1821, Mexico won its independence from Spain, and San Antonio came under Mexican rule. In 1835, Texas revolted against Mexico. On March 6, 1836, 4,000 Mexican soldiers attacked the Alamo, defended by 189 men, who held out for thirteen days. Eventually the entire Texan garrison was executed and the battle of the Alamo became a national landmark. Texas became an independent republic in 1836 and a state in 1845.

The San Antonio Museum of Art (SAMoA) opened in 1981 in a building that for almost 100 years had housed the Lone Star Brewery. The historic preservation is a success. Modern free-standing stairs and a balcony contrast with the bricks, wooden beams, and lofty archways of the old brewery.

The museum has an excellent encyclopedic collection, featuring art from ancient Egypt, Greece, and Rome. The collection of ancient glass is noteworthy. The museum also has a good Asian art collection including works from China, Japan, Korea, and other countries.

The museum's American collection mirrors our cultural history with works by John Singleton Copley, Benjamin West, Gilbert Stuart, the Hudson River School, and representative works by artists of the nineteenth and twentieth centuries. There is great emphasis on the work of regional artists.

Culturally, San Antonio always remained close to Mexico and it is fitting that the SAMoA houses the Nelson A. Rockefeller Center for Latin American Art. Collecting art was one of Nelson Rockefeller's passions. He assumed the presidency of New York's Museum of Modern Art (p. 297)—founded by his mother in 1929—when he was thirty years old and played a key role in the development of the museum. He founded the Museum of Primitive Art in New York, now housed in the Michael C. Rockefeller Wing of New York's Metropolitan Museum of Art (p. 293). He also contributed to the Hood Museum of Art, Dartmouth College (p. 251), his alma mater. San Antonio was the beneficiary of the fifty years he spent collecting 2,500 pieces of South American art. Rockefeller first visited Mexico in 1933 and became enchanted by its cultures. His tastes were eclectic. He acquired art from well-established artists and studied and bought pre-Columbian art, but he was especially delighted by Mexico's folk art available at local markets. In 1998, almost twenty years after his death, his daughter Ann R. Roberts gave what remained of her father's Latin American collection to the SAMoA. The museum's own collection and other major gifts complemented the Rockefeller donation, and the Nelson A. Rockefeller Center for South American Art, housed in a new two-story wing, became a reality.

The ground floor is shared by Pre-Columbian and Folk Art collections. The former, mostly assembled by Elizabeth Huth Coates, is comprehensive. There are examples of Olmec art, as well objects made by the west coast cultures (Jalisco, Colima, and Nayarit). There are classic period objects from the Teotihuacan, Oaxaca, Veracruz, and Maya regions and post-Classic objects from the Aztec, Mixtec, and Toltec periods. Andean holdings include fine ceramics, gold, and textiles.

The Folk Art holdings of SAMoA are subdivided into decorative, utilitarian (clothing, household furnishings), and ceremonial objects. Visitors' favorite is the *Negrito Mask* whose pearl- and flower-encrusted crown contrasts with its black face and very white eyes. The mask, the painted earthenware model of a cathedral, and the figures of monkeys and cranes appeal to the child in all of us.

The second floor of the museum is shared by Colonial, Republican, early modern, and mid-twentieth-century art. Because the Roman Catholic Church was the principal patron, most of the 100 paintings and objects of the seventeenth- and eighteenth-century Spanish Colonial period are religious. There are statues and pictures of saints, of the Virgin, and of the holy family. Anonymous artists painted most of the work in popular style and much of it is reminiscent of the folk art. Liturgical silver, secular textiles, and furniture represent the decorative arts of this period. Of interest are facsimiles of codices kept by the Conquistadores.

Mexican and South American masters—Diego Rivera, David Alfaro Siqueiros, and others—as well as changing exhibits are also displayed on the second floor.

Vermont

BENNINGTON

The Bennington Museum

Address: W. Main Street, Bennington, VT 05201

Telephone: (802) 447-1571

Web: www.benningtonmuseum.com

Hours: Daily, *Nov–May*: 9–5; *June–Oct*: 9–6. Closed New Year's, Thanksgiving, and Christmas days.

Strengths: Grandma Moses. Bennington pottery. 19th- and early-20th-century American glass. Historical memorabilia concerning Vermont.

Other: Museum shop. Schoolhouse.

Activities for Children: The collections of the museum are of interest to children.

Parking: On site.

Anna Mary Robertson Moses (1860–1961), better known as Grandma Moses, would have felt right at home in the Bennington Museum, which houses the largest public collection of her works. America's most beloved folk artist would also have liked the museum's surroundings: the rolling landscape, the white clapboard houses, the gigantic trees, and the one-room schoolhouse she attended in Eagle Bridge, New York, more than 130 years ago. The museum moved the school to its present site on the museum grounds in 1972. Grandma Moses lived ten miles across the border, in New York State. She started painting when she was in her seventies. Eventually a friend persuaded her try to sell some of her work at the Hoosick Falls Womens' Exchange located in the town's drugstore. There it was noticed by Otto Kallir, a New York art dealer, who gave her a one-woman show in 1940. Moses's work was also included in the *Unknown Artists* exhibit at New York's MoMA in 1939. When Moses was 100 she illustrated Clement Clark Moore's *Twas the Night before Christmas.*

Initially the Bennington museum collected Moses's work because she was a local artist. By now it owns thirty-four paintings and, according to Executive Director Steven Miller, "We now buy every painting we can." The paintings are wishful escapes to what we like to believe rural activities were like in the olden days. We see skaters twirling on a frozen pond in a winter landscape, cows and horse-drawn carts in front of *The Checked House,* maple sugaring, a view of Bennington, and other images painted in a deceptively simple, childlike style sometimes called American primitive.

The Bennington's Moses collection was enlarged in the late 1990s by a curious event. Two sisters, Mary and Edna Colt, had befriended Grandma Moses and in the process had acquired several of her pictures. At Edna's death these were willed to the Bennington Museum, packed up, and allegedly mailed, but they never arrived at their destination. Years later, several wooden crates arrived at the museum. They were unpacked with great caution, and to everybody's joy, seven paintings by Grandma Moses emerged unscathed.

The Bennington Museum acquired many artifacts associated with the artist's life: an extensive photographic record of her life, including pictures of the dress she wore at her ninetieth birthday party and of the cake decorated by Norman Rockwell.

Like The Berkshire Museum in Pittsfield, Massachusetts (see p. 217), the Bennington Museum dates from a time when museums were more general than they are today. The institution goes back to 1875 and it has occupied its column-fronted building since 1928.

The museum owns paintings by Ralph Earl, Ammi Phillips, Erastus Salisbury Field, and William Morris Hunt as well as works relating to Vermont's history. It is well known for its 4,000 pieces of Bennington Pottery. Bennington, we learn, was one of America's most important centers of ceramic production, exhibiting its wares at America's first World's Fair, in New York in 1853. In 2000 the museum's collection of redware and stoneware was rearranged in stunning new galleries. Objects range from the very mundane (kegs, jars, and crocks, noted for their elaborate cobalt decorations of flowers, birds, and animals) to the unique. Bennington's American glass collection, with over 5,000 objects of pressed and free-blown glass, is extraordinary. There is also an excellent furniture exhibit.

Of historical interest is a room that illustrates Vermont's participation in all of America's wars, including the French and Indian War, the American Revolution, the Spanish American War, the Civil War, and the Mexican war. Children will like the old toys and dolls.

Virginia

NORFOLK

The Chrysler Museum of Art

Address: 245 Olney Road, Norfolk, VA 23510

Telephone: (757) 664-6200

Web: www.chrysler.org

Hours: Thur–Sat 10–5; Wed 10–9; Sun 1–5. Closed Mon, Tues, and New Year's, Independence, Thanksgiving, and Christmas days. Daily tours.

Strength: Encyclopedic. Italian, French, and American art. Glass collection.

Special Events: Temporary traveling shows. Live concerts first Thurs evenings.

Other: Historic houses: The Willoughby-Baylor House, from 1794; and the Moses Myers House, the elegant residence of Norfolk's first Jewish citizen, from the late 18th century. Tours for both houses start at 401 E. Freemason Street. They are closed Sun, Mon, and Tues from Jan through March. Large art reference library open to the public. Restaurant. Museum shop.

Activities for Children: Weekend hands-on family activities geared to temporary shows or a particular part of the permanent collection.

Parking: On site.

Some great museums have humble beginnings. The origins of what is now the Chrysler Museum can be traced to Irene Leache and Anna Cogswell Wood, who founded the Leache-Wood Female Seminary in Norfolk in 1871. As befits a school in Thomas Jefferson's home state,

Georges de La Tour's *Saint Philip*, at The Chrysler Museum of Art.

fine arts were an important subject at the seminary. Irene Leache died in 1900, and in her memory her friend and collaborator established several organizations with the goal of founding an art museum.

It took until 1933 for the first wing of the Norfolk Museum of Arts and Science to open in a Florentine Renaissance style building. The art collection of the museum slowly outgrew its quarters and in 1967 Walter P. Chrysler, Jr., entered the scene.

His father, Walter Sr., was the founder of the Chrysler Corporation, but Walter Jr. was more interested in art than in cars. At fourteen, he bought his first painting—a small Auguste Renoir watercolor—and never looked back. After college, during the 1930s, he went to Europe befriending—and buying art from—Pablo Picasso, Georges Braque, Juan Gris, Henri Matisse, Fernand Léger, and other avant-garde painters. Back in New York he participated in the creation of MoMA, administered the Chrysler Building, and volunteered for service in the Navy during World War Two. When stationed in Norfolk he met, and eventually married, Jean Ester Outland.

By then his art collection had become the focus of his life. He concentrated on European and American paintings, but inspired by his Long Island neighbor Louis Comfort Tiffany, fell in love with glass. Eventually Chrysler assembled 8,000 glass objects.

Chrysler Sr. said to his son while contemplating some of his own cherished possessions, "They are yours to enjoy only for a brief period of time. But remember they . . . belong to everyone." Chrysler Jr. searched for a home for his treasures, and selected the museum in Norfolk, henceforth to be known as The Chrysler Museum of Art. Walter himself directed the institution from 1971 to 1976 and chaired the Board until 1984. A succession of major renovations transformed the original wings into a large museum with over sixty galleries, space for changing exhibitions, a theater, and other amenities. The location of the building on an inlet of the Elizabeth River makes it look like a floating Venetian Palace. The atmosphere of grandeur continues in the entrance, with its great hall and double stairs leading to the upper floors.

Ambling through the galleries of the Chrysler is intensely pleasurable. The American folk paintings, donated by Walter's sister Bernice Chrysler and her husband, E. W. Garbisch, are outstanding. Edward Hicks, of the *Peaceable Kingdom*, surprises us with a charming image of *Washington at the Delaware*. Erastus Salisbury Field's *Last Supper*, a New England version of the Leonardo da Vinci masterpiece in Milan, is charming. There are portraits by John Singleton Copley and landscapes by Albert Bierstadt and Thomas Cole as well as by American Impressionists. There is also an extensive collection of twentieth-century American art. The Chrysler owns half of Thomas Hart Benton's large 1932 mural *Unemployment, Radical Protest, Speed*, deaccessioned by the Whitney Museum (the New Britain Museum of American Art owns other parts of the mural—see p. 111). The harried nanny, hurrying a baby carriage along in *New York Pavements*, is an unusually cheerful Edward Hopper work.

Among the European works is Georges de La Tour's *Saint Philip*. In this very early de La Tour the painter characteristically illuminated this plain man's forehead, twisted belt, hands, and staff. Originally the serene and intense work was part of a series of thirteen depicting Christ and his apostles. Only three of these survive; the two others are on display in a French provincial museum.

The Chrysler's collection of nineteenth- and twentieth-century art is a delight, including such works as Charles-Emile Jacque's *Shepherd and his Flock*, Henri Fantin-Latour's *Portrait of Léon Maître*, and choice French Impressionists and Post-Impressionists.

The result of Walter Chrysler's love affair with glass is another wonderful feature. Not only can we revel in an extensive historic collection, including the works by Tiffany, Carder, Galle, Orrefors, and Lalique, but the museum actively collects and exhibits modern art glass. The museum also actively collects photographs, with a special emphasis on images of the Civil War and the civil rights movement.

RICHMOND

Virginia Museum of Fine Arts

Address: 2800 Grove Avenue, Richmond, VA 23221

Telephone: (804) 340-1400

Web: www.vmfa.state.va.us

Hours: Tues–Wed, Fri–Sun 11–5; Thurs 11–8. Closed Mon and New Year's, Independence, Thanksgiving, and Christmas days. Tours Tues–Sun at 2:30 and Thurs at 6 and 7.

Strengths: 19th and 20th-century European art. British Sporting Art. Decorative arts (silver, Art Nouveau, Fabergé).

Other: Concerts. Lectures. By appointment: Special tours for visually impaired/blind individuals (reserve at 804-340-1435, 3 or more weeks in advance). Special interest "Tours of the Month." Pleasant cafés. Museum shop.

Activities for Children: Educational Resource room with art-related books, puzzles, crayons, games, and CD-ROMs. Also family days and other free or low-cost programs. An excellent treasure hunt map, the Family Gallery Guide, singles out highlights throughout the museum.

Parking: On site (enter lot from either Grove or Boulevard).

One would expect Virginia, one of America's oldest and most aristocratic states, to have a very old museum. The aftereffects of the Civil War, and of the Depression, however, hampered progress. The Virginia Museum of Fine Arts (VMFA) only opened the doors of its Georgian-style building in 1936. At the time, this state-operated museum owned only 100 works of art.

The museum grew quickly, however, partly because it had the very good fortune of being a close neighbor of Paul Mellon, one of America's major museum builders. (Also see the National Gallery of Art, p. 125, and the Yale University Art Gallery, p. 116.) There were other major donors, as well, including Sidney and Francis Lewis and Lillian Thomas Pratt. Within a matter of a few decades the VMFA sprouted several wings and today its 18,000 objects are, to use the words of the museum's brochure, variously "Indescribable, Cool, Dazzling, Spellbinding, and Classy." The works also range in size from huge to minuscule, and in spirit from religious and inspiring to fun and irreverent. The objects range from Fabergé eggs made from gold and precious stones in Imperial Russia, to tribal fetishes made from wood, feathers, and string, to furniture made of cardboard by Frank Gehry.

Breeding horses and collecting art were two of Paul Mellon's major passions. Bunny, his wife, was an award-winning gardener. The Sporting Art collection and the mostly French paintings they gave to the VMFA reflect these pleasures. From Théodore Géricault's *The Mounted Jockey,* Eugène Delacroix's *Study of a Brown-Black Horse,* and Pablo Picasso's *Jester on Horseback,* to Eastman Johnson's moving and magnificent *A Ride for Liberty—The Fugitive Slaves,* witnessed by the artist during the Civil War, horses figure in many pictures. Other masterpieces include Kees van Dongen's impressionistic picture of a *Parisian Lady,* wearing a black hour-glass dress and a large fur-trimmed hat, silhouetted with her black puppy against a yellow background. There is Albert Marquet's *Le Louvre,* an aerial view in which a corner of the famous museum peeks out above a canopy of spring-green trees and the River Seine flows by. Paul Cézanne's portrait of his early patron, Victor Chocquet, is also included.

There are galleries housing superior collections of Egyptian, Asian, Indian, Himalayan, Byzantine, Medieval, Decorative, earlier European, American, African, and late-twentieth-century art. The VMFA's holdings of decorative art, especially Art Nouveau, Art Deco, and Arts and Crafts, are particularly fine. It is a matter of taste whether you prefer the twists, curves, and curls of Hector Guimard's *Cabinet,* the geometric lines of Charles Rennie Mackintosh's chairs, the shimmer of Louis Comfort Tiffany's "peacock-hued" *Punch Bowl,* or the sinuous design of René Lalique's *Brooch,* but admirers won't be disappointed.

The museum's extensive holdings of Fabergé are also outstanding. The collection unexpectedly came to the museum from the estate of Mrs. Lillian Thomas Pratt, one of four major Fabergé collectors in the

U.S. The House of Fabergé's most famous creations were the jewel-encrusted Easter eggs given by the Czar to the Czarina, and the VFMA now owns five of these fabulous objects—including the blue-and-gold Imperial *Czarevich Easter Egg* from 1912. There also are enameled candy boxes, jeweled parasol handles, picture frames, and the especially delectable miniature crystal flowerpots filled with a single enameled flower.

WILLIAMSBURG

Abby Aldrich Rockefeller Folk Art Museum

Address: 307 S. England Street, Williamsburg, VA 23187

Telephone: (757) 220-7670

Web: www.colonialwilliamsburg.org

Hours: Daily 10–5, 365 days a year. A 30-min introductory tour is offered regularly.

Strength: American folk art mostly dating from 1740–1865, including paintings, sculptures, weathervanes, coverlets, fracturs (birth and baptismal certificates), toys, decoys, and other works.

Special Events: Annual exhibitions devoted to doll houses, miniature rooms, and Christmas.

Other: Temporary exhibits. Museum shop.

Activities for Children: Hands-on activities focused on special exhibitions. Occasional workshops at which children make folk-art objects.

Parking: On site, or park at Colonial Williamsburg visitors' center and take the shuttle bus.

Folk art can be totally captivating and joyous, especially when it is as carefully selected as are the examples on view at the Abby Aldrich Rockefeller Folk Art Museum (FAM). Viewers smile when looking at the sleeping *Baby In Red Chair, The Quilting Party,* or Reuben Law Reed's *Washington and Lafayette at the Battle of Yorktown,* in which the father of our country and his French ally are mounted on large white and brown stallions. In addition to visual delight the pictures tell us that the values of an earlier America were simpler. In these pre-camera days, paintings were the only means of recording likenesses and the FAM is filled with portraits of ordinary folks. Many works emphasize

Baby in Red Chair, by an unknown artist, is at the Abby Aldrich Rockefeller Folk Art Museum.

the benefits of a virtuous, God-fearing life; toys are nonmechanical, and shop signs straightforward.

The possessions of the museum are extremely varied. There are quilts, landscapes, cityscapes, seascapes, mourning pictures, still lives, chests, butter molds, coverlets, and much more. The FAM owns thirty-five paintings by Edward Hicks, including several versions of his *Peaceable Kingdom*, fifteen works by Ammi Phillips, and many by Erastus Salisbury Field (also see Springfield Museums, p. 219).

Abby Aldrich Rockefeller's interest in folk art was sparked by art dealer Edith Gregor Halpert (also see the Marion Koogler McNay Art Museum, p. 390), who suggested that Mrs. Rockefeller acquire both the "ancestors" and the "descendants" of her modern American art collection. The nucleus of the FAM collection (424 works) was bought during the 1920s, when folk art was out of favor. Mrs. Rockefeller went about assembling folk art, defined as work produced by untrained artists, in her usual enthusiastic, tasteful, and thorough manner. At one point she felt that Southern folk art was underrepresented in her collection and she sent an associate on a four-month tour of the region. He discovered *The Old Plantation* (1790–1800), showing African Americans at a dance playing a variety of instruments.

The collection of the Folk Art Museum reflects Mrs. Rockefeller's deep commitment. "Few, if any of my mother's many interests in art gave her as much pleasure than her collection of American folk art," her son Winthrop Rockefeller wrote in 1959 in a book about the museum, "and none, I think, more clearly demonstrates her deep pride in the cultural life of the American people." During Mrs. Rockefeller's lifetime only part of the collection was on view. In 1957, in her memory, husband John D. Jr. liberally endowed America's first museum devoted to folk art. The exhibition space was tripled in 1992.

Washington

SEATTLE

Frye Art Museum

Address: 704 Terry Avenue, Seattle, WA 98104

Telephone: (206) 622-9250

Web: www.fryeart.org

Hours: Tues–Wed, Fri 10–5; Thurs 11–9; Sun 12–5. Closed Mon and major holidays.

Strengths: Representational art. Extensive collection of 19th-century German art (particularly the Munich School). Survey of American painting. Northwest and Alaskan regional art.

Special Events: Concerts. Poetry readings.

Other: Pleasant restaurant. Museum shop.

Activities for Children: Low-cost hands-on programs and workshops.

Parking: Free, on site.

The Frye Art Museum (the Frye) is a pleasant mixture of the contemporary and the old-fashioned. Excellent temporary exhibits showcase living artists of the American Northwest; the museum also collects photographs and continues to add judiciously to its collection. The original 1950s building, designed by Paul Thiry, was modernized and enlarged by Rick Sudbury in 1997. From its portico there is an impressive view of downtown Seattle. Large, contemporary reflecting pools surround a stunning small rotunda, the starting point of the original thirty-by-sixty-foot, toplit gallery.

The contemporary feeling of the building contrasts with the academic, mostly German, art collected by the Fryes themselves. To stress the link between old and new, the revamped galleries, suffused with natural light, still feature the quirky, S-shaped velvet seats that used to be found in museums throughout the world.

Both Charles and Emma Frye were born in Iowa. These second-generation Germans arrived in Seattle in 1888 where Charles became a successful meat packer. During their leisure time the childless couple devoted themselves to art and music. They bought their first painting at the Chicago World's Fair in 1893 and gradually acquired a large collection of mostly German paintings, emphasizing the mid-nineteenth-century Munich School.

It comes as a surprise to most visitors that from 1870 to 1900 Munich was Europe's top art center, briefly rivaling Paris. At the time, "Mad" Ludwig of Bavaria sponsored Richard Wagner and Bismarck forged a unified German Reich. A portrait of the German chancellor by Franz Seraph von Lenbach is on view, as well as pictures by Friedrich von Kaulbach, Gabriel Max, and their contemporaries. Munich attracted hundreds of art students from around the world, including the Americans William Merritt Chase and Frank Duveneck. In 1893, after paintings of the Barbizon school, Gustave Courbet, Edouard Manet, and even Childe Hassam reached Munich, the city's artists revolted against officially sanctioned academic art and organized a "secession."

Like the Seattle Art Museum (see p. 407), the Frye has a painting of the *Judgement of Paris,* this one by Franz von Stuck. The Frye's Greek goddesses are nude, wearing elaborate crowns, and Paris is a shepherd wearing a golden helmet. The original Frye collection also features works by Adolphe William Bouguereau, Barbizon artists, and a great many livestock paintings.

The collections of the museum evolved with the times. There are portraits by Gilbert Stuart, a view of Venice by Thomas Moran, a rare small seascape by Albert Bierstadt, and works by Winslow Homer, John Henry Twachtman, and many others. A place of honor is reserved for Eustace P. Ziegler's *Alaska Sentinels*, a stunning view of a stand of redwoods. Ziegler (1881–1969) was enthralled by Alaska and recorded the magnificence of our northernmost state in paintings, many of which are now on view in Anchorage. Emma died in 1934 and Charles in 1940. As directed by the Frye will, Walser S. Greathouse, their lawyer, executor, and sole trustee, settled business matters and established the museum and Eustace Ziegler installed the works of art.

Henry Art Gallery

Address: 15th Avenue NE and NE 41st Street, Seattle, WA 98195

Telephone: (206) 543-2280

Web: www.henryart.org

Hours: Tues–Wed, Fri–Sun 11–5; Thurs 11–8. Closed Mon and New Year's, Independence, Thanksgiving, and Christmas days. Tours on selected Thurs and Sat at 2.

Strengths: Survey of American art. Photography.

Special Events: Temporary shows. Lectures. Art dialogue.

Other: Small café. Museum shop.

Activities for Children: Hands-on activities. Family programs. Public Art. Walking tour map.

Parking: Pay garages; usually free parking available on Sun.

Horace C. Henry, the founder of Washington State's first museum, arrived in Seattle in 1890. The state was one year old, the city thirty-nine, and Henry forty-six. He was a building contractor and among other projects was awarded a lucrative railroad contract. He had always been interested in art and had started buying paintings while living in Minneapolis. His purchases mirrored the taste of his time. He acquired Adolphe-William Bouguereau, Wilhelm G. F. Haseman, Narcisco Diaz de la Peña, Meyer von Bremen, and other painters mostly forgotten today, but he also bought works by Barbizon painters, George Inness, Alexander Wyant, William Keith, Henry Ward Ranger, and others. He preferred pictures of young girls and of landscapes; his *Adirondack Lake* by Winslow Homer and *Old House and Garden, East* by Childe

Hassam are still museum favorites. Henry bought art during his frequent travels around the U.S. and even in Paris. Like Minnesota's T. B. Walker (p. 238), and Washington, D.C.'s James Corcoran (p. 121), he first displayed his pictures at home, even building a special addition. By 1911 he owned 185 paintings.

For a while Henry supported the efforts of the Seattle Art Society, but eventually, mostly because he wanted to preserve his collection as a whole, he joined forces with the University of Washington to found a museum. When the museum's architect, Carl F. Gould, built it in 1929 it was supposed to be part of a large art complex, the grandiose entrance to the entire campus; however, those plans were never realized. Today the Henry Art Gallery's original squat structure, whose style is described as "Gould's collegiate Gothic," contrasts with the later buildings of the university and also with its own contemporary addition, built seventy years later. The toplit galleries are well organized and tastefully appointed. Their intimate size and beautiful light add to the pleasure of the visit. In 1997, Charles Gwathmey, who had designed the addition to New York's Guggenheim (p. 281) and Miami's new Museum of Contemporary Art (p. 145), mightily enlarged the Henry—it grew from 10,000 to 46,000 square feet. The combination of the old red brick with Gwathmey's glass, buff cast-stone panels, concrete, and stainless steel is creative. Most exciting is a turreted walkway that connects the street to the entrance of the museum.

The collection, too, has grown—to 20,500 objects—and now includes a judicious survey of American art including works by Gilbert Stuart, Winslow Homer, Stuart Davis, and Robert Motherwell as well as extensive photography and video holdings. As is the case with most small museums, despite the new addition much of the collection is in storage. The museum organizes thoughtful temporary shows.

Seattle Art Museum

Address: *SAM Downtown*: 100 University Street, Seattle, WA 98101; *Seattle Asian Art Museum (SAAM)*: Volunteer Park at 1400 E. Prospect Street, Volunteer Park, Seattle, WA 98112

Telephone: *SAM*: (206) 654-3255; *SAAM*: (206) 654-3206

Web: www.seattleartmuseum.org

Hours: Tues–Wed, Fri–Sun 10–5; Thurs 10–9. Closed Mon except Martin Luther King Jr., Presidents', Memorial, and Labor days; also closed New Year's, Thanksgiving, and Christmas days. Docent-led tours daily at 1 and 2, and on Thurs at 6:15 and 7:15. Also free "create your own" audio tours.

Strengths: Asian, African, Northwest Coast Native American art. Kress collection of Italian Renaissance, Baroque, and Northern European art. Porcelain.

Special Events: After Hours Thurs eves 5:30–8:30: Live music, poetry reading, gallery tours, cash bar.

Other: *At SAM*: Pleasant café off the museum's "spirit path." *At SAAM*: 55 familiar and exotic teas are available at Kao Tea Garden. In 2003 SAM's new Olympic Sculpture Park, for outdoor sculpture, will open on a 7.4 acre site on Seattle's central waterfront.

Activities for Children: Various workshops and family programs are available in SAM's third-floor Art Activity Room and in SAAM's Fuller Garden Court: e.g., paper cutting and folding activities, learning dances, "journey" to the Philippines.

Parking: *At SAM*: Paid, in adjacent garages. *At SAAM*: On site.

The first thing you notice as you approach the Seattle Art Museum (SAM) is Jonathan Borofsky's forty-eight-foot-tall sculpture of the *Hammering Man*. (Other versions of the work are at the Museum of Contemporary Art, San Diego—see p. 79—and the University of California Berkeley Art Museum—see p. 54.) The sculpture, fashioned from sheets of blackened steel, contrasts with the sleek, almost windowless, rounded structure of the museum itself.

In 1933, soon after it was founded, SAM occupied quarters in Volunteer Park, situated on a hill high above Seattle. Robert E. Fuller, the founding director and SAM's principal donor, remained at its helm for thirty years. When SAM outgrew its building it moved downtown to a five-story high-rise designed by Robert Venturi. It kept its old home, however, transforming it into a purely Asian museum—the Seattle Asian Art Museum (SAAM).

The collections at both museums are highly focused, consisting mostly of European and African art, Native and contemporary art of the Northwest, porcelain, and Asian art. It is the latter that dominates. Indeed, according to museum literature, Robert Fuller "avidly pursued

Seattle Art Museum with the 48-ft.-tall sculpture, *Hammering Man*, by Jonathan Borofsky.

his passion for all things Chinese." Dr. Sherman E. Lee, one of the foremost authorities on Asian art in the world and a future director of the Cleveland Museum of Art (p. 327), assisted him from 1948 to 1952.

The long entrance hall of SAM Downtown is a "spirit path" whose ceiling is bisected by a series of graceful modulated arches, a motif Venturi also used in the Museum of Contemporary Art, San Diego (p. 79). Two immense stone guardians, a camel and two rams dating from the fifteenth century, stand watch. The Asian influence, including the restrained manner of displaying only a limited number of choice objects, prevails throughout the museum. Specific Asian possessions include a section of the *Deer Scroll*, considered to be a National Treasure of Japan. The scroll, dating from the early seventeenth century, blends poetry, calligraphy, and painting. Other scrolls depict cranes, squirrels, and blossoming plum trees.

The European art holdings consist mostly of Renaissance and Northern European works, many the gift of the Samuel H. Kress Foundation. Among them is a powerful late portrait by Anthony Van Dyck of *Pompose II de Bellière*, the young French ambassador to the Netherlands. There is a charming rendition of the world's most famous beauty contest, *The Judgment of Paris* by Lucas Cranach the Elder. As in the painting of the same subject at Seattle's Frye Art Museum (see p. 404), the women are nude but Paris, the judge, is clad in the heavy armor of a Renaissance knight.

SAM also has an impressive African collection. During an intense collecting period of twenty years, Katherine C. White assembled a surprising collection of more than 3,000 objects of mostly African art—masks, sculptures, textiles, basketry, and decorative arts from 100 different African cultures. Ms. White moved to Seattle in 1979 and died within the year. Thanks to her will, coupled with financial support from Boeing, SAM became the fortunate recipient of these treasures and almost instantly became internationally known for its African possessions. A large display of fantastic masks, each one mounted on a freestanding post, transmit a sense of mystery and power seldom encountered in similar exhibits. The feeling is heightened by a video showing how similar masks are used in actual ceremonies.

It is fitting that Seattle has a magnificent collection of the art of its original inhabitants. The collection, considered one of the finest in the world, is subdivided into the Woven Treasures, featuring baskets, textiles, and clothing; Carved Treasures; and the Spiritual World. Two immense carved *House Poles* seem to hold up the ceiling of the museum. Their combination of animals, including the mythical thunderbird spreading his wings, and humans seem entirely "at home" in the Venturi building.

The role that chance plays in the formation of a museum cannot be stressed often enough. During the 1940s a group of women formed the Seattle Ceramic Society, which proceeded to acquire the most exquisite porcelains. The examples include Chinese export porcelains from when manufacture was a jealously guarded state secret, and European porcelains. Jacques-André Joseph Aved's portrait of *Madame Brion, Seated, Taking Tea* among her porcelain treasures may remind the attentive viewer of the *Princess in the Land of Porcelain* in Washington, D.C.'s Freer Gallery (p. 134).

Most of the museum's extensive 7,000-work Asian collection is housed in the original museum's spectacular Art Moderne building designed by Carl F. Gould, who also built Seattle's so very different Henry Art Gallery (see previous entry). For out-of-towners, the trip up

Capitol Hill—five miles from downtown—is astounding. The Seattle Asian Art Museum sits in a park filled with flowers and giant old trees, some of which can be glimpsed from the rear windows. Isamu Noguchi's *Black Sun,* a doughnut-shaped ring, towers above an old reservoir. Beyond it is a view of Pudget Sound and the peaks of the Olympic Mountain chain. Two camels, reproductions of the one in SAM Downtown's "spirit path," guard the entrance to the museum. The galleries are filled with serene works from India, Korea, China, Japan, and India. Buddhas and goddesses stretch out their many arms. A polychromed wooden, fourteenth-century *Monk* from China is shown *At the Moment of Enlightenment.* Chinese and Japanese ceramics surprise because they are so contemporary-looking. The museum's jades and snuff bottles, many of them assembled by Robert Fuller and his mother, are particularly noteworthy.

TACOMA

Tacoma Art Museum

Address: 1123 Pacific Avenue, Tacoma WA 98402

Telephone: (253) 272-4258

Web: www.tacomaartmuseum.org

Hours: Tues–Sun 10–5; Thurs 10–8. Closed Mon and major holidays.

Strengths: Northwestern art. Japanese woodblock prints. Chihuly glass.

Special Events: Unusual temporary exhibits. Festivals. Family Art Adventures 12:30–3 second Sun; Artwalk third Thurs; Senior Art Explorers 10:30–3 last Wed; Toddler Time 10–12 first Tues; others.

Other: Museum store. Sara Little Center for Design Research, with 5,000 objects of personal adornment, ritual, and daily use; open by appointment.

Parking: On street.

The Tacoma Art Museum (TAM) started as the very casual women's Tacoma Art League in 1891. Matters got more organized in 1934, when the club became the Tacoma Art Association headquartered on the fourth floor of a tower of the College of Puget Sound. The Association, still run by women volunteers, organized four to six exhibitions a year. Twenty-three years later, when everyone was tired of climbing all those steps, TAM moved. At first it occupied various quarters, including the old city jail and a storefront buffering a Bible store and a liquor store. In 1971 it was given the old bank building where it is housed today and will remain until 2003, at which time a new building located in Tacoma's emerging art center should be ready.

From early on the TAM and its predecessors concentrated on art of the Northwest, and its collection of often unfamiliar artists is growing. The museum owns work by Michael Stafford, Sally Haley, Mark Tobey, Fay Jones, and many others. The museum also owns a group of works by the Ashcan School, a group of artists who, around the turn of the nineteenth century, insisted on painting the "warts" of the world.

So far, three major collections have been left to the TAM. In 1971 the museum received the Carolyn Schneider Collection, consisting mostly of works on paper by leading American artists active during the middle of the twentieth century. Tacoma resident Constance R. Lyon's impressive collection of Japanese prints of the Edo period (1615–1868) were left to the TAM, which continues to enlarge this legacy. The museum was also the recipient of the Lindberg Collection, consisting mostly of nineteenth- and twentieth-century European works. The museum is particularly proud of its Impressionists and purchased two sculptures by Edgar Degas to enhance the *Dancers* included in the Lindberg bequest. Currently most of the permanent collection is in storage.

Tacoma is the birthplace of Dale Chihuly, the glassmaker whose work is increasingly encountered in museums across America. Chihuly is building a glass museum that will be linked to the new TAM by a bridge. Both buildings are neighbors of Tacoma's old Union Station, now used as a courthouse. This recycling does not detract from the building's majestic architecture, typical of the days when the railroad was king. Union Station, with its soaring cupola and large windows, has already been "adopted" by Chihuly. His large Persian glass flowers adorn the windows, fantastic murals adorn two walls, and currently a large, royal-blue standing chandelier dominates the center. Striking as these old and new building are, however, they will always be dwarfed by snow-covered Mount Hood, which reminds the visitor of the spectacular beauty of the American West.

While waiting for the new glass museum, visitors can study Chihuly's work at the old TAM. Seven composite pieces, donated by the artist in memory of his father and brother, are displayed at eye level. The works consist of Chihuly's characteristic nestled, intricate organic shapes fashioned out of extremely thin, delicately colored glass. Northwest Coast Indian baskets, stored in Tacoma's Historical Society, inspired the brown *Tabac Basket Series with Black Lip Wraps*. Shells, sea urchins, and other creatures come alive in the artist's pink and white *Sea Forms*. Examples of the artist's Venetian series are red as is a large red vase flecked in gold surrounded by a snake like organic form intertwined with a green leaf.

Wisconsin

MILWAUKEE

Milwaukee Art Museum

Address: 700 N. Lincoln Memorial Drive, Milwaukee, WI 53202

Telephone: (414) 224-3200

Web: www.mam.org

Hours: Tues–Wed, Fri–Sat 10–5; Thurs 12–9; Sun 12–5. Closed Mon and New Year's, Thanksgiving, and Christmas days.

Strengths: European Old Masters. 19th- and 20th-century American and European art. Decorative arts, contemporary arts and crafts, and outsider art.

Special Events: First Fri: Dancing to live music. Senior days.

Other: Interactive technology center that helps visitors learn more about artwork on display. Bistro walk café overlooking Lake Michigan. Museum shop.

Activities for Children: Family days.

Parking: Low-cost, just north and west of museum.

Northern Europeans, mostly Germans, flooded Milwaukee during the late nineteenth century. At one time German was widely spoken in the city and German artists specialized in painting large panoramas of Biblical or historic scenes. Displayed in the round, the immense canvases served as a backdrop to music and narration. (One surviving work of this genre, Vanderlyn's *Panoramic View of Versailles,* can still be seen at New York's Metropolitan Museum of Art—see p. 293.) In 1900 the Milwaukee panoramic artists and their friends founded the Milwaukee Art Institute and mounted art exhibitions. This was not the town's only artistic enterprise. In 1888, Fredrick Layton, an English-born meatpacker, built the Layton Art Gallery. The thirty-eight paintings he donated formed the nucleus of the future collection of the Milwaukee Art Museum (MAM). The city's two art organizations went their separate ways until after World War Two, when they joined forces with several other groups and decided to create an art center memorializing that war's dead.

Eero Saarinen built the new center on a site located on the shore of Lake Michigan. The overall plan is a floating, cantilevered cross, which, according to museum literature, "is now considered a classic in the development of modern architecture."

In 1975 there was a major addition to the Saarinen building and fifteen years later the collection, now numbering over 20,000 works, needed additional room. Santiago Calatrava, a Spanish-born architect, designed a large rectangular extension at right angles to the old museum. This almost doubled the exhibition space. The new wing terminates in a grand reception hall that soars to a height of sixty feet. As befits a building in Frank Lloyd Wright's home state, the shiplike tip of this hall visually blends with the waters of Lake Michigan. A moveable sunscreen, resembling a giant bird about to take flight, is perched on the roof. The function of this light and temperature controlling brise-soleil is both practical and ceremonial.

Ultimately a museum is defined by its possessions. During the past 112-plus years the MAM has received numerous donations and today its collections range from ancient to contemporary art, with special emphasis on art from the fifteenth century on. Most European and American schools are amply represented (Medieval and Renaissance art, European Old Masters, American art of the nineteenth and twentieth centuries, including Impressionists, Post-Impressionists, Realism, Ashcan School, etc.).

The art world was shocked when the museum acquired Francisco de Zurbarán's mystical *Saint Francis* for $60,000, a tidy sum in 1958. The austere saint, his face obscured by his cowl, his hands clutching a skull, contrasts with more joyous religious paintings, notably the altarpiece by Nardo di Cione, a fourteenth-century Florentine artist. In 1969 Peg Bradley gave the museum more than 600 works of her lovingly assembled collection of late nineteenth- and twentieth-century modern and contemporary European and American art. As befits a museum with German roots, the gift featured a large collection of works by German Expressionists, including the largest grouping of works by Gabriele Münter outside Germany. We note the painter's *Boating, 1910,* in which a formally dressed party rows in a spectacular lake toward blue mountains. The René von Schleinitz Collection of nineteenth-century German academic genre paintings and ornately decorated beer steins celebrates Milwaukee's German heritage in a totally different way.

The MAM owns the Prairie Archives of Decorative Arts, including those of Frank Lloyd Wright and other objects and documents by, or relating to, leading designers of the twentieth century. The museum also features a large collection of prints and drawings as well as the archives of the Landfall Press of Chicago, one of America's premier fine art printer/publishers. The museum also keeps up with the cutting edge of contemporary art; there are works by Cy Twombly, Eva Hesse, Anselm Kiefer, Duane Hanson, and many others.

Index

This index is a guide to the strengths and highlights of the museums in this book as listed in the summary information. It is not meant to be comprehensive of the contents of each museum, but it will help you locate quickly key collections you have read about here.

El Greco, 327
Ellesmer manuscript, *Canterbury Tales*, 96
enamels, 278
  French Limoges, 325
English, *see* British
Ernst, Max, 385
Etruscan sculpture, 363
European:
  contemporary, 136, 358, 388
  antiquity to 20th century, 374, 388
  18th century, 150
  14th through 19th century, 158
  Impressionists, 108
  19th century, 99, 146, 150, 215, 265, 358, 400, 413
  Old Masters, 87, 195, 413
  portrait miniatures, 322
  prints, 177
  sculpture, 136, 142, 273, 318, 343
  17th century, 150
  textiles, 142
  20th century, 99, 108, 130, 146, 358, 400, 413
  12th century, 130, 358
  Western, 269, 278
  works on paper, 52
  see also specific countries
European sculpture court, 293
Expressionists, German, 93, 158, 211, 244, 320

Fabergé, 183, 400
Fauvism, 93
Federal art, American, 140
  portraits, 186
Ferrand, Beatrix, 123
Field, Erastus Salisbury, 219
15th century:
  drawings and prints, 303
  European paintings, 158
  Northern European tapestries, 180
film, 297
first editions, 303
Fischer, George, 52
Flemish, 83, 269
folk art, 158, 262
  American, 193, 255, 334, 402
14th century:
  drawings and prints, 303
  European paintings, 158

fracturs, 402
Fragonard, Jean Honoré, 278
Francis Little House (Wright), 236, 346
French, 87, 183, 209, 397
  Colonial art, 183
  decorative arts, 58, 269
  early 20th century, 52, 269
  18th century, 83, 96, 269, 325
  Impressionists, 163, 205, 336, 351
  Limoges enamels, 325
  19th century, 82, 96, 269, 278, 325
  period furniture, 370
  pewter, 370
  porcelain, 370
  Post-Impressionism, 390
  17th century, 278
  16th century, 82
furniture, 202, 278
  English period, 370
  French period, 370
  period, 325
furniture, American, 195
  19th century, 158
  17th century, 108
  20th century, 158

Gainsborough, Thomas, 278, 303
gardens, 123, 276
  sculpture, 60, 273, 297, 312, 315, 329
Gauguin, Paul, 169
genre paintings, 217
German:
  18th-century porcelain, 370
  Expressionists, 93, 158, 211, 244, 320
  paintings, 74, 404
glass, 183, 332, 392, 397
  American 19th and early 20th century, 395
  ancient, 332
  art, 153
  Asian, 134
  Chihuly, 411
  paper weights, 163
  studio, 169, 332
  Tiffany, 368
Gothic, 363
  architecture, 353
  chapel, 233
Goya, Francisco de, 68, 327
Greco, El, 327

Greek, ancient, 57, 134, 153, 198, 212
  coins, 212
  8th to 1st century B.C.E., 121
  pottery, 249
  sculpture, 363
Gutenberg Bible, 96

Hall of Architecture, 358
Hartley, Marsden, 190
Himalayan, 71, 255
Hindu sculptures, 374
Hispanic Colonial, see Spanish Colonial
Hispano-Moresque lusterware, 285
history, historical:
  manuscripts, documents, and maps, 341
  memorabilia, Vermont, 395
  of New York, 301
Hoffman, Malvina, 172
Hofmann, Hans, 54
Homer, Winslow, 188, 190, 223
Hudson River School, 108, 111, 217, 374

icons, Russian, 82
illuminated manuscripts, 58, 96, 198, 303
illustrations, 221
  American, 348
  magazine, 118
Impressionists, 68, 108, 198, 209, 219, 293, 327, 355, 370, 374
  American, 44, 108, 140, 167
  French, 163, 205, 223, 336, 351
Indian, 68, 134, 198, 212, 380
  paintings, 71
  temple figures, 85
Indian, American, see Native American
Ingres, Jean-Auguste-Dominique-, 278
Inness, George, 253
installations:
  multimedia, 289
  sound and art, 213
International art, after 1945, 383
Inuit art, 273
Iranian art, 134
Islamic art, 60, 212

Italian, 209, 397
  decorative art, 269
  design, 106
  majolica, 121
  Renaissance, 41, 116, 143, 269, 293, 339, 368, 372, 407
  16th to 19th century, 82

jade, 85
  Asian, 134
  Chinese, 71
Japanese, 60, 134, 199, 205, 212, 374, 380
  netsuke, 71
  woodblock prints, 411
  woodblock prints, Ukiyo-e period, 366
Jennewein, C. Paul, 153
Jewish, Judaica, 236, 289

Kandinsky, Wassily, 281
Katz, Alex, 193
Kent, Rockwell, 186, 190
Kentucky, 180
Khmer sculpture, 85
Korean, 134, 212, 380

lacquerware, Asian, 134
lamps, Tiffany, 301
landscape photography, American, 378
landscapes, 278
  American, 102, 140, 158, 366
  American 19th century, 339
  British 18th and 19th century, 370
  Dutch, 215
  English, 215
  Maine, 190
Lasansky, Mauricio, 172
Latin American, 99, 285
  Pre-Columbian to 20th century, 392
Lehigh Valley, regional art of, 346
Limoges enamels, French, 325
Louisiana, 183
lusterware, Hispano-Moresque, 285

magazine illustrations, 118
Magritte, René, 385
Maine, 186, 188, 190
majolica, Italian, 121